Spanish
FOR
DUMMIES®
2ND EDITION

by Berlitz, Susana Wald, and Cecie Kraynak, MA

WILEY-
INDIA

Spanish For Dummies®, 2nd Edition

Authorized reprint by Wiley India Pvt. Ltd., 4435-36/7, Ansari Road, Daryaganj,
New Delhi – 110002.

Copyright © 2011 by Wiley Publishing, Inc., Indianapolis, Indiana

This edition is auth

Reprint: 2012

Printed at: *Sanat Printers, Kundli, Haryana*

ISBN: 978-81-265-3465-4

About the Authors

Susana Wald is a writer and a simultaneous and literary translator in Hungarian, Spanish, English, and French. As a publisher, she has been working with books and authors for many years. She has been a teacher in Chile and Canada and has known the joy of learning from her students and their untiring enthusiasm and tolerance. She is also an artist and has had her work shown in many countries in North, Central, and South America and in Europe.

Cecie Kraynak, MA, has taught and tutored Spanish at the junior-high, high-school, and college levels for more than 25 years. She is a frequent traveler to Spanish-speaking countries and has studied abroad at the University of the Americas in Cholula, Mexico, and the Universidad Complutense in Madrid, Spain. She earned her bachelor's degree in Spanish and secondary education in 1980 and her master's degree in Spanish literature in 1983 from Purdue University. Cecie authored *Spanish Verbs For Dummies* (Wiley) and has edited numerous books on learning Spanish. She is currently the ESL coordinator for the South Montgomery Schools in New Market, Indiana.

Berlitz® has meant excellence in language services for more than 130 years. At more than 400 locations and in 50 countries worldwide, Berlitz® offers a full range of language and language-related services, including instruction, cross-cultural training, document translation, software localization, and interpretation services. Berlitz® also offers a wide array of publishing products, such as self-study language courses, phrase books, travel guides, and dictionaries.

The world-famous Berlitz Method® is the core of all Berlitz® language instruction. From the time of its introduction in 1878, millions have used this method to learn new languages. For more information about Berlitz® classes and products, please consult your local telephone directory for the Language Center nearest you or visit the Berlitz® Web site at www.berlitz.com, where you can enroll in classes or shop directly for products online.

Dedication

Cecie: In memory of my father, Frank Howard, who never lost his sense of adventure.

Author's Acknowledgments

Cecie: Thanks to acquisitions editor Michael Lewis for choosing me to work on this second edition of *Spanish For Dummies* and working closely with me during the initial stages to formulate the vision for this book. Thanks also go to project editor Georgette Beatty for carefully shaping the manuscript and shepherding the text through production; to copy editor Megan Knoll for purging the manuscript of any typos and ugly grammatical errors; and to both of them for using their knowledge of Spanish to make this book all that much better. Thanks also to the technical reviewers, Alicia Añino and Greg Harris, for their expertise and careful attention to detail. Last but not least, thanks to my husband, Joe, who assisted in preparing the numerous manuscript submissions.

Publisher's Acknowledgments

We're proud of this book; please send us your comments at http://dummies.custhelp.com. For other comments, please contact our Customer Care Department within the U.S. at 877-762-2974, outside the U.S. at 317-572-3993, or fax 317-572-4002.

Some of the people who helped bring this book to market include the following:

Acquisitions, Editorial, and Media Development

Senior Project Editor: Georgette Beatty

(Previous Edition: Kathleen M. Cox)

Acquisitions Editor: Michael Lewis

Copy Editor: Megan Knoll

(Previous Edition: Kathleen Dobie, Patricia Pan, Billie Williams)

Assistant Editor: David Lutton

Technical Editors: Alicia Añino, Greg Harris

Assistant Project Manager: Jenny Swisher

Associate Producer: Josh Frank

Quality Assurance: Doug Kuhn

CD Producer: Her Voice Unlimited, LLC

Editorial Manager: Michelle Hacker

Editorial Assistant: Jennette ElNaggar

Art Coordinator: Alicia B. South

Cover Photo: ©iStockphoto.com/Yang Yin

Cartoons: Rich Tennant
 (www.the5thwave.com)

Composition Services

Project Coordinator: Sheree Montgomery

Layout and Graphics: Claudia Bell, Carl Byers, Christin Swinford

Proofreaders: Jessica Kramer, Tricia Liebig

Indexer: Valerie Haynes Perry

Illustrator: Elizabeth Kurtzman

Publishing and Editorial for Consumer Dummies

Diane Graves Steele, Vice President and Publisher, Consumer Dummies

Kristin Ferguson-Wagstaffe, Product Development Director, Consumer Dummies

Ensley Eikenburg, Associate Publisher, Travel

Kelly Regan, Editorial Director, Travel

Publishing for Technology Dummies

Andy Cummings, Vice President and Publisher, Dummies Technology/General User

Composition Services

Debbie Stailey, Director of Composition Services

Contents at a Glance

Table of Contents

Introduction

*A*s society becomes more international in nature, knowing how to say at least a few words and phrases in other languages becomes increasingly useful. Global business environments often necessitate overseas travel or at least the ability to communicate via e-mail and over the phone. You just may have friends and neighbors who speak other languages, or you may want to get in touch with your heritage by learning a little bit of the language that your ancestors spoke.

Whatever your reason for wanting to acquire some Spanish, *Spanish For Dummies,* 2nd Edition, can help. Two experts at helping readers develop knowledge — Berlitz®, experts in teaching foreign languages, and Wiley Publishing, publishers of the best-selling *For Dummies* series — have teamed up to produce a book that gives you the skills you need for basic conversational communication in Spanish. We're not promising fluency here, but if you want to greet someone, purchase a ticket, or order off a menu in Spanish, you need look no further than *Spanish For Dummies,* 2nd Edition.

Spanish is one of the great European languages, rich in heritage from its more than nine centuries of existence. This is the language that comes from the region of Spain that English-speakers call Castile. As Christopher Columbus and other Spanish explorers came to the New World, Spanish became the language of the majority of the peoples from Florida to Tierra del Fuego (with the exception of Brazil, where Portuguese is spoken). When you go to places like Argentina, Bolivia, Chile, Uruguay, Paraguay, Peru, Ecuador, Colombia, Venezuela, Mexico, Guatemala, Puerto Rico, Cuba, Costa Rica, Panama, Honduras, or Nicaragua, you speak in or are spoken to in Spanish. If you visit cities like Santiago de Chile, Montevideo, Asuncion, Buenos Aires, Lima, Caracas, Bogota, Mexico City, Quito, San Juan, and many, many others, the people predominantly speak Spanish. And when you speak their language or even attempt to communicate with them in their native tongue, you add a richer dimension to your experience. Some folks say that language can be a barrier. And we believe that by removing this barrier, you open a world of possibilities.

So you have several good reasons to embrace this beautiful language. You may want to understand the culture and the people. You may also want your Spanish-speaking friends and neighbors at home to understand you, in their own language. So even if your Spanish isn't perfect, you'll be appreciated and encouraged in your attempts to immerse yourself in the Spanish-speaking world.

About This Book

Spanish For Dummies, 2nd Edition, can help you reach moments of true understanding in a different language. Use the text as a language and cultural guide for those moments when you really need to know how and why things are done. This book concentrates on Latin American Spanish, meaning the Spanish spoken in Mexico, Central America, and South America.

This book isn't a class that you have to drag yourself to twice a week for a specified period of time. You can use the book however you want to, whether your goal is to know some words and phrases to help you get around when you visit Mexico and the countries of Central or South America, travel to Spain, or simply want to be able to say, "Hello, how are you?" to your Spanish-speaking neighbor. Go through this book at your own pace, reading as much or as little at a time as you like. You don't have to trudge through the chapters in order, either; just read the sections that interest you.

And don't forget to practice by using the CD at the back of this book for help in pronunciation and inflection. The only way to really know and love a language is to speak it. Throughout the book, we give you lots of words, phrases, and dialogues, complete with pronunciations. The CD includes only a sampling of them, but we've provided a broad selection that should serve most of your basic needs.

Conventions Used in This Book

To make this book easy for you to navigate, we've set some conventions:

- ✔ Spanish terms are set in **boldface** to make them stand out. They're accompanied by pronunciations, set in normal type with stressed syllables in *italics* (see the following bullet), and English translations, also set in *italics*. (Exception: Words to Know boxes underline stressed syllables and don't specially format Spanish words or the translations.)

- ✔ Within the pronunciation brackets, we separate all the words that have more than one syllable with a hyphen, like this: (*kah*-sah).

- ✔ Verb conjugations (lists that show you the forms of a verb) are given in tables in this order: the *I* form, the *you* (singular, familiar) form, the *he/she/you* (singular, formal) form, the *we* form, the *you* (plural, familiar) form, and the *they/you* (plural, formal) form. Pronunciations follow in the second column. Here's an example:

Conjugation	*Pronunciation*
yo llevo	yoh *yeh*-bvoh
tú llevas	tooh *yeh*-bvahs
él, ella, usted lleva	ehl, *eh*-yah, oohs-*tehd yeh*-bvah
nosotros, nosotras llevamos	noh-*soh*-trohs, noh-*soh*-trahs yeh-*bvah*-mohs
vosotros, vosotras lleváis	bvoh-*soh*-trohs, bvoh-*soh*-trahs yeh-*bva*ees
ellos, ellas, ustedes llevan	*eh*-yohs, *eh*-yahs, oohs-*teh*-dehs *yeh*-bvahn

Language learning is a peculiar beast, so this book includes a few elements that other *For Dummies* books don't. Following are the new elements you encounter:

✔ **Talkin' the Talk dialogues:** The best way to pick up a language is to see and hear how it's used in conversation, so we include dialogues throughout the book. The dialogues come under the heading "Talkin' the Talk" and show you the Spanish words, the pronunciation, and the English translation.

✔ **Words to Know blackboards:** Memorizing key words and phrases is also important in language learning, so we collect the important words that appear in a Talkin' the Talk dialogue and write them on a chalkboard with the heading "Words to Know."

✔ **Fun & Games activities:** If you don't have actual Spanish-speakers to practice your new language skills on (and even if you do), you can use the Fun & Games activities to reinforce what you learn. These word games are fun ways to challenge yourself and gauge your progress. You can find the answers to each exercise in Appendix D.

Also note that because each language has its own ways of expressing ideas, the English translations that we provide for the Spanish terms may not be exactly literal. We want you to know the gist of what's being said, not just the words that are being said. For example, you can translate the Spanish phrase **de nada** (deh *nah*-dah) literally as *of nothing*, but the phrase really means *you're welcome* (as in, *think nothing of it*). This book gives the *you're welcome* translation.

What You're Not to Read

We like to think that you'll read every word in this book, but we also know that you're eager to start immersing yourself in Spanish. So feel free to skip the sidebars (those gray-shaded boxes sprinkled throughout the chapters); they're full of interesting information but not essential to your study of Spanish.

Foolish Assumptions

To write this book, we had to make some assumptions about who you are and what you want from a book called *Spanish For Dummies,* 2nd Edition. Here are the assumptions that we've made about you:

- ✔ You know no Spanish — or if you took Spanish back in school, you don't remember a word of it.
- ✔ You're primarily interested in communicating verbally in Spanish, not in reading or writing Spanish, though this book can help with that, too.
- ✔ You're not looking for a book that will make you fluent in Spanish; you just want to know some words, phrases, and sentence constructions so that you can communicate basic information in Spanish.
- ✔ You don't want to have to memorize long lists of vocabulary words or a bunch of boring grammar rules, but you do want some guidance on grammar to deepen your understanding and use of the language.
- ✔ You want to have fun and learn a little bit of Spanish at the same time.

If these statements apply to you, you've found the right book!

How This Book Is Organized

This book is divided by topic into parts, and then into chapters. The following sections tell you what types of information you can find in each part.

Part 1: Getting Started

This part lets you get your feet wet by giving you some Spanish basics, including how to recite your ABCs; pronounce words and phrases like a native speaker; and meet, greet, and exchange pleasantries with other Spanish speakers. We bring you up to speed in a hurry on basic Spanish grammar, so you're better equipped to formulate your own Spanish expressions. You discover how to count in Spanish (up to a million!), tell time, talk about days and dates, and convert your favorite measurements into metric equivalents. Finally, we introduce you to Spanish in your home, where you can pick up all sorts of useful words and phrases.

Part II: Spanish in Action

In this part, you begin putting your Spanish to good use. Instead of focusing on grammar points, as many language textbooks do, this part focuses on everyday situations that you may find yourself in if you're visiting or living in a Spanish-speaking country or dealing with your Spanish-speaking neighbors. This part hones your small-talk skills and takes you on shopping and dining excursions; you also discover how to ask for directions, go out on the town, conduct business, and enjoy some recreational and outdoor activities. At the end of this part, you should be able to do some basic navigation in the Spanish language.

Part III: Spanish on the Go

This part gives you the tools you need to take your Spanish on the road, whether it's to a local Spanish restaurant or to a museum in Mexico. This part is devoted to the traveler in you, helping you survive the customs process, check into hotels, nab a taxi, exchange dollars for pesos, and have a great time doing it. Sprinkled throughout are cultural tidbits that introduce you to people, places, and things that are important in Spanish-speaking cultures.

Part IV: The Part of Tens

If you're looking for small, easily digestible pieces of information about Spanish, this part is for you. Here, you find ten ways to pick up Spanish quickly, ten things you should never say in Spanish, ten catchy Spanish expressions to know, and ten phrases that make you sound like a native Spanish speaker.

Part V: Appendixes

This part of the book includes important information that you can use for reference. We include two mini-dictionaries (Spanish-to-English and English-to-Spanish), verb tables that show you how to conjugate regular and irregular verbs, a listing of the tracks included on the audio CD (and where in the book those dialogues are so that you can follow along), and the all-important answer keys for the Fun & Games sections at the end of each chapter.

Icons Used in This Book

You may be looking for particular information while reading this book. To make certain types of information easier for you to find, we've placed the following icons in the left-hand margins throughout the book:

Pay close attention to the information marked with this icon; it's something so important that you should commit it to memory.

This icon highlights tips that can make learning Spanish easier.

Languages are full of quirks that may trip you up if you're not prepared for them. This icon points to discussions of these weird grammar rules.

If you're looking for information and advice about culture and travel, look for these icons. They draw your attention to interesting tidbits about the countries in which Spanish is spoken.

The audio CD that comes with this book gives you the opportunity to listen to real Spanish speakers so that you can get a better understanding of what Spanish sounds like. This icon marks the Talkin' the Talk dialogues that you can find on the CD.

Where to Go from Here

The best way to learn a language is to immerse yourself in it. Listen to the way Spanish sounds, concentrate on the pronunciation, and look at how it's written. By listening and repeating, you enter a new world of ideas and peoples. Acquiring Spanish through immersion really does feel like a sort of magic.

If you've never taken Spanish lessons before, you may want to read the chapters in Part I before tackling the later chapters. Part I gives you some of the basics you need to know about the language.

Discovering a language is all about jumping in and giving it a try (no matter how bad your pronunciation is at first). So make the leap! Start at the beginning, pick a chapter that interests you, or pop the CD into your stereo or computer and listen to a few dialogues. Just be sure to speak as well as listen and have fun along the way!

Part I
Getting Started

The 5th Wave   By Rich Tennant

"Then one day a friend asked him what he would say if he ever met Penelope Cruz."

In this part . . .

This part lets you get your feet wet by introducing you to Spanish basics, including a brief primer on everything you need to know about Spanish grammar to start speaking it. You discover how to recite your ABCs; pronounce words and phrases like a native speaker; and meet, greet, and exchange pleasantries with other Spanish speakers. We show you how to count in Spanish (up to a million!), tell time, talk about days and dates, and convert your favorite measurements into metric equivalents. Finally, we encourage you to start speaking Spanish at home, where you can pick up all sorts of useful words and phrases.

Chapter 1
Spanish in a Nutshell

- -

- -

*E*veryone wants to know Spanish, but learning it takes considerable time and effort. That's okay. Rome wasn't built in a day, and we didn't learn Spanish overnight.

However, you can wrap your brain around basic Spanish grammar and get up to speed on Spanish words and phrases in a matter of minutes. That's what this chapter is all about. Here we provide the short 'n' sweet version of the rest of this book, so you can start speaking and understanding Spanish immediately.

Tackling Basic Grammar

Studying grammar (language rules) is kind of a buzz killer. You want to start speaking Spanish *now*. But grammar is an essential ingredient and actually provides a shortcut to learning and understanding a second language:

Vocabulary + Grammar + Practice = Fluency

Know the vocabulary, plug the words into the grammar, and you're ready not only to state your business but also to ask questions and understand the answers.

Chapter 2 is chock full of basic Spanish grammar, but you don't need to know everything all at once. Start with the most basic phrase — a simple sentence, a noun followed by a verb, a person or thing performing an action.

When constructing bare-bones sentences, follow a few basic rules of Spanish grammar:

- ✔ The subject noun performs the action (the verb).

- ✔ If you use an article, such as **el** or **la** (meaning *the*), it must agree with the noun in *gender* — masculine nouns use **el,** whereas feminine nouns use **la.**

- ✔ The verb must agree with the subject noun in person (I, we, you, he, she, they) and number. In English, for example, *I walk to the store* but *He walks to the store*. The process of converting verbs into the different forms is called *conjugation*.

Conjugating a verb in Spanish is a process of changing the ending of the verb to match up with the subject pronoun or its equivalent in a sentence. Here's a sample with the Spanish verb **hablar** (*to speak*):

Subject Pronoun	*Verb*	*English*
yo (*I*)	**hablo**	*I speak*
tú (*you* [informal, singular])	**hablas**	*you speak*
Usted (*you* [formal, singular])	**habla**	*you speak*
él/ella (*he/she*)	**habla**	*he/she speaks*
nosotros/nosotras (*we*)	**hablamos**	*we speak*
vosotros/vosotras (*you* [informal, plural])	**habláis**	*you speak*
Ustedes (*you* [formal, plural])	**hablan**	*you speak*
ellos/ellas (*they*)	**hablan**	*they speak*

Yeah, it gets more complicated than that. Spanish has irregular verbs that don't follow the rules (see Appendix B for a sampling), and, like most languages, its verbs conjugate differently to reflect tense, as in past, present, and future tense. For now, however, knowing what this conjugation stuff is all about is a big step.

Easing into Common Expressions

In Chapter 3, we present numerous common Spanish expressions (as well as the scoop on pronunciations, greetings, introductions, and more) that enable you to speak Spanish pronto. Until then, here are a few essential and very common expressions:

¡**Hola!** (¡*oh*-lah!) (*Hello!*)

¿**Quiubo?** (¿kee-*ooh*-boh?) (*Hello, what's happening?*)

Adiós. (ah-dee*ohs*.) (*Good-bye.*)

Por favor. (pohr fah-*bvohr*.) (*Please.*)

Gracias. (*grah*-seeahs.) (*Thank you.*)

Lo siento. (loh see*ehn*-toh.) (*I'm sorry.*)

¿**Habla usted inglés?** (¿*ah*-bvlah oohs-*tehd* een-*glehs*?) (*Do you speak English?*)

No hablo mucho español. (no *ah*-bvloh *mooh*-choh eh-spah-*nyohl.*) (*I don't speak much Spanish.*)

No sé. (noh seh.) (*I don't know.*)

Claro. (*clah*-roh.) (*I understand.* [Literally: *Clear.*])

The following phrases can get you through a number of awkward pauses as you think of the right word during a conversation:

¡**Olé!** (¡oh-*leh!*) (*Great!; Superb!; Keep going!*)

¿**De veras?** (¿deh *bveh*-rahs?) (*Really?*) This phrase signals slight disbelief.

¡**No me digas!** (¡noh meh *dee*-gahs!) (*You don't say!*) This phrase also indicates disbelief.

Counting on Numbers, Times, and Days

Navigating any country requires a knowledge of numbers, dates, times, and measurements. Without such knowledge, you can't possibly show up for dinner at the right time (let alone the right day of the week), and you can't ask for a specific number or amount of whatever it is you want. Chapter 4 brings you up to speed on all these topics in a hurry. Until then, the following can get you to your first date or meeting:

- Ask *What day?*: ¿**Qué día?** (¿keh *dee*-ah?)

- Ask *What time?*: ¿**A qué hora?** (¿ah keh *oh*-rah?)

- **Name the days of the week starting with Monday:** **lunes** (*looh*-nehs), **martes** (*mahr*-tehs), **miércoles** (mee*ehr*-koh-lehs), **jueves** (hooheh-bvehs), **viernes** (bvee*ehr*-nehs), **sábado** (*sah*-bvah-doh), **domingo** (doh-*meen*-goh).

- **Count to 12 in Spanish:** **uno** (*ooh*-noh), **dos** (dohs), **tres** (trehs), **cuatro** (koo*ah*-troh), **cinco** (*seen*-koh), **seis** (*seh*ees), **siete** (see*eh*-teh), **ocho** (*oh*-choh), **nueve** (nooh*eh*-bveh), **diez** (dee*ehs*), **once** (*ohn*-seh), **doce** (*doh*-seh).

✔ **Tell what hour of the day it is:** To say *It's 1:00,* use **Es la una** (ehs la *ooh*-nah). *It's noon* is **Es el mediodía** (ehs ehl meh-deeoh-*dee*-ah), and *It's midnight* is **Es la medianoche** (ehs lah meh-deeah-*noh*-cheh). For all other times of the day after 1:00, use **Son las** + the number; for example **Son las dos** (sohn lahs dohs) (*It's 2:00*).

Speaking Spanish around the House

Most people start learning Spanish at home or school before venturing into Spanish-speaking territory. Either way, your house or apartment is a great place to pick up lots of useful Spanish vocabulary and phrases. Naming most of the rooms in your home is the first step:

✔ **la cocina** (lah koh-*see*-nah) (*the kitchen*)

✔ **el comedor** (ehl koh-meh-*dohr*) (*the dining room*)

✔ **el salón** (ehl sah-*lohn*) (*the living room*)

✔ **el baño** (ehl *bvah*-nyoh) (*the bathroom*)

✔ **el dormitorio** (ehl dohr-mee-*toh*-reeoh) (*the bedroom*)

Your home is packed with all sorts of stuff, but only a few are bare essentials:

✔ **la nevera** (lah neh-*bveh*-rah) (*the refrigerator*)

✔ **el horno microondas** (ehl *ohr*-noh *mee*-kroh-*ohn*-dahs) (*the microwave*)

✔ **el mando a distancia** (ehl *mahn*-doh ah dees-*tahn*-seeah) (*the TV remote control*)

Chapter 5 introduces you to Spanish words for most other household items and can even help talk you through numerous household activities.

Putting Spanish into Action

Eventually, you want to take your Spanish outside the safe confines of your home or classroom and start using it in your day-to-day conversations. The chapters in Part II provide you with words, phrases, dialogues, and more for common scenarios, including making small talk, asking for directions, and going shopping. The following sections provide a preview of what to expect.

Use it or lose it. Actively pursue opportunities to speak Spanish. You may feel a little uncomfortable speaking it at first, but the more you practice and learn from your mistakes, the more fluent you become.

Making small talk

Much of the chatter you hear on a daily basis is small talk that typically commences with a question:

¿Cómo te llamas? (*¿koh*-moh teh *yah*-mahs?) (*What's your name?*)

¿Dónde vives? (*¿dohn*-deh *bvee*-bvehs?) (*Where do you live?*)

¿Qué hace usted? (¿keh *ah*-seh oohs-*tehd?*) (*What do you do?*)

¿Cómo está usted? (*¿koh*-moh ehs-*tah* oohs-*tehd?*) (*How are you* [formal]?)

¿Cuántos años tienes? (¿kooh*ahn*-tohs *ahn*-yohs tee*ehn*-ehs?) (*How old are you* [informal]? [Literally: *How many years do you have?*])

To answer these questions, start with the following:

Me llamo . . . . (meh *yah*-moh . . . .) (*My name is . . . .*)

Vivo en . . . . (*bvee*-bvoh ehn . . . .) (*I live in . . . .*)

Yo soy un estudiante. (yoh sohy oohn ehs-tooh-dee*ahn*-teh.) (*I'm a male student.*)

Estoy muy bien. (ehs-*tohy* moo*hee* bee*ehn*) (*I'm very well.*) or **Estoy así así.** (*ehs*-tohy ah-*see* ah-*see.*) (*I'm so-so.*)

Yo tengo veinticinco años. (yoh *tehn*-go bveheen-tee-*seen*-koh *ahn*-yohs.) (*I am 25 years old.*)

This small sample of small talk phrases are great ice breakers, but they can't get you through an entire conversation. Check out Chapter 6 for more Spanish small talk questions, words, and phrases.

Asking for directions

Asking for directions in Spanish isn't all that difficult. The tough part is understanding the answer to your question. The most effective way to overcome this challenge is to carry a map of the area and ask people to show you on the map:

Hola. ¿Por favor, puede Ud. decirme como llegar a . . .? (*oh*-lah. ¿pohr fah-*bvohr*, pooh*eh*-deh oohs-*tehd* deh-*seer*-meh *koh*-moh yeh-*gahr* ah . . . ?) (*Hello. Can you please tell me how to get to . . . ?*)

Por favor, enséñeme en este mapa. (pohr fah-*bvohr*, ehn-*seh*-nyeh-meh ehn *ehs*-teh *mah*-pah.) (*Please show me on this map.*)

¿Dónde estamos ahora? (¿*dohn*-deh ehs-*tah*-mohs ah-*oh*-rah?) (*Where are we now?*)

¿A cuánto estamos a . . . ? (¿ah kooh*ahn*-toh ehs-*tah*-mohs ah . . . ?) (*How far is it to . . . ?*)

Asking for and giving directions is ultimately more complex than these phrases account for. You need to know direction words for here and there, above, below, to the left, to the right, inside, outside, north, south, and so on. See Chapter 7 for details.

Eating out and buying food

Wrestling with a foreign language can really work up an appetite, so kill two birds with one stone — head to the market or a local Spanish or Mexican restaurant and rustle up some grub.

Whether you're at the market or a restaurant, pointing can help you get through your early experiences in ordering food and beverages. Accompany your pointing gesture with the following:

Yo quiero éste. (yoh kee*eh*-roh *ehs*-teh.) (*I want this one.*)

Eventually, you want to do more than the caveman ordering technique. In Chapter 8, we give you all the Spanish you need to know to make reservations at a **restaurante** (rrehs-tahooh-*rahn*-teh), order your meal and a beverage, and purchase groceries and fresh produce at the local **mercado** (mehr-*kah*-doh) (*market*) or **supermercado** (sooh-pehr-mehr-*kah*-doh) (*supermarket*).

Going shopping

Regardless of where you happen to be (either in your hometown or in a new locale), you need to buy stuff, and that's not as easy as it sounds when you're shopping in an area where Spanish is the official language. Knowing words for the bare necessities can help:

✔ **la camisa** (lah kah-*mee*-sah) (*the shirt*)

✔ **el champú** (ehl chahm-*pooh*) (*the shampoo*)

✔ **la falda** (lah *fahl*-dah) (*the skirt*)

✔ **el jabón** (ehl Hah-*bvohn*) (*the soap*)

✔ **los pantalones** (lohs pahn-tah-*loh*-nehs) (*the pants*)

✔ **el papel higiénico** (ehl pah-*pehl* ee-He*eeh*-nee-koh) (*the toilet paper*)

✔ **la pasta de dientes** (lah *pahs*-tah deh dee*ehn*-tehs) (*the toothpaste*)

✔ **los zapatos** (lohs sah-*pah*-tohs) (*the shoes*)

If you need more stuff than that or help with finding what you're looking for, head to Chapter 9, which features much more vocabulary along with verbs and phrases for getting help, trying on clothes, asking for specific colors and fabrics, and making comparisons.

Heading out on the town

Half the fun of traveling consists of exploring what various areas have to offer in the way of activities and entertainment. You don't want to sit around your room all day counting the geckos, so head to Chapter 10, where you discover how to conjugate and use the verb **salir** (sah-*leer*) (*to go out, to leave*). And be sure to invite some of your new friends along with the verb **invitar** (een-bvee-*tahr*).

Chapter 10 offers several ideas for making dates, going out on the town, having fun, and talking all about the good times you've had — in Spanish, of course!

Doing business and communicating

Speaking Spanish at work offers new opportunities for picking up additional vocabulary, phrases, and grammar. You're likely to be working in **la oficina** (lah oh-fee-*see*-nah) (*the office*); using **la computadora** (lah kohm-pooh-tah-*doh*-rah) (*the computer*), **el teléfono** (ehl teh-*leh*-foh-noh) (*the telephone*), and **la fotocopiadora** (lah foh-toh-koh-peeah-*doh*-rah) (*the photocopier*); talking with your colleagues around **el enfriador de agua** (ehl ehn-freeah-*dohr* deh *ah*-goohah) (*the water cooler*); and using all sorts of **los suministros de la oficina** (lohs sooh-mee-*nees*-trohs deh lah oh-fee-*see*-nah) (*the office supplies*).

You also need to be able to find your way around the different buildings, rooms, and departments, such as **la sala de descanso** (lah *sah*-lah deh dehs-*kahn*-soh) (*the break room*), **el cuarto de almacenamiento** (ehl kooh*ahr*-toh deh ahl-mah-seh-nah-mee*ehn*-toh) (*the storage room*), and **la salida** (lah sah-*lee*-dah) (*the exit*). And you want to know how to talk about various office activities, including answering the phone, making copies, and using a computer.

Chapter 11 covers all this info and more, including introducing you to the imperative mood, so that you can delegate tasks with the command form of verbs, and the preterite tense, so that you can talk about things that happened in the past.

Enjoying the great outdoors and more

All work and no play can make for a dullard in any language, so in Chapter 12, we focus on Spanish words, phrases, and dialogue dealing with indoor and outdoor recreational activities. Here a few examples to get you started:

> **¿Juega al ajedrez?** (¿Hooh*eh*-gah ahl ah-Heh-*drehs?*) (*Do you play chess?*)

> **¿Te gusta leer?** (¿teh *goohs*-tah leh-*ehr?*) (*Do you like to read?*)

> **¿Te gusta caminar?** (¿teh *goohs*-tah kah-mee-*nahr?*) (*Do you like to walk (hike)?*)

> **¿Qué te gusta jugar?** (¿keh teh *goohs*-tah hooh-*gahr?*) (*What do you like to play?*)

Taking Spanish on the Go

Immersing yourself in a country where Spanish is the official language is perhaps the most effective way to become comfortable with conversational Spanish. That's why we devote an entire part to chapters on travelling with Spanish. The following sections bring you up to speed on the bare basics of what to expect in Part III.

Preparing for a trip

The most enjoyable and hassle-free trips begin with proper preparation. You need to decide where you want to go with the verb **ir** (eer) (*to go*), secure **el pasaporte** (ehl pahs-ah-*pohr*-teh) (*the passport*) and **el visado** (ehl bvee-*sah*-doh) (*the visa*) ahead of time, schedule **el vuelo** (ehl bvooh*eh*-loh) (*the flight*), and **hacer la maleta** (ah-*sehr* lah mah-*leh*-tah) (*to pack your luggage*).

Chapter 13 covers all these items and more along with introducing you to a new verb tense for discussing your future travel plans.

Making sense of money

When traveling outside your home country, you need to deal with foreign currencies and be able to perform everyday financial transactions, such as getting **el dinero** (ehl dee-*neh*-roh) (*the money*) out of an ATM and using **la tarjeta de crédito** (lah tahr-*Heh*-tah deh *kreh*-dee-toh) (*the credit card*) to pay for stuff.

Chapter 14 provides plenty of guidance on how to manage your money and perform financial transactions in Spanish, whether you're dealing with a teller or an ATM. We also provide you with everything you need to know to get the best exchange rate for your dollar.

Getting around with local transportation

Unless you're planning on touring your country of destination on foot or bicycle (which can be interesting modes of travel), you need to be able to make your way around via plane, train, taxi, bus, trolley, or other forms of public transportation. Start by asking,

> **¿Dónde está . . . ?** (*¿dohn*-deh ehs-*tah . . . ?*) (*Where is . . . ?*)

followed by the mode of transportation you're looking for:

- ✔ **el aeropuerto** (ehl ah-eh-roh-pooh*ehr*-toh) (*the airport*)
- ✔ **la estación de tren** (lah ehs-tah-see*ohn* deh trehn) (*the train station*)
- ✔ **el taxi** (ehl *tahk*-see) (*the taxi*)
- ✔ **la estación de autobuses** (lah ehs-tah-see*ohn* deh ahooh-toh-*bvooh*-sehs) (*the bus station*)
- ✔ **la oficina de renta de autos** (lah oh-fee-*see*-nah deh *rrehn*-tah deh ahooh-tohs) (*the car rental office*)

You then need to purchase a ticket or pay a fare, drive (if you're renting a car), and perhaps even deal with customs officers. And you have to do all these tasks on schedule. Turn to Chapter 15 for assistance.

Securing a place to stay

Even if you're out all day exploring, you need a place to crash and to store your belongings — you need a hotel or motel room or the equivalent. Sounds easy enough until you start dealing with the details, such as the cost per night, the location of the room, the size of the bed, and so on. The following questions can help you find a room that meets your needs and budget:

> **¿Tiene una habitación disponible?** (¿tee*eh*-neh *ooh*-nah ah-bvee-tah-see*ohn* dees-poh-*nee*-bvleh?) (*Do you have a room available?*)

> **¿Es la habitación bastante grande para dos personas?** (¿ehs lah ah-bvee-tah-see*ohn* bvahs-*tahn*-teh *grahn*-deh *pah*-rah dohs pehr-*soh*-nahs?) (*Is the room large enough for two people?*)

> **¿Tiene un baño privado?** (¿tee*eh*-neh oohn *bvah*-nyoh pree-*bvah*-doh?) (*Does it have a private bathroom?*)

> **¿Tiene dos camas?** (¿tee*eh*-neh dohs *kah*-mahs?) (*Does it have two beds?*)

> **¿Cuánto cuesta por una noche?** (¿kooh*ahn*-toh kooh*ehs*-tah pohr *ooh*-nah *noh*-cheh?) (*How much is the cost for one night?*)

> **¿Acepta tarjetas de crédito?** (¿ah-*sehp*-tah tahr-*Heh*-tahs deh *kreh*-dee-toh?) (*Do you accept credit cards?*)

Most of these questions can be answered **Sí.** (*Yes.*) or **No.** (*No.*), which should make understanding the answers easier.

If you need more than these basics to secure lodgings, head to Chapter 16, where we explain how to make reservations, check out the room before you check in, register, and ask for extra towels and other essentials.

Taking action during emergencies

Hopefully, wherever you travel, you won't need to deal with any serious emergencies, but if you do, we have you covered in Chapter 17. The first thing is to let someone know you need help:

> **¡Por favor ayúdeme!** (¡pohr fah-*bvohr* ah-*yooh*-deh-meh!) (*Please help me!*)

Then comes the tough part — describing the type of help you need. Chapter 17 is designed to help you get help, whether you're experiencing a medical, law enforcement, legal, or general emergency, such as a fire. We also provide guidance on how to offer help to others.

Fun & Games

The following word search contains several Spanish words that we introduce in this chapter. We've listed the English translations here; find and circle the Spanish equivalents in the word search. (See Appendix D for the answer key.)

L	T	U	A	J	T	J	B	K	S	O	L	A	H	O	R	A
N	C	O	M	E	D	O	R	P	I	K	A	J	C	A	E	M
P	X	K	C	Y	V	I	A	R	H	A	B	L	A	M	O	S
H	O	L	A	R	A	P	O	R	A	Z	Z	D	R	X	Y	O
J	N	H	Y	Í	A	T	O	E	B	G	G	Z	S	A	Y	F
M	A	R	D	M	I	N	V	T	L	R	Q	K	U	R	W	I
N	Q	Q	G	M	U	I	B	Z	O	A	Y	U	T	P	G	C
Z	E	Q	R	B	P	R	E	I	V	C	I	K	H	B	Z	I
D	A	O	O	O	A	A	G	D	R	I	W	A	Z	H	A	N
M	D	P	F	O	D	R	E	S	T	A	C	I	Ó	N	W	A
N	Q	W	A	M	F	J	F	H	Z	S	M	F	Y	C	U	Z
J	N	X	J	T	A	E	U	C	W	E	L	W	W	I	O	D
A	N	T	T	R	O	N	P	N	W	R	N	A	D	U	N	O
B	L	G	E	I	W	S	P	Z	N	Y	J	D	H	D	Ñ	D
Ó	G	V	O	S	I	Y	G	L	L	S	W	I	F	A	A	F
N	E	K	Z	P	U	C	G	Q	V	Z	H	Ó	B	D	W	Q
N	P	K	T	R	E	N	X	B	J	P	N	S	O	D	I	X

Good-bye	We talk
Now	I talk
Bathroom	Hello
City	Soap
Dining room	Map
Day	Refrigerator
Bedroom	Office
Station	Train
Thank you	Shoes

Chapter 2

Warming Up with Spanish Grammar Basics

....

In This Chapter

▶ Understanding simple sentence construction

▶ Asking basic questions in Spanish

▶ Starting out right with subject pronouns

▶ Adding action with regular and irregular verbs

▶ Liberating that whole gender thing with articles and adjectives

....

Speaking a language is like driving a car. When you know what you're doing, driving becomes second nature. You don't even think about accelerating, steering, braking, or even reading the road signs — you just drive. Spanish is the same. As soon as you know the vocabulary and grammar, you read, write, and speak almost instinctively.

Knowing what you're doing means knowing the rules of the road, and for Spanish, those rules constitute grammar. You don't need to know a whole lot of grammar to start speaking the language, but keeping some basic rules in mind can help you wrap your brain around the topic and provide you with the framework for a clearer understanding of what you're studying and why. This chapter brings you up to speed in a hurry.

Breaking Down Simple Sentence Structure

Naturally, when you meet people, you want to talk to them. And how do you go about that? In sentences, of course. In Spanish, as in English, you form a sentence by combining a subject, a verb, and perhaps further descriptive information. For example:

La casa es grande. (lah *kah*-sah ehs *grahn*-deh.) (*The house is big.*)

Here, the subject of the sentence is **la casa** (lah *kah*-sah) (*the house*); then comes the verb, **es** (ehs) (*is*); after that comes the adjective, **grande** (*grahn*-deh) (*big*), which describes the house. Here are some more examples:

> **La mujer es bella.** (lah mooh-*Hehr* ehs *bveh*-yah.) (*The woman is beautiful.*)
>
> **El hombre es alto.** (ehl *ohm*-bvreh ehs *ahl*-toh.) (*The man is tall.*)
>
> **Las calles son anchas.** (lahs *kah*-yehs sohn *ahn*-chahs.) (*The streets are wide.*)

Before you begin to examine the basic building blocks of a sentence, familiarize yourself with the two essential components of every sentence — subject and predicate.

- ✔ The *subject* is the entity performing the action along with anything that describes the subject. The subject, when stated, is always a noun or a pronoun.
- ✔ The *predicate* is everything else — the action (or verb) and everything related to that action.

To form a negative sentence you simply add a **no** in front of the verb as shown in the following examples:

> **El carro no es nuevo.** (ehl *kah*-rroh noh ehs nooh*eh*-bvoh.) (*The car isn't new.*)
>
> **El perro no es bueno.** (ehl *peh*-rroh noh ehs bvooh*eh*-noh.) (*The dog isn't good.*)
>
> **El hombre no es bajo.** (ehl *ohm*-bvreh noh ehs *bvah*-Hoh.) (*The man isn't short.*)

Forming Questions: The Basics

We have some good news for you: Forming a question in Spanish is easy. All you have to do is invert the order of the verb and the subject. Where you say **Ésta es . . . .** (*ehs*-tah ehs . . . .) in a regular sentence, for a question you say **¿Es ésta . . . ?** (¿ehs *ehs*-tah . . . ?). This setup works the same as it does in English, when you say *This is . . . .* and *Is this . . . ?*

Check out this example:

> **Ésta es la puerta.** (*ehs*-tah ehs lah pooh*ehr*-tah.) (*This is the door.*)
>
> **¿Es ésta la puerta?** (¿ehs *ehs*-tah lah pooh*ehr*-tah?) (*Is this the door?*)

To answer a question in the affirmative, you follow exactly the same sentence model used in English. That is, you add the word *yes* in front of the response, followed by a comma. For example:

> **¿Es la escuela nueva?** (¿ehs lah ehs-koo*heh*-lah noo*heh*-bvah?) (*Is the school new?*)

> **Sí, la escuela es nueva.** (see, lah ehs-koo*heh*-lah ehs noo*heh*-bvah.) (*Yes, the school is new.*)

Now, suppose you want to answer in the negative. All you have to do is insert the word no at the beginning of your answer and before the verb (almost the way you do in English, but easier). An example:

> **¿Es ése el carro?** (¿ehs *eh*-seh ehl *kah*-rroh?) (*Is that the car?*)

> **No, ése no es el carro.** (noh, *eh*-seh noh ehs ehl *kah*-rro.) (*No, that isn't the car.*)

The following sentences were affirmative statements in the preceding section, and now we're using them to demonstrate the questioning (interrogative) and denying (negative) responses:

> **¿Es bella la mujer?** (¿ehs *bveh*-yah lah mooh-*Hehr?*) (*Is the woman beautiful?*)

> **No, la mujer no es bella.** (noh, lah mooh-*Hehr* noh ehs *bveh*-yah.) (*No, the woman isn't beautiful.*)

> **¿Es alto el hombre?** (¿ehs *ahl*-toh ehl *ohm*-bvreh?) (*Is the man tall?*)

> **No, el hombre no es alto.** (noh, ehl *ohm*-bvreh noh ehs *ahl*-toh.) (*No, the man isn't tall.*)

> **¿Son anchas las calles?** (¿sohn *ahn*-chahs lahs *kah*-yehs?) (*Are the streets wide?*)

> **No, las calles no son anchas.** (noh, lahs *kah*-yehs noh sohn *ahn*-chahs.) (*No, the streets aren't wide.*)

Note in these examples that the Spanish questions place the adjective before the subject, while in English the adjective follows the subject.

English often includes the verb *do* in questions, but Spanish makes things easier on you. In Spanish, the word *do* is understood as part of the verb when a question is asked:

> **¿Vas al cine?** (¿bvahs ahl *see*-neh?) (*Do you go to the movies?*)

> **Sí, voy.** (see, bvohy.) (*Yes, I [do] go.*)

¿**Va tu padre al cine?** (¿bvah tooh *pah*-dreh ahl *see*-neh?) (*Does your father go to the movies?*)

No, él no va. (noh, ehl noh bvah.) (*No, he doesn't go.*)

Meeting Subject Pronouns Face to Face

A *subject pronoun* is a word used in place of a subject noun. Instead of saying "Lucy fried an egg," for example, you can say, "She fried an egg." *She* (the subject pronoun) takes the place of *Lucy* (the subject noun).

In English, you use subject pronouns all the time in place of, or to avoid, repeating subject nouns. It saves a lot of time and effort, to write (or say) "They left" rather than "Mr. Anthony Bolavolunta and Miss Cleopatra Johnson left." The subject pronouns *I, you, he, she, we,* and *they* enable you to speak more clearly and concisely after the subject has been stated and understood. Subject nouns and pronouns alike are followed by the appropriate forms of the verbs expressing particular actions.

You don't use Spanish subject pronouns as frequently as their English counterparts, because a Spanish verb ending generally indicates the subject. (See the later section "Introducing Regular and Irregular Verbs" for more information.) You use Spanish subject pronouns, therefore, mainly to be polite, to emphasize or stress the subject, or to be perfectly clear as to who the subject is.

Just like in English, Spanish subject pronouns have a person (first, second, or third) and a number (singular or plural), as you can see in Table 2-1. (The second-person plural form **vosotros/vosotras** is used in spoken Spanish mainly in Spain. Check out the sidebar "When in Spain, vosotros rules" later in this chapter for details.)

Table 2-1		Spanish Subject Pronouns		
Person	*Singular*	*Meaning*	*Plural*	*Meaning*
1st person	**yo** (yoh)	*I*	**nosotros/nosotras** (noh-*soh*-trohs/ noh-*soh*-trahs)	*we*
2nd person informal	**tú** (tooh)	*You*	**vosotros/vosotras** (bvoh-*soh*-trohs/ bvoh-*soh*-trahs)	*you*
2nd person formal	**usted (Ud.)** (oohs-*tehd*)	*You*	**ustedes (Uds.)** (oohs-*teh*-dehs)	*you*

Person	Singular	Meaning	Plural	Meaning
3rd person	**él** (ehl)	*he*	**ellos** (*eh*-yohs)	*they* (for a group of all males or both males and females)
	ella (*eh*-yah)	*she*	**ellas** (*eh*-yahs)	*they* (for a group of all females)

You don't express the English pronoun *it* as a subject in Spanish; it can be understood from the meaning of the sentence:

¿Qué es? (¿keh ehs?) (*What is it?*)

Es una herramienta. (ehs *ooh*-nah eh-rrah-mee-*ehn*-tah.) (*It's a tool.*)

The following sections help you select the correct subject pronouns for all circumstances in all parts of the Spanish-speaking world.

A few words about yo

Unlike the English subject pronoun *I*, which is always capitalized, the Spanish pronoun **yo** is capitalized only at the beginning of a sentence. Because the conjugated verb ending used for **yo** makes it clear that the subject of the sentence is *I*, **yo** can actually be omitted from the sentence and the sentence can simply start with the verb. Here's an example:

(Yo) Me voy. ([yoh] meh bvohy.) (*I'm leaving.*)

Nosotros and nosotras

When you're talking about someone else and yourself at the same time, you must use *we* (**nosotros/nosotras**). **Nosotros** refers to more than one male or to a combined group of males and females, no matter the number of each gender present. **Nosotras** refers to a group of females only:

Jorge y yo (Nosotros) jugamos al tenis. (*Hohr*-Heh ee yoh [noh-*soh*-trohs] Hooh-*gah*-mohs ahl *teh*-nees.) (*Jorge and I [We] play tennis.*)

Luz y yo (Nosotras) jugamos al tenis. (loohs ee yoh [noh-*soh*-trahs] Hooh-*gah*-mohs ahl *teh*-nees.) (*Luz and I [We] play tennis.*)

It's you, you know: The tú/usted issue

People use both body language and spoken language to convey how they want a relationship to develop. Relationships tend to be more formal in Spanish than in English. If you need to be formal in English, you have to show it by your body movements or by the tone of your voice. In Spanish, the distinction between **tú** (tooh) and **usted** (oohs-*tehd*) allows you to introduce this formality right into the language.

In the olden days, English speakers said *thou* and *you*. People said *thou* to their beloved and *you* to their beloved's parents. Anyone listening to a conversation knew whether the speakers were intimate or had a more formal relationship.

Spanish speakers kept this habit. Spanish speakers say **tú** as English speakers used to say "thou" and **usted** to signify a more respectful way of talking to someone such as a new acquaintance, an older person, or someone whom they want to show respect or keep a certain distance from, such as is required in a business relationship. Most adults address children by using **tú.**

At some point in a relationship between people who speak Spanish, a shift occurs from the formal **usted** to the more informal and intimate **tú.** Two people of the same age, the same social status, or the same educational level, or people who want to express a certain intimacy, very soon arrive at a point where they want to talk to each other in a more informal or intimate manner. It's at this point that they use the word **tú** when addressing each other. In Spanish, you call this **tutearse** (tooh-teh*ahr*-seh) — that is, *to talk tú.* On the other hand, if you don't want to have a closer, more intimate relationship with someone, or if you want to keep the relationship more professional and less chummy, you should stick to calling that person **usted.** These formalities make relationships more graceful and varied. Being graceful in your speech and your relationships is much appreciated in Spanish-speaking places.

Following are some examples of sentences that use **tú** and **usted:**

> **¿Vas tú con Juan en el auto rojo?** (¿bvahs tooh kohn Hooh*ahn* ehn ehl *ahooh*-toh *rroh*-Hoh?) (*Do you* [friendly, informal] *go with Juan in the red car?*)

> **¿Cómo se llama usted?** (¿*koh*-moh seh *yah*-mah oohs-*tehd*?) (*What's your* [respectful, formal] *name?*)

> **Usted tiene una casa muy bella.** (oohs-*tehd* tee*eh*-neh *ooh*-nah *kah*-sah *mooh*ee *bveh*-yah.) (*You* [respectful, formal] *have a very beautiful house.*)

When in Spain, vosotros rules

The pronoun **vosotros** is used in spoken Spanish mainly in Spain. In all other Spanish-speaking countries, **vosotros** is taught in the schools, but most countries never use it in normal conversation. In Latin America, you hear **ustedes**; there's no distinction between formal and informal in the plural you.

Here are all the various *you* forms, using **trabajar** (*to work*) as an example:

tú trabajas (*you work*): singular, informal

usted trabaja (*you work*): singular, formal

vosotros trabajáis (*you work*): plural, informal in Spain

ustedes trabajan (*you work*): plural, formal in Spain; formal *and* informal in Latin America

You may hear a variation of the **vosotros** in Argentina or Colombia, **Vos trabajás** (*you work*). From a grammatical standpoint, this form is totally incorrect, so don't try to copy it.

When people in Spain want to address several people informally, they use the word **vosotros** (bvoh-*soh*-trohs), which is the plural form of **tú**. Spanish-speaking Americans almost never use **vosotros**. In Spanish-speaking Latin America, people instead say **ustedes** (meaning *you,* in the plural). This **ustedes** can be a formal way of addressing two or more people, or it can be very informal — the situation dictates the difference. Here are some examples of **ustedes** in action both ways:

> **¿Adónde van ustedes dos?** (¿ah-*dohn*-deh bvahn oohs-*teh*-dehs dohs?) (*Where are the two of you going?*) [Can be formal or very informal]

> **¿Ustedes van conmigo, ¿Verdad?** (¿oohs-*teh*-dehs bvahn kohn-*mee*-goh, ¿bvehr-*dahd?*) (*You guys are going with me. Right?*) [Informal]

> **¿Bailan ustedes el tango?** (¿*bvah*ee-lahn oohs-*teh*-dehs ehl *tahn*-goh?) (*Do you dance the tango?*) [Formal]

The nearby sidebar "When in Spain, vosotros rules" gives you more information.

You always write the abbreviations for *you* singular and plural as **Ud.** (**usted**) and **Uds.** (**ustedes**) with capital letters, even though you write the English equivalent *you* with a lowercase letter unless it appears at the beginning of a sentence. When **usted** and **ustedes** aren't abbreviated, they're capitalized only at the beginning of a sentence. When you read these abbreviations aloud, you say the whole word. Here are some examples:

¿Busca Ud. (usted) algo? (¿*boohs*-kah oohs-*tehd ahl*-goh?) (*Are you looking for something?*)

¿Necesitan Uds. (ustedes) ayuda? (¿neh-seh-*see*-tahn oohs-*teh*-dehs ah-*yooh*-dah?) (*Do you need help?*)

Ellos versus ellas

Ellos (*they*) refers to more than one male or to a combined group of males and females, no matter the number of each gender present. **Ellas** refers to a group of females only:

Juan y Jorge (Ellos) escuchan. (Hooh*ahn* ee *Hohr*-Heh [*eh*-yohs] ehs-*kooh*-chahn.) (*Juan and Jorge [They] listen.*)

Juan y Luz (Ellos) escuchan. (Hooh*ahn* ee loohs [*eh*-yohs] ehs-*kooh*-chahn.) (*Juan and Luz [They] listen.*)

El niño y mil niñas (Ellos) escuchan. (ehl *neen*-yoh ee meel *neen*-yahs [*eh*-yohs] ehs-*kooh*-chahn.) (*The boy and 1,000 girls [They] listen.*)

Luz y Susana (Ellas) escuchan. (loohs ee sooh-*sah*-nah [*eh*-yahs] ehs-*kooh*-chahn.) (*Luz and Susana [They] listen.*)

Introducing Regular and Irregular Verbs

When a verb is in the infinitive form in English, it begins with *to* — for example, "to run," "to talk," and "to think." The indication is of an action (or a state of being) without a specific subject carrying out, being, or doing that action. When you add a subject to the sentence (someone or something that performs the action), you must then use the correct *conjugation* of the verb; for example, I eat, you eat, and we eat, but he, she, or it eats.

Spanish verb infinitives all end with one of three letter combinations: **-ar,** **-er,** or **-ir.** Regardless of a verb's ending, however, it's classified as regular or irregular, as you find out in the following sections. Regular verbs follow a standard conjugation scheme, while irregular verbs don't.

✔ **Regular verbs:** Conjugating regular verbs is easy. When you know how to conjugate one regular **-ar** verb, you can determine the conjugation of all regular **-ar** verbs. The same goes for all **-er** and **-ir** regular verbs — get to know just one set of rules, and you can apply them to an entire group of verbs.

✔ **Irregular verbs:** The conjugated forms of irregular verbs, however, are less predictable. Therefore, you need to memorize more forms of each irregular verb to ensure that you use it correctly. (Don't worry if you make a mistake; most Spanish-speakers can figure out what you want to say even if your verb ending isn't quite right.)

Regular verbs

In all regular verbs in Spanish, the first part of the verb — its *root* — remains unchanged. For example, the verb **preparar** (preh-pah-*rahr*) (*to prepare*) is a regular verb ending in **-ar**. The root **prepar-** remains unchanged throughout conjugation. The following table shows you how you conjugate this verb — and all other regular **–ar** verbs — in the present tense.

Conjugation	*Pronunciation*
yo preparo	yoh preh-*pah*-roh
tú preparas	tooh preh-*pah*-rahs
él, ella, usted prepara	ehl, *eh*-yah, oohs-*tehd* preh-*pah*-rah
nosotros, nosotras preparamos	noh-*soh*-trohs, noh-*soh*-trahs preh-pah-*rah*-mohs
vosotros, vosotras preparáis	bvoh-*soh*-trohs, bvoh-*soh*-trahs preh-pah-*rah*ees
ellos, ellas, ustedes preparan	*eh*-yohs, *eh*-yahs, oohs-*teh*-dehs preh-*pah*-rahn

The following table shows you how to conjugate all regular **-er** verbs in the present tense. For our example, we've chosen the regular **-er** verb **comprender** (kohm-prehn-*dehr*) (*to understand*). The root of this verb is **comprend-**.

Conjugation	*Pronunciation*
yo comprendo	yoh kohm-*prehn*-doh
tú comprendes	tooh kohm-*prehn*-dehs
él, ella, usted comprende	ehl, *eh*-yah, oohs-*tehd* kohm-*prehn*-deh
nosotros, nosotras comprendemos	noh-*soh*-trohs, noh-*soh*-trahs kohm-*prehn*-deh-mohs
vosotros, vosotras comprendéis	bvoh-*soh*-trohs, bvoh-*soh*-trahs kohm-prehn-*deh*ees
ellos, ellas, ustedes comprenden	*eh*-yohs, *eh*-yahs, oohs-*teh*-dehs kohm-*prehn*-dehn

The following table shows you how to conjugate all regular **-ir** verbs in the present tense, using the regular **-ir** verb **aburrir** (ah-bvooh-*rreer*) (*to annoy, to vex, to bore*) as an example. The root is **aburr-**.

Conjugation	Pronunciation
yo aburro	yoh ah-*bvooh*-rroh
tú aburres	tooh ah-*bvooh*-rrehs
él, ella, usted aburre	ehl, *eh*-yah, oohs-*tehd* ah-*bvooh*-rrehn
nosotros, nosotras aburrimos	noh-*soh*-trohs, noh-*soh*-trahs ah-bvooh-*rree*-mohs
vosotros, vosotras aburrís	bvoh-*soh*-trohs, bvoh-*soh*-trahs ah-bvooh-*rrees*
ellos, ellas, ustedes aburren	*eh*-yohs, *eh*-yahs, oohs-*teh*-dehs ah-*bvooh*-rrehn

To keep things simple, stick with the present tense when you're first starting out with speaking Spanish. In Chapter 11, you discover how to issue commands with the imperative and conjugate verbs in the preterite (past) tense. Chapter 13 introduces the simple future tense conjugation.

Talkin' the Talk

Rosario is preparing dinner for her boyfriend Alejandro. The following is a telephone conversation she has with a friend about what she is preparing for the romantic dinner. (Track 2)

(Telephone rings . . .)

Rosario: **Bueno.**
bvooh*eh*-noh.
Hello.

Lupe: **Hola, Rosario. Soy Lupe. ¿Qué haces?**
oh-lah, rroh-*sah*-reeoh. sohy *looh*-peh. ¿keh *ah*-sehs?
Hello, Rosario. It's Lupe. What are you doing?

Rosario: **Preparo una cena romántica para mi novio Alejandro.**
preh-*pah*-roh *ooh*-nah *seh*-nah rroh-*mahn*-tee-kah *pah*-rah mee *noh*-bveeoh ah-leh-*Hahn*-droh.
I'm preparing a romantic dinner for my boyfriend Alejandro.

Lupe: **¿Qué preparas?**
¿keh preh-*pah*-rahs?
What are you preparing?

Rosario: **Preparo una paella especial con arroz, camarones, cebollas, y judías verdes.**
preh-*pah*-roh *ooh*-nah pah-*eh*-yah ehs-peh-see*ahl* kohn ah-*rrohs,* kah-mah-*roh*-nehs, seh-*bvoh*-yahs, ee Hooh-*dee*-ahs *bvehr*-dehs.
I'm preparing a special paella with rice, shrimp, onions, and green beans.

Lupe: **¡Excelente! Es muy especial y muy romántico.**
¡ehk-seh-*lehn*-teh! ehs *moo*hee ehs-peh-see*ahl* ee *moo*hee rroh-*mahn*-tee-koh.
Excellent! It's very special and very romantic.

Rosario: **Pues, adiós. Necesito terminar de preparar la cena.**
pooh*ehs,* ah-dee-*ohs.* neh-seh-*see*-toh tehr-mee-*nahr* deh preh-pah-*rahr* lah *seh*-nah.
Well, good-bye. I need to finish preparing dinner.

Lupe: **Hasta mañana.**
ahs-tah mahn-*yah*-nah.
See you tomorrow.

Words to Know

la cena	lah <u>seh</u>-nah	the dinner
romántica	rroh-<u>mahn</u>-tee-kah	romantic
el novio	ehl <u>noh</u>-bvee-oh	the boyfriend
el arroz	ehl ah-<u>rrohs</u>	the rice
los camarones	lohs kah-mah-<u>roh</u>-nehs	the shrimp
las cebollas	lahs seh-<u>bvoh</u>-yahs	the onions
las judías verdes	lahs Hooh-<u>dee</u>-ahs <u>bvehr</u>-dehs	the green beans

Irregular verbs

Conjugating irregular verbs is challenging because these verbs don't follow the standard Spanish verb conjugation rules that we describe in the preceding section. The good news is that even irregular verbs can be predictable in their unpredictability. That is to say that even the most irregular Spanish verbs have some pattern or method to their madness.

An example is the verb **tener** (teh-*nehr*) (to have). As the following table shows, the root of the verb, **ten-,** changes into **teng-** and **tien-** in much of the present tense. Look carefully at the endings, though, and you can see that they remain the same.

Conjugation	*Pronunciation*
yo tengo	yoh *tehn*-goh
tú tienes	tooh tee*eh*-nehs
él, ella, usted tiene	ehl, *eh*-yah, oohs-*tehd* tee*eh*-neh
nosotros, nosotras tenemos	noh-*soh*-trohs, noh-*soh*-trahs teh-*neh*-mohs
vosotros, vosotras tenéis	bvoh-*soh*-trohs, bvoh-*soh*-trahs teh-*neh*ees
ellos, ellas, ustedes tienen	*eh*-yohs, *eh*-yahs, oohs-*teh*-dehs tee*eh*-nehn

Another irregular Spanish verb that means *to have* is **haber** (ah-*bvehr*). Though its meaning is the same as **tener,** conjugated in the preceding table, **haber** is used as an auxiliary verb to form the compound verb tenses — as is the case with the English helping verb *to have,* which is used in such conjugations as *He has written* or *I have stopped.*

Another very useful irregular verb is the verb **poder,** which means *to be able to* (often translated as *can,* such as in the sentence "I can speak Spanish!") Here are the conjugations of the verb **poder:**

Conjugation	*Pronunciation*
yo puedo	yoh pooh*eh*-doh
tú puedes	tooh pooh*eh*-dehs
él, ella, usted puede	ehl, *eh*-yah, oohs-*tehd* pooh*eh*-deh
nosotros, nosotras podemos	noh-*soh*-trohs, noh-*soh*-trahs poh-*deh*-mohs
vosotros, vosotras podéis	bvoh-*soh*-trohs, bvoh-*soh*-trahs poh-*deh*ees
ellos, ellas, ustedes pueden	*eh*-yohs, *eh*-yahs, oohs-*teh*-dehs pooh*eh*-dehn

Check out Appendix B to see a variety of irregular verbs conjugated.

Talkin' the Talk

 In the following conversation, the Gonzalez sisters are attending a family reunion after not seeing each other for five years. They have a lot of catching up to do. (Track 3)

Verónica: **Hola, Susana. ¿Cómo estás?**
oh-lah, sooh-*sah*-nah. *¿koh*-moh ehs-*tahs?*
Hello, Susana. How are you?

Susana: **Estoy muy bien. ¿Y tú? Hace mucho tiempo. ¿Cuántos años tiene tu hijo ahora?**
ehs-*tohy mooh*ee beee*ehn.* ¿ee tooh? ah-seh *mooh*-choh tee-*ehm*-poh. ¿kooh*ahn*-tohs *ahn*-yohs teee*eh*-neh tooh ee-Hoh ah-*oh*-rah?
I am very well. And you? It's been a long time. How old is your son now?

Verónica: **Estoy muy bien también. Mi hijo, Francisco, ya tiene doce años y es muy alto para su edad.**
ehs-*tohy mooh*ee bvee*ehn* tahm-bvee*ehn.* mee ee-Hoh, frahn-*sees*-koh, yah teee*eh*-neh *doh*-seh ah-nyohs ee ehs *mooh*ee *ahl*-toh *pah*-rah sooh eh-*dahd.*
I am also well. My son, Francisco, is already 12 years old and is very tall for his age.

Y ahora tengo las gemelas Calíope y Camila. Ellas tienen cuatro años. Son preciosas.
ee ah-*oh*-rah *tehn*-goh lahs Heh-*meh*-lahs kah-*lee*-oh-peh ee kah-*mee*-lah. *eh*-yahs teee*eh*-nehn kooh*ah*-troh ah-nyohs. sohn preh-seee*oh*-sahs.
And now I have the twins, Calíope and Camila. They're 4 years old. They're precious.

¿Y tú y tu esposo? ¿Cuántos hijos tienen Uds.?
¿ee tooh ee tooh ehs-*poh*-soh? ¿kooh*ahn*-tohs ee-Hohs teee*eh*-nehn oohs-*teh*-dehs?
And you and your husband? How many children do you have?

Susana: **Nosotros tenemos tres hijos — un niño y dos niñas.**
noh-*soh*-trohs teh-*neh*-mohs trehs ee-Hohs oohn *nee*-nyoh ee dohs *nee*-nyahs.
We have three children — a boy and two girls.

Verónica: **¿Cuántos años tienen ellos?**
¿kooh*ahn*-tohs *ah*-nyohs teee*eh*-nehn *eh*-yohs?
How old are they?

Susana: **Nuestro hijo Roberto tiene cinco años, nuestra hija Sara tiene tres años, y la chiquita, Ramona, tiene catorce meses.**
nooh*ehs*-troh ee-Hoh rroh-*bvehr*-toh teee*eh*-neh *seen*-koh *ahn*-yohs, nooh*ehs*-trah ee-Hah *sah*-rah teee*eh*-neh trehs *ahn*-yohs, ee lah chee-*kee*-tah rrah-*moh*-nah teee*eh*-neh kah-*tohr*-seh meh-sehs.
Our son Roberto is 5 years old, our daughter Sara is 3 years old, and the youngest, Ramona, is 14 months.

Verónica: **¡Qué maravilloso! Estoy muy contenta de verte después de tanto tiempo y hablar de nuestras familias.**
¡keh mah-rah-bvee-*yoh*-soh! ehs-*tohy* mooh*ee* kohn-*tehn*-tah deh *bvehr*-teh dehs-pooh*ehs* deh *tahn*-toh teee*ehm*-poh ee ah-*bvlahr* deh nooh*ehs*-trahs fah-*mee*-leeahs.
How wonderful! I'm so happy to see you after such a long time and to talk about our families.

Susana: **Estoy de acuerdo.**
ehs-*tohy* deh ah-kooh*ehr*-doh.
I agree.

Words to Know

hace mucho tiempo	ah-seh mooh-choh teeehm-poh	it's been a long time
el hijo	ehl ee-Hoh	the son
la hija	lah ee-Hah	the daughter
ahora	ah-oh-rah	now
también	tahm-bveeehn	also
la edad	lah eh-dahd	the age
las gemelas	lahs Heh-meh-lahs	the twins (female)
preciosa	preh-see-oh-sah	precious
el esposo	ehl ehs-poh-soh	the husband
el niño	ehl nee-nyoh	the boy
la niña	lah nee-nyah	the girl
contenta	kohn-tehn-tah	content, happy

Understanding That Whole Gender Thing

In Spanish, everything in creation (not just people) has gender! When you refer to people and animals, understanding gender use in Spanish is easy because gender is a part of their essences, just as with flowers; everyone knows that flowers are pollinated, needing both genders to produce fruit and seeds.

So why not refer to all things that grow with names that are marked by gender? And if things that grow have gender, why not give everything (and every word) that privilege? Many languages, including Spanish (but excluding English) spread this gender thing into their universes. In the following sections, we cover the gender of articles and adjectives.

Getting particular with articles

In English, you use the articles *the* (singular and plural), *a* or *an* (singular), and *some* (plural) without knowing the subject's gender. However, with Spanish articles, you can point out when you're referring to one or several specific beings or things, and in the same breath, you can specify their gender.

The definite articles (representing the English *the*) in Spanish are

- **el** (ehl): Masculine, singular
- **la** (lah): Feminine, singular
- **los** (lohs): Masculine, plural
- **las** (lahs): Feminine, plural

The indefinite articles (meaning *a* or *an/some*) in Spanish are

- **un** (*oohn*): Masculine, singular
- **una** (*ooh*-nah): Feminine, singular
- **unos** (*ooh*-nohs): Masculine, plural
- **unas** (*ooh*-nahs): Feminine, plural

So how do you know when to use which gender on your article? Here are some simple rules you can follow to help you.

- If the noun represents a person, you know whether the person is masculine or feminine, and that's your indicator.
- When the noun ends in *o,* it's usually male.
- When the noun ends in *a,* it's usually female.
- When a noun ends in an *e,* it's usually masculine. There are exceptions to this rule, such as **estudiante** (*student*), which can be either feminine or masculine, and **madre** (*mother*), which is feminine. (Remember, if a person is represented, look to the gender of the person for your clue!)
- When a noun ends in a consonant, it's usually feminine. One exception to this rule is **jardín** (*garden*), which is masculine.

For example, in English, the word *piano* has no gender. But in Spanish, the word *piano* (pee*ah*-noh) ends in an *o* and is masculine. Consequently, *piano* has a masculine definite article before it, **el piano** (ehl pee*ah*-noh) (*the piano*), or the masculine indefinite article **un piano** (oohn pee*ah*-noh) (*a piano*).

Here are some additional examples:

> ✔ **el niño** (ehl *nee*-nyoh) (*the boy*)
>
> **los niños** (lohs *nee*-nyohs) (*the boys* [or *children*])
>
> **un niño** (oohn *nee*-nyoh) (*a boy*)
>
> **unos niños** (*ooh*-nohs *nee*-nyohs) (*some boys* [or *children*])
>
> ✔ **la niña** (lah *nee*-nyah) (*the girl*)
>
> **las niñas** (lahs *nee*-nyahs) (*the girls*)
>
> **una niña** (*ooh*-nah *nee*-nyah) (*a girl*)
>
> **unas niñas** (*ooh*-nahs *nee*-nyahs) (*some girls*)

Look at the **los niños** entry in the preceding list and notice that the translation is plural for both "the boys" and "the children." When you have mixed company (both the male and female genders are present), you use the male plural article. So **los niños** can mean *boys* or *boys and girls*. You follow the same pattern with **unos**.

To pluralize a noun in Spanish, follow three simple rules:

> ✔ **Rule #1:** If a noun ends in a vowel, add *s*.
>
> ✔ **Rule #2:** If a noun ends in a consonant, add *es*.
>
> ✔ **Rule #3:** If a word ends in a *z*, change the *z* to *c* and then add *es*.

Here are a few examples to illustrate:

> ✔ **la chica** (lah *chee*-kah) (*the girl*)
>
> **las chicas** (lahs *chee*-kahs) (*the girls*)
>
> **una chica** (*ooh*-nah *chee*-kah) (*a girl*)
>
> **unas chicas** (*ooh*-nahs *chee*-kahs) (*some girls*)
>
> ✔ **la mujer** (lah mooh-*Hehr*) (*the woman*)
>
> **las mujeres** (lahs mooh-*Hehr*-ehs) (*the women*)
>
> **una mujer** (*ooh*-nah mooh-*Hehr*) (*a woman*)
>
> **unas mujeres** (*ooh*-nahs mooh-*Heh*-rehs) (*some women*)
>
> ✔ **la luz** (lah loohs) (*the light*)
>
> **las luces** (lahs *looh*-sehs) (*the lights*)
>
> **una luz** (*ooh*-nah loohs) (*a light*)
>
> **unas luces** (*ooh*-nahs *looh*-sehs) (*some lights*)

A professional job

When the word for a particular profession is masculine, you form the feminine term by adding an *a* to the end of the word. Thus, **doctor** becomes **doctora.** From there, you can choose the appropriate article with the help of the nearby section "Getting particular with articles":

la doctora (lah dohk-*toh*-rah) (*the female doctor*)

las doctoras (lahs dohk-*toh*-rahs) (*the female doctors*)

una doctora (*ooh*-nah dohk-*toh*-rah) (*a female doctor*)

unas doctoras (*ooh*-nahs dohk-*toh*-rahs) (*some female doctors*)

Not as tough as it looks, is it? However, every rule has its exceptions, and this one is no different. Some Spanish professions use the same term regardless of whether the professional is male or female. Here are a few examples of these exceptions:

el/la cantante (ehl/lah kahn-*tahn*-teh) (*the male/female singer*)

el/la dentista (ehl/lah dehn-*tees*-tah) (*the male/female dentist*)

el/la electricista (ehl/lah eh-lehk-tree-*sees*-tah) (*the male/female electrician*)

el/la policía (ehl/lah poh-lee-*see*-ah) (*the male/female police officer*)

Adding more description with adjectives

Adjectives are the essence of colorful language! A noun tells you what you're talking about, and a pronoun tells whom you're talking about. But adjectives tell you what these things and people are like, including their genders and numbers.

Suppose you want to say *I have a white car.* In Spanish you say, **Tengo un carro blanco.** (*tehn*-goh oohn *kah*-rroh *bvlahn*-koh.). Remember, the final *o* tips you off that **carro** is masculine. A masculine noun gets a masculine adjective: **blanco** (*bvlahn*-koh).

To say *The girl is tall*, you'd say, **La chica es alta.** (lah *chee*-kah ehs *ahl*-tah.). *Girl* is a feminine noun, so you describe it with a feminine adjective. In this case, both end in *a*.

When you talk about things in the plural, you add the letter *s* to the adjective to show that you're talking about more than one. So, **blanco** (*bvlahn*-koh) becomes **blancos** (*bvlahn*-kohs), **alta** (*ahl*-tah) becomes **altas** (*ahl*-tahs), and so on. More examples follow:

Las mujeres son altas. (lahs mooh-*heh*-rehs sohn *ahl*-tahs.) (*The women are tall.*)

Los hombres altos van en un auto rojo. (lohs *ohm*-bvrehs *ahl*-tohs bvahn ehn oohn *ahooh*-toh *rroh*-hoh.) (*The tall men go in a red car.*)

Las casas son grandes. (lahs *kah*-sahs sohn *grahn*-dehs.) (*The houses are large.*)

Los caminos son largos. (lohs kah-*mee*-nohs sohn *lahr*-gohs.) (*The roads are long.*)

Fun & Games

Time for an activity — a crossword puzzle! Provide the correct verb form for the subject/verb pair given in the clues. Hint: All the verbs in this puzzle are regular verbs. To find the correct form, you should use the examples given in the chapter for conjugating regular **-ar, -er,** and **-ir** verbs accordingly. See Appendix D for the answer key.

Across

1 él vivir

3 Uds. retirar

7 él barrer

8 Uds. soplar

9 yo viajar

12 nosotras preparar

13 Ud. hablar

14 ella caminar

Down

1 ellos vender

2 vosotros visitar

4 ella abrir

5 tú mencionar

6 yo comer

7 tú bailar

8 Ud. sospechar

10 ella desear

11 ellos nadar

Chapter 3

Getting Started with Basic Expressions

Speaking Spanish is a whole lot different from writing it, and because this book is more about speaking Spanish than writing it, we want to get you speaking it as quickly and as often as possible. You don't need to be able to recite entire paragraphs. Start slowly by finding out how to say some expressions people use on a daily basis, such as **¡Hola!** (*¡oh-*lah!) (*Hello!*) and **Adiós** (ah-dee*ohs.*) (*Good-bye.*). Of course, you need to pronounce these simple expressions properly so that the people you're talking to know what you're trying to say.

In this chapter, we start you off as slowly as possible with the Spanish alphabet and essential pronunciation rules and guidelines. After you've made your way through the preliminaries, you get to start speaking Spanish with some of the most common everyday expressions.

Reciting Your ABCs

The most elementary building blocks of any language are the letters of its alphabet. Fortunately, the pronunciations of the Spanish letters are nearly identical to the English alphabet; however, the names of the letters are slightly different. Here is the basic Spanish alphabet and its pronunciation (you can hear it on Track 1 of this book's audio CD):

a (ah)	**b** (bveh)	**c** (seh)	**d** (deh)
e (eh)	**f** (*eh*-feh)	**g** (Heh)	**h** (*ah*-cheh)
i (ee)	**j** (*Hoh*-tah)	**k** (kah)	**l** (*eh*-leh)
m (*eh*-meh)	**n** (*eh*-neh)	**ñ** (*eh*-nyeh)	**o** (oh)
p (peh)	**q** (kooh)	**r** (*eh*-reh)	**s** (*eh*-seh)
t (teh)	**u** (ooh)	**v** (bveh)	**w** (*doh*-bleh bveh) (*ooh*-bveh *doh*-bvleh) (Spain)
x (*eh*-kees)	**y** (ee gree-*eh*-gah)	**z** (*seh*-tah)	

Spanish also includes some double letters in its alphabet: **ch** (cheh), **ll** (*eh*-yeh or ye), and **rr** (a trilled *r*).

Pronunciations in this book appear in parentheses (*pronunciation brackets*). Within the pronunciation brackets, we separate syllables with a hyphen (*kah-sah*) and identify stressed syllables with italics. We say much more about stress in the following section.

Understanding Pronunciation and Stress

In Spanish, one syllable always gets more stress than the others — you say it louder than the others. In single-syllable words, knowing what to stress is obvious. But many words have more than one syllable, and that's when the situation becomes, well, stressful. In the following sections, we describe placing stress, using accents, and pronouncing diphthongs.

Looking for stress in the usual places

Can you believe that you're looking for stress? In Spanish, the right stress at the right time is a good thing, and fortunately, stress in Spanish is easy to control. If you have no written accent, you have two rules to follow:

✔ The word is stressed on the next to last syllable if it ends in a vowel, an *n,* or an *s.* Here are some examples:

• **pollo** (*poh*-yoh) (*chicken*)

• **caminan** (kah-*mee*-nahn) (*they walk*)

• **mariposas** (mah-ree-*poh*-sahs) (*butterflies*)

✔ The word is stressed on the last syllable when it ends in a consonant that isn't an *n* or *s*. Look at these examples:

- **cantar** (kahn-*tahr*) (*to sing*)
- **feliz** (feh-*lees*) (*happy*)

If a word doesn't follow one of these two rules, it has an accent mark on it to indicate where you should place the stress; see the following section for more information.

Scouting out accented syllables

One good thing about having the accent mark on a syllable is that you can tell immediately where the stress is just by looking at the word.

The accent mark doesn't affect how the vowel is pronounced, just which syllable is stressed. Here are some examples of words with accent marks:

balcón (bahl-*kohn*) (*balcony*)

carácter (kah-*rahk*-tehr) (*character, personality*)

fotógrafo (foh-*toh*-grah-foh) (*photographer*)

pájaro (*pah*-Hah-roh) (*bird*)

The accent mark isn't always an indication of stress on a syllable. It's also used in some single-syllable words to distinguish the meaning of two words that are otherwise identical, as shown in Table 3-1.

Table 3-1	One-Syllable Words That Change Meaning When Accented		
Accented Form	**Meaning**	**Unaccented Form**	**Meaning**
dé	*give* (imperative of **dar**)	**de**	*of, from*
él	*he, him*	**el**	*the*
más	*more*	**mas**	*but*
mí	*me*	**mi**	*my*
sé	*I know, be* (imperative of **ser**)	**se**	*one's self*
sí	*yes*	**si**	*if*
té	*tea*	**te**	*you*
tú	*you*	**tu**	*your*

Change a letter, change the meaning

Changing one letter, such as in **marea** (mah-reh-ah) (*tide*) and **mareo** (mah-reh-oh) (*dizziness*), can change the meaning of a word. This letter phenomenon occurs in Spanish as well as in English, and finding such words is fun. In the case of the earlier example, the two words do come from the same root **mar** (mahr) (*sea*).

And associating the tide to one's dizziness isn't all that difficult. But in other places you can have oceans of difference. Here are some more examples: **casa** (*kah*-sah) (*house*) and **cosa** (*koh*-sah) (*thing*); and **pito** (*pee*-toh) (*whistle*), **pato** (*pah*-toh) (*duck*), and **peto** (*peh*-toh) (*bib, breastplate*).

Pronouncing diphthongs

Diphthong comes from Greek, where *di* means "two," and *thong* comes from a very similar word meaning "sound" or "voice." (Don't worry, we had to look it up in the dictionary ourselves.) Very simply, diphthong means "double sound."

The Spanish word is **diptongo** (deep-*tohn*-goh). Dipthongs are the combination of two vowels, a weak vowel with a strong one. For instance, *i* and *o* combine to make *io* as in **patio** (*pah*-teeoh) (*courtyard, patio*).

In the following sections, we explain how to join weak and strong vowels, place accents on diphthongs, and separate strong vowels from each other.

Joining the weak to the strong

Dipthongs are always made up of a weak and a strong vowel. Calling vowels "weak" or "strong" is a convention of the Spanish language. The convention comes from the fact that the strong vowel is always dominant in the diphthong. *I* and *u* are weak vowels, leaving *a, e,* and *o* as strong ones.

To visualize this weak or strong concept, consider a piccolo flute and a bass horn. The sound of the piccolo is definitely more like the Spanish *i* and *u*, while the bass horn sounds more like the Spanish *a, e,* and especially *o*.

The vowels in a diphthong belong together in the same syllable. In fact, they're stuck like superglue; they can't be separated unless the weak vowel has a written accent.

In the dipthong, the stress naturally falls on the strong vowel. An accent mark alerts you when the stress falls on the weak vowel. In the combination of two weak vowels, the stress is on the second one. Try these examples of diphthongs:

> **¡Adiós!** (¡ah-dee*ohs!*) (*Good-bye!*)
>
> **bueno** (bvooh*eh*-noh) (*good*)
>
> **cuando** (kooh*ahn*-doh) (*when*)
>
> **fiar** (fee*ahr*) (*to sell on credit*)
>
> **fuera** (fooh*eh*-rah) (*outside*)

Separating the strong from the strong

When two strong vowels are combined, they don't form a diphthong. Instead, the vowels retain their separate pronunciations, so you must put them into separate syllables. Here are some examples:

> **aorta** (ah-*ohr*-tah) (*aorta*) (See! Just as in English!)
>
> **feo** (*feh*-oh) (*ugly*)
>
> **marea** (mah-*reh*-ah) (*tide*)
>
> **mareo** (mah-*reh*-oh) (*dizziness*)

Retooling Punctuation Rules

As you work with Spanish, you may notice unfamiliar punctuation before questions and exclamations. Spanish indicates the mood (or tone) of what you're saying both at the beginning and at the end of a phrase that's a question or an exclamation by inserting upside-down question mark (¿), as in **¿Decía?** (¿deh-*see*-ah?) (*You were saying?*) or exclamation point (¡), as in **¡Decía!** (¡deh-*see*-ah) (*You were saying!*).

As far as we know, Spanish is the only language that provides this sort of punctuation. However, the punctuation is very useful when you have to read something aloud because you know beforehand how to modulate your voice when the phrase is coming up. It's the verbal equivalent of making gestures, which you can see in the following examples:

> **¿Dónde está?** (¿*dohn*-deh ehs-*tah?*) (*Where is it?*)
>
> **¡Qué maravilla!** (¡keh mah-rah-*bvee*-yah!) (*How wonderful!*)

Reflecting on Reflexive Verbs and Pronouns

One significant difference between Spanish and English is that Spanish uses reflexive verbs and pronouns. Whenever you look at yourself, bathe yourself, wake (yourself) up, or worry yourself silly, you're involved in a reflexive action. You, the subject, are doing something to yourself, the object. In English, reflexive actions become a little fuzzy because so much is considered understood. Spanish, however, designates reflexive action by requiring the use of a reflexive verb *and* a reflexive pronoun, such as *myself, yourself,* or *herself.* The following sections tell you more about this interesting phenomenon.

Turning the subject into the object with reflexive verbs

When creating a reflexive verb construction, you need a subject, a reflexive verb, and a reflexive pronoun, but not necessarily in that order. When you conjugate the reflexive verbs in English, you place the pronoun after the conjugated verb. In other words, you say *you bathe yourself.* But in Spanish, the order is *you yourself bathe.*

The following table shows a reflexive verb **bañarse** (bvah-ny*ahr*-seh) (*to bathe oneself*) in all its present tense conjugations:

Conjugation	*Pronunciation*
yo me baño	yoh meh *bvah*-nyoh
tú te bañas	tooh teh *bvah*-nyahs
él, ella, usted se baña	ehl, *eh*-yah, oohs-*tehd* seh *bvah*-nyah
nosotros, nosotras nos bañamos	noh-*soh*-trohs, noh-*soh*-trahs nohs bvah-*nyah*-mohs
vosotros, vosotras os bañáis	bvoh-*soh*-trohs, bvoh-*soh*-trahs ohs bvah-*nyah*ees
ellos, ellas, ustedes se bañan	*eh*-yohs, *eh*-yahs, oohs-*teh*-dehs seh *bvah*-nyahn

Many of these reflexive verbs involve the mention of a body part, and because the owner of the body part is already clear (due to the reflexive verb), you don't use a possessive pronoun. Instead of saying, *I brush my hair,* for example, you say, *I brush the hair.* (**Me cepillo el pelo.**) (meh seh-*pee*-yoh ehl *peh*-loh.) because the reflexive pronoun already signals that it's your hair.

Table 3-2 gives a list of some commonly used reflexive verbs; note that some have stem changes (see Chapter 6 for more about stem-changing verbs).

Table 3-2 Common Reflexive Verbs

Spanish Verb (Used with a Reflexive Pronoun)	English	Pronunciation	Spanish Verb (Used with a Reflexive Pronoun)	Pronunciation	English
aburrirse	to become bored	ah-bvooh-rreer-seh	equivocarse	eh-kee-bvoh-kahr-seh	to be mistaken
acostarse (o to ue)	to go to bed	ah-kohs-tahr-seh	hacerse	ah-sehr-seh	to become
afeitarse	to shave one's self	ah-fehee-tahr-seh	irse	eer-seh	to go away
bañarse	to bathe one's self	bvah-nyahr-seh	lavarse	lah-bvahr-seh	to wash one's self
callarse	to be silent	kah-yahr-seh	levantarse	leh-bvahn-tahr-seh	to stand up, to get up
casarse (con)	to get married; to marry (someone)	kah-sahr-seh (kohn)	llamarse	yah-mahr-seh	to call one's self
cepillarse el pelo	to brush one's hair	seh-pee-yahr-seh ehl peh-loh	maquillarse	mah-kee-yahr-seh	to put on makeup
cepillarse los dientes	to brush one's teeth	seh-pee-yahr-seh lohs deeehn-tehs	olvidarse (de)	ohl-bvee-dahr-seh (deh)	to forget
despertarse (e to ie)	to wake up	dehs-pehr-tahr-seh	peinarse	pehee-nahr-seh	to comb one's hair
divertirse (e to ie)	to have fun	dee-bvehr-teer-seh	preocuparse por	preh-oh-kooh-pahr-seh pohr	to worry (about)
dormirse (o to ue)	to fall asleep	dohr-meer-seh	quejarse (de)	keh-Hahr-seh (deh)	to complain
ducharse	to take a shower	dooh-chahr-seh	quitarse	kee-tahr-seh	to take off, to remove (clothing)
encontrarse (o to ue)	to be located, to meet	ehn-kohn-trahr-seh	reírse (de)	rreh-eer-seh (deh)	to laugh at
enfadarse (con)	to get angry	ehn-fah-dahr-seh (kohn)	sentarse (e to ie)	sehn-tahr-seh	to sit down
enfermarse	to get sick	ehn-fehr-mahr-seh	sentirse (e to ie)	sehn-teer-seh	to feel
enojarse	to become angry	eh-noh-Hahr-seh	vestirse (e to i)	bvehs-teer-seh	to get dressed

Accompanying reflexive verbs with reflexive pronouns

You always conjugate a reflexive verb with the reflexive pronoun that agrees with the subject. Generally, these pronouns precede the conjugated verbs. The verb conjugation isn't affected by the use of the pronoun. Table 3-3 demonstrates each reflexive pronoun with an example verb.

Table 3-3	Properly Using Reflexive Pronouns		
Infinitive	*Subject*	*Reflexive Pronoun*	*Verb*
dormirse (*o* to *ue*) (*to fall asleep*)	**yo**	**me** (meh)	**duermo**
despertarse (*e* to *ie*) (*to wake up*)	**tú**	**te** (teh)	**despiertas**
vestirse (*e* to *i*) (*to get dressed*)	**él, ella, Ud.**	**se** (seh)	**viste**
enfermarse (*to get sick*)	**nosostros**	**nos** (nohs)	**enfermamos**
callarse (*to be silent*)	**vosotros**	**os** (ohs)	**calláis**
ducharse (*to take a shower*)	**ellos, ellas, Uds.**	**se** (seh)	**duchan**

Here are some examples that show you how to use these reflexive pronouns:

¿De qué se queja Ud? (¿deh keh seh *keh*-Hah oohs-*tehd?*) (*What are you complaining about?*)

Me quejo de los precios. (meh *keh*-Hoh deh lohs *preh*-seeohs.) (*I'm complaining about the prices.*)

¿A qué hora se acuestan los niños? (¿ah keh *oh*-rah seh ah-kooh*ehs*-tahn lohs *nee*-nyohs?) (*At what time do the children go to bed?*)

Los niños se acuestan a las nueve. (lohs *nee*-nyohs seh ah-kooh*ehs*-tahn ah lahs nooh*eh*-bveh.) (*The children go to bed at 9:00.*)

To negate a reflexive verb, you put **no** or the proper negative word before the reflexive pronoun:

¿Se enoja Ud. a menudo? (¿seh eh-*noh*-Hah oohs-tehd ah meh-*nooh*-doh?) (*Do you often get angry?*)

No, no me enojo a menudo. (noh, noh meh eh-*noh*-Hoh ah meh-*nooh*-doh.) (*No, I don't get angry often.*)

Nunca me enojo. (*noohn*-kah meh eh-*noh*-Hoh.) (*I never get angry.*)

No me enojo nunca. (noh meh eh-*noh*-Hoh *noohn*-kah.) (*I never get angry.*)

Putting reflexive pronouns in their places

You generally place reflexive pronouns before the conjugated verbs:

Me aplico en la clase de español. (meh ah-*plee*-koh ehn lah *klah*-seh deh ehs-pah-*nyohl.*) (*I apply myself in Spanish class.*)

¿Por qué te pones enojado? (¿pohr keh teh *poh*-nehs eh-noh-*Hah*-doh?) (*Why are you becoming angry?*)

Ella no se siente bien. (*eh*-yah noh seh see*ehn*-teh bvee*ehn.*) (*She doesn't feel well.*)

In sentences with two verbs that follow one subject (as in the first two examples that follow) or in sentences with a present participle (as in the second two examples that follow), you have the choice of placing the reflexive pronoun before the conjugated verb or after and attached to the infinitive or the present participle. When you attach the pronoun to a present participle, the stressed vowel requires an accent:

Voy a maquillarme. (bvohy ah mah-kee-*yahr*-meh.) (*I'm going to put on my makeup.*)

Me voy a maquillar. (meh bvohy ah mah-kee-*yahr.*) (*I'm going to put on my makeup.*)

Estoy maquillándome. (ehs-*tohy* mah-kee-*yahn*-doh-meh.) (*I'm putting on my makeup.*)

Me estoy maquillando. (meh ehs-*tohy* mah-kee-*yahn*-doh.) (*I'm putting on my makeup.*)

In general, to correctly place the accent on a present participle-pronoun combo, count back three vowels and add the accent:

Ella está peinándose. (*eh*-yah ehs-*tah* pehee-*nahn*-doh-seh.) (*She's combing her hair.*)

If the statement is negative, **no** goes either directly in front of the verb (when the pronoun is attached to the present participle) or in front of the pronoun (when the pronoun precedes the conjugated verb). Any stated subject appears first.

✔ Without a stated subject:

No voy a maquillarme. (noh bvohy ah mah-kee-*yahr*-meh.) (*I'm not going to put on my makeup.*)

> **No me voy a maquillar.** (noh meh bvohy ah mah-kee-*yahr*.) (*I'm not going to put on my makeup.*)

✔ With a stated subject:

> **Yo no voy a maquillarme.** (yoh noh bvohy ah mah-kee-*yahr*-meh.) (*I'm not going to put on my makeup.*)

> **Yo no me voy a maquillar.** (yoh noh meh bvohy ah mah-kee-*yahr*.) (*I'm not going to put on my makeup.*)

When used with a command (see Chapter 11 for more about commands), a reflexive pronoun precedes a negative command and follows (and is attached to) an affirmative command (formal or informal):

> **Lávese. (Lávate.)** (*lah*-bveh-seh. [*lah*-bvah-teh.]) (*Wash yourself.*)

> **No se lave. (No te laves.)** (noh seh *lah*-bveh. [noh teh *lah*-bvehs.]) (*Don't wash yourself.*)

Keep these general rules about accentuation in mind:

✔ When one pronoun is attached, count back three vowels and add an accent:

> **Acuéstate temprano.** (ah-kooh*ehs*-tah-teh tehm-*prah*-noh.) (*Go to bed early.*)

✔ When two pronouns are attached, count back four vowels and add an accent:

> **Póngaselo.** (*pohn*-gah-seh-loh.) (*Put it on.*)

Greetings and Introductions: Formal or Informal

As you begin a relationship, Latin Americans believe that keeping a certain formality is best. Only when you already know the person should you use the friendlier, informal phrases. Because Latinos look at building relationships this way, try to respect that view when you're in Spanish-speaking countries or with Latinos in the United States. It's just being polite, Latin American-style. A relationship with a customer in a business situation, however, is normally kept at a formal level.

Latinos don't use **tú** (tooh), the informal *you*, when addressing someone to whom they want to show respect or someone they're meeting for the first time (see Chapter 2 for more about **tú**). However, Latin Americans know that people in the States tend to treat each other very informally, so some may treat you as someone they already know. You may feel a bit leery of this behavior, though: The uncharacteristic informality may make you wonder whether there's some special reason for treating you with such familiarity. On the other hand, an overly friendly Spanish-speaker may simply be trying to put you at ease.

The following sections give you the lowdown on all sorts of Spanish greetings and introductions, from formal to informal.

Latin Americans are generally easygoing people who love to converse. Feel free to initiate contact with them, using the greetings we present in the following sections. If you feel interest on both your part and theirs to keep the contact going, you can introduce yourself, but wait for your acquaintance to give you his or her name. Only if the other person doesn't give you his or her name should you ask what it is. In some specific situations, a third person introduces you, but usually you're expected to introduce yourself.

Introducing yourself with the verb llamarse in any situation

Now is a good time to include the conjugation of **llamarse** (yah-*mahr*-seh) (*to call one's self*), the equivalent of *name is*, which you use when you introduce yourself.

The verb **llamar** is a regular **-ar** verb (see Chapter 2 for more about regular verbs); however, the **se** at the end of it tells you that the verb is reflexive. A *reflexive* verb is one that acts on the noun (or subject) of the sentence. For instance, the sentence **Yo me llamo** (yoh meh *yah*-moh) literally means *I call myself*. In this case, *I* is the subject of the sentence, and *call myself* reflects back to *I*. We discuss reflexive verbs in more detail earlier in this chapter.

Take a look at the following table for the conjugation of **llamarse** in the present tense. Pay attention to the reflexive pronouns — they stay the same for all reflexive verbs.

Conjugation	Pronunciation
yo me llamo	yoh meh *yah*-moh
tú te llamas	tooh teh *yah*-mahs
él, ella, usted se llama	ehl, *eh*-yah, oohs-*tehd* seh *yah*-mah
nosotros, nosotras nos llamamos	noh-*soh*-trohs, noh-*soh*-trahs nohs yah-*mah*-mohs
vosotros, vosotras os llamáis	bvoh-*soh*-trohs, bvoh-*soh*-trahs ohs yah-*mah*ees
ellos, ellas, ustedes se llaman	*eh*-yohs, *eh*-yahs, oohs-*teh*-dehs seh *yah*-mahn

Spanish-speakers often drop the pronoun off their sentences, and the same holds true for the verb **llamarse**. So a person usually introduces herself with just **Me llamo . . .** , not **Yo me llamo . . . .**

Meeting on formal terms

Formal introductions mean that you don't talk in a chummy, informal way to a person with whom you have no relationship as of yet. It's a way of showing respect toward a new acquaintance and doesn't mean you're being cold or distant. People who don't know each other use the **usted** (oohs-*tehd*) verb form (the third-person formal) when addressing one another (see Chapter 2).

When you're talking to a child, you speak less formally, although the child will likely address you formally by inserting **don** (dohn) or **doña** (*doh*-nyah) in front of your name. Calling someone **don** or **doña** can be a way of showing that you're addressing an older and respected person. (To the child, the adult looks old.)

In Latin America especially, *how* you greet people is very important. Latin Americans tend to be very respectful toward each other and newcomers. So as a rule, when you greet someone for the first time in Latin America, it's best not to say **¡Hola!**, which translates to *Hello!* or *Hi!* — a greeting that's considered quite informal. Instead, you can use the more formal **¡Buenos días!** (¡bvooh*eh*-nohs *dee*-ahs!) (*Good morning!*), **¡Buenas tardes!** (¡bvooh*eh*-nahs *tahr*-dehs!) (*Good afternoon!*), or **¡Buenas noches!** (¡bvooh*eh*-nahs *noh*-chehs!) (*Good evening!*).

Talkin' the Talk

In a more formal situation, people introduce each other differently. Listen to Pedro García Fernández as he approaches a table at a sidewalk cafe with a person already sitting there. (Track 4)

Pedro:	**¿Me permite?**
	¿meh pehr-*mee*-teh?
	May I?

Jane:	**Sí, ¡adelante!**
	see, ¡ah-deh-*lahn*-teh!
	Yes, [go] ahead!

Pedro:	**Buenas tardes. Me llamo Pedro García Fernández.**
	bvooh*eh*-nahs *tahr*-dehs. meh *yah*-moh *peh*-droh gahr-*see*-ah fehr-*nahn*-dehs.
	Good afternoon. My name is Pedro García Fernández.

Jane:	**Mucho gusto, señor García. Me llamo Jane Wells.** *mooh-choh goohs-toh, seh-nyohr gahr-see-ah. meh* *yah-moh Jane Wells.* *A pleasure, Mr. García. My name is Jane Wells.*
Pedro:	**Igualmente.** *ee-goohahl-mehn-teh.* *Likewise.*

Words to Know

adelante	ah-deh-<u>lahn</u>-teh	go ahead (Literally: forward)
¿Me permite?	¿meh pehr-<u>mee</u>-teh?	May I?
mucho gusto	<u>mooh</u>-choh <u>goohs</u>-toh	a pleasure
igualmente	ee-goohahl-<u>mehn</u>-teh	likewise

Making more-solemn introductions

Some situations call for a certain level of solemnity. An example is when you're being introduced to a very important or famous person. Like English, a few specific phrases signal this formality, as the following examples demonstrate:

¿Me permite presentarle a . . . ? (¿meh pehr-*mee*-teh preh-sehn-*tahr*-leh ah . . . ?) (*May I introduce you to. . . ?*)

Es un gusto conocerle. (ehs oohn *goohs*-toh koh-noh-*sehr*-leh.) (*It's a pleasure to meet you.*)

El gusto es mío. (ehl *goohs*-toh ehs *mee*-oh.) (*The pleasure is mine.*)

Getting chummy: Informal greetings

When you're greeting someone you're familiar with (or you're being introduced to a child), you can use a more informal greeting without fear of offending the other person. Of course, you use the informal **tú** verb forms when addressing someone you're familiar with, but you're also more casual in the greetings themselves, such as **¿Qué tal?** (¿keh tahl?) (*How's it going?*), **¿Qué pasa?** (¿keh *pah*-sah?) (*What's happening?*), or just a simple **Hola.** (*oh*-lah.) (*Hi.*).

Talkin' the Talk

Discover how John and Julia, two teenagers, greet each other informally.

John: **¡Hola! ¿Cómo te llamas?**
             ¡oh-lah! ¿*koh*-moh teh *yah*-mahs?
             Hi! What's your name?

Julia: **Me llamo Julia. ¿Y tú?**
             meh *yah*-moh *Hooh*-leeah. ¿ee tooh?
             My name is Julia. And yours?

John: **Yo me llamo John.**
             yoh meh *yah*-moh John.
             My name is John.

Deconstructing Spanish Names

Suppose you meet a woman named María Carmen Fernández Bustamante (mah-*ree*-ah *kahr*-mehn fehr-*nahn*-dehs bvoohs-tah-*mahn*-teh). Fernández is her father's last name, and Bustamante is her mother's last name. You may call her **señorita** (seh-nyoh-*ree*-tah) or *Miss* Fernández because of the three-part structure of her name. (In an English-speaking country, she would rearrange her name to María Carmen Bustamante Fernández because English speakers put the father's name at the end and use the person's last name as a reference.)

So far, so good. But if Miss Fernández marries, she adds on more names. In our example, she marries **señor** (seh-*nyohr*) (*Mr.*) Juan José García Díaz (Hooh*ahn* Hoh-*seh* gahr-*see*-ah *dee*-ahs). She is still called Fernández, but after her father's name she adds **de** (deh) (*of*) and her husband's surname, which is García. Now, she is **señora** (seh-*nyoh*-rah) María Carmen Fernández de García (mah-*ree*-ah *kahr*-mehn fehr-*nahn*-dehs deh gahr-*see*-ah).

Note that Spanish-speakers capitalize **señor** or **señora** when abbreviated, the same way people in the States capitalize Mr. and Mrs. See the nearby sidebar "Capitalizing abbreviations" for more information.

Within the social circles of some countries, the surname of a married woman's husband gets more emphasis; in other places, her father's surname is stressed. For example, you hear the husband's surname used more often in Argentina than in Mexico.

The effect of these conventions is that women keep their family names, which are considered very important and meaningful. A child's surnames indicate both his or her father and mother. **Señor** García, in our example, has a child, Mario, by a previous marriage to a woman whose surname was Ocampo. Because children carry the surnames of both parents, Mario is called Mario García Ocampo. And when **señor** García and María Carmen Fernández de García's daughter, Ana, is born, her name is Ana García Fernández. Ana and Mario are siblings, having the same father and different mothers. The Spanish use of both the father's and mother's surnames immediately indicates the relationship between the siblings.

Among Spanish-speaking peoples, using both parents' first names for their same-sex children is customary. So in a family where the mother, Marta Inés, has three daughters, she may call one Marta Julieta, another Marta Felicia, and the third Marta Juana. When the father's name is used for the son, the two are called identical names, because *Jr.* isn't used in Spanish. But you can tell the men apart because their mother's surnames are different.

Capitalizing abbreviations

Only in abbreviations (as well as proper names) do Spanish speakers use capitals. Here's how it goes:

señor	Sr.	seh-*nyohr*	*Mr.* or *sir*
señora	Sra.	seh-*nyoh*-rah	*Mrs.* or *madam*
señorita	Srta.	seh-nyoh-*ree*-tah	*Miss*
usted	Ud.	oohs-*tehd*	*you* (formal, singular)
ustedes	Uds.	oohs-*teh*-dehs	*you* (formal, plural)

Asking and Answering "How Are You?" with the Verbs Ser and Estar

In Spanish, you have two ways to ask, *To be or not to be?* You can say **¿Ser o no ser?** (¿sehr oh noh sehr?) when the state of being is unlikely to change (you'll always be a person, for example), and you use **¿Estar o no estar?** (¿ehs-*tahr* oh noh ehs-*tahr?*) if the state of being is changeable (you won't always be tired . . . hopefully!). In the following sections, we talk about both of these verbs and provide other phrases for asking people how they are.

Being in a permanent way with the verb ser

Ser (sehr) (*to be*) refers to a state of being that is *permanent,* like the fact that you're you. This verb also refers to all descriptions that are expected to be permanent, such as places of origin (nationalities); certain characteristics or qualities such as shape (height and weight) or age (old or young) that are unlikely to change anytime soon; profession; and descriptions of the date, time, or place of an event.

The verb **ser** is the one most frequently used in Spanish. And, of course, just like the English *to be,* it's an irregular verb. (We discuss irregular verbs in Chapter 2.) The following table shows how **ser** is conjugated in the present tense.

Conjugation	Pronunciation
yo soy	yoh sohy
tú eres	tooh *eh*-rehs
él, ella, usted es	ehl, *eh*-yah, oohs-*tehd* ehs
nosotros, nosotras somos	noh-*soh*-trohs, noh-*soh*-trahs *soh*-mohs
vosotros, vosotras sois	bvoh-*soh*-trohs, bvoh-*soh*-trahs *soh*ees
ellos, ellas, ustedes son	*eh*-yohs, *eh*-yahs, oohs-*teh*-dehs sohn

Here are some examples of using forms of the verb **ser:**

> **¿De dónde es Ud.?** (¿deh *dohn*-deh ehs oohs-*tehd?*) (*Where are you* [formal, singular] *from?*)

> **¿De dónde eres tú?** (¿deh *dohn*-deh *eh*-rehs tooh?) (*Where are you* [informal, singular] *from?*)

> **Soy mujer.** (sohy mooh-*Hehr.*) (*I'm a woman.*)

Soy canadiense. (sohy kah-nah-dee-*ehn*-seh.) (*I'm Canadian.*)

Soy de Winnipeg. (sohy de Winnipeg.) (*I'm from Winnipeg.*)

Eres muy bella. (*eh*-rehs *moo*hee *bveh*-yah.) (*You're very beautiful.*)

Ella es maestra. (*eh*-yah ehs mah-*ehs*-trah.) (*She's a teacher.*)

Nosotros somos de aquí. (noh-*soh*-trohs *soh*-mohs deh ah-*kee*.) (*We are from here.*)

Vosotras sois muy generosas. (bvoh-*soh*-trahs *soh*ees *moo*hee Heh-neh-*roh*-sahs.) (*You* [informal, plural] *are very generous.*)

Ellos son muy altos. (*eh*-yohs sohn moohy *ahl*-tohs) (*They're very tall.*)

¿Son ustedes uruguayos? (¿sohn oohs-*teh*-dehs ooh-rooh-gooh*ah*-yohs?) (*Are you* [formal, plural] *Uruguayan?*)

Talkin' the Talk

Imagine that you're in a café, the meeting place for socializing in most Latin American countries, and you can overhear several conversations. Listening to the people at the first table, you hear the following:

Roberto: **¿Y usted Jane, de qué ciudad es?**
¿ee oohs-*tehd* Jane, deh keh seeooh-*dahd* ehs?
And you, Jane, what city are you from?

Jane: **Soy de New Berlin, en el estado de Nueva York.**
sohy deh New Berlin, ehn ehl ehs-*tah*-doh deh nooh*eh*-bvah yohrk.
I'm from New Berlin in the state of New York.

Roberto: **¿Es una ciudad grande?**
¿ehs *ooh*-nah seeooh-*dahd grahn*-deh?
Is it a very large city?

Jane: **Es un pueblo chico, pero muy bonito.**
ehs oohn pooh*eh*-bvloh *chee*-koh, *peh*-roh *moo*hee bvoh-*nee*-toh.
It's a small town, but it's very nice.

Roberto: **Bueno, ésta es también una ciudad chica.**
bvooh*eh*-noh, *ehs*-tah ehs tahm-bvee*ehn ooh*-nah seeooh-*dahd chee*-kah.
Well, this is also a small city.

Jane: **¡Para nada!, es bastante grande.**
¡*pah*-rah *nah*-dah!, ehs bvahs-*tahn*-teh *grahn*-deh.
Not at all, it's quite big.

Words to Know

ciudad	seeooh-<u>dahd</u>	city
grande	<u>grahn</u>-deh	big; large
pueblo	poo<u>heh</u>-bvloh	town
chico	<u>chee</u>-koh	little; small
bonito	bvoh-<u>nee</u>-toh	nice
bastante	bvahs-<u>tahn</u>-teh	quite; enough

Being right now with the verb estar

Spanish is a very precise language. In Spanish, you have two forms of *to be,* each with a different meaning, to supply more precision to your statements. Unlike in English, when you talk about *being* in Spanish, the verb you use removes any guesswork about what your meaning is.

As we discuss in the preceding section, when you speak of permanently being someone or something in Spanish, you use the verb **ser.** But when you're talking about a state of being that isn't permanent — such as being someplace (you won't be there forever), or being some temporary way (being ill, for instance) — you use the verb **estar** (ehs-*tahr*). The following table conjugates the present tense of the verb **estar:**

Conjugation	*Pronunciation*
yo estoy	yoh ehs-*tohy*
tú estás	tooh ehs-*tahs*
él, ella, usted está	ehl, *eh*-yah, oohs-*tehd* ehs-*tah*
nosotros, nosotras estamos	noh-*soh*-trohs, noh-*soh*-trahs ehs-*tah*-mohs
vosotros, vosotras estáis	bvoh-*soh*-trohs, bvoh-*soh*-trahs ehs-*tahees*
ellos, ellas, ustedes están	eh-yohs, *eh*-yahs, oohs-*teh*-dehs ehs-*tahn*

To talk about how you're feeling, you use the verb **estar,** as shown in the following examples.

¿Cómo está usted? (¿*koh*-moh ehs-*tah* oohs-*tehd?*) (*How are you* [formal]?)

¿Cómo estás? (¿*koh*-moh ehs-*tahs?*) (*How are you* [informal]?)

Yo estoy muy alegre. (yoh ehs-*tohy* mooh*ee* ah-*leh*-greh.) (*I'm very happy.*)

Carmen está enferma. (*kahr*-mehn ehs-*tah* ehn-*fehr*-mah.) (*Carmen is sick.*)

Nosotros estamos aburridos. (noh-*soh*-trohs ehs-*tah*-mohs ah-bvooh-*rree*-dohs.) (*We're bored.*)

Talkin' the Talk

 Here's a dialogue to help you practice this new way of being, the one that isn't forever. While having a cup of coffee in a neighborhood café, you overhear the following conversation. (Track 5)

Guillermo:	**¿Cómo están ustedes?**
	¿*koh*-moh ehs-*tahn* oohs-*teh*-dehs?
	How are you?

Sra. Valdés:	**Estamos muy bien, gracias.**
	ehs-*tah*-mohs *mooh*ee bvee*ehn*, *grah*-seeahs.
	We're very well, thank you.

Guillermo:	**¿Están de paseo?**
	¿ehs-*tahn* deh pah-*seh*-oh?
	Are you taking a walk?

Sra. Valdés:	**Estamos de vacaciones.**
	ehs-*tah*-mohs deh bvah-kah-see*oh*-nehs.
	We're on vacation.

Guillermo:	**¿Están contentos?**
	¿ehs-*tahn* kohn-*tehn*-tohs?
	Are you happy?

Sra. Valdés:	**Estamos muy felices.**
	ehs-*tah*-mohs *mooh*ee feh-*lee*-sehs.
	We're very happy.

Guillermo:	**¿Cómo está su hija?**
	¿*koh*-moh ehs-*tah* sooh ee-Hah?
	How is your daughter?

Sra. Valdés:	**Más o menos, no está muy feliz.**
	mahs oh *meh*-nohs, noh ehs-*tah* mooh*ee* feh-*lees.*
	So-so, she's not very happy.

Americans all

You probably like to tell people where you're from, and you like to know where the people you meet are from, too. Almost everyone likes to talk about nationalities. And when you talk about nationalities with Latin Americans, you're wise to remember one crucial point: Latin Americans are Americans, too. So to say **americano** (ah-meh-ree-*kah*-noh) when you mean someone from the United States doesn't quite cover the ground. You make yourself better understood if you say **estadounidense** (ehs-tah-doh-ooh-nee-*dehn*-seh), meaning specifically from the U.S. of A.

Asking how people are with other phrases

When you're greeting people, you don't always want to say the same thing — you can say *hello* without simply saying *hello*. We've looked around for some of the more interesting ways to greet the people that you may come across when you're out and about, and here are a few.

¿Cómo le va? (¿*koh*-moh leh bvah?) (*How are you doing?*)

¿Cómo van las cosas? (¿*koh*-moh bvahn lahs *koh*-sahs?) (*How are things [going]?*)

¿Quiubo? (¿keeooh-bvoh?) (*How are things?* [Literally: *What was there?*]) (Chile)

¿Qué pasó? (¿keh pah-*soh?*) (*How are things?* [Literally: *What happened?*]) (Mexico)

Saying "Please," "Thank You," "Good-bye," and Other Pleasantries

When you're engaged in small talk, you can often get by with a few standard expressions, such as the following:

Por favor. (pohr fah-*bvohr*.) (*Please.*)

Muchas gracias. (*mooh*-chahs *grah*-seeahs.) (*Thank you very much.*)

No, gracias. (noh, *grah*-seeahs.) (*No, thank you.*)

Nada, gracias. (*nah*-dah, *grah*-seeahs.) (*Nothing, thanks.*)

Lo siento. (loh see*ehn*-toh.) (*I'm sorry.*)

Mi culpa. (mee *koohl*-pah.) (*My fault.*)

Con permiso. (kohn pehr-*mee*-soh.) (*Excuse me.*) (In the way)

Discúlpeme. (dees-*koohl*-peh-meh) (*Excuse me.*) (Interruption)

¿Qué necesita usted? (¿keh neh-seh-*see*-tah oohs-*tehd?*) (*What do you need?*)

Quiero unas baterías. (kee*eh*-roh *ooh*-nahs bah-tehr-*ee*-ahs.) (*I want some batteries.*)

No entiendo. (noh ehn-tee*ehn*-doh) (*I don't understand.*)

¿Repita, por favor? (¿rreh-*pee*-tah, pohr fah-*bvohr?*) (*Can you repeat that, please?*)

Necesito información, por favor. (neh-seh-*see*-toh een-fohr-mah-see-*ohn,* pohr fah-*bvohr.*) (*I need information, please.*)

Necesito ayuda. (neh-seh-*see*-toh ah-*yooh*-dah.) (*I need some help.*)

¿Adónde va usted? (¿ah-*dohn*-deh bvah oohs-*tehd?*) (*Where are you going?*)

No sé. (noh seh.) (*I don't know.*)

When you're done talking and are ready to part company, you have several options for saying good-bye, including the following; you can use them formally or informally.

Adiós. (ah-dee*ohs*.) (*Good-bye.*)

Ciao. (chow.) (*Ciao.*)

Hasta luego. (*ahs*-tah looh*eh*-goh.) (*See you later.*)

Hasta mañana. (*ahs*-tah mah-*nyah*-nah.) (*See you tomorrow.*)

Hasta la vista. (*ahs*-tah lah *bvees*-tah.) (*See you later.*)

Speaking about Speaking:
The Verb Hablar

To complete your conversations, you need to know about the verb **hablar** (ah-*bvlahr*) (*to speak; to talk*). You'll be happy to know that **hablar** is a regular verb, so you don't need to memorize how it works. (We cover regular verbs in Chapter 2.) This verb is from the group that ends in **-ar.** The root of this verb is **habl-,** and the table that follows shows how it's conjugated in the present tense.

Conjugation	*Pronunciation*
yo hablo	yoh *ah*-bvloh
tú hablas	tooh *ah*-bvlahs
él, ella, usted habla	ehl, *eh*-yah, oohs-*tehd ah*-bvlah
nosotros, nosotras hablamos	noh-*soh*-trohs, noh-*soh*-trahs ah-*bvlah*-mohs
vosotros, vosotras habláis	bvoh-*soh*-trohs, bvoh-*soh*-trahs ah-*bvlah*ees
ellos, ellas, ustedes hablan	*eh*-yohs, *eh*-yahs, oohs-*teh*-dehs *ah*-bvlahn

Here are some examples of **hablar** in action:

> **¿Habla usted inglés?** (*¿ah*-bvlah oohs-*tehd* een-*glehs?*) (*Do you speak English?*)

> **Hablo inglés.** (*ah*-bvloh een-*glehs.*) (*I speak English.*)

> **¿Hablas español?** (*¿ah*-bvlahs ehs-pah-*nyohl?*) (*Do you speak Spanish?*)

> **Hablamos español.** (ah-*bvlah*-mohs eh-spah-*nyohl.*) (*We speak Spanish.*)

> **Ellas no hablan mucho español.** (*eh*-yahs no *ah*-bvlahn *mooh*-choh ehs-pah-*nyohl.*) (*They [the girls] don't speak much Spanish.*)

Talkin' the Talk

At the café, you hear talk about speaking.

Antonia: **¿Habla usted español?**
¿ah-bvlah *oohs*-tehd ehs-pah-*nyohl?*
Do you speak Spanish?

Reynaldo: **Sí. ¿Qué idiomas habla usted?**
see. ¿keh ee-dee*oh*-mahs *ah*-bvlah oohs-*tehd?*
Yes. What languages do you speak?

Antonia: **Yo hablo inglés y francés.**
yoh *ah*-bvloh een-*glehs* ee frahn-*sehs.*
I speak English and French.

Reynaldo:	**¿Es muy difícil hablar inglés?**
	¿ehs *moohee* dee-*fee*-seel *ah*-bvlahr een-*glehs*?
	Is it very difficult to speak English?
Antonia:	**No, ¡es muy fácil!**
	noh, ¡ehs *moohee fah*-seel!
	No, it's very easy!
Reynaldo:	**¿Y es difícil hablar francés?**
	¿ee ehs dee-*fee*-seel *ah*-bvlahr frahn-*sehs*?
	And is it difficult to speak French?
Antonia:	**No, no es en absoluto difícil.**
	noh, noh ehs ehn ahbv-soh-*looh*-toh dee-*fee*-seel.
	No, it's not at all difficult.

Words to Know

el idioma	ehl ee-dee*oh*-mah	the language
difícil	dee-<u>fee</u>-seel	difficult; hard
fácil	<u>fah</u>-seel	easy
en absoluto	ehn ahb-soh-<u>looh</u>-toh	at all

Fun & Games

Translate the English sentences below into Spanish. All the statements are based on information in this chapter. Sit back, relax, and marvel at how much Spanish you know. See Appendix D for the answer key.

Good afternoon! _____

My name is Jane Wells. _____

Where are you (informal, singular) from? _____

I'm Canadian. _____

What city are you from? _____

Is it a very large city? _____

Yes, it's a very large city. _____

We're on vacation. _____

Are you happy? _____

We're very happy. _____

Chapter 4

Getting Your Numbers, Times, and Measurements Straight

. . . .

In This Chapter

▶ Counting to ten and beyond

▶ Figuring out what time it is

▶ Setting dates and writing them down

▶ Adjusting to the metric system

. . . .

*F*unctioning in any language requires that you be able to recite your ABCs, count to ten, describe things in very basic terms, and deal with schedules and appointments. Although Chapter 3 covers the ABCs, this chapter deals with all the other basics, including counting, telling time, naming the days of the week and months of the year, and knowing your weights and measures.

Counting to 100 and Beyond

One of the first skills you acquire is to count in your native language. Likewise, one of the first skills you need to pick up in Spanish is the ability to count, at least up to ten. The following sections show you how to count in Spanish — both with cardinal numbers (one, two, three) and ordinal numbers (first, second, third).

Counting with cardinal numbers

You can get by with asking for one thing, or more than one thing, or even some things in Spanish . . . for a while. But eventually, you want to ask for two things, or ten things, or even more. When numbers are important, you need to know how to say them, so we show you how in the following sections.

Listing numbers from zero on

Here's how to count from 1 to 2 billion in Spanish:

Number	Spanish	Number	Spanish
0	**cero** (*seh*-roh)	19	**diecinueve** (deeeh-see-nooh*eh*-bveh)
1	**uno** (*ooh*-noh)	20	**veinte** (bveh*een*-teh)
2	**dos** (dohs)	21	**veintiuno** (bveheen-tee-*ooh*-noh)
3	**tres** (trehs)	22	**veintidós** (bveheen-tee-*dohs*)
4	**cuatro** (kooh*ah*-troh)	23	**veintitrés** (bveheen-tee-*trehs*)
5	**cinco** (*seen*-koh)	24	**veinticuatro** (bveheen-tee-kooh*ah*-troh)
6	**seis** (*seh*ees)	25	**veinticinco** (bveheen-tee-*seen*-koh)
7	**siete** (see*eh*-teh)	26	**veintiséis** (bveheen-tee-*seh*ees)
8	**ocho** (*oh*-choh)	27	**veintisiete** (bveheen-tee-see*eh*-teh)
9	**nueve** (nooh*eh*-bveh)	28	**veintiocho** (bveheen-tee-*oh*-choh)
10	**diez** (dee*eh*s)	29	**veintinueve** (bveheen-tee-nooh*eh*-bveh)
11	**once** (*ohn*-seh)	30	**treinta** (*treh*een-tah)
12	**doce** (*doh*-seh)	40	**cuarenta** (koohah-*rehn*-tah)
13	**trece** (*treh*-seh)	50	**cincuenta** (seen-kooh*ehn*-tah)
14	**catorce** (cah-*tohr*-seh)	60	**sesenta** (seh-*sehn*-tah)
15	**quince** (*keen*-seh)	70	**setenta** (seh-*tehn*-tah)
16	**dieciséis** (deeeh-see-*seh*ees)	80	**ochenta** (oh-*chehn*-tah)
17	**diecisiete** (deeeh-see-see*eh*-teh)	90	**noventa** (noh-*bvehn*-tah)
18	**dieciocho** (deeeh-see-*oh*-choh)	100	**cien (ciento)** (see*ehn*) (see*ehn*-toh)

Number	Spanish	Number	Spanish
101	**ciento uno** (see*ehn*-toh *ooh*-noh)	900	**novecientos** (noh-bveh-see*ehn*-tohs)
200	**doscientos** (doh-see*ehn*-tohs)	1,000	**mil** (meel)
300	**trescientos** (treh-see*ehn*-tohs)	2,000	**dos mil** (dohs meel)
400	**cuatrocientos** (koo-hah-troh-see*ehn*-tohs)	100,000	**cien mil** (see*ehn* meel)
500	**quinientos** (kee-nee*ehn*-tohs)	1,000,000	**un millón** (oohn mee-*yohn*)
600	**seiscientos** (sehees-see*ehn*-tohs)	2,000,000	**dos millones** (dohs mee-*yoh*-nehs)
700	**setecientos** (seh-teh-see*ehn*-tohs)	1,000,000,000	**mil millones** (meel mee-*yoh*-nehs)
800	**ochocientos** (oh-choh-see*ehn*-tohs)	2,000,000,000	**dos mil millones** (dohs meel mee-*yoh*-nehs)

If you're accustomed to ordering by the dozen, add the following to your list of numbers:

- **una docena** (*ooh*-nah doh-*seh*-nah) (*a dozen*)
- **media docena** (*meh*-deeah doh-*seh*-nah) (*a half dozen*)

English speakers generally write the number *1* in one short, downward stroke. In the Spanish-speaking world, however, the number *1* has a little hook on top, which makes it look like a *7*. So, in order to distinguish a *1* from a *7*, you put a line through the *7*, which makes it look like this: *7̶*.

Using a few handy guidelines for cardinal numbers

Keep the following rules in mind when using cardinal numbers in Spanish:

- **Uno** (*1*), used only when counting, becomes **un** before a masculine noun and **una** before a feminine noun whether the noun is singular or plural (for more about gender issues, check out Chapter 2):
  - **uno, dos, tres** (*one, two, three*)
  - **un niño y una niña** (*a boy and a girl*)
  - **sesenta y un dólares** (*61 dollars*)

✔ You use the conjunction **y** (*and*) only for numbers between 16 and 99. You don't use it directly after hundreds:

- **ochenta y ocho** (*88*)

- **doscientos treinta y siete** (*237*)

✔ You generally write the numbers 16 through 19 and 21 through 29 as one word. The numbers 16, 22, 23, and 26 have accents on the last syllable:

- *16:* **dieciséis**

- *22:* **veintidós**

- *23:* **veintitrés**

- *26:* **veintiséis**

✔ When used before a masculine noun, **veintiún** (*21*) has an accent on the last syllable:

- **veintiún días** (*21 days*)

- **veintiuna semanas** (*21 weeks*)

✔ **Ciento** (*100*) becomes **cien** before nouns of either gender and before the numbers **mil** (*1,000*) and **millones.** Before all other numbers, you use **ciento. Un** (*1*), which you don't use before **cien(to)** or **mil,** comes before **millón** (*1,000,000*). When a noun follows **millón,** you put the preposition **de** between **millón** and the noun. **Millón** drops its accent in the plural **(millones):**

- **cien sombreros** (*100 hats*)

- **cien blusas** (*100 blouses*)

- **cien mil millas** (*100,000 miles*)

- **cien millones de dólares** (*100 million dollars*)

- **ciento noventa acres** (*190 acres*)

- **mil posibilidades** (*1,000 possibilities*)

- **un millón de razones** (*1,000,000 reasons*)

✔ Compounds of **ciento** (**doscientos, trescientos,** and so on) must agree with the gender of a noun that follows them:

- **cuatrocientos pesos** (*400 pesos*)

- **seisientas pesetas** (*600 pesetas*)

✔ You use cardinal numbers when expressing the first part of an address:

- **mil seiscientos Pennsylvania Avenue** (*1600 Pennsylvania Avenue*)

With numerals and decimals, Spanish uses commas where English uses periods, and vice versa:

English	Spanish
6,000	6.000
0.75	0,75
$14.99	$14,99

Getting sequential with ordinal numbers

You may identify what you did during the day by reciting what you did first, second, third, and so on. Those very words *first, second,* and *third* are *ordinal numbers.* They tell you order and sequence.

When given directions, you hear a lot of phrases describing things like the third block to the left or the fourth floor. So ordinal numbers are extremely useful. Here are the first ten:

- **primero** (pree-*meh*-roh) (*first*)
- **segundo** (seh-*goohn*-doh) (*second*)
- **tercero** (tehr-*seh*-roh) (*third*)
- **cuarto** (kooh*ahr*-toh) (*fourth*)
- **quinto** (*keen*-toh) (*fifth*)
- **sexto** (*sehks*-toh) (*sixth*)
- **séptimo** (*sehp*-tee-moh) (*seventh*)
- **octavo** (ohk-*tah*-bvoh) (*eighth*)
- **noveno** (noh-*bveh*-noh) (*ninth*)
- **décimo** (*deh*-see-moh) (*tenth*)

Here are some phrases to help you practice using ordinal numbers:

- **Vivo en el octavo piso.** (*bvee*-bvoh ehn ehl ohk-*tah*-bvoh *pee*-soh.) (*I live on the eighth floor.*)
- **En la tercera calle hay un museo.** (ehn lah tehr-*seh*-rah *kah*-yeh ahy oohn mooh-*seh*-oh.) (*At the third street there is a museum.*)

- **Mi casa es la cuarta casa de la esquina.** (mee *kah*-sah ehs lah kooh*ahr*-tah *kah*-sah deh lah ehs-*kee*-nah.) (*My house is the fourth house from the corner.*)

- **En el primer piso hay una florería.** (ehn ehl pree-*mehr* pee-soh ahy ooh-nah floh-reh-*ree*-ah.) (*On the first floor there is a flower shop.*)

The following list outlines everything you must remember when using ordinal numbers in Spanish:

- Spanish speakers rarely use ordinal numbers after 10th. After that, they usually use cardinal numbers in both the spoken and written language:

  - **el séptimo mes** (*the 7th month*)

  - **el siglo quince** (*the 15th century*)

- Ordinal numbers must agree in gender (masculine or feminine) with the nouns they modify. You can make ordinal numbers feminine by changing the final *-o* of the masculine form to *-a:*

  - **el cuarto día** (*the fourth day*)

  - **la cuarta vez** (*the fourth time*)

  Primero and **tercero** drop the final *-o* before a masculine singular noun:

  - **el primer muchacho** (*the first boy*)

  - **el tercer hombre** (*the third man*)

- The Spanish ordinal numbers may be abbreviated. You use the superscript **o** for masculine nouns and the superscript **a** for feminine nouns. And you use **er** only for the abbreviations of **primer** and **tercer:**

  - **primero(a):** $1^{o(a)}$

  - **segundo(a):** $2^{o(a)}$

  - **primer:** 1er

  - **tercer:** 3er

- A cardinal number that replaces an ordinal number above 10th is always masculine, because the masculine word **número** (*number*) is understood:

  - **la calle (número) ciento dos** (*102nd Street*)

- In dates, **primero** is the only ordinal number you use. All other dates call for the cardinal numbers:

  - **el primero de mayo** (*May 1st*)

  - **el doce de enero** (*January 12th*)

- In Spanish, cardinal numbers precede ordinal numbers:

  - **las dos primeras escenas** (*the first two scenes*)

Telling Time

Knowing how to speak and understand time-related words and phrases is a must for anyone studying a foreign language. In the following sections, we explain how to note the time exactly and provide a number of common time-related expressions.

Asking for (and responding about) the time

If you hear **¿Qué hora es?** (¿keh *oh*-rah ehs?), someone wants to know the time. If it's 1:00, you answer **Es la una.** (ehs lah *ooh*-nah.) (*It's 1:00.*). For any hour other than 1:00, you use **Son las . . .** and the appropriate number for the hour you want to express: **Son las dos.** (sohn lahs dohs.) (*It's 2:00.*).

Noon and midnight have their own special designations:

- ✔ **el mediodía** (ehl meh-deeoh-*dee*-ah) (*noon*)
- ✔ **la medianoche** (lah meh-deeah-*noh*-cheh) (*midnight*)

To express time in Spanish, you can imagine the face of the clock divided into two halves, with the minutes after the hour on the right side and the minutes before the hour to the left. Thus, to express the time after the hour (up to and including half past the hour), use **y** (ee) (*and*) and the number of minutes. To express time before the next hour, use the number of the next hour and then **menos** (*meh*-nohs) (*less*) and the number of the minutes left to go in the hour. As Western ways have spread around the globe and time is often read from digital clocks, Spanish-speakers sometimes express time exactly by simply stating the number of minutes after the hour with **y** (ee) (*and*). The following shows how to express time after and before the hour (using both methods):

Time	Spanish
2:05	**las dos y cinco** (lahs dohs ee *seen*-koh)
3:10	**las tres y diez** (lahs trehs ee dee*ehs*)
4:15	**las cuatro y cuarto** (lahs kooh*ah*-troh ee kooh*ahr*-toh) or **las cuatro y quince** (lahs kooh*ah*-troh ee *keen*-seh)
5:20	**las cinco y veinte** (lahs *seen*-koh ee bveh*een*-teh)
6:25	**las seis y veinticinco** (lahs seh*ees* ee bveh*een*-tee-*seen*-koh)
7:30	**las siete y media** (lahs see*eh*-teh ee *meh*-deeah) or **las siete y treinta** (lahs see*eh*-teh ee treh*een*-tah)

(continued)

Time	Spanish
7:35	**las ocho menos veinticinco** (lahs *oh*-choh *meh*-nohs bveheen-tee-*seen*-koh) or **las siete y treinta y cinco** (lahs see*eh*-teh ee treh*een*-tah ee *seen*-koh)
8:40	**las nueve menos veinte** (lahs nooh*eh*-veh *meh*-nohs bveh*een*-teh) or **las ocho y cuarenta** (lahs oh-choh ee koohah-*rehn*-tah)
9:45	**las diez menos cuarto** (lahs dee*ehs meh*-nohs kooh*ahr*-toh) or **las nueve y cuarenta y cinco** (lahs nooh*eh*-veh ee koohah-*rehn*-tah ee *seen*-koh)
10:50	**las once menos diez** (lahs *ohn*-seh *meh*-nohs dee*ehs*) or **las diez y cincuenta** (lahs dee*ehs* ee seen-kooh*ehn*-tah)
11:55	**las doce menos cinco** (lahs *doh*-seh *meh*-nohs seen-koh) or **las once y cincuenta y cinco** (lahs *ohn*-seh ee seen-kooh*ehn*-tah ee *seen*-koh)

If you want to discuss at what time a particular event will occur, you can use a question — **¿A qué hora . . . ?** (ah keh *oh*-rah . . .) (*At what time . . .*) — and answer by stating the time as we show you earlier in the section:

> **¿A qué hora vienen?** (¿ah keh *oh*-rah bvee*ehn*-ehn?) (*At what time are they coming?*)
>
> **A la una.** (ah lah *ooh*-nah.) (*At 1:00.*)
>
> **A las tres y cuarto.** (ah lahs trehs ee kooh*ahr*-toh.) (*At 3:15.*)

Exploring common expressions of time

When expressing time, the words and expressions in the following table may come in handy:

Spanish	English
un segundo (oohn seh-*goohn*-doh)	*a second*
un minuto (oohn mee-*nooh*-toh)	*a minute*
un cuarto de hora (oohn kooh*ahr*-toh deh *oh*-rah)	*a quarter of an hour*
una hora (*ooh*-nah *oh*-rah)	*an hour*
media hora (*meh*-deeah *oh*-rah)	*half hour*
por la mañana (pohr lah mah-*nyah*-nah)	*in the morning (a.m.)*
por la tarde (pohr lah *tahr*-deh)	*in the afternoon (p.m.)*

Spanish	English
por la noche (pohr lah *noh*-cheh)	*in the evening (p.m.)*
¿a qué hora? (¿ah keh *oh*-rah?)	*at what time?*
a las nueve en punto (ah lahs nooh*eh*-bveh ehn *poohn*-toh)	*at exactly 9:00*
a eso de las dos (ah *eh*-soh deh lahs dohs)	*at about 2:00*
en una hora (ehn *ooh*-nah *oh*-rah)	*in an hour*
dentro de un rato (*dehn*-troh deh oohn *rrah*-toh)	*in a while*
hasta las diez (*ahs*-tah lahs dee*eehs*)	*until 10:00*
antes de las nueve (*ahn*-tehs deh lahs nooh*eh*-bveh)	*before 9:00*
después de las siete (dehs-pooh*ehs* deh lahs see*eh*-teh)	*after 7:00*
¿desde qué hora? (¿*dehs*-deh keh *oh*-rah?)	*since what time?*
desde las ocho (*dehs*-deh lahs *oh*-choh)	*since 8:00*
hace una hora (*ah*-seh *ooh*-nah *oh*-rah)	*one hour ago*
temprano (tehm-*prah*-noh)	*early*
adelantado (ah-deh-lahn-*tah*-do)	*early (in arriving)*
tarde (*tahr*-deh)	*late*
de retraso (deh rreh-*trah*-soh)	*late (in arriving)*

Using the Calendar and Dates

Dates are important parts of everyday life (in more ways than one!). If you're writing a paper with a strict due date, leaving on vacation and need flight confirmations, or scheduling appointments for your clients and customers, you need to know how to express dates. In the following sections, you discover everything you need to know about Spanish days, weeks, months, seasons, and dates.

Discussing the days of the week

If you hear **¿Qué día es hoy?** (¿keh *dee*-ah ehs ohy?), someone must have forgotten what day of the week it is. You should respond with **Hoy es . . .** (ohy ehs . . .) (*Today is . . .*) and then provide the name of one of the days listed here:

Spanish	English
lunes (*looh*-nehs)	*Monday*
martes (*mahr*-tehs)	*Tuesday*
miércoles (mee*ehr*-koh-lehs)	*Wednesday*
jueves (hooh*eh*-bvehs)	*Thursday*
viernes (bvee*ehr*-nehs)	*Friday*
sábado (*sah*-bvah-doh)	*Saturday*
domingo (doh-*meen*-goh)	*Sunday*

Unlike the English calendar, the Spanish calendar starts with Monday. Here are two more guidelines for talking about days of the week in Spanish:

✔ Unless you use them at the beginning of a sentence, you don't capitalize the days of the week in Spanish:

Lunes es un día de vacaciones. (*looh*-nehs ehs oohn *dee*-ah deh bvah-kah-see*oh*-nehs.) (*Monday is a vacation day.*)

Lunes y martes son días de vacaciones. (*looh*-nehs ee *mahr*-tehs sohn *dee*-ahs deh bvah-kah-see*oh*-nehs.) (*Monday and Tuesday are vacation days.*)

✔ You use **el** to express *on* when referring to a particular day of the week and **los** to express *on* when the action occurs repeatedly:

No trabajo el sábado. (noh trah-*bvah*-Hoh ehl *sah*-bvah-doh.) (*I'm not working on Saturday.*)

No trabajo los sábados. (noh trah-*bvah*-Hoh lohs *sah*-bvah-dohs.) (*I don't work on Saturdays.*)

Naming the months and seasons

If you hear **¿En qué mes . . .?** (¿ehn keh mehs . . . ?), someone is asking you in what month a certain event takes place. The curious person may be asking about the beginning or end of the school year, a special holiday celebration, the occurrence of a business meeting, or expected travel plans. The following table provides the names of the months in Spanish:

Spanish	English
enero (eh-*neh*-roh)	*January*
febrero (feh-*bvreh*-roh)	*February*
marzo (*mahr*-soh)	*March*

Spanish	English
abril (ah-*bvreel*)	*April*
mayo (*mah*-yoh)	*May*
junio (*hooh*-neeoh)	*June*
julio (*hooh*-leeoh)	*July*
agosto (ah-*gohs*-toh)	*August*
septiembre (sehp-tee*ehm*-bvreh)	*September*
octubre (ohk-*tooh*-bvreh)	*October*
noviembre (noh-bvee*ehm*-bvreh)	*November*
diciembre (dee-cee*ehm*-bvreh)	*December*

Like days of the week, the months aren't capitalized in Spanish unless they appear at the beginning of a sentence:

> **Junio es un mes agradable.** (*hooh*-neeoh ehs oohn mehs ah-grah-*dah*-bvleh.) (*June is a nice month.*)

> **Junio y julio son meses agradables.** (*hooh*-neeoh ee *hooh*-leeoh sohn *meh*-sehs ah-grah-*dah*-bvlehs.) (*June and July are nice months.*)

In Spanish, the seasons are masculine except for spring:

- ✔ **el invierno** (ehl een-bvee*ehr*-noh) (*the winter*)
- ✔ **la primavera** (lah pree-mah-*bveh*-rah) (*the spring*)
- ✔ **el verano** (ehl bveh-*rah*-noh) (*the summer*)
- ✔ **el otoño** (ehl oh-*toh*-nyoh) (*the autumn/fall*)

Expressing dates in the proper format

If you want to ask a passerby or an acquaintance about the date, politely inquire **¿Cuál es la fecha de hoy?** (¿kooh*ahl* ehs lah *feh*-chah deh ohy?) (*What is today's date?*) The person should respond with **Hoy es . . .** (ohy ehs . . .) (*Today is . . .*) and then use the following formula to express the correct date:

> day + **el** + cardinal number (except for **primero**) + **de** + month + **de** + year

The following is an example translation that uses this formula:

> **Hoy es viernes, el quince de abril de dos mil once.** (ohy ehs bvee*ehr*-nehs ehl *keen*-seh deh *ah*-bvreel deh dohs meel *ohn*-seh.) (*Today is Friday, April 15, 2011.*)

Now that you have a handy formula, you need to know a few more details about writing dates in Spanish:

✔ You express the first day of each month with **primero** (pree-*meh*-roh). You use cardinal numbers for all other days:

 • **el primero de enero** (ehl pree-*meh*-roh deh eh-*neh*-roh) (*January 1st*)

 • **el siete de enero** (ehl see*eh*-teh deh eh-*neh*-roh) (*January 7th*)

 • **el treinta de octubre** (ehl treh*een*-tah deh ohk-*tooh*-bvreh) (*October 30th*)

✔ Use **el** (ehl) to express *on* with Spanish dates:

 • **Partimos el once de octubre.** (pahr-*tee*-mohs ehl *ohn*-seh deh ohk-*tooh*-bvreh.) (*We are leaving on October 11th.*)

✔ In Spanish, you express years in thousands and hundreds, not just in hundreds:

 • **mil cuatrocientos noventa y dos** (meel koohah-troh-see*ehn*-tohs noh-*bvehn*-tah ee dohs) (*1492 [one thousand four hundred ninety-two]*)

When you write dates as numbers in Spanish, they follow the sequence day/month/year, which may confuse English speakers — especially for dates below the 12th of the month. You write *February 9th* as 2/9 in English, but in Spanish it's 9/2.

When speaking of dates in everyday language, the words and expressions that follow may come in handy:

Spanish	English	Spanish	English
un día (oohn *dee*-ah)	*a day*	**anteayer** (ahn-teh-ah-*yehr*)	*day before yesterday*
una semana (*ooh*-nah seh-*mah*-nah)	*a week*	**ayer** (ah-*yehr*)	*yesterday*
un mes (oohn mehs)	*a month*	**hoy** (ohy)	*today*
un año (oohn *ah*-nyoh)	*a year*	**mañana** (mah-*nyah*-nah)	*tomorrow*
en (ehn)	*in*	**mañana por la mañana** (mah-*nyah*-nah pohr lah mah-*nyah*-nah)	*tomorrow morning*

Spanish	English	Spanish	English
hace (*ah*-seh)	*ago*	**mañana por la tarde** (mah-*nyah*-nah pohr lah *tahr*-deh)	*tomorrow afternoon*
por (pohr)	*per*	**mañana por la noche** (mah-*nyah*-nah pohr lah *noh*-cheh)	*tomorrow night*
durante (dooh-*rahn*-teh)	*during*	**pasado mañana** (pah-*sah*-doh mah-*nyah*-nah)	*day after tomorrow*
próximo(a) (*prohk*-see-moh)	*next*	**desde** (*dehs*-deh)	*from*
pasado(a) (pah-*sah*-doh/dah)	*last (the one passed)*	**de hoy en una semana** (deh ohy ehn *ooh*-nah seh-*mah*-nah)	*a week from today*
último(a) (*oohl*-tee-moh/mah)	*last (in a series)*	**de mañana en dos semanas** (deh mah-*nyah*-nah ehn dohs seh-*mah*-nahs)	*two weeks from tomorrow*
la víspera (lah *bvees*-peh-rah)	*eve*	**dentro de una (dos) semana(s)** (*dehn*-troh deh *ooh*-nah/*dohs* seh-*mah*-nah/nahs)	*within one (two) week(s)*

Talkin' the Talk

Listen as Cruz tells her friend Talia about her vacation plans. (Track 6)

Cruz: **¡Vamos de vacaciones a Puerto Rico en un mes!**
¡*bvah*-mohs deh bvah-kah-see*oh*-nehs ah pooh*ehr*-toh *rree*-koh ehn oohn mehs!
We're going on vacation to Puerto Rico in a month!

Talia: **¡Que suerte tienes! Hemos pasado un invierno terrible aquí.**
¡keh sooh*ehr*-teh tee*eh*-nehs! *eh*-mohs pah-*sah*-doh oohn een-bvee*ehr*-noh teh-*rree*-bvleh ah-*kee*.
You're so lucky! We've had a terrible winter here.

Cruz: **Sí, yo sé. El mes de febrero es especialmente difícil para mí cada año. Es un mes corto, pero para mí es largo.**

see, yoh seh. ehl mehs deh feh-*bvreh*-roh ehs ehs-peh-seeahl-*mehn*-teh dee-*fee*-seel *pah*-rah mee *kah*-dah *ah*-nyoh. ehs oohn mehs *kohr*-toh, *peh*-roh *pah*-rah mee ehs *lahr*-goh.

Yes, I know. The month of February is especially difficult for me every year. It's a short month, but for me it's long.

Talia: **Estoy de acuerdo. Casi siempre hace muy mal tiempo en el mes de febrero. ¿En qué día salen?**

ehs-*tohy* deh ah-kooh*ehr*-doh. *kah*-see seee*ehm*-preh *ah*-seh *mooh*ee mahl tee*ehm*-poh ehn ehl mehs deh feh-*bvreh*-roh. ¿ehn keh *dee*-ah *sah*-lehn?

I agree with you. It's almost always very bad weather in the month of February. What day do you leave?

Cruz: **Salimos el cinco de abril. Es un sábado.**

sah-*lee*-mohs ehl *seen*-koh deh ah-*bvreel*. ehs oohn *sah*-bvah-doh.

We leave April 5th. It's a Saturday.

Talia: **¿A qué hora sale tu vuelo?**

¿ah keh *oh*-rah *sah*-leh tooh bvooh*eh*-loh?

What time does your flight leave?

Cruz: **A las cinco y media de la mañana. Es muy temprano, pero entonces podemos ir a la playa por la tarde.**

ah lahs *seen*-koh ee *meh*-deeah deh lah mah-*nyah*-nah. ehs *mooh*ee tehm-*prah*-noh, *peh*-roh ehn-*tohn*-sehs poh-*deh*-mohs eer ah lah *plah*-yah pohr lah *tahr*-deh.

At 5:30 a.m. It's very early, but then we can go to the beach in the afternoon.

Talia: **¡Seguramente Uds. van a pasar un tiempo excelente en Puerto Rico!**

¡seh-gooh-rah-*mehn*-teh oohs-*teh*-dehs bvahn ah *pah*-sahr oohn tee*ehm*-poh ehk-seh-*lehn*-teh ehn pooh*ehr*-toh *rree*-koh!

You guys are certainly going to have an excellent time in Puerto Rico!

Words to Know

el mes	ehl mehs	the month
febrero	feh-_bvreh_-roh	February
¡Que suerte tienes!	¡keh sooh_ehr_-teh tee_eh_-nehs!	You're so lucky!
el invierno	ehl een-bvee_ehr_-noh	the winter
el año	ehl _ah_-nyoh	the year
hace muy mal tiempo	_ah_-seh moohee mahl tee_ehm_-poh	it's very bad weather
abril	ah-_bvreel_	April
sábado	_sah_-bvah-doh	Saturday

Familiarizing Yourself with the Metric System

Knowing your numbers in Spanish gets you only so far. When you're referencing weights, volumes, and distances, you also need to mention units of measure. Mexico, Spain, and other Spanish-speaking countries use the metric system (not the U.S. customary system common in the United States), so you need to know your conversions. In the following sections, we describe units of weight and volume along with linear measurements.

Units of weight and volume

The metric system measures weight in grams and kilograms, and volume in milliliters and liters (not the ounces, pounds, cups, pints, and so on you may be accustomed to). Here are some rough conversions (and Spanish terms for the units):

✔ *One gram* is **un gramo** (oohn *grah*-moh) — roughly equivalent to the weight of water filling a thimble.

✔ A **kilo** (*kee*-loh) is a bit more than two pounds. **Kilo** actually comes from the word **kilogramo** (kee-loh-*grah*-moh) (*kilogram*), which is one thousand grams.

✔ A **litro** (*lee*-troh) (*liter*) is a bit more than a quart or exactly half as much as you get in one of those two-liter soda bottles.

✔ A **milílitro** (mee-*lee*-lee-troh) (*milliliter*) is one one-thousandth of a liter. A teaspoon contains about 5 milliliters. A cup contains about 250 milliliters.

Talkin' the Talk

 Listen as Amalia bargains with a vendor over oranges at a fruit and vegetable stand. (Track 7)

Amalia:	**¿A cuánto las naranjas?** ¿ah kooh*ahn*-toh lahs nah-*rahn*-Hahs? *How much for the oranges?*
Vendor:	**A diez pesos las veinticinco.** ah dee*ehs peh*-sohs lahs bveheen-tee-*seen*-koh. *Ten pesos for 25.*
Amalia:	**¿A cuánto los aguacates?** ¿ah kooh*ahn*-toh lohs ah-gooh*ah-kah*-tehs? *How much for the avocados?*
Vendor:	**Quince pesos el kilo.** *keen*-seh *peh*-sohs ehl *kee*-loh. *Fifteen pesos for one kilo.*
Amalia:	**¡Es muy caro!** ¡ehs *moohee kah*-roh! *It's very expensive.*
Vendor:	**Es más barato que ayer.** ehs mahs bvah-*rah*-toh keh ah-*yehr.* *It's cheaper than yesterday.*
Amalia:	**¿Tiene bananas?** ¿tee*eh*-neh bvah-*nah*-nahs? *Do you have bananas?*

Vendor:	**¿Sí, de cuáles?**
	¿see, deh koohah-lehs?
	Yes, which kind?
Amalia:	**De esos. ¿Cuánto son?**
	deh eh-sohs. ¿koohahn-toh sohn?
	Those. How much are they?
Vendor:	**Tres pesos el kilo.**
	trehs peh-sohs ehl kee-loh.
	Three pesos per kilo.
Amalia:	**Medio kilo, por favor. ¿A cuánto los ajos?**
	meh-deeoh kee-loh, pohr fah-bvohr. ¿ah koohahn-toh lohs ah-Hos?
	A half kilo please. How much is the garlic?
Vendor:	**A cinco pesos el ramillete.**
	ah seen-koh peh-sohs ehl rrah-mee-yeh-teh.
	Five pesos per bunch [of heads].

Words to Know

naranjas	nah-rahn-hahs	oranges
aguacates	ah-goohah-kah-tehs	avocados
caro	kah-roh	expensive
más barato	mahs bvah-rah-toh	cheaper
bananas	bvah-nah-nahs	bananas
ajo	ah-Hoh	garlic
ramillete	rrah-mee-yeh-teh	bunch

Linear measurements

Although the United States measures length in inches, feet, and yards, distances in miles, and speeds in miles per hour (mph), Spanish-speaking countries use centimeters, meters, and kilometers to measure length. Here are the translations:

- ✔ **centímetro** (sehn-*tee*-meh-troh) (*centimeter*)
- ✔ **metro** (*meh*-troh) (*meter*)
- ✔ **kilómetro** (kee-*loh*-meh-troh) (*kilometer*)

To get a feel for linear and distance measurements in the metric system, consider the following conversions:

- ✔ An inch is about 2½ centimeters.
- ✔ A meter is a little longer than a yard.
- ✔ A quarter mile is about 400 meters.
- ✔ A mile is 1.6 kilometers.
- ✔ 60 miles per hour is about 100 kilometers per hour.

Fun & Games

The following is a crossword puzzle with all the clues in English. All you have to do is provide the Spanish equivalents for these words and you've got what you need to fill in the puzzle! See Appendix D for the answer key.

Across

1 summer
4 eight
7 month
8 second
11 August
13 fifty
14 May
15 spring
18 thirty
20 hundred
21 eighty
22 three
23 winter
25 eleven

Down

1 Friday
2 fifth
3 Sunday
5 today
6 fifteen
7 Tuesday
9 January
10 four
12 week
16 March
17 Thursday
19 nine
20 fourteen
24 ninth

Chapter 5

Speaking Spanish at Home

....

In This Chapter
▶ Naming the rooms in a home (and the stuff in them)
▶ Talking about your daily plans
▶ Cooking up some mealtime conversation
▶ Taking part in typical household tasks
▶ Mastering the possessive in and around your home

....

*B*efore you take your Spanish skills on the road, spend some time at home brushing up on basic vocabulary and expressions you use around your house or apartment. This chapter leads you on a Spanish-speaking tour of your home and then assists you in engaging in common household activities in Spanish. Plus, you find out how to tag items in the house as *yours*. Consider this chapter your own personal Spanish immersion at-home program!

Taking a Tour of Your Home

Every room of your home is probably packed with items people talk about on a daily basis — chairs, tables, lamps, appliances, pots, pans, dishes, you name it. The following sections take you on a tour of a typical home.

As you tour your home, you may want to label common household items with their Spanish names and refer to them by those Spanish names throughout the day. Sometimes, writing and speaking the name of the item is enough to help you remember. And if you happen to forget, the labels function as a quick reminder. Just be sure to use labels that are easy to peel off.

Regardless of where you are in your home, you encounter several words that apply to just about every room:

▶ **la alfombra** (lah ahl-*fohm*-bvrah) (*the carpet, the rug*)

▶ **el interruptor de luz** (ehl een-teh-rroohp-*tohr* deh loohs) (*the light switch*)

✔ **la lámpara** (lah *lahm*-pah-rah) (*the lamp*)

✔ **los muebles** (lohs mooh*eh*-bvlehs) (*the furniture*)

✔ **la pared** (lah pah-*rehd*) (*the wall*)

✔ **la puerta** (lah pooh*ehr*-tah) (*the door*)

✔ **el suelo** (ehl sooh*eh*-loh) (*the floor*)

✔ **el techo** (ehl *teh*-choh) (*the ceiling*)

✔ **la ventana** (lah bvehn-*tah*-nah) (*the window*)

The kitchen

You probably know your way around a kitchen in English, but navigating that same kitchen **(la cocina)** (lah koh-*see*-nah) in Spanish can be a real challenge. Here are some words for referencing the big stuff — the sink, stove, refrigerator, and so on.

✔ **el congelador** (ehl kohn-Heh-lah-*dohr*) (*the freezer*)

✔ **la encimera** (lah ehn-see-*meh*-rah) (*the countertop*)

✔ **la estufa** (lah eh-*stooh*-fah) (*the stove*)

✔ **el fregadero** (ehl freh-gah-*deh*-roh) (*the sink*)

✔ **el gabinete** (ehl gah-bvee-*neh*-teh) (*the cabinet*)

✔ **el horno** (ehl *ohr*-noh) (*the oven*)

✔ **el horno microondas** (ehl *ohr*-noh mee-kroh-*ohn*-dahs) (*the microwave oven*)

✔ **el lavaplatos** (ehl lah-bvah-*plah*-tohs) (*the dishwasher*)

✔ **la nevera** (lah neh-*bveh*-rah) (*the refrigerator*)

Most kitchens contain a hefty collection of smaller appliances, cookware, and other items, including the following:

✔ **el abrelatas** (ehl ah-bvreh-*lah*-tahs) (*the can opener*)

✔ **el basurero** (ehl bvah-sooh-*reh*-roh) (*the garbage can*)

✔ **el batidor manual** (ehl bvah-tee-*dohr* mah-nooh*ahl*) (*the whisk*)

✔ **la cafetera de filtro automática** (lah kah-feh-*teh*-rah deh *feel*-troh ahooh-toh-*mah*-tee-kah) (*the automatic coffee maker*)

✔ **el caldero** (ehl kahl-*deh*-roh) (*the pot*)

✔ **las cucharas dosificadoras** (lahs kooh-*chah*-rahs doh-see-fee-kah-*doh*-rahs) (*the measuring spoons*)

- ✔ **el destapador** (ehl dehs-tah-pah-*dohr*) (*the bottle opener*)
- ✔ **la espátula** (lah ehs-*pah*-tooh-lah) (*the spatula*)
- ✔ **el escurridor** (ehl ehs-kooh-rree-*dohr*) (*the colander*)
- ✔ **la jarra medidora** (lah *Hah*-rrah meh-dee-*doh*-rah) (*the measuring cup*)
- ✔ **la licuadora** (lah lee-kooah-*doh*-rah) (*the blender*)
- ✔ **la sartén** (lah sahr-*tehn*) (*the frying pan*)
- ✔ **la tabla de cortar** (lah *tah*-bvlah deh kohr-*tahr*) (*the cutting board*)
- ✔ **la tapa** (lah *tah*-pah) (*the lid*)
- ✔ **el tostador** (ehl tohs-tah-*dohr*) (*the toaster*)

The dining room

Whether you're being asked to set the table or you need a napkin, having a few terms stored in your memory bank for the dining room **(el comedor)** (ehl koh-meh-*dohr*) can come in handy.

- ✔ **la cuchara** (lah kooh-*chah*-rah) (*the spoon*)
- ✔ **el cuchillo** (ehl kooh-*chee*-yoh) (*the knife*)
- ✔ **el mantel** (ehl mahn-*tehl*) (*the tablecloth*)
- ✔ **la mesa** (lah *meh*-sah) (*the table*)
- ✔ **el plato** (ehl *plah*-toh) (*the plate*)
- ✔ **la servilleta** (lah sehr-bvee-*yeh*-tah) (*the napkin*)
- ✔ **la silla** (lah *see*-yah) (*the chair*)
- ✔ **la taza** (lah *tah*-sah) (*the cup*)
- ✔ **el tazón** (ehl tah-*sohn*) (*the bowl*)
- ✔ **el tenedor** (ehl teh-neh-*dohr*) (*the fork*)
- ✔ **el vaso** (ehl *bvah*-soh) (*the glass*)

The living room

When you're in the living room **(el salón)** (ehl sah-*lohn*), the most important question you need to know in any language is **¿Dónde está el mando a distancia?** (¿*dohn*-deh ehs-*tah* ehl *mahn*-doh ah dees-*tahn*-seeah?) (*Where's the TV remote control?*) To round out your living room vocabulary, we include some additional words to know in the following list:

✔ **el escritorio** (ehl ehs-kree-*toh*-reeoh) (*the desk*)

✔ **la mesita** (lah meh-*see*-tah) (*the end table*)

✔ **la mesita central** (lah meh-*see*-tah sehn-*trahl*) (*the coffee table*)

✔ **la pintura** (lah peen-*tooh*-rah) (*the painting*)

✔ **el sillón reclinable** (ehl see-*yohn* rreh-klee-*nah*-bvleh) (*the recliner*)

✔ **el sofá** (ehl soh-*fah*) (*the sofa*)

✔ **el tele** (ehl *teh*-leh) (*the TV set*)

✔ **el teléfono** (ehl teh-*leh*-foh-noh) (*the telephone*)

✔ **el televisor** (ehl teh-leh-bvee-*sohr*) (*the television set*)

The bedroom

Chances are good that you'll mostly be doing something other than talking in **el dormitorio** (ehl dohr-mee-*toh*-reeoh) (*the bedroom*). Hopefully after reading a few chapters in this book and listening to the CD, you start to dream in Spanish. Until that happens, brush up on your bedroom vocab. (For more bedtime Spanish, see the section "Taking part in bedtime banter" later in this chapter.)

✔ **la almohada** (lah ahl-moh-*ah*-dah) (*the pillow*)

✔ **el armario** (ehl ahr-*mah*-reeoh) (*the closet*)

✔ **la cama** (lah *kah*-mah) (*the bed*)

✔ **mi cuarto** (mee kooh*ahr*-toh) (*my room*)

✔ **la cobija** (lah koh-*bvee*-Hah) (*the blanket*)

✔ **el despertador** (ehl dehs-pehr-tah-*dohr*) (*the alarm clock*)

✔ **el gavetero** (ehl gah-bveh-*teh*-roh) (*the chest of drawers*)

✔ **la mesita de noche** (lah meh-*see*-tah deh *noh*-cheh) (*the nightstand*)

✔ **la sábana** (lah *sah*-bvah-nah) (*the sheet*)

The bathroom

El baño (ehl *bvah*-nyoh) (*the bathroom*) may be one of the smallest rooms in the house, but it's often packed with the most stuff, including the following bare necessities (see Chapter 9 for additional bathroom items that you can buy at the pharmacy):

- ✔ **la bañera** (lah bvah-*nyeh*-rah) (*the bathtub*)
- ✔ **el botiquín** (ehl boh-tee-*keen*) (*the medicine cabinet*)
- ✔ **el cepillo** (ehl seh-*pee*-yoh) (*the brush*)
- ✔ **el champú** (ehl chahm-*pooh*) (*the shampoo*)
- ✔ **la ducha** (lah *dooh*-chah) (*the shower*)
- ✔ **el espejo** (ehl ehs-*peh*-Hoh) (*the mirror*)
- ✔ **el excusado** (ehl eks-*kooh*-sah-doh) (*the toilet*)
- ✔ **el jabón** (ehl Hah-*bvohn*) (*the soap*)
- ✔ **el lavamanos** (ehl lah-bvah-*mah*-nohs) (*the sink*)
- ✔ **el papel higiénico** (ehl pah-*pehl* ee-Hee*eh*-nee-koh) (*the toilet paper*)
- ✔ **el peine** (ehl *peh*ee-neh) (*the comb*)
- ✔ **la toalla** (lah toh-*ah*-yah) (*the towel*)

The laundry room

La lavandería (lah lah-bvahn-deh-*ree*-ah) (*the laundry room*) is where you stick most of the stuff you don't want visitors to see, including your washer, dryer, and perhaps most of your cleaning equipment and supplies. For now, familiarize yourself with the basic terminology.

- ✔ **el detergente** (ehl deh-tehr-*Hehn*-teh) (*the detergent*)
- ✔ **el gancho** (ehl *gahn*-choh) (*the clothes hanger*)
- ✔ **la lavadora** (lah lah-bvah-*doh*-rah) (*the washing machine*)
- ✔ **la lejía** (lah leh-*Hee*-ah) (*the bleach*)
- ✔ **la plancha** (lah *plahn*-chah) (*the iron*)
- ✔ **la secadora** (lah seh-kah-*doh*-rah) (*the dryer*)
- ✔ **el suavizante** (ehl soohah-bvee-*sahn*-teh) (*the fabric softener*)
- ✔ **la tabla de planchar** (lah *tah*-bvlah deh plahn-*chahr*) (*the ironing board*)

The garage

El garaje (ehl gah-*rah*-Heh) (*the garage*) is usually more than just the place where you park your car. It's typically a workroom of sorts, complete with a collection of tools. Here's a list of common items you're likely to find in **el garaje:**

✔ **los alicates** (lohs ah-lee-*kah*-tehs) (*the pliers*)

✔ **la bicicleta** (lah bvee-see-*kleh*-tah) (*the bicycle*)

✔ **la caja de herramientas** (lah *kah*-Hah deh eh-rrah-mee*ehn*-tahs) (*the toolbox*)

✔ **el camión** (ehl kah-mee*ohn*) (*the truck*)

✔ **la camioneta** (lah kah-meeoh-*neh*-tah) (*the van*)

✔ **el carro** (ehl *kah*-rroh) (*the car*)

✔ **la cinta métrica** (lah *seen*-tah *meh*-tree-kah) (*the tape measure*)

✔ **los clavos** (lohs *klah*-bvohs) (*the nails*)

✔ **la cortadora de césped** (lah kohr-tah-*doh*-rah deh *sehs*-pehd) (*the lawnmower*)

✔ **el destornillador** (ehl dehs-tohr-nee-yah-*dohr*) (*the screwdriver*)

✔ **la llave** (lah *yah*-bveh) (*the wrench*)

✔ **la llave inglesa** (lah *yah*-bveh een-*gleh*-sah) (*the crescent wrench*)

✔ **el martillo** (ehl mahr-*tee*-yoh) (*the hammer*)

✔ **el serrucho** (ehl seh-*rrooh*-choh) (*the saw*)

✔ **los tornillos** (lohs tohr-*nee*-yohs) (*the screws*)

Other areas

We cover the primary rooms in a home in the preceding sections, but we haven't yet touched on some secondary areas — the basement and attic and various passageways (hallways and staircases, for example). That's about to change. Here, we introduce you to Spanish terms for these often used yet often overlooked areas.

✔ **el ático** (ehl *ah*-tee-koh) (*the attic*)

✔ **la entrada** (lah ehn-*trah*-dah) (*the entrance, the entryway*)

✔ **la escalera** (lah ehs-kah-*leh*-rah) (*the staircase*)

✔ **el estudio** (ehl ehs-*tooh*-deeoh) (*the study*)

✔ **el pasillo** (ehl pah-*see*-yoh) (*the hallway*)

✔ **el portal** (ehl pohr-*tahl*) (*the entrance, the doorway*)

✔ **el recibidor** (ehl rreh-see-bvee-*dohr*) (*the entrance hall*)

✔ **el sótano** (ehl *soh*-tah-noh) (*the basement*)

Talkin' the Talk

 Valería has just moved into her new house and needs help moving the furniture from the garage, where the movers have left it, into the various rooms. She has asked her friends Javier and Manolo to come over to help her with the heavy lifting and has promised to prepare them dinner in her new kitchen to repay them for their help. (Track 8)

Valería:	**Hola Javier y Manolo. Gracias por venir a ayudarme.** *oh*-lah Hah-bveee*ehr* ee mah-*noh*-loh. *grah*-seeahs pohr bveh-*neer* ah ah-yooh-*dahr*-meh. *Hi Javier and Manolo. Thanks for coming over to help me.*
Javier:	**No es ningún problema. Siempre estamos contentos de trabajar por una comida gratis.** noh ehs neen-*goohn* proh-*bvleh*-mah. seee*ehm*-preh ehs-*tah*-mohs kohn-*tehn*-tohs ah trah-bvah-*Hahr* pohr *ooh*-nah koh-*mee*-dah *grah*-tees. *It's not a problem. We're always happy to work for a free meal.*
Manolo:	**Pues, ¿dónde debemos empezar?** pooh*ehs*, ¿*dohn*-deh deh-*bveh*-mohs ehm-peh-*sahr?* *Well, where should we start?*
Valería:	**Primero podemos llevar mi cama, mi gavetero, y este escritorio arriba al dormitorio.** pree-*meh*-roh poh-*deh*-mohs yeh-*bvahr* mee *kah*-mah, mee gah-bveh-*teh*-roh, ee ehs-teh ehs-kree-*toh*-reeoh ah-*rree*-bvah ahl dohr-mee-*toh*-reeoh. *First we can carry my bed, my dresser, and this desk upstairs to the bedroom.*
Javier:	**¿Dónde está el dormitorio?** ¿*dohn*-deh ehs-*tah* ehl dohr-mee-*toh*-reeoh? *Where is the bedroom?*
Valería:	**Suben por las escaleras y pasan por el pasillo.** *sooh*-bvehn pohr lahs ehs-kah-*leh*-rahs ee *pah*-sahn pohr ehl pah-*see*-yoh. *You go up the stairs and down the hallway.*

Manolo:	**Entonces solamente necesitamos mover el sofá, las dos mesitas, el sillón reclinable, y el tele al salón.**
	ehn-tohn-sehs soh-lah-mehn-teh neh-seh-see-tah-mohs moh-bvehr ehl soh-fah, lahs dohs meh-see-tahs, ehl see-yohn rreh-klee-nah-bvleh, ee ehl teh-leh ahl sah-lohn.
	Then we just need to move the sofa, the two end tables, the recliner, and the TV into the living room.
Valería:	**¡Fantástico!**
	¡fahn-tahs-tee-koh!
	Fantastic!
Javier:	**¿Es el cuarto pequeño al lado de la cocina la lavandería?**
	¿ehs ehl koohahr-toh peh-keh-nyoh ahl lah-doh deh lah koh-see-nah lah lah-bvahn-deh-ree-ah?
	Is the small room next to the kitchen the laundry room?
Valería:	**Sí, tienes razón. La lavadora y la secadora van allí.**
	see, teeeh-nehs rrah-sohn. lah lah-bvah-doh-rah ee lah seh-kah-doh-rah bvahn ah-yee.
	Yes, you're right. The washer and dryer go there.
	Ahora necesitamos mover la mesa y las sillas a la cocina, y entonces yo puedo desempacar los platos y los utensilios de cocina.
	ah-oh-rah neh-seh-see-tah-mohs moh-bvehr lah meh-sah ee lahs see-yahs ah lah koh-see-nah, ee ehn-tohn-sehs yoh pooheh-doh dehs-ehm-pah-kahr lohs plah-tohs ee lohs ooh-tehn-see-leeohs deh koh-see-nah.
	Now we need to move the table and chairs into the kitchen, and then I can unpack the dishes and cookware.
	¡Y pronto podemos comer!
	¡ee prohn-toh poh-deh-mohs koh-mehr!
	And in no time we can eat!
Manolo:	**¡Eso es una idea excelente!**
	¡eh-soh ehs ooh-nah ee-deh-ah ehk-seh-lehn-teh!
	That's an excellent idea!

Words to Know

venir	bveh-<u>neer</u>	to come
ayudar	ah-yooh-<u>dahr</u>	to help
ningún	neen-<u>goohn</u>	none, not any
gratis	<u>grah</u>-tees	free
pues	pooh<u>ehs</u>	well
subir	sooh-<u>bveer</u>	to go up, to climb
pasar	pah-<u>sahr</u>	to pass, to walk through
entonces	ehn-<u>tohn</u>-sehs	then
tener razón	teh-<u>nehr</u> rah-<u>sohn</u>	to be right
desempacar	dehs-ehm-pah-<u>kahr</u>	to unpack

Discussing Your Daily Plans

Family members often meet over breakfast to discuss their daily plans, or at least exchange essential bits of information in the mad race to get out the door. In the following sections, we introduce you to common words and phrases you may use when discussing your daily schedule, whatever it happens to be.

Going with the verb ir

The following minitable shows you how to conjugate the present tense of the verb **ir** (eer) (*to go*) — a very useful verb when you're on the go! **Ir** is a very irregular verb — so much so that you have to take it on faith from us that the following table shows the correct conjugations, because you sure couldn't tell just by looking at it.

Conjugation	Pronunciation
yo voy	yoh bvohy
tú vas	tooh bvahs
él, ella, usted va	ehl, *eh*-yah, oohs-*tehd* bvah
nosotros, nosotras vamos	noh-*soh*-trohs, noh-*soh*-trahs *bvah*-mohs
vosotros, vosotras vais	bvoh-*soh*-trohs, bvoh-*soh*-trahs *bvah*ees
ellos, ellas, ustedes van	*eh*-yohs, *eh*-yahs, oohs-*teh*-dehs bvahn

You (or I, he, she, we, or they) can talk about going to a variety of places:

Voy a la casa de mi amigo. (bvohy ah lah *kah*-sah deh mee ah-*mee*-goh.) (*I go to my friend's house.*)

¿Cuándo vas a casa? (¿kooh*ahn*-doh bvahs ah *kah*-sah?) (*When do you go home?*)

Ella va a la ciudad para trabajar. (*eh*-yah bvah ah lah seeooh-*dahd* pah-rah trah-bvah-*Hahr*.) (*She goes to the city to work.*)

Él va al otro lado de la calle. (ehl bvah ahl *oh*-troh *lah*-doh deh lah *kah*-yeh.) (*He goes across the street.*)

Nosotros vamos al aeropuerto mañana. (noh-*soh*-trohs *bvah*-mohs ahl ah-ee-roh-pooh*ehr*-toh mah-*nyah*-nah.) (*We go to the airport tomorrow.*)

Los estudiantes van afuera para jugar. (lohs ehs-tooh-dee*ahn*-tehs bvahn ah-fooh*eh*-rah *pah*-rah Hooh-*gahr*.) (*The students go outside to play.*)

Ellos van al cine. (*eh*-yohs bvahn ahl *see*-neh.) (*They go to the movies.*)

Describing what you like with the verb gustar

When you talk about liking something in Spanish, including activities that are a part of your daily plans, you use the verb **gustar** (goohs-*tahr*) (*to like; to enjoy*). Because **gustar** is a bit of a strange bird, we've included a translation in the following conjugation table to help you choose the correct form.

Conjugation	Pronunciation	Translation
me gusta	meh *goohs*-tah	*I like*
te gusta	teh *goohs*-tah	*you* [informal] *like*
le gusta	leh *goohs*-tah	*he, she, you* [formal] *like(s)*

nos gusta	nohs *goohs*-tah	*we like*
os gusta	ohs *goohs*-tah	*you* [informal] *like*
les gusta	lehs *goohs*-tah	*they, you* [formal] *like*

The following expressions can help you express what you like:

> **Me gusta pasear.** (meh *goohs*-tah pah-seh-*ahr.*) (*I like to walk.*)

> **Le gusta jugar con el gato.** (leh *goohs*-tah Hooh-*gahr* kohn ehl *gah*-toh.) (*She likes to play with the cat.*)

> **¿Les gusta comer algo?** (¿lehs *goohs*-tah koh-*mehr* ahl-goh?) (*Would you* [formal, plural] *like something to eat?*)

When what you like is plural, you must pluralize the form of the verb by adding *n:*

> **Nos gustan los gatos.** (nohs *goohs*-tahn lohs *gah*-tohs.) (*We like cats.*)

If you actually love something, you can use the verb **encantar** (ehn-kahn-*tahr*) (*to love*) to show a stronger emotion. This verb follows the same conjugation pattern as **gustar:**

> **Les encantan las películas románticas.** (lehs ehn-*kahn*-tahn lahs peh-*lee*-kooh-lahs rroh-*mahn*-tee-kahs.) (*They love romantic movies.*)

Heading off to work

As you head off to work **(el trabajo)** (ehl trah-*bvah*-Hoh), you're more likely to discuss plans around your workday rather than the work itself. The following phrases are likely to come in handy:

> **Necesito salir temprano para el trabajo hoy.** (neh-seh-*see*-toh sah-*leer* tehm-*prah*-noh *pah*-rah ehl trah-*bvah*-Hoh ohy.) (*I need to leave early for work today.*)

> **Voy a llegar tarde a casa hoy.** (bvohy ah yeh-*gahr tahr*-deh ah *kah*-sah ohy.) (*I'll be home late today.*)

> **¿Quieres almorzar juntos?** (¿kee*eh*-rehs ahl-mohr-*sahr Hoohn*-tohs?) (*Would you like to have lunch together?*)

> **Tengo una reunión importante hoy.** (*tehn*-goh *ooh*-nah rrehooh-nee*ohn* eem-pohr-*tahn*-teh ohy.) (*I have an important meeting today.*)

> **¿A qué hora debo de llegar a casa hoy?** (¿ah keh *oh*-rah *deh*-bvoh deh yeh-*gahr* ah *kah*-sah ohy?) (*What time must I be home today?*)

¿Tienes unos planes después del trabajo hoy? (¿tee*eh*-nehs *ooh*-nohs *plah*-nehs dehs-pooh*ehs* dehl trah-*bvah*-Hoh ohy?) (*Do you have any plans after work today?*)

No, no tengo planes después del trabajo. (noh, noh *tehn*-goh *plah*-nehs dehs-pooh*ehs* dehl trah-*bvah*-Hoh.) (*No, I don't have plans after work.*)

Flip to Chapter 11 if you're interested in finding out some terms related to working in an office.

Leaving for school

Whether you're heading out to school **(la escuela)** (lah ehs-kooh*eh*-lah) or speaking to someone who's leaving for school, you want to be able to ask questions and interpret answers. Here are some important school terms to know:

- ✔ **el autobús escolar** (ehl ahooh-toh-*bvoohs* ehs-koh-*lahr*) (*the school bus*)
- ✔ **el bolígrafo** (ehl bvoh-*lee*-grah-foh) (*the pen*)
- ✔ **la carpeta** (lah kahr-*peh*-tah) (*the folder*)
- ✔ **la clase de ciencias** (lah *klah*-seh deh see*ehn*-seeahs) (*the science class*)
- ✔ **la clase de historia** (lah *klah*-seh deh ees-*toh*-reeah) (*the history class*)
- ✔ **la clase de matemáticas** (lah *klah*-seh deh mah-teh-*mah*-tee-kahs) (*the math class*)
- ✔ **el examen** (ehl ehk-*sah*-mehn) (*the test*)
- ✔ **el informe** (ehl een-*fohr*-meh) (*the report*)
- ✔ **el lápiz** (ehl *lah*-pees) (*the pencil*)
- ✔ **los libros** (lohs *lee*-bvrohs) (*the books*)
- ✔ **la mochila** (lah moh-*chee*-lah) (*the backpack*)
- ✔ **la tarea** (lah tah-*reh*-ah) (*the homework*)

Talkin' the Talk

Zarita is discussing her day with her mother Nadia before she leaves for school. (Track 9)

Nadia: **Buenos días, Zarita. ¿Pasa algo especial en la escuela hoy?**
bvooh*eh*-nohs *deeahs*, sah-*ree*-tah. ¿*pah*-sah *ahl*-goh ehs-peh-see*ahl* ehn lah ehs-kooh*eh*-lah ohy?
Good morning, Zarita. Is anything special going on at school today?

Zarita:	**No, de veras no hay nada especial hoy.** noh, deh *bveh*-rahs noh ahy *nah*-dah ehs-peh-see*ahl* ohy. *No, there's really nothing special today.*
Nadia:	**¿Tienes toda la tarea terminada?** ¿tee*eh*-nehs *toh*-dah lah tah-*reh*-ah tehr-mee-*nah*-dah? *Do you have all of your homework finished?*
Zarita:	**Sí, salvo un informe para la clase de historia que es para el viernes.** see, *sahl*-bvoh oohn een-*fohr*-meh *pah*-rah lah *klah*-seh deh ees-*toh*-reeah keh ehs *pah*-rah ehl bvee*ehr*-nehs. *Yes, except for a report for history class that's due on Friday.*
Nadia:	**¿Cómo va en la clase de historia, en general?** ¿*koh*-moh bvah ehn lah *klah*-seh deh ees-*toh*-reeah, ehn Hehn-eh-*rahl?* *How's it going in history class, in general?*
Zarita:	**Así así, pero de veras no me gusta escribir los informes.** ah-*see* ah-*see*, *peh*-roh deh *bveh*-rahs noh meh *goohs*-tah ehs-kree-*bveer* lohs een-*fohr*-mehs. *Okay, but I really don't like to write reports.*
Nadia:	**¿Llegas a casa inmediatamente después de la escuela hoy?** ¿*yeh*-gahs ah *kah*-sah een-meh-deeah-tah-*mehn*-teh dehs-pooh*ehs* deh lah ehs-koohe*h*-lah ohy? *Are you coming home right after school today?*
Zarita:	**Tengo que practicar con el equipo de fútbol hasta las seis.** *tehn*-goh keh prahk-tee-*kahr* kohn ehl eh-*kee*-poh deh *fooht*-bvohl *ahs*-tah lahs *seh*ees. *I have to practice with the soccer team until 6:00.*
Nadia:	**Está bien. Hasta luego.** ehs-*tah* bveee*hn*. *ahs*-tah looheh*h*-goh. *Okay. I'll see you later.*
Zarita:	**Bien. Tengo que irme. El autobús está aquí. ¡Hasta luego!** bveee*hn*. *tehn*-goh keh *eer*-meh. ehl ahooh-toh-*bvoohs* ehs-*tah* ah-*kee*. ¡*ahs*-tah looheh*h*-goh! *Okay. I have to go.The bus is here. See you later!*

Words to Know

¿Pasa algo especial?	¿pah-sah ahl-goh ehs-peh-seeahl?	Is anything special going on?
la escuela	lah ehs-kooheh-lah	the school
de veras	deh bveh-rahs	really
la tarea	lah tah-reh-ah	the homework
terminada	tehr-mee-nah-dah	finished
salvo	sahl-bvoh	except
un informe	oohn een-fohr-meh	a report
la clase	lah klah-seh	the class
escribir	ehs-kree-bveer	to write

Eating at Home

To this day, food remains the universal language and one of the best tools for introducing students to new languages and cultures. Knowing some basic words and phrases before sitting down for a meal at home can make the experience more enjoyable and certainly improves the opportunities for engaging in stimulating dinner conversation. In the following sections, we provide handy phrases for setting the table and asking for food and drinks; we also explain how to conjugate three important verbs related to eating and drinking. Flip to Chapter 8 for terms and tips for dining out and going to the market.

Cooking with the verb cocinar

Cocinar (koh-see-*nahr*) means *to cook,* and whether or not you like to cook, *someone* has to do it or no one will eat. **Cocinar** is a regular **-ar** verb and is very easy to conjugate, as you can see in the following verb chart:

Conjugation	*Pronunciation*
yo cocino	yoh koh-*see*-noh
tú cocinas	tooh koh-*see*-nahs
él, ella, usted cocina	ehl, *eh*-yah, oohs-*tehd* koh-*see*-nah
nosotros, nosotras cocinamos	noh-*soh*-trohs, noh-*soh*-trahs koh-see-*nah*-mohs
vosotros, vosotras cocináis	bvoh-*soh*-trohs, bvoh-*soh*-trahs koh-see-*nah*ees
ellos, ellas, ustedes cocinan	*eh*-yohs, *eh*-yahs, oohs-*teh*-dehs koh-*see*-nahn

Here are a couple of examples of this verb in use:

Mi padre siempre cocina los sábados. (mee *pah*-dreh see*ehm*-preh koh-*see*-nah lohs *sah*-bvah-dohs.) (*My father always cooks on Saturdays.*)

Nosotros cocinamos paella para ocasiones especiales. (noh-*soh*-trohs koh-see-*nah*-mohs pah-*eh*-yah *pah*-rah oh-kah-see*oh*-nehs ehs-peh-see*ah*-lehs.) (*We cook paella for special occasions.*)

Setting the table

You may find these phrases useful when you set the table:

¡A poner la mesa! (¡ah poh-*nehr* lah *meh*-sah!) (*Set the table!*)

Aquí están los platos y los vasos. (ah-*kee* ehs-*tahn* lohs *plah*-tohs ee lohs *bvah*-sohs.) (*Here are the dishes and glasses.*)

¿Qué cubiertos? (¿keh kooh-bvee*ehr*-tohs?) (*What cutlery?*)

Cuchara, cuchillo, y tenedor. (kooh-*chah*-rah kooh-*chee*-yo ee teh-neh-*dohr*.) (*Spoon, knife, and fork.*)

Aquí están las servilletas. (ah-*kee* ehs-*tahn* lahs sehr-bvee-*yeh*-tahs.) (*Here are the napkins.*)

No se olvide de poner el pimentero en la mesa. (noh seh ohl-*bvee*-deh deh poh-*nehr* ehl pee-mehn-*teh*-roh ehn lah *meh*-sah.) (*Don't forget to put the pepper shaker on the table.*)

Más sal en el salero. (mahs sahl ehn ehl sah-*leh*-roh.) (*More salt in the salt shaker.*)

Giving and receiving food and drinks at meals

Here are some common terms connected with meals:

- **el almuerzo** (ehl ahl-mooh*ehr*-soh) (*lunch*)
- **la cena** (lah *seh*-nah) (*supper*)
- **la comida** (la koh-*mee*-dah) (*dinner, meal, food*)
- **el desayuno** (ehl deh-sah-*yooh*-noh) (*breakfast*)
- **tener hambre** (teh-*nehr ahm*-bvreh) (*to be hungry*)
- **tener sed** (teh-*nehr* sehd) (*to be thirsty*)

You may hear these phrases, or speak them yourself, when giving or receiving foods and beverages:

Está picante. (ehs-*tah* pee-*kahn*-teh.) (*It's hot* [flavor/spice].)

Está caliente. (ehs-*tah* kah-lee*ehn*-teh.) (*It's hot* [temperature].)

Está frío. (ehs-*tah* free*oh*.) (*It's cold.*)

Es sabroso. (ehs sah-*bvroh*-soh.) (*It's tasty.*)

Lamento, no tenemos . . . . (lah-*mehn*-toh, noh teh-*neh*-mohs . . . .) (*Sorry, we don't have . . . .*)

¿Qué ingredientes tiene? (¿keh een-greh-dee*ehn*-tehs tee*eh*-neh?) (*What are the ingredients?*)

¡Salud! (sah-*loohd*) (*Cheers!*)

These words can help you when you're asking for something to drink; Chapter 8 gives you a more extensive list of drink options.

- **un refresco** (oohn rreh-*frehs*-koh) (*a soda*)
- **un trago** (oohn *trah*-goh) (*a shot, a drink*)
- **un vaso de agua** (oohn *bvah*-soh deh *ah*-goohah) (*a glass of water*)
- **un vaso de leche** (oohn *bvah*-soh deh *leh*-cheh) (*a glass of milk*)
- **un vaso de vino** (oohn *bvah*-soh deh *bvee*-noh) (*a glass of wine*)

Using three verbs at the table

In Spanish, you talk about eating with the verb **comer** (koh-*mehr*) and drinking with the verb **beber** (bveh-*bvehr*). The verb **tomar** (toh-*mahr*) does double duty; you can use it for eating and drinking. Find out the details in the following sections.

To eat: The verb comer

Comer means *to eat*. A regular verb from the **-er** group, the root of this verb is **com-** (kohm), as the following table shows:

Conjugation	Pronunciation
yo como	yoh *koh*-moh
tú comes	tooh *koh*-mehs
él, ella, usted come	ehl, *eh*-yah, oohs-*tehd koh*-meh
nosotros, nosotras comemos	noh-*soh*-trohs, noh-*soh*-trahs koh-*meh*-mohs
vosotros, vosotras coméis	bvoh-*soh*-trohs, bvoh-*soh*-trahs koh-*meh*ees
ellos, ellas, ustedes comen	*eh*-yohs, *eh*-yahs, oohs-*teh*-dehs *koh*-mehn

To drink: The verb beber

Beber (bveh-*bvehr*), which means *to drink,* is a regular verb; it's from the **-er** group. The root of the verb is **beb-** (bvehbv), as you can see in the following table:

Conjugation	Pronunciation
yo bebo	yoh *bveh*-bvoh
tú bebes	tooh *bveh*-bvehs
él, ella, usted bebe	ehl, *eh*-yah, oohs-*tehd bveh*-bveh
nosotros, nosotras bebemos	noh-*soh*-trohs, noh-*soh*-trahs bveh-*bveh*-mohs
vosotros, vosotras bebéis	bvoh-*soh*-trohs, bvoh-*soh*-trahs bveh-*bveh*ees
ellos, ellas, ustedes beben	*eh*-yohs, *eh*-yahs, oohs-*teh*-dehs *bveh*-bvehn

To eat and to drink: The verb tomar

Tomar (toh-*mahr*) literally means *to take* and often indicates exactly that (such as in the phrase **tomar el autobús** [toh-*mahr* ehl ahooh-toh-*bvoohs*] [*to take the bus*]). But when you say **tomar un refresco** (toh-*mahr* oohn rreh-*frehs*-koh), you're talking about *drinking a soda,* not literally taking one. Similarly, when you say **tomar una hamburguesa** (toh-*mahr* ooh-nah ahm-bvoohr-*geh*-sah), you're talking about *eating a hamburger,* and you know that's what you mean in these cases because **tomar** is followed by something you eat or drink.

Tomar is a regular verb of the **-ar** group. The root of the verb is **tom-** (tohm); check out the table that follows for the conjugation:

Conjugation	Pronunciation
yo tomo	yoh *toh*-moh
tú tomas	tooh *toh*-mahs
él, ella, usted toma	ehl, *eh*-yah, oohs-*tehd toh*-mah
nosotros, nosotras tomamos	noh-*soh*-trohs, noh-*soh*-trahs toh-*mah*-mohs
vosotros, vosotras tomáis	bvoh-*soh*-trohs, bvoh-*soh*-trahs toh-*mah*ees
ellos, ellas, ustedes toman	*eh*-yohs, *eh*-yahs, oohs-*teh*-dehs *toh*-mahn

Engaging in Common Household Activities

Although cooking and eating consume a large part of most people's daily household activities (see the preceding sections), you can find plenty more to do around your home, including watching TV, playing games, doing chores, and, when all of those other activities exhaust you, going to bed. The following sections provide key words and phrases for communicating as you engage in these activities around your home.

Doing anything with the verb hacer

A most basic verb is the verb **hacer** (ah-*sehr*) which means *to do* or *to make*. It's slightly irregular in the present tense, as you can see in the following verb chart. It follows the rules of conjugation for regular **-er** verbs except in the **yo** form — it changes the *c* to a *g*.

Conjugation	Pronunciation
yo hago	yoh *ah*-goh
tú haces	tooh *ah*-sehs
él, ella, usted hace	ehl, *eh*-yah, oohs-*tehd ah*-seh
nosotros, nosotras hacemos	noh-*soh*-trohs, noh-*soh*-trahs ah-*seh*-mohs
vosotros, vosotras hacéis	bvoh-*soh*-trohs, bvoh-*soh*-trahs ah-*seh*ees
ellos, ellas, ustedes hacen	*eh*-yohs, *eh*-yahs, oohs-*teh*-dehs *ah*-sehn

Here are a couple of examples of how to use **hacer:**

> **Ella hace un crucigrama.** (*eh*-yah *ah*-seh oohn krooh-see-*grah*-mah.) (*She's doing a crossword puzzle.*)

> **Nosotros hacemos un rompecabezas.** (noh-*soh*-trohs ah-*seh*-mohs oohn rrohm-peh-kah-*bveh*-sahs.) (*We're doing a puzzle.*)

Keeping up with household chores

Whether you and other household members keep your living space tidy or hire someone to do it for you, you need to be able to discuss what needs to be done and reference essential tools and cleaning supplies. Here are some words to get you started:

- ✔ **la aspiradora** (lah ahs-pee-rah-*doh*-rah) (*the vacuum*)
- ✔ **el cubo** (ehl *kooh*-bvoh) (*the bucket*)
- ✔ **el detergente (en polvo)** (ehl deh-tehr-*Hehn*-teh [ehn *pohl*-bvoh]) (*the [powdered] detergent*)
- ✔ **la escoba** (lah ehs-*koh*-bvah) (*the broom*)
- ✔ **el recogedor** (ehl rreh-koh-Heh-*dohr*) (*the dustpan*)
- ✔ **el trapeador** (ehl trah-peh-ah-*dohr*) (*the mop*)

Of course, you also want to know the names for those common chores themselves (if only so that you can complain about doing them). Check out the following list:

- ✔ **barrer** (bvah-*rrehr*) (*to sweep [with a broom]*)
- ✔ **trapear** (trah-peh-*ahr*) (*to mop*)
- ✔ **pasar la aspiradora** (pah-*sahr* lah ahs-pee-rah-*doh*-rah) (*to vacuum*)
- ✔ **quitar el polvo** (kee-*tahr* ehl pohl-*bvoh*) (*to dust*)
- ✔ **sacar la basura** (sah-*kahr* lah bvah-*sooh*-rah) (*to take out the trash*)

Head to Chapter 11 to find out how to form commands with these chore verbs so that you can assign these tasks to someone else.

Household chores usually require a good deal of cleaning, so familiarize yourself with the verb **limpiar** (leem-pee*ahr*) (*to clean*). **Limpiar** is a regular verb that belongs to the **-ar** verb group. The root of **limpiar** is **limpi-**(*leem*-pee), as you can see in the following verb chart:

Conjugation	Pronunciation
yo limpio	yoh *leem*-peeoh
tú limpias	tooh *leem*-peeahs
él, ella, usted limpia	ehl, *eh*-yah, oohs-*tehd leem*-peeah
nosotros, nosotras limpiamos	noh-*soh*-trohs, noh-*soh*-trahs leem-pee*ah*-mohs
vosotros, vosotras limpiáis	bvoh-*soh*-trohs, bvoh-*soh*-trahs leem-pee-*ah*ees
ellos, ellas, ustedes limpian	*eh*-yohs, *eh*-yahs, oohs-*teh*-dehs *leem*-peeahn

Talkin' the Talk

Solana and Octavio have a list of chores that need to be done. Now they just need to review the list together and decide who will perform each chore.

Solana: **Octavio, ¿prefieres pasar la aspiradora por las alfombras o barrer y trapear el suelo de la cocina?**
ohk-*tah*-bveeoh, ¿preh-fee*eh*-rehs pah-*sahr* lah ahs-pee-rah-*doh*-rah pohr lahs ahl-*fohm*-bvrahs oh bvah-*rrehr* ee trah-peh-*ahr* ehl sooh*eh*-loh deh lah koh-*see*-nah?
Octavio, do you prefer to vacuum the carpets or sweep and mop the kitchen floor?

Octavio: **Prefiero pasar la aspiradora por las alfombras. También puedo sacar la basura.**
preh-fee*eh*-roh pah-*sahr* lah ahs-pee-rah-*doh*-rah pohr lahs ahl-*fohm*-bvrahs. tahm-bee*eh*n pooh*eh*-doh sah-*kahr* lah bvah-*sooh*-rah.
I prefer to vacuum. I can take out the trash, too.

Solana: **Yo puedo empezar a lavar la ropa, y tú puedes poner la ropa en la secadora.**
yoh pooh*eh*-doh ehm-peh-*sahr* ah lah-*bvahr* lah *roh*-pah, ee tooh pooh*eh*-dehs poh-*nehr* lah *rroh*-pah ehn lah seh-kah-*doh*-rah.
I can start washing the clothes, and you can put the clothes in the dryer.

Octavio: **¿Eso es todo en la lista?**
¿*eh*-soh ehs *toh*-doh ehn lah *lees*-tah?
Is that everything on the list?

Solana: **Sí, es todo. Gracias por tu ayuda.**
            see, ehs *toh*-doh. *grah*-seeahs pohr tooh
            ah-*yooh*-dah.
            Yes, that's everything. Thanks for your help.

Words to Know

pasar la aspiradora	pah-<u>sahr</u> lah ahs-pee-rah-<u>doh</u>-rah	to vacuum
barrer	bvah-<u>rrehr</u>	to sweep
trapear	trah-peh-<u>ahr</u>	to mop
empezar	ehm-peh-<u>sahr</u>	to start
lavar	lah-<u>bvahr</u>	to wash

Taking part in bedtime banter

In most homes, bedtime is a ritual surrounded by common phrases. When bedtime finally arrives, you may find the following phrases very useful.

Tengo mucho sueño. (*tehn*-goh *mooh*-choh sooh*eh*-nyoh.) (*I am very tired.*)

Voy a acostarme. (bvohy ah ah-kohs-*tahr*-meh.) (*I am going to bed.*)

¿Cuándo vas a acostarte? (¿kooh*ahn*-doh bvahs ah ah-kohs-*tahr*-teh?) (*When are you going to bed?*)

Necesito levantarme temprano mañana. (neh-seh-*see*-toh leh-bvahn-*tahr*-meh tehm-*prah*-noh mah-*nyah*-nah.) (*I need to get up early tomorrow.*)

¿A qué hora necesitas despertarte mañana? (¿ah keh *oh*-rah neh-seh-*see*-tahs dehs-pehr-*tahr*-teh mah-*nyah*-nah?) (*What time do you need to wake up tomorrow?*)

Favor de poner el despertador para las seis de la mañana. (fah-*bvohr* deh poh-*nehr* ehl dehs-pehr-tah-*dohr* pah-rah lahs *seh*ees deh lah mah-*nyah*-nah.) (*Please set the alarm clock for 6:00 a.m.*)

¿Hay más pasta de dientes? (¿ahy mahs *pahs*-tah deh deeh*ehn*-tehs?) (*Is there more toothpaste?*)

¿Necesitas otra cobija? (¿neh-seh-*see*-tahs *oh*-trah koh-*bvee*-Hah?) (*Do you need another blanket?*)

Necesitas lavarte la cara. (neh-seh-*see*-tahs lah-*bvahr*-teh lah *kah*-rah.) (*You need to wash your face.*)

Necesitas cepillarte los dientes. (neh-seh-*see*-tahs seh-pee-*yahr*-teh lohs dee*ehn*-tehs.) (*You need to brush your teeth.*)

Necesitas ducharte. (neh-seh-*see*-tahs dooh-*chahr*-teh.) (*You need to take a shower.*)

Check out Chapter 16 for full details about the verbs **dormir** (dohr-*meer*) (*to sleep*) and **despertarse** (dehs-pehr-*tahr*-seh) (*to wake up*).

Yours, Mine, and Ours: Being Possessive

In Spanish, you can use the words that signal possession in singular or plural form, depending on the number of items you're referring to. For example, when you're dealing with possessive adjectives, you say **mi llave** (mee *yah*-bveh) (*my key*), if you refer to one key. More often than not, however, you say **mis llaves** (mees *yah*-bvehs) (*my keys*) because you likely possess more than one key.

You follow the same rules when you use a possessive pronoun, such as when you say **esta llave es mía** (*ehs*-tah *yah*-bveh ehs *mee*-ah) (*this key is mine*), or, in the case of several, **estas llaves son mías** (*ehs*-tahs *yah*-bvehs sohn *mee*-ahs) (*these keys are mine*).

Notice that because **llave** is feminine, you use **mía,** the female-gender possessive. This rule sounds more complicated than it actually is. Just use the number (singular or plural) and the gender (male or female) of the nouns you talk about as you would when applying an adjective to them (see Chapter 2).

The following sections provide more details on possessive adjectives and possessive pronouns.

Possessive adjectives

The following list shows you all the possible possessive adjectives; the designations "singular" and "plural" refer to how you're using the subject *you,* not to the object you're attaching the adjective to:

- **mi/mis** (mee/mees) (*my*)
- **tu/tus** (tooh/toohs) (*your* [singular, familiar])
- **su/sus** (sooh/soohs) (*his, her, its, your* [singular, formal])

✔ **nuestro/nuestros** (nooh*ehs*-troh/nooh*ehs*-trohs) (*our* [used when the possessed person, animal, or object is masculine])

✔ **nuestra/nuestras** (nooh*ehs*-trah/nooh*ehs*-trahs) (*our* [used when the possessed person, animal, or object is feminine])

✔ **vuestro/vuestros** (bvooh*ehs*-troh/bvooh*ehs*-trohs) (*your* [plural, familiar] [used when the possessed person, animal, or object is masculine])

✔ **vuestra/vuestras** (bvooh*ehs*-trah/bvooh*ehs*-trahs) (*your* [plural, familiar] [used when the possessed person or animal or object is feminine])

✔ **su/sus** (sooh/soohs) (*their, your* [plural, formal])

Here are some examples of how to use possessive adjectives:

Este es mi dormitorio. (*ehs*-teh ehs mee dohr-mee-*toh*-reeoh.) (*This is my bedroom.*)

Tus llaves están en la mesa. (toohs *yah*-bvehs ehs-*tahn* ehn lah *meh*-sah.) (*Your keys are on the table.*)

Tus toallas están secas. (toohs toh-*ah*-yahs ehs-*tahn seh*-kahs.) (*Your towels are dry.*)

Su hermano tiene mi libro. (sooh ehr-*mah*-noh tee*eh*-neh mee *lee*-bvroh.) (*Your brother has my book.*)

Este es su sillón reclinable nuevo. (*ehs*-teh ehs sooh see-*yohn* rreh-klee-*nah*-bvleh nooh*eh*-bvoh.) (*This is his new recliner.*)

Nuestras sábanas están limpias. (nooh*ehs*-trahs *sah*-bvah-nahs ehs-*tahn leem*-peeahs.) (*Our sheets are clean.*)

Possessive pronouns

The following list shows you the basic possessive pronouns:

✔ **el mío/los míos** (ehl *mee*-oh/lohs *mee*-ohs) (*mine* [used when the possessed person, animal, or object is masculine])

✔ **la mía/las mías** (lah *mee*-ah/lahs *mee*-ahs) (*mine* [used when the possessed person, animal, or object is feminine])

✔ **el tuyo/los tuyos** (ehl *tooh*-yoh/lohs *tooh*-yohs) (*yours* [singular, familiar] [used when the possessed person, animal, or object is masculine])

✔ **la tuya/las tuyas** (lah *tooh*-yah/lahs *tooh*-yahs) (*yours* [singular, familiar] [used when the possessed person, animal, or object is feminine])

✔ **el suyo/los suyos** (ehl *sooh*-yoh/lohs *sooh*-yohs) (*his, hers, its, yours* [singular, formal] [used when the possessed person, animal, or object is masculine])

✔ **la suya/las suyas** (lah *sooh*-yah/lahs *sooh*-yahs) (*his, hers, its, yours* [singular, formal] [used when the possessed person, animal, or object is feminine])

✔ **el nuestro/los nuestros** (ehl nooh*ehs*-troh/lohs nooh*ehs*-trohs) (*ours* [used when the possessed person, animal, or object is masculine])

✔ **la nuestra/las nuestras** (lah nooh*ehs*-trah/lahs nooh*ehs*-trahs) (*ours* [used when the possessed person, animal, or object is feminine])

✔ **el vuestro/los vuestros** (ehl bvooh*ehs*-troh/lohs bvooh*ehs*-trohs) (*yours* [plural, familiar] [used when the possessed person, animal, or object is masculine])

✔ **la vuestra/las vuestras** (lah bvooh*ehs*-trah/lahs bvooh*ehs*-trahs) (*yours* [plural, familiar] [used when the possessed person, animal, or object is feminine])

✔ **el suyo/los suyos** (ehl *sooh*-yoh/lohs *sooh*-yohs) (*theirs, yours* [plural, formal] [used when the possessed person, animal, or object is masculine])

✔ **la suya/las suyas** (lah *sooh*-yah/lahs *sooh*-yahs) (*theirs, yours* [plural, formal] [used when the possessed person, animal, or object is feminine])

Here are some examples of possessive pronouns for you to practice. Notice that the article is usually omitted after the verb **ser,** unless needed for emphasis.

Esa cama es mía. (*eh*-sah *kah*-mah ehs *mee*-ah.) (*That bed is mine.*)

La mía es más grande. (lah *mee*-ah ehs mahs *grahn*-deh) (*Mine is much larger.*)

Los calcetines son míos. (lohs kahl-seh-*tee*-nehs sohn *mee*-ohs.) (*The socks are mine.*)

Esa maleta es la tuya. (*eh*-sah mah-*leh*-tah ehs lah *tooh*-yah.) (*That suitcase is yours.*)

Ese otro plato es el suyo. (*eh*-seh *oh*-troh *plah*-toh ehs ehl *sooh*-yoh.) (*That other plate is yours* [formal].)

Ese vaso es suyo. (*eh*-seh *bvah*-soh ehs *sooh*-yoh.) (*That glass is hers.*)

El suyo está aquí. (ehl *sooh*-yoh ehs-*tah* ah-*kee*) (*His is here.*)

Las camas que están en el otro cuarto son suyas. (lahs *kah*-mahs que ehs-*tahn* ehn ehl *oh*-troh kooh*ahr*-toh sohn *sooh*-yahs.) (*The beds in the other room are yours* [formal, plural].)

Las nuestras están en el segundo piso. (lahs nooh*ehs*-trahs ehs-*tahn* ehn ehl seh-*goohn*-doh *pee*-soh) (*Ours are on the second floor.*)

Esas sillas son nuestras. (*eh*-sahs *see*-yahs sohn nooh*ehs*-trahs.) (*Those chairs are ours.*)

Fun & Games

In the following cutaway view of the home, write the Spanish word for each room next to the number of that room (include the article; for example, **la cocina**):

1. _____

2. _____

3. _____

4. _____

5. _____

6. _____

7. _____

Write the Spanish word for each household item next to the letter of the item (include the article):

a. _____

b. _____

c. _____

d. _____

e. _____

f. _____

g. _____

h. _____

i. _____

j. _____

k. _____

l. _____

m. _____

n. _____

See Appendix D for the answer key.

Part II
Spanish in Action

"When making small talk in Spanish, remember 'The Five Ws'—who, what, when, where, and why me?"

In this part . . .

In this part, you step out into the real world and start communicating in Spanish in common, real-world situations. Instead of hammering grammar points as many language textbooks do, this part focuses on everyday situations that you may find yourself in if you're in a Spanish-speaking country or dealing with your Spanish-speaking neighbors at home. Along the way, we do introduce some grammar lessons in bite-sized bits so that you can grasp the essentials at a more reasonable pace.

This part hones your small-talk skills, enables you to ask for directions and understand what you're told, takes you on dining and shopping excursions and out on the town, shows you how to conduct business in Spanish, and lets you unwind with some recreational activities. At the end of this part, you should be able to do some basic navigation with the Spanish language.

Chapter 6

Getting to Know You: Making Small Talk

· ·

In This Chapter

▶ Starting with simple questions

▶ Discussing the weather

▶ Talking about your family

▶ Chatting about where you live and what you do

▶ Understanding diminutives

· ·

Small talk is the universally recognized means of discussing common, easily understood interests and concerns, and it's the best way to quickly get acquainted with new people from all walks of life wherever you may find yourself. This chapter helps you make small talk with your Spanish-speaking neighbors so that you can begin to achieve a better understanding of them and how they go about their daily lives.

Asking Key Questions: Six Ws and Two Hs

You may have heard about "The Five Ws," which represent the questions that you need to ask to cover the basic information about a situation (who, what, where, when, and why). We've added three more questions to this group that you may find useful when you meet someone. Here are the key questions:

✔ **¿Quién?** (¿keee*ehn*?) (*Who?*)

✔ **¿Qué?** (¿keh?) (*What?*)

✔ **¿Dónde?** (¿*dohn*-deh?) (*Where?*)

✔ **¿Cuándo?** (¿kooh*ahn*-doh?) (*When?*)

✔ **¿Por qué?** (¿pohr keh?) (*Why?*)

✔ **¿Cuál?** (¿koohahl?) (*Which?*)

✔ **¿Cómo?** (¿koh-moh?) (*How?, What?*)

✔ **¿Cuánto?** (¿koohahn-toh?) (*How much?*)

The following are examples of how to use these words:

¿Quién es él? (¿keeehn ehs ehl?) (*Who is he?*)

¿Qué hace usted? (¿keh ah-seh oohs-tehd?) (*What do you do?*)

¿Dónde viven ustedes? (¿dohn-deh bvee-bvehn oohs-teh-dehs?) (*Where do you [plural] live?*)

¿Cuándo llegan ellos? (¿koohahn-doh yeh-gahn eh-yohs?) (*When do they arrive?*)

¿Por qué está usted aquí? (¿pohr keh ehs-tah oohs-tehd ah-kee?) (*Why are you [formal] here?*)

¿Cuál hotel es mejor? (¿koohahl oh-tehl ehs meh-Hohr?) (*Which hotel is better?*)

¿Cómo es el camino? (¿koh-moh ehs ehl kah-mee-noh?) (*How is the road? or What's the road like?*)

¿Cuánto cuesta el cuarto? (¿koohahn-toh koohehs-tah ehl koohahr-toh?) (*How much is the room?*)

All of the words have accent marks added to them when used in a question or an exclamation. In this case, the accent marks don't show stress. When these same words are used in a regular statement of fact (neither questioning nor exclamatory), no accent is used.

Talkin' the Talk

Carlos is on Flight 223 from Mendoza to Buenos Aires. He has introduced himself to his seatmates, so he knows their names, but he wants to make small talk about himself.

Carlos: **¡Qué vuelo tan agradable!**
              ¡keh bvooheh-loh tahn ah-grah-*dah*-bvleh!
              What a pleasant flight!

Juan: **Sí, es un vuelo tranquilo.**
              see, ehs oohn bvooheh-loh trahn-*kee*-loh.
              Yes, it's a smooth flight.

Carlos: **¿Viaja a menudo en avión?**
¿bvee*ah*-Hah ah meh-*nooh*-doh ehn ah-bvee*ohn*?
Do you fly often?

Juan: **No, éste es mi primer vuelo.**
noh, *ehs*-teh ehs mee pree-*mehr* bvooheh-loh.
No, this is my first flight.

Carlos: **¿De dónde es usted?**
¿deh *dohn*-deh ehs oohs-*tehd*?
Where are you from?

Juan: **Soy de Buenos Aires. ¿Y usted?**
sohy deh bvooheh-nohs *ahee*-rehs. ¿ee oohs-*tehd*?
I'm from Buenos Aires. And you?

Carlos: **Yo soy de Nueva York.**
yoh sohy deh nooheh-bvah yohrk.
I'm from New York.

¿Cómo es Buenos Aires?
¿*koh*-moh ehs bvooheh-nohs *ahee*-rehs?
What's Buenos Aires like?

Juan: **Es una ciudad grande y maravillosa.**
ehs *ooh*-nah seeooh-*dahd grahn*-deh ee
mah-rah-bvee-*yoh*-sah.
It's a large and wonderful city.

Words to Know

vuelo	bvooh*eh*-loh	flight
tan	tahn	so
agradable	ah-grah-*dah*-bvleh	pleasant
tranquilo	trahn-*kee*-loh	smooth
a menudo	ah meh-*nooh*-doh	often
primer	pree-*mehr*	first
maravillosa	mah-rah-bvee-*yoh*-sah	wonderful

Chatting about the Weather

In temperate climates, weather is much less of an issue than it is in countries where conditions vary a great deal. Some cities in southern Mexico, for example, don't even do weather reports. Even so, the weather is always a relatively safe topic of conversation wherever your travels take you.

To ask about the weather **(el tiempo)** (ehl tee*ehm*-poh), you say **¿Qué tiempo hace?** (¿keh tee*ehm*-poh *ah*-seh?) (*What's the weather like?*). In response, you may hear one of the following answers:

- ✔ **Está húmedo.** (ehs-*tah ooh*-meh-doh) (*It's humid.*)
- ✔ **Está nublado.** (ehs-*tah* nooh-*bvlah*-doh) (*It's cloudy.*)
- ✔ **Hace calor.** (*ah*-seh kah-*lohr*) (*It's hot.*)
- ✔ **Hace fresco.** (*ah*-seh *frehs*-koh) (*It's cool.*)
- ✔ **Hace frío.** (*ah*-seh *free*-oh) (*It's cold.*)
- ✔ **Hace sol.** (*ah*-seh sohl) (*It's sunny.*)
- ✔ **Hay niebla.** (ahy nee*eh*-bvlah) (*It's foggy.*)
- ✔ **Llueve.** (yooh*eh*-bveh) (*It's raining.*)
- ✔ **Nieva.** (nee*eh*-bvah) (*It's snowing.*)

Here are some other weather terms to be familiar with:

- ✔ **el clima** (ehl *klee*-mah) (*the climate*)
- ✔ **un relámpago** (oohn rreh-*lahm*-pah-goh) (*a flash of lightning*)
- ✔ **la temperatura** (lah tehm-peh-rah-*tooh*-rah) (*the temperature*)
- ✔ **un trueno** (oohn trooh*eh*-noh) (*a thunderclap*)

Talkin' the Talk

Mario has just returned from a six-month assignment in Argentina. Now back at his home office, Mario and his co-worker Rosa talk about the weather in Buenos Aires. (Track 10)

Rosa: **¿Cómo es el clima de Buenos Aires?**
          ¿*koh*-moh ehs ehl *klee*-mah deh bvooh*eh*-nohs
          ahee-rehs?
          What's Buenos Aires' climate like?

Mario: **Es muy agradable y templado.**
ehs *moohee* ah-grah-*dah*-bvleh ee tehm-*plah*-doh.
It's very pleasant and mild.

Rosa: **¿Llueve mucho?**
¿yooh*eh*-bveh *mooh*-choh?
Does it rain a lot?

Mario: **Sí, llueve todo el año, pero no mucho.**
see, yooh*eh*-bveh *toh*-doh ehl *ah*-nyoh, *peh*-roh noh
mooh-choh.
Yes, it rains all year round, but not too much.

Rosa: **¿Y también hace sol?**
¿ee tahm-bvee*ehn* ah-seh sohl?
And is it also sunny?

Mario: **Sí, hace sol casi todos los días.**
see, *ah*-seh sohl *kah*-see *toh*-dohs lohs *dee*-ahs.
Yes, it's sunny almost every day.

Rosa: **¿No nieva nunca?**
¿noh neee*eh*-bvah *noohn*-kah?
Does it ever snow?

Mario: **No, en Buenos Aires nunca nieva.**
noh, ehn bvooh*eh*-nohs *ah*ee-rehs *noohn*-kah
neee*eh*-bvah.
No, in Buenos Aires it never snows.

Words to Know

templado	tehm-<u>plah</u>-doh	mild
todo el año	<u>toh</u>-doh ehl <u>ah</u>-nyoh	all year round
nunca	<u>noon</u>-kah	never
casi	<u>kah</u>-see	almost

Describing Family Members

The individual is the basic element of U.S. and Canadian societies. In Latin America, on the other hand, the family **(la familia)** (lah fah-*mee*-leeah) is the basic unit. People work, live, and function in accord with their families. When visiting your Spanish-speaking neighbors, therefore, you'll be more comfortable if you pay attention to the way Latinos stress the importance of the family and of family relationships.

The following list gives basic names for family members. Figure 6-1 shows a typical family tree, which may help you in remembering the Spanish words for various family members:

- ✔ **la abuela** (lah ah-bvooh*eh*-lah) (*the grandmother*)
- ✔ **el abuelo** (ehl ah-bvooh*eh*-loh) (*the grandfather*)
- ✔ **la cuñada** (lah kooh-*nyah*-dah) (*the sister-in-law*)
- ✔ **el cuñado** (ehl kooh-*nyah*-doh) (*the brother-in-law*)
- ✔ **la esposa** (lah ehs-*poh*-sah) (*the wife*)
- ✔ **el esposo** (ehl ehs-*poh*-soh) (*the husband*)
- ✔ **la hermana** (lah ehr-*mah*-nah) (*the sister*)
- ✔ **el hermano** (ehl ehr-*mah*-noh) (*the brother*)
- ✔ **la hija** (lah *ee*-Hah) (*the daughter*)
- ✔ **el hijo** (ehl *ee*-Hoh) (*the son*)
- ✔ **la madre** (lah *mah*-dreh) (*the mother*)
- ✔ **la madrina** (lah mah-*dree*-nah) (*the godmother*)
- ✔ **la nieta** (lah neee*eh*-tah) (*the granddaughter*)
- ✔ **el nieto** (ehl neee*eh*-toh) (*the grandson*)
- ✔ **la nuera** (lah nooh*eh*-rah) (*the daughter-in-law*)
- ✔ **el padre** (ehl *pah*-dreh) (*the father*)
- ✔ **el padrino** (ehl pah-*dree*-noh) (*the godfather*)
- ✔ **la prima** (lah *pree*-mah) (*the female cousin*)
- ✔ **el primo** (ehl *pree*-moh) (*the male cousin*)
- ✔ **la sobrina** (lah soh-*bvree*-nah) (*the niece*)
- ✔ **el sobrino** (ehl soh-*bvree*-noh) (*the nephew*)

- ✔ **la suegra** (lah sooh*eh*-grah) *(the mother-in-law)*
- ✔ **el suegro** (ehl sooh*eh*-groh) *(the father-in-law)*
- ✔ **la tía** (lah *tee*-ah) *(the aunt)*
- ✔ **el tío** (ehl *tee*-oh) *(the uncle)*
- ✔ **el yerno** (ehl *yehr*-noh) *(the son-in-law)*

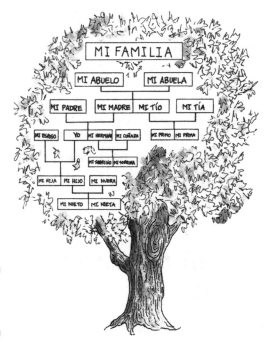

Figure 6-1:
A family tree
in Spanish.

Talking about Where You Live with the Verb Vivir

After someone has invited you over, you may very well want to return the favor. And "Where do you live?" is as frequent a question as "Where do you work?" when making small talk. The verb **vivir** (bvee-*bveer*) is a regular verb (we introduce regular verbs in Chapter 2), and it means *to live.* You can see how to conjugate its present tense in the following table:

Conjugation	Pronunciation
yo vivo	yoh *bvee*-bvoh
tú vives	tooh *bvee*-bvehs
él, ella, usted vive	ehl, *eh*-yah, oohs-*tehd bvee*-bveh
nosotros, nosotras vivimos	noh-*soh*-trohs, noh-*soh*-trahs bvee-*bvee*-mohs
vosotros, vosotras vivís	bvoh-*soh*-trohs, bvoh-*soh*-trahs bvee-*bvees*
ellos, ellas, ustedes viven	*eh*-yohs, *eh*-yahs, oohs-*teh*-dehs *bvee*-bvehn

Check out these examples of **vivir:**

Yo vivo en una casa grande. (yoh *bvee*-bvoh ehn *ooh*-nah *kah*-sah *grahn*-deh.) (*I live in a large house.*)

Ellos viven en un apartamento en el centro de la ciudad. (*eh*-yohs *bvee*-bvehn ehn oohn ah-pahr-tah-*mehn*-toh ehn ehl *sehn*-troh deh lah seeeooh-*dahd.*) (*They live in an apartment in the center of the city.*)

Mis abuelos viven en un pueblo cerca del Océano Pacífico. (mees ah-bvooh*eh*-lohs *bvee*-bvehn ehn oohn pooh*eh*-bvloh *sehr*-kah dehl oh-*seh*-ah-noh pah-*see*-fee-koh.) (*My grandparents live in a town near the Pacific Ocean.*)

Discussing Work with the Verbs Trabajar and Entender

Work and professions are always useful subjects for small talk. The verb for *to work* is **trabajar** (trah-bvah-*Hahr*); it's a regular **-ar** verb. Chapter 11 gives you the lowdown on all kinds of work-related terms, but the following are some useful words to get you started:

- ✔ **la compañía** (lah kohm-pah-*nyee*-ah) (*the company*)
- ✔ **el/la director/a** (ehl/lah dee-rehk-*tohr*/ah) (*the manager*)
- ✔ **los empleados** (lohs ehm-pleh-*ah*-dohs) (*the employees*)
- ✔ **la fábrica** (lah *fah*-bvree-kah) (*the factory*)
- ✔ **la jefa** (lah *Heh*-fah) (*the [female] boss*)
- ✔ **el jefe** (ehl *Heh*-feh) (*the[male] boss*)
- ✔ **el sueldo** (ehl sooh*ehl*-doh) (*the wage, the pay*)
- ✔ **el trabajo** (ehl trah-*bvah*-Hoh) (*the job*)

Here are few examples of phrases you may hear when discussing work:

Ella trabaja en una fábrica. (*eh*-yah trah-*bvah*-Hah ehn *ooh*-nah *fah*-bvree-kah.) (*She works in a factory.*)

Todos los empleados reciben el sueldo mínimo cuando empiezan. (*toh*-dohs lohs ehm-pleh-*ah*-dohs rreh-*see*-bvehn ehl sooh*ehl*-doh *mee*-nee-moh kooh*ahn*-doh ehm-pee*eh*-sahn.) (*All of the employees receive minimum wage when they start.*)

El trabajo del director es muy difícil. (ehl trah-*bvah*-Hoh dehl dee-rehk-tohr ehs *mooh*ee dee-*fee*-seel.) (*The manager's job is very difficult.*)

When discussing work and professions, you want to be sure that you understand the people you're talking to, so you use the irregular verb **entender** (ehn-tehn-*dehr*) (*to understand*). Because **entender** is irregular, you conjugate it in the present tense as shown in the following table (find out more about irregular verbs in Chapter 2):

Conjugation	*Pronunciation*
yo entiendo	yoh ehn-tee*ehn*-doh
tú entiendes	tooh ehn-tee*ehn*-dehs
él, ella, usted entiende	ehl, *eh*-yah, oohs-*tehd* ehn-tee*ehn*-deh
nosotros, nosotras entendemos	noh-*soh*-trohs, noh-*soh*-trahs ehn-tehn-*deh*-mohs
vosotros, vosotras entendéis	bvoh-*soh*-trohs, bvoh-*soh*-trahs ehn-tehn-*deh*ees
ellos, ellas, ustedes entienden	*eh*-yohs, *eh*-yahs, oohs-*teh*-dehs ehn-tee*ehn*-dehn

When you use the verb **entender** with the preposition **de** (deh) (*of*), you're saying that the subject knows how to do whatever the verb indicates.

Here are some examples to help you use the irregular verb **entender:**

Yo entiendo de enfermería. (yoh ehn-tee*ehn*-doh deh ehn-fehr-meh-*ree*-ah.) (*I know about nursing.*)

Francisca entiende de cocina. (frahn-*sees*-kah ehn-tee*ehn*-deh deh koh-*see*-nah.) (*Francisca knows about cooking.*)

Pedro no entiende. (*peh*-droh noh ehn-tee*ehn*-deh.) (*Pedro doesn't understand.*)

Nosotros entendemos el problema. (noh-*soh*-trohs ehn-tehn-*deh*-mohs ehl proh-*bvleh*-mah.) (*We understand the problem.*)

Ellos entienden lo que decimos. (*eh*-yohs ehn-tee*ehn*-dehn loh keh deh-*see*-mohs.) (*They understand what we are saying.*)

When you hear the term *stem-changing verbs,* you may imagine some weird grammatical creature in a sci-fi flick that morphs as terrified beginning Spanish students attempt to conjugate it. Dealing with stem-changing verbs isn't exactly that bad, but it requires some patience and understanding. To help you cope, keep the following points in mind:

- ✔ Focus on present-tense conjugations for now. You can look over the verb conjugation tables in Appendix B to see other tenses.

- ✔ You encounter three primary types of stem-changing verbs in which the vowel in the stem changes from *e* to *i*, *e* to *ie*, or *o* to *ue*.

- ✔ You occasionally see a fourth type of stem-changing verb — the verb **jugar** has a stem change of *u* to *ue*.

- ✔ Stem changes occur in all the present-tense forms of these verbs *except* for the **nosotros** and the **vosotros** forms.

Sometimes the conjugation format for stem-changing verbs is referred to as "the boot" because if you draw a dark line around the forms of the verb that have a stem change, they resemble a boot. Check out Figure 6-2 to see what we mean.

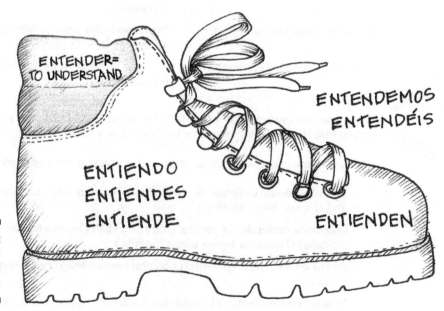

Figure 6-2:
The stem-changing boot.

Talkin' the Talk

 Listen to Jane and Pedro in a café talking about their jobs. (Track 11)

Jane: **¿Dónde trabaja usted?**
          ¿dohn-deh trah-bvah-Hah oohs-tehd?
          Where do you work?

Pedro: **Trabajo en México; soy ingeniero.**
          trah-*bvah*-Hoh ehn *meh*-Hee-koh; sohy
          een-Heh-nee*eh*-roh.
          I work in Mexico [City]; I'm an engineer.

Jane: **¿Para qué compañía trabaja?**
          ¿pah-rah keh kohm-pah-nyee-ah trah-bvah-Hah?
          What company do you work for?

Pedro: **Soy empresario independiente.**
          sohy ehm-preh-*sah*-reeoh een-deh-pehn-dee*eh*-teh.
          I'm an independent entrepreneur.

Jane: **¿Cuántos empleados tiene?**
          ¿koohahn-tohs ehm-pleh-ah-dohs teeeh-neh?
          How many employees do you have?

Pedro: **Tengo nueve empleados. ¿Y usted, qué hace?**
          *tehn-goh nooheh-bveh ehm-pleh-ah-dohs. ¿ee oohs-
          tehd, keh ah-seh?*
          I have nine employees. And you, what do you do?

Jane: **Soy dentista.**
          sohy dehn-*tees*-tah.
          I'm a dentist.

Pedro: **¿Y dónde tiene su consultorio?**
          ¿ee dohn-deh teeeh-neh sooh kohn-soohl-toh-reeoh?
          And where is your office?

Jane: **En Puebla.**
          ehn pooh*eh*-bvlah.
          In Puebla.

Words to Know

ingeniero	een-Heh-nee_eh_-roh	engineer
empresario	ehm-preh-_sah_-reeoh	entrepreneur
independiente	een-deh-pehn-dee_ehn_-teh	independent
dentista	dehn-_tees_-tah	dentist
consultorio	kohn-soohl-_toh_-reeoh	office

Engaging in "Small" Talk with Diminutives

In English when you want to say that something is small, you have to add the adjective *small* or *little* in front of the noun. Not so in Spanish. In Spanish, you add a few letters to the noun, called a *suffix,* meaning that you paste it to the end of the word. With that suffix, you create a diminutive, and people know that you're talking about something or someone small. The suffixes you add to the words are **-ito** (*ee*-toh) or **-ita** (*ee*-tah). For example, a **niño** (*nee*-nyoh) (*boy/child*) turns little when you add the suffix **-ito: niñito** (nee-*nyee*-toh) (*little boy/child*). Other examples include using **Juanito** or **Juanita** to differentiate a son or daughter from a father or mother with the same first name (Juan or Juana), referring to your small house **(casa)** as **mi casita,** and calling a puppy or little dog a **perrito.**

Talkin' the Talk

Shirley chats about kids with Juan Carlos's family.

Florencia: **Dime Shirley, ¿tienes hijos?**
dee-meh Shirley, ¿*teeeh*-nehs ee-Hohs?
Tell me Shirley, do you have children?

Shirley: **Tengo un hijo. Aquí está su foto.**
tehn-goh oohn ee-Hoh. ah-*kee* ehs-*tah* sooh *foh*-toh.
I have a son. Here's his photo.

Florencia: **A ver . . . un muchachito muy guapito.**
ah bvehr . . . oohn mooh-chah-*chee*-toh *mooh*ee
goohah-*pee*-toh.
Let's see . . . a very handsome little boy.

Shirley: **Sí. ¿Y tú?**
see. ¿ee tooh?
Yes. And you?

Florencia: **Yo tengo una hija y un hijito.**
yoh *tehn*-goh *ooh*-nah ee-Hah ee oohn ee-*Hee*-toh.
I have a daughter and a little son.

Shirley: **¿Cuántos años tienen?**
¿kooh*ahn*-tohs *ah*-nyohs tee*eh*-nehn?
How old are they?

Florencia: **Mi hija tiene seis años y mi hijito tres. Aquí viene mi hija.**
mee ee-Hah tee*eh*-neh *se*hees *ah*-nyohs ee mee ee-
Hee-toh trehs. ah-*kee* bvee*eh*-neh mee ee-Hah.
My daughter is six and my little son three. Here comes my daughter.

Shirley: **Hola, ¿cómo te llamas?**
oh-lah, ¿*koh*-moh teh *yah*-mahs?
Hello, what's your name?

Rosita: **Me llamo Rosita.**
meh *yah*-moh rroh-*see*-tah.
My name is Rosita.

Shirley: **¡Qué bello nombre!**
¡keh *bveh*-yoh *nohm*-breh!
What a beautiful name!

Words to Know

dime	dee-meh	tell me
bello	bveh-yoh	beautiful
nombre	nohm-bvreh	name

Fun & Games

You've been invited to attend a Spanish-speaking wedding. Both the bride and groom have very large families, so you have several relationships to figure out and small-talk words to brush up on. The night before the wedding, your host quizzes you on question words and family members. Unscramble the following English words and then provide the Spanish translation. See Appendix D for the answer key.

- ✔ eaelmf coinsu _____
- ✔ chwih _____
- ✔ cleun _____
- ✔ draggundreath _____
- ✔ dreamthrong _____
- ✔ fatgodher _____
- ✔ franterdagh _____
- ✔ herfat _____
- ✔ hewn _____
- ✔ hwy _____
- ✔ moodgreth _____
- ✔ nos _____
- ✔ ons-ni-awl _____
- ✔ redaught-ni-wal _____
- ✔ remoth _____
- ✔ resist _____
- ✔ robreth-ni-lwa _____
- ✔ rrteboh _____
- ✔ sandgron _____
- ✔ emla sincou _____
- ✔ strise-ni-wla _____
- ✔ tanu _____
- ✔ thaw _____
- ✔ thredaug _____

Chapter 7

Asking for Directions

· ·

In This Chapter

▶ Pinpointing locations

▶ Receiving directions

▶ Getting around with the help of a map

▶ Heading up with **subir** and down with **bajar**

▶ Expressing distance with **cerca** (*near*) and **lejos** (*far*)

· ·

*I*n this chapter, you discover how to use **¿Dónde?** (*¿dohn*-deh?) (*Where?*) and other common Spanish words and phrases to figure out where you're going and how to get there. Yep, you get directions on how to ask for directions. Even more importantly, as you become familiar with these words and phrases, you understand not only the questions but also the answers that people provide.

If the imperative commands in this chapter seem like Greek to you, head to Chapter 11, where we discuss forming commands in detail.

Asking "Where Is . . . ?" and "Where Are . . . ?"

In its most basic application, the *Where?* question helps you determine where something is. When you're lost, for example, you probably wonder *Where am I?* When you're looking for a particular place, such as a theater, you may ask *Where is the dinner theater?* When you misplace something, such as a pen, you may ask *Where is the pen?*

Because you're asking where things *are* (where they *be*), you pair the Spanish word **¿dónde?** with the verb expressing being in a temporary sense — **estar** (ehs-*tahr*), covered in Chapter 3.

When you use **¿dónde?** in a question, you add the accent over the *o*, but when you use it in a phrase such as **el pueblo donde ellos viven** (ehl pooh*eh*-bvloh *dohn*-deh *eh*-yohs bvee-bvehn) (*the town where they live*), the *o* doesn't get an accent mark, as we mention in Chapter 6.

Sample the following sentences that use **¿dónde?** and **estar:**

> **¿Dónde está el Museo de Larco?** (*¿dohn*-deh ehs-*tah* ehl mooh-*seh*-oh deh *lahr*-koh?) (*Where is the Larco Museum?*)

> **¿Dónde estamos ahora?** (*¿dohn*-deh ehs-*tah*-mohs ah-*oh*-rah?) (*Where are we now?*)

> **¿Dónde estás?** (*¿dohn*-deh ehs-*tahs?*) (*Where are you?*)

> **¿Dónde están los perros?** (*dohn*-deh ehs-*tahn* lohs *peh*-rrohs?) (*Where are the dogs?*)

And here is a sentence for the person who wants to know everything:

> **¡Quiero saber el cómo, el cuándo, y el dónde!** (¡kee*eh*-roh sah-*bvehr* ehl *koh*-moh ehl kooh*ahn*-doh ee ehl *dohn*-deh!) (*I want to know the how, the when, and the where!*)

Describing Position Relative to Yourself

You can identify the space around your body in six ways:

- ✔ **delante (de)** (deh-*lahn*-teh [deh]) (*in front [of]*):

  Paula camina delante de Clara. (pah*ooh*-lah kah-*mee*-nah deh-*lahn*-teh deh *klah*-rah.) (*Paula walks in front of Clara.*)

- ✔ **detrás (de)** (deh-*trahs* [deh]) (*behind*):

  Clara va detrás de Paula. (*klah*-rah bvah deh-*trahs* deh pah*ooh*-lah.) (*Clara goes behind Paula.*)

- ✔ **a la derecha (de)** (ah lah deh-*reh*-chah [deh]) (*to the right [of]*):

  A la derecha de Paula está Felipe. (ah lah deh-*reh*-chah deh pah*ooh*-lah ehs-*tah* feh-*lee*-peh.) (*To the right of Paula is Felipe.*)

- ✔ **a la izquierda (de)** (ah lah ees-kee*ehr*-dah [deh]) (*to the left [of]*):

  José se sienta a la izquierda de Clara. (Hoh-*seh* seh see*ehn*-tah ah lah ees-kee*ehr*-dah deh *klah*-rah.) (*José sits to the left of Clara.*)

- ✔ **debajo (de)** (deh-*bvah*-Hoh [deh]) (*beneath; under*):

  Hay pasto debajo de los pies de José. (ahy *pahs*-toh deh-*bvah*-Hoh deh lohs pee*ehs* deh Hoh-*seh*.) (*There's grass under Jose's feet.*)

➤ **por encima (de)** (pohr ehn-*see*-mah [deh]) (*above*):

La rama está por encima de la cabeza de Paula. (lah *rrah*-mah ehs-*tah* pohr ehn-*see*-mah deh lah kah-*bveh*-sah deh pah*ooh*-lah.) (*The branch is above Paula's head.*)

Before you go any farther, you need to understand the distinction between two very similar words: **derecho** and **derecha**. What was that, you say? Look again. The only difference between the two words is that one word ends in *o* and the other in *a*, but the meaning is no longer the same!

➤ **derecho** (deh-*reh*-choh) (*straight; straight ahead*):

Siga derecho por esta calle. (*see*-gah deh-*reh*-choh pohr *ehs*-tah *kah*-yeh.) (*Keep going straight on this street.*)

➤ **derecha** (deh-*reh*-chah) (*right*):

En la esquina doble a la derecha. (ehn lah ehs-*kee*-nah *doh*-bvleh ah lah deh-*reh*-chah.) (*At the corner, turn to the right.*)

Understanding Directions: It's a Prepositional Thing

You often use words to tell where people or things are in relation to other people and things. You can use these terms to describe the relationships:

➤ **al lado (de)** (ahl *lah*-doh [deh]) (*beside, next to, at the side [of]*)

➤ **enfrente (de)** (ehn-*frehn*-teh [deh]) (*in front [of]*)

➤ **dentro (de)** (*dehn*-troh [deh]) (*inside [of]*)

➤ **adentro** (ah-*dehn*-troh) (*inside*)

Because **dentro** also means *inside*, **adentro** may express movement, as when someone or something moves toward an interior. The same goes for the following two bullets **fuera** and **afuera**.

➤ **fuera** (foo*eh*-rah) (*outside*)

➤ **afuera** (ah-foo*eh*-rah) (*outside*)

➤ **bajo** (*bvah*-Hoh) (*under; below*)

➤ **debajo (de)** (deh-*bvah*-Hoh [deh]) (*underneath*)

➤ **arriba** (ah-*rree*-bvah) (*above*)

➤ **junto a** (*Hoohn*-toh ah) (*next to*)

➤ **encima de** (ehn-*see*-mah deh) (*on top [of]*)

Practicing these directions comes in handy. The sentences that follow use spatial-direction terms:

La pastelería está al lado del banco. (lah pahs-teh-leh-*ree*-ah ehs-*tah* ahl *lah*-doh dehl *bvahn*-koh.) (*The pastry shop is next to the bank.*)

Al frente del banco hay una zapatería. (ahl *frehn*-teh dehl *bvahn*-koh ahy *ooh*-nah sah-pah-teh-*ree*-ah.) (*In front of the bank there is a shoe store.*)

Cuando hace buen tiempo, comemos el almuerzo afuera. (koo*hahn*-doh *ah*-seh boo*hehn* tee*ehm*-poh, koh-*meh*-mohs ehl ahl-moo*hehr*-soh ah-fooh*eh*-rah.) (*When the weather is nice we eat lunch outside.*)

Hay un gato dentro de la caja. (ahy oohn gah-toh dehn-troh deh lah kah-Hah.) (*There's a cat inside the box.*)

Cuando llueve, ponen las mesas adentro. (koo*hahn*-doh yooh*eh*-bveh *poh*-nehn lahs *meh*-sahs ah-*dehn*-troh.) (*When it rains, they put the tables inside.*)

El tren subterráneo corre debajo de la calle. (ehl trehn soohbv-teh-*rrah*-neh-oh *koh*-rreh deh-*bvah*-Hoh deh lah *kah*-yeh.) (*The subway runs under the street.*)

Ellos ponen sus libros encima de la mesa. (*eh*-yohs *poh*-nehn soohs *lee*-bvrohs ehn-*see*-mah deh lah *meh*-sah.) (*They put their books on the table.*)

Talkin' the Talk

After checking in at her hotel, Catalina asks the hotel receptionist for directions to the restaurant and the pool. (Track 12)

Catalina: **¿Dónde está el restaurante?**
¿*dohn*-deh ehs-*tah* ehl rrehs-tahooh-*rahn*-teh?
Where's the restaurant?

Receptionist: **Está arriba, en el segundo piso.**
ehs-*tah* ah-*rree*-bvah, ehn ehl seh-*goohn*-doh *pee*-soh.
It's upstairs, on the second floor.

Catalina: **¿En qué piso está la piscina?**
¿ehn keh *pee*-soh ehs-*tah* lah pee-*see*-nah?
On what floor is the pool?

Receptionist: **Está en el quinto piso.**
ehs-*tah* ehn ehl *keen*-toh *pee*-soh.
It's on the fifth floor.

Puede tomar el ascensor.
pooh*eh*-deh toh-*mahr* ehl ah-sehn-*sohr.*
You may take the elevator.

Catalina: **¿Cómo llego al ascensor?**
¿koh-moh yeh-*goh* ahl ah-sehn-*sohr?*
How do I get to the elevator?

Receptionist: **El ascensor está allí a la izquierda.**
ehl ah-sehn-*sohr* ehs-*tah* ah-*yee* ah lah
ees-kee*ehr*-dah.
The elevator is there to the left.

Words to Know

restaurant	rrehs-tahooh-*rahn*-teh	restaurant
arriba	ah-*rree*-bvah	upstairs
piso	*pee*-soh	floor
piscina	pee-*see*-nah	pool
ascensor	ah-sehn-*sohr*	elevator

Navigating with a Map

You can get around a new place more easily if you find your way on a map or have someone show you on the map how to get to the place you're looking for. In the following sections, we provide handy terms and phrases that you can practice when you navigate with a map.

Talking about the points on a compass and other helpful terms

Some directions are used throughout the world to explain how to get somewhere or find something by using the points on a compass. The following terms help you specify north from south and east from west:

- ✔ **el norte** (ehl *nohr*-teh) (*the north*)

- ✔ **el sur** (ehl soohr) (*the south*)

- ✔ **el este** (ehl *ehs*-teh) (*the east*)

- ✔ **el oriente** (ehl oh-ree*ehn*-teh) (*the east* [Literally: *where the sun originates*])

- ✔ **el oeste** (ehl oh-*ehs*-teh) (*the west*)

- ✔ **el poniente** (ehl poh-nee*ehn*-teh) (*the west* [Literally: *where the sun sets*])

The following words are helpful when asking or giving general directions:

- ✔ **la avenida** (lah ah-bveh-*nee*-dah) (*the avenue*)

- ✔ **el barrio** (ehl *bvah*-rreeoh) (*the neighborhood*)

- ✔ **el bulevar** (ehl bvooh-leh-*bvahr*) (*the boulevard*)

- ✔ **la calle** (lah *kah*-yeh) (*the street*)

- ✔ **la cuadra** (lah kooh*ah*-drah) (*the block*)

- ✔ **la esquina** (lah ehs-*kee*-nah) (*the corner*)

- ✔ **el jardín** (ehl Hahr-*deen*) (*the garden; a small park*)

- ✔ **la manzana** (lah mahn-*sah*-nah) (*the block*)

- ✔ **el parque** (ehl *pahr*-keh) (*the park*)

- ✔ **la plaza** (lah *plah*-sah) (*the square, the plaza*)

- ✔ **el río** (ehl *rree*-oh) (*the river*)

The verbs **doblar** (doh-*bvlahr*) (*to turn*) and **seguir** (seh-*geer*) (*to follow, to continue*) are handy verbs for giving directions. **Doblar** is a regular **-ar** verb and follows the rules for all regular **-ar** verbs. **Seguir**, on the other hand, is an irregular, stem-changing verb; its stem changes from *e* to *i* in all of the conjugated forms except for the **nosotros/nosotras** and **vosotros/vosotras** forms. The **yo** form is **sigo** (*see*-goh) — the *u* drops out due to Spanish spelling rules so that the pronunciation remains correct.

Understanding some basic phrases

Here are some mapping phrases you may hear as you navigate with a map:

- ✔ **La avenida Venus está al este de mi casa.** (lah ah-bveh-*nee*-dah *bveh*-noohs ehs-*tah* ahl *ehs*-teh deh mee *kah*-sah.) (*Venus Avenue is east of my house.*)

- ✔ **Al oeste está la calle Las Violetas.** (ahl oh-*ehs*-teh ehs-*tah* lah *kah*-yeh lahs bveeoh-*leh*-tahs.) (*To the west is Violetas Street.*)

- ✔ **El parque está al norte.** (ehl *pahr*-keh ehs-*tah* ahl *nohr*-teh.) (*The park is to the north.*)

- ✔ **Al sur se va hacia el río.** (ahl soohr seh bvah ah-*see*-ah ehl *rree*-oh.) (*To the south is the river.* [Literally: *To the south, one goes toward the river.*])

- ✔ **El oriente es donde el sol se levanta.** (ehl oh-ree*ehn*-teh ehs *dohn*-deh ehl sohl seh leh-*bvahn*-tah.) (*The east is where the sun rises.*)

- ✔ **El poniente es donde el sol se pone.** (ehl poh-nee*ehn*-teh ehs *dohn*-deh ehl sohl seh *poh*-neh.) (*The west is where the sun sets.*)

Asking for directions can be problematic. The people who answer your questions know the city, and the answers seem so obvious to them! So to keep you going and sharpen your ear, here are some questions you may ask and possible answers you may hear when finding your way around a new city or town:

¿**Cómo llego a la Avenida de los Ángeles?** (¿*koh*-moh *yeh*-goh ah lah ah-bveh-*nee*-dah deh lohs *ahn*-Heh-lehs?) (*How do I get to the Avenue of the Angels?*)

Siga derecho hasta que llegue a una avenida ancha. (*see*-gah deh-*reh*-choh *ah*-stah keh *yeh*-geh ah *ooh*-nah ah-bveh-*nee*-dah *ahn*-chah.) (*Continue going straight until you come to a wide avenue.*)

¿**Dónde hay un parque grande?** (¿*dohn*-deh ahy oohn *pahr*-keh *grahn*-deh?) (*Where is there a large park?*)

Vaya derecho en la Calle Principal, y junto al río hay un parque grande. (*bvah*-yah deh-*reh*-choh ehn lah *kah*-yeh preen-see-*pahl* ee *Hoohn*-toh ahl *rree*-oh ahy oohn *pahr*-keh *grahn*-deh.) (*Go straight on Main Street, and on the riverside there is a large park.*)

¿**Dónde está el Palacio Nacional?** (¿*dohn*-deh ehs-*tah* ehl pah-*lah*-seeoh nah-seeoh-*nahl*?) (*Where is the National Palace?*)

Camine derecho por cuatro cuadras a la plaza que está en el centro de la ciudad. (kah-*mee*-neh deh-*reh*-choh pohr kooh*ah*-troh kooh*ah*-drahs ah lah plah-*sah* keh *ehs*-tah ehn ehl *sehn*-troh deh lah seeooh-*dahd*.) (*Walk straight for four blocks to the square that's in the center of the city.*)

¿Cómo llego al centro de la ciudad? (¿*koh*-moh *yeh*-goh ahl *sehn*-troh deh lah seeooh-*dahd?*) (*How do I arrive at the center of the city?*)

Doble a la izquierda en la avenida que se llama La Alameda. (*doh*-bvleh ah lah ees-kee*ehr*-dah ehn lah ah-bveh-*nee*-dah keh seh *yah*-mah lah ah-lah-*meh*-dah) (*Turn left at the avenue that is called La Alameda.*)

Talkin' the Talk

 Ana Luisa is an artist who's anxious to visit the Graphic Arts Museum. She plans to walk there from her hotel so she can avoid the heavy traffic. (Track 13)

Ana Luisa: **Disculpe, ¿cómo llego al Museo de la Estampa?**
dees-*koohl*-peh, ¿*koh*-moh *yeh*-goh ahl mooh-*seh*-oh deh lah ehs-*tahm*-pah?
Excuse me, how do I get to the Graphic Arts Museum?

Receptionist: **Muy fácil. Sale del hotel.**
moohee fah-seel. *sah*-leh dehl oh-*tehl*.
Very easy. You go out of the hotel.

Ana Luisa: **¿Dónde está la salida?**
¿*dohn*-deh ehs-*tah* lah sah-*lee*-dah?
Where is the exit?

Receptionist: **La salida está a la derecha.**
lah sah-*lee*-dah ehs-*tah* ah lah deh-*reh*-chah.
The exit is to the right.

Al salir, vaya a la izquierda.
ahl sah-*leer*, *bvah*-yah ah lah ees-kee*ehr*-dah.
As you get out, you go to the left.

Camine hasta la segunda calle.
kah-*mee*-neh *ahs*-tah lah seh-*goohn*-dah *kah*-yeh.
Walk to the second street.

Doble a la derecha y camine una cuadra.
doh-bvleh ah lah deh-*reh*-chah ee kah-*mee*-neh *ooh*-nah kooh*ah*-drah.
Turn to the right and walk one block.

Llega al museo.
yeh-gah ahl mooh-seh-oh.
You arrive at the museum.

Ana Luisa: **Gracias por su ayuda.**
grah-seeahs pohr sooh ah-yooh-dah.
Thanks for your help.

Words to Know

disculpe	dees-<u>koohl</u>-peh	excuse me
llegar	yeh-<u>gahr</u>	to arrive
muy fácil	moohee <u>fah</u>-seel	very easy
caminar	kah-mee-<u>nahr</u>	to walk
salida	sah-<u>lee</u>-dah	exit
ayuda	ah-<u>yooh</u>-dah	help

Dealing with Normal Ups and Downs: The Verbs Subir and Bajar

Usually when you're getting or giving directions, you're dealing with two dimensions, as on a map. In some cases, however, you need to navigate the third dimension by going up and down hills, ascending or descending stairs, riding the elevator up or down, and so on. In situations such as these, you need to know how to use the verbs **subir** (sooh-*bveer*) (*to ascend; to go up*) and **bajar** (bvah-*Hahr*) (*to descend; to go down*). The following sections show you how to conjugate these two verbs in the present tense and use them in sentences.

Heading up with the verb subir

The following minitable shows you how to conjugate the present tense of the verb **subir** (sooh-*bveer*) (*to go up; to ascend*). Its root is **sub-** (soohbv), and it's a regular -**ir** verb (see Chapter 2 for more information).

Conjugation	Pronunciation
yo subo	yoh *sooh*-bvoh
tú subes	tooh *sooh*-bvehs
él, ella, usted sube	ehl, *eh*-yah, oohs-*tehd sooh*-bveh
nosotros, nosotras subimos	noh-*soh*-trohs, noh-*soh*-trahs sooh-*bvee*-mohs
vosotros, vosotras subís	bvoh-*soh*-trohs, bvoh-*soh*-trahs sooh-*bvees*
ellos, ellas, ustedes suben	*eh*-yohs, *eh*-yahs, oohs-*teh*-dehs *sooh*-bvehn

Practicing verb conjugations is essential; that way, they soon become second nature. But until they do become second nature, here are some phrases to help you:

Yo subo las escaleras todos los días. (yoh *sooh*-bvoh lahs ehs-kah-*leh*-rahs toh-*dohs* lohs *dee*-ahs.) (*I go up the stairs every day.*)

Subes por esa calle, a la izquierda. (*sooh*-bvehs pohr *eh*-sah *kah*-yeh, *ah* lah ees-kee*ehr*-dah.) (*You* [informal] *go up on that street, to the left.*)

Nosotros subimos con ustedes. (noh-*soh*-trohs sooh-*bvee*-mohs kohn oohs-*teh*-dehs) (*We go up with you.*)

Ellos suben por esa escalera. (*eh*-yohs *sooh*-bvehn pohr *eh*-sah ehs-kah-*leh*-rah.) (*They go up that staircase.*)

Heading down with the verb bajar

What goes up must come down, right? The descending verb is **bajar** (bvah-*Hahr*) (*to descend; to go down*). **Bajar** is a regular verb (see Chapter 2 for more details), and its root is **baj-** (bvahH). Here's how you conjugate **bajar** in the present tense:

Conjugation	Pronunciation
yo bajo	yoh *bvah*-Hoh
tú bajas	tooh *bvah*-Hahs
él, ella, usted baja	ehl, *eh*-yah, oohs-*tehd bvah*-Hah
nosotros, nosotras bajamos	noh-*soh*-trohs, noh-*soh*-trahs bvah-*Hah*-mohs
vosotros, vosotras bajáis	bvoh-*soh*-trohs, bvoh-*soh*-trahs bvah-*Hah*ees
ellos, ellas, ustedes bajan	eh-yohs, eh-yahs, oohs-*teh*-dehs *bvah*-Hahn

When you need to go down, right down you go! Practice, practice, practice!

> **Tú bajas del auto con el perro.** (tooh *bvah*-Hahs dehl ah*ooh*-toh kohn ehl *peh*-rroh.) (*You* [informal] *get down out of the car with the dog.*)

> **Ella baja por la escalera.** (*eh*-yah *bvah*-Hah pohr lah ehs-kah-*leh*-rah.) (*She goes down the stairs.*)

> **Bajamos por esta calle.** (bvah-*Hah*-mohs pohr *ehs*-tah *kah*-yeh.) (*We go down this street.*)

> **Ellos dicen que bajan al restaurante a comer.** (*eh*-yohs dee-sehn keh *bvah*-Hahn ahl rrehs-tahooh-*rahn*-teh ah *koh*-mehr.) (*They say that they are going down to the restaurant to eat.*)

Going Here, There, and Everywhere

In Spanish, you can indicate *here, there,* and *over there* depending on the distance from the speaker. Because *here, there,* and *over there* are adverbs, they always work with verbs and words that talk about space:

- **acá** (ah-*kah*) (*here*)
- **aquí** (ah-*kee*) (*here*)
- **allí** (ah-*yee*) (*there*)
- **allá** (ah-*yah*) (*over there*)

The following sentences enable you to practice situations in which you may use *here, there,* or *over there:*

> **Acá está el museo.** (ah-*kah* ehs-*tah* ehl mooh-*seh*-oh.) (*Here's the museum.*)

> **Aquí está tu libro.** (ah-*kee* ehs-*tah* tooh *lee*-bvroh.) (*Here's your book.*)

> **Allí, en la esquina, está el banco.** (ah-*yee*, ehn lah ehs-*kee*-nah, ehs-*tah* ehl *bvan*-koh.) (*There, on the corner, is the bank.*)

> **¡Corre allá!** (*¡koh*-rreh ah-*yah!*) (*Run over there!*)

Sometimes you talk about no-places and all-places: *nowhere* and *everywhere,* along with *anywhere.* You can use the following phrases to express the idea of all places or no particular places in Spanish:

- **en ninguna parte** (ehn neen-*gooh*-nah *pahr*-teh) (*nowhere, anywhere*)
- **en todas partes** (ehn *toh*-dahs *pahr*-tehs) (*everywhere*)

The following sentences can help you practice using these phrases:

En todas partes hay gente simpática. (ehn *toh*-dahs *pahr*-tehs ahy *Hehn*-teh seem-*pah*-tee-kah.) (*There are nice people everywhere.*)

En ninguna parte encuentro mis llaves. (ehn neen-*gooh*-nah *pahr*-teh ehn-kooh*ehn*-troh mees *yah*-bvehs.) (*I can't find my keys anywhere.*)

Cerca and Lejos: How Far Should You Go?

In this section, you can explore the words **cerca** (*sehr*-kah) (*near, close*) and **lejos** (*leh*-Hohs) (*far*). Use these two words when you want to discuss how great the distance, and the possible amount of effort, required to arrive at a specific place. Check out these examples:

Mi casa está muy lejos del centro de la ciudad. (mee *kah*-sah ehs-*tah* moohee *leh*-Hohs dehl *sehn*-troh deh lah seeooh-*dahd.*) (*My house is very far from the center of the city.*)

Su casa está muy cerca de la biblioteca. (sooh *kah*-sah ehs-*tah* moohee *sehr*-kah deh lah bvee-bvleeoh-*teh*-kah.) (*His house is very near the library.*)

Ellos viven muy lejos de sus abuelos. (*eh*-yohs *bvee*-bvehn moohee *leh*-Hohs deh soohs ah-bvooh*eh*-lohs) (*They live very far from their grandparents.*)

Talkin the Talk

Inés is deciding how to spend her day. Should she attend the cinema, visit a museum, or do both? First, she needs to find out how near these places are to her and to each other.

Inés: **¿Está lejos el cine Las Flores?**
¿ehs-*tah* *leh*-Hohs ehl *see*-neh lahs *floh*-rehs?
Is the Las Flores cinema far?

Martín: **No, está muy cerca — a sólo dos cuadras.**
noh, ehs-*tah* moohee *sehr*-kah ah *soh*-loh dohs koo*ah*-drahs.
No, it's quite near — only two blocks away.

Inés: **¿Y el Teatro Bolívar?**
¿ee ehl teh-*ah*-troh bvoh-*lee*-bvahr?
And the Bolivar Theater?

Martín: **El teatro Bolívar sí está lejos.**
ehl teh-*ah*-troh bvoh-*lee*-bvahr *see* ehs-*tah leh*-Hohs.
The Bolivar Theater is far.

Tiene que tomar el subte.
tee*eh*-neh keh toh-*mahr* ehl *soohbv*-teh.
You have to take the subway.

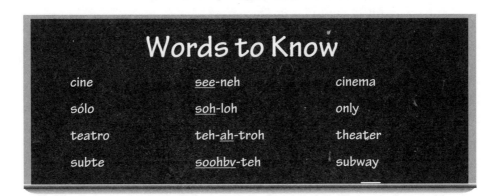

Words to Know

cine	*see*-neh	cinema
sólo	*soh*-loh	only
teatro	teh-*ah*-troh	theater
subte	*soohbv*-teh	subway

Felipe and Bárbara Rodriguez, who speak very little English, are coming to your birthday party. You sent directions to everyone along with their invitations, but they were in English. Bárbara has asked you to translate your directions for them; see Appendix D for the answer key.

Go to the square. _____

Walk two blocks to the small park. _____

Go straight to Alabaster Ave. _____

Turn left. _____

Continue north to Camisa St. _____

Turn right. _____

Continue two more blocks and turn left on Reina Blvd.
_____

My house is behind the park. _____

Chapter 8

Dining Out and Going to the Market

- -

In This Chapter

▶ Making reservations at a Latin American or Spanish restaurant

▶ Placing your food and beverage order

▶ Eating moles (the sauces, not the critters) and other delicacies

▶ Picking up the tab

▶ Shopping at different markets

- -

*F*ood is an important element of any culture. Each country and region in Latin America has different-tasting food, making restaurant-hopping and trying new dishes there among the most diverse experiences possible. The same is true in sunny Spain, where deep-fried fish, mountain-cured ham, and a variety of other tasty treats awaits you. As you work up your appetite for Latin American and Spanish cuisine at home or abroad, brush up on your Spanish so that you're prepared to do a little restaurant-hopping of your own and gather goodies at the local markets.

In this chapter, we bring you up to speed on essential Spanish words and phrases for eating out and shopping at markets and supermarkets so that you can order meals (and drinks) at your favorite restaurants and shop for food at the market, fairly confident that you're getting what you want.

Eating Out

Nothing seems simpler than eating out. All you have to bring to the table is a good appetite, right? Usually, that's true — until you decide to eat out at a restaurant where the menu's in Spanish and the servers speak little or no English. The following sections re-create the entire experience for you from the time you make your reservation to the time you pay the bill . . . minus the fine cuisine, of course.

Not all **restaurantes** (rrehs-tahooh-*rahn*-tehs) (*restaurants*) are the same; this list highlights some vocab to help you distinguish among the different types of establishments you may encounter.

✔ **el bar** (ehl bvahr) (*the bar*)

✔ **el café** (ehl kah-*feh*) (*the coffeehouse*)

✔ **la cafetería** (lah kah-feh-teh-*ree*-ah) (*the cafeteria*)

✔ **el mesón** (ehl meh-*sohn*) (*the tavern*)

✔ **la taberna** (lah tah-*bvehr*-nah) (*the tavern*)

Making a restaurant reservation

To make a reservation, you need the verb **reservar** (reh-sehr-*bvahr*) (*to reserve*). **Reservar** is a regular **-ar** verb, so it isn't difficult to conjugate, as you can see in the following verb chart:

Conjugation	*Pronunciation*
yo reservo	yoh rreh-*sehr*-bvoh
tú reservas	tooh rreh-*sehr*-bvahs
él, ella, usted reserva	ehl, eh-yah, oohs-tehd rreh-*sehr*-bvah
nosotros, nosotras reservamos	noh-*soh*-trohs, noh-*soh*-trahs rreh-sehr-*bvah*-mohs
vosotros, vosotras reserváis	bvoh-*soh*-trohs, bvoh-*soh*-trahs rreh-sehr-*bvah*ees
ellos, ellas, ustedes reservan	*eh*-yohs, *eh*-yahs, oohs-*teh*-dehs rreh-*sehr*-bvahn

Following are some useful phrases that may come in handy when you're making a reservation and sitting down at a restaurant:

Necesitamos una mesa para seis personas, por favor. (neh-seh-see-*tah*-mohs *ooh*-nah *meh*-sah *pah*-rah *seh*ees pehr-*soh*-nahs, pohr fah-*bvohr*.) (*We need a table for six people, please.*)

Tengo una reservación para dos personas. (*tehn*-goh *ooh*-nah rreh-sehr-bvah-see*ohn pah*-rah dohs pehr-*soh*-nahs.) (*I have a reservation for two people.*)

Necesitamos otro cubierto, por favor. (neh-seh-see-*tah*-mohs *oh*-troh kooh-bvee*ehr*-toh, pohr fah-*bvohr*.) (*We need another place setting, please.*)

Refer to Chapter 4 for the dates and times that you need to make your reservations.

The vast majority of restaurants in Latin America don't require reservations.

Getting what you want with the verb querer

The verb **querer** (keh-*rehr*) is often used to convey *to want* or *to wish*. **Querer** is an irregular verb of the stem-changing variety. In the following conjugation in the present tense, notice that the root **quer-** (kehr) is transformed into **quier-** (kee*ehr*). The *e* of the root (or stem) changes to *ie* in all of the conjugations except the **nosotros/nosotras** and **vosotros/vosotras** forms. (Flip to Chapter 6 for more about stem-changing verbs.)

Conjugation	*Pronunciation*
yo quiero	yoh kee*eh*-roh
tú quieres	tooh kee*eh*-rehs
él, ella, usted quiere	ehl, eh-yah, oohs-tehd kee*eh*-reh
nosotros, nosotras queremos	noh-*soh*-trohs, noh-*soh*-trahs keh-*reh*-mohs
vosotros, vosotras queréis	bvoh-*soh*-trohs, bvoh-*soh*-trahs keh-*reh*ees
ellos, ellas, ustedes quieren	*eh*-yohs, *eh*-yahs, oohs-*teh*-dehs kee*eh*-rehn

Talkin' the Talk

Señor Porter wants to take his wife to a nice restaurant on her birthday.

Señor Porter: **Quiero reservar una mesa para dos personas.**
kee*eh*-roh rreh-sehr-*bvahr* ooh-nah *meh*-sah pah-rah dohs pehr-*soh*-nahs.
I want to reserve a table for two people.

Waiter:	**¡Cómo no! ¿Para qué hora?**
	¡koh-moh noh! *¿pah*-rah keh *oh*-rah?
	Of course! For what time?
Señor Porter:	**Para las ocho de la noche.**
	pah-rah lahs *oh*-choh deh lah *noh*-cheh.
	For 8:00 p.m.
Waiter:	**¿A nombre de quién?**
	¿ah *nohm*-bvreh deh kee*ehn*?
	Under what name?
Señor Porter:	**El señor Porter.**
	ehl *seh-nyohr* Porter.
	Mr. Porter.
Waiter:	**Bien, les esperamos.**
	bvee*ehn*, lehs ehs-peh-*rah*-mohs.
	Good, we look forward to seeing you.
Señor Porter:	**Muchas gracias.**
	mooh-chahs *grah*-seeahs.
	Many thanks.

Calling a waiter

A waiter in Argentina is a **mozo** (*moh*-soh) or *young man*. But calling someone **mozo** in Chile is offensive. In Chile, you say **garzón** (gahr-*sohn*), which is derived from the French word for *young man* — the similarly spelled and identically pronounced **garçon**.

If you call the waiter by either of these terms in Mexico, he may not react. You can better get his attention by saying **joven** (*Hoh*-bvehn), meaning *young man,* even if he isn't so young. In Spain, a *waiter* is a **camarero** (kah-mah-*reh*-roh).

When a woman is serving you, call her simply **señorita** (seh-nyoh-*ree*-tah), *Miss,* no matter where you are, which brings up another interesting cultural note. In the United States, the occupation of waiting tables is dominated by women, but in most of Europe, Mexico, and Central and South America, waiting tables is primarily a masculine occupation.

Recognizing and asking for foods on the menu

A menu in a foreign language can be intimidating, as shown in Figure 8-1. But Latin American and Spanish cuisine has many tasty and exotic foods that you don't want to miss, as you find out in the following sections.

To discuss which of those delicacies you're going to order, use the verb **pedir** (peh-*deer*) (*to order, to ask for*). **Pedir** is a stem-changing verb that changes from *e* to *i* in all of the conjugations except the **nosotros/nosotras** and **vosotros/vosotras** forms. (See Chapter 6 for more on stem-changing verbs.)

The most popular dishes

This list identifies the most popular dishes in Spanish-speaking countries:

- ✔ **Empanada** (ehm-pah-*nah*-dah) actually means *in bread*. In Mexico, an **empanada** is a folded and stuffed corn tortilla. You can get **empanadas** made out of wheat dough, which is folded, stuffed, and then fried, in Argentina and Chile. They're usually filled with spicy meat and vegetable mixes and are the Hispanic equivalent of an eggroll or the Eastern European pierogi. Argentinians like theirs small. Chileans make theirs big. Either way, they're delicious!

- ✔ In Spain, a **tortilla** (tohr-*tee*-yah) is a potato, onion, and egg omelette that's often served at room temperature. Figure 8-2 provides a recipe for **tortilla de patatas** (tohr-*tee*-yah deh pah-*tah*-tahs) (*potato omelet*); it features **huevos** (hooh*eh*-bvohs) (*eggs*), **patatas** (pah-*tah*-tahs) (*potatoes*), **cebolla** (seh-*bvoh*-yah) (*onion*), **aceite** (ah-*seh*ee-teh) (*oil*), and **sal** (sahl) (*salt*).

- ✔ In Mexico, **elote** (eh-*loh*-teh) is the name of tender corn, the kind you eat from the cob. The same thing in Argentina, Chile, Peru, and Bolivia is called **choclo** (*choh*-kloh).

- ✔ Green beans in Mexico are called **ejotes** (eh-*Hoh*-tehs). In South America, you find them under names like **porotos verdes** (poh-*roh*-tohs *bvehr*-dehs) or **porotitos** (poh-roh-*tee*-tohs). When the beans are dry, they're called **porotos** (poh-*roh*-tohs) in most of Spanish-speaking America — except in Mexico, where they're known as **frijoles** (free-*Hoh*-lehs). Nowhere else can you see as great a variety of beans as in a Peruvian market. They come in enough colors and shapes and sizes to make your mouth water. You may want to try them all.

✔ In Chile, **filete** (fee-*leh*-teh) is the cut of beef called *sirloin* in the United States. In Argentina, the same cut is called **lomo** (*loh*-moh).

✔ The basic Argentinean meal is **bife, con papas y ensalada** (*bvee*-feh, kohn *pah*-pahs ee ehn-sah-*lah*-dah), which translates to *grilled steak, with potatoes and salad.* On an Argentinean grill, you're likely to find a number of meats familiar to you, along with others that you've probably never eaten. Among the more exotic are **chinchulín** (cheen-chooh-*leen*), which is braided and grilled beef bowels. ¡**Delicioso!** Another delicacy is **molleja** (moh-*yeh*-Hah), which is the thyroid gland of a cow.

✔ In Mexico, however, **molleja** (moh-*yeh*-Hah) is chicken gizzard. And in Chile, the same chicken gizzard is **contre** (*kohn*-treh).

✔ The liver that you eat in Chile is called **pana** (*pah*-nah); in most other places in Latin America, liver is **hígado** (*ee*-gah-doh).

✔ In Spain, **jamón serrano** (Hah-*mohn* seh-*rrah*-noh), salt cured ham typical of the mountain regions, is a great delicacy.

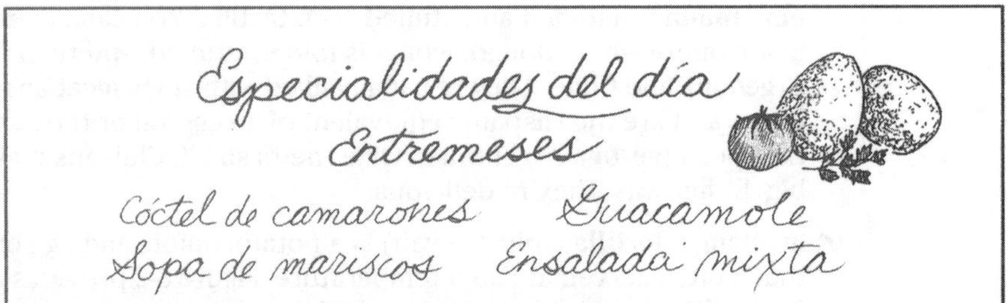

Especialidades del día

Entremeses

Cóctel de camarones   Guacamole

Sopa de mariscos   Ensalada mixta

Platos principales

Huachinango a la veracruzana

Pollo con mango

Mole amarillo con carne de res

Figure 8-1:
Menu items
in Spanish.

TORTILLA DE PATATAS

RECETA FÁCIL (PARA TRES PERSONAS)   LA RECETA

INGREDIENTES
4 HUEVOS   1 CEBOLLA
3 PATATAS   100 mL DE ACEITE DE OLIVA
                  SAL

PASO 1: LAVE Y CORTE LAS PATATAS Y
LAS CEBOLLAS EN REBANADAS.

PASO 2: CALIENTE EL ACEITE (MENOS 3 CUCHARADAS)
EN UNA SARTÉN.

PASO 3: AÑADE LAS REBANADAS DE PATATA Y CEBOLLA.

PASO 4: ALTERNE CAPAS DE PATATA Y CEBOLLA.

PASO 5: COCINE A FUEGO LENTO, REVOLVIENDO
OCASIONALMENTE HASTA
QUE LAS PAPAS ESTÉN TIERNAS.

PASO 6: BATA LOS HUEVOS EN UN TAZÓN GRANDE
CON UN TENEDOR. AGREGUE LA SAL AL GUSTO.

PASO 7: ESCURRA LAS PATATAS Y LAS CEBOLLAS Y
AÑADALÁS A LOS HUEVOS, PRESIONANDO PARA
QUE LOS HUEVOS CUBRIRLAS POR COMPLETO,
Y DEJAR QUE REPOSE DURANTE 15 MINUTOS.

PASO 8: CALIENTE 2 CUCHARADAS DEL ACEITE EN UNA
SARTÉN GRANDE.

PASO 9: AGREGUE LA MEZCLA DE PAPA DE HUEVO.
SE PROPAGA RÁPIDAMENTE.

PASO 10: BAJE EL FUEGO A MEDIO-ALTO Y AGITAR
LA CACEROLA PARA EVITAR QUE SE PEGUE.

PASO 11: CUANDO LAS PAPAS EMPIECEN A DORARSE,
PONGA UNA PLACA EN LA PARTE SUPERIOR
Y TAPA LA SARTÉN PARA COCINAR OTRO LADO.
AGREGANDO OTRA CUCHARADA DE ACEITE.
(PUEDE VOLTEAR 3 O 4 VECES PARA UNA
MEJOR COCCIÓN.)

Figure 8-2:
A sample
recipe in
Spanish.

Fish and other kinds of seafood

If you love fish and seafood, the places to go are Chile and Peru. The
best fish in the world swim in the Humboldt Current, which comes
from Antarctica.

✔ You find delights such as **loco** (*loh*-koh), a truly gigantic scallop, and **congrio** (*kohn*-greeoh), or *conger eel,* a type of fish.

✔ You can also find **albacora** (ahl-bvah-*koh*-rah) (*swordfish*), **cangrejo** (kahn-*greh*-Hoh) (*giant crab*), **jaiba** (*Ha*hee-bvah) (*small crab*), **langosta** (lahn-*gohs*-tah) (*lobster*), **langostino** (lahn-gohs-*tee*-noh) (*prawn*), **camarón** (kah-mah-*rohn*) (*shrimp*) (such as you may have in your **cóctel de camarones** [*kohk*-tehl deh kah-mah-*roh*-nehs] [*shrimp cocktail*]), and other delights to crowd your **sopa marinera** (*soh*-pah mah-ree-*neh*-rah) or **sopa de mariscos** (*soh*-pah deh mah-*rees*-kohs) (*seafood soup*).

✔ Peruvians make **ceviche** (seh-*bvee*-cheh) out of raw fish or raw seafood. In **ceviche,** raw fish or seafood is marinated in lemon juice, salt, and hot peppers. The fish or seafood is still raw after this treatment, but it looks less transparent, as though it were cooked. Sensational! **Ceviches** come in many varieties, but one commonality is that Latinos like their **ceviche** very hot (spicy).

Additional specialties

You also may want to order some of these specialties:

✔ Although that creamy green fruit is called **aguacate** (ah-goohah-*kah*-teh) in Mexico and **palta** (*pahl*-tah) in Argentina, Uruguay, and Chile, it's still the same *avocado.*

✔ In the south of Mexico, when you say **pan** (pahn), meaning *bread,* people usually think of something that the baker made to taste sweet. In South America, **pan** is closer to what folks eat in the United States.

✔ **Torta** (*tohr*-tah) in Mexico is a sandwich in a bun; a **sándwich** (*sahnd*-weech) is made with bread baked in a mold and sliced. But most everywhere else in Latin America, **torta** means *cake,* and **sándwich** means *sandwich* no matter how it's served.

✔ **Memelas** (meh-*meh*-lahs) in Mexico are tortillas that are pinched on the side to form a hollow, which is filled with pastes (such as almond paste) and delicacies.

✔ **Gazpacho** (gahs-*pah*-choh) is a chilled tomato and vegetable soup from Spain flavored with olive oil, garlic, and vinegar.

✔ In Spain, **paella** (pah-*eh*-yah) is a favorite dish made of seafood and saffron rice.

Talkin' the Talk

 Now for great eating! You can use the following conversation as an example to order some soup or salad. (Track 14)

Waiter:	**¿Están listos para ordenar?** ¿ehs-*tahn* lees-tohs *pah*-rah ohr-deh-*nahr*? *Are you ready to order?*
Señora Porter:	**Yo quiero una ensalada mixta.** yoh kee*eh*-roh *ooh*-nah ehn-sah-*lah*-dah *meeks*-tah. *I want a mixed [several vegetables] salad.*
Señor Porter:	**Y para mí, una sopa de mariscos.** ee *pah*-rah mee, *ooh*-nah *soh*-pah deh mah-*rees*-kohs. *And for me, seafood soup.*
Waiter:	**¿Y de plato fuerte?** ¿ee deh *plah*-toh fooh*ehr*-teh? *And as the main course?*
Señor Porter:	**¿Qué nos recomienda?** ¿keh nohs rreh-koh-mee*eh*-dah? *What do you suggest?*
Waiter:	**Tenemos dos platos especiales: mole amarillo con carne de res, y huachinango a la veracruzana.** teh-*neh*-mohs dohs *plah*-tohs ehs-peh-see*ah*-lehs: *moh*-leh ah-mah-*ree*-yoh kohn *kahr*-neh deh rrehs, ee oohah-chee-*nahn*-goh ah lah bveh-rah-krooh-*sah*-nah. *We have two specialties: yellow mole with beef, and red snapper Veracruz style.*
Señora Porter:	**¿Qué es el huachinango a la veracruzana?** ¿keh ehs ehl oohah-chee-*nahn*-goh ah lah bveh-rah-krooh-*sah*-nah? *What is the red snapper Veracruz style?*

Waiter:	**Es pescado con tomates, chile, cilantro, y cebolla.**
	ehs pehs-*kah*-doh kohn toh-*mah*-tehs, *chee*-leh, see-*lahn*-troh, ee seh-*bvoh*-yah.
	It's fish with tomatoes, hot peppers, cilantro, and onions.

Señora Porter:	**Yo quiero pollo frito.**
	yoh keee*eh*-roh *poh*-yoh *free*-toh.
	I want fried chicken.

Waiter:	**No tenemos pollo frito. Tenemos pollo asado en salsa de mango.**
	noh teh-*neh*-mohs *poh*-yoh *free*-toh. teh-*neh*-mohs *poh*-yoh ah-*sah*-doh ehn *sahl*-sah deh *mahn*-goh.
	We don't have fried chicken. We have roasted chicken with mango sauce.

Señora Porter:	**¿Con qué está acompañado?**
	¿kohn keh ehs-*tah* ah-kohm-pah-*nyah*-doh?
	What does it come with?

Waiter:	**Con elotes frescos, y calabacitas entomatadas.**
	kohn eh-*loh*-tehs *frehs*-kohs, ee kah-lah-bvah-*see*-tahs ehn-toh-mah-*tah*-dahs.
	With fresh corn, and zucchini in tomato sauce.

Señora Porter:	**Bueno, voy a probar el pollo con mango.**
	bvooh*eh*-noh, bvohy ah proh-*bvahr* ehl *poh*-yoh kohn *mahn*-goh.
	Good, I'll try the chicken with mango.

Taking a bathroom break

Inevitably, you want to wash your hands, freshen your makeup, or do something else that requires the use of a public bathroom. Bathrooms in Latin America are very similar to those in the United States and Canada — the more expensive the restaurant, the more elegant the bathroom. The following phrases can help you find the room you need:

¿Dónde están los baños? (¿*dohn*-deh ehs-*tahn* lohs *bvah*-nyohs?) (*Where are the bathrooms?*)

Los baños están al fondo, a la derecha. (lohs *bvah*-nyohs ehs-*tahn* ahl *fohn*-doh, ah lah deh-*reh*-chah.) (*The bathrooms are in the back, to the right.*)

¿Es éste el baño? (¿ehs *ehs*-teh ehl *bvah*-nyoh?) (*Is this the bathroom?*)

No, éste no es el baño. Es ése. (noh, *ehs*-teh noh ehs ehl *bvah*-nyoh. ehs *eh*-seh.) (*No, this isn't the bathroom. It's that one.*)

Words to Know

listo	<u>lees</u>-toh	ready
ordenar	ohr-deh-<u>nahr</u>	to order
ensalada mixta	ehn-sah-<u>lah</u>-dah <u>meeks</u>-tah	mixed salad
plato fuerte	<u>plah</u>-toh foo<u>hehr</u>-teh	main course
platos especiales	<u>plah</u>-tohs ehs-peh-see<u>ah</u>-lehs	specialties
mole amarillo con carne de res	<u>moh</u>-leh ah-mah-<u>ree</u>-yoh kohn <u>kahr</u>-neh deh rrehs	yellow mole with beef
huachinango a la veracruzana	oohah-chee-<u>nahn</u>-goh ah lah bveh-rah-krooh-<u>sah</u>-nah	red snapper Veracruz style
pescado	pehs-<u>kah</u>-doh	fish
pollo frito	<u>poh</u>-yoh <u>free</u>-toh	fried chicken
calabacitas entomatadas	kah-lah-bvah-<u>see</u>-tas ehn-toh-mah-<u>tah</u>-dahs	zucchini in tomato sauce
pollo asado en salsa de mango	<u>poh</u>-yoh ah-<u>sah</u>-doh ehn <u>sahl</u>-sah deh <u>mahn</u>-goh	roasted chicken with mango sauce

Sampling the sauces: Hot, cold, and spicy!

Some people say that what's truly special about Latin American foods is the sauce. This statement is especially true of the sauces served in Mexico, which have an infinite variety of flavors and textures.

Moles served hot and hotter

Mole (*moh*-leh), a word used in Mexico, means *sauce*. These Mexican moles are served hot with meats and chicken:

✔ **Mole negro** (*moh*-leh *neh*-groh) (*black mole*) looks black — naturally! — and is made with all toasted ingredients: cocoa, chilies, almonds, onions, garlic, and bread. It can be very spicy or less so.

✔ **Mole colorado** (*moh*-leh koh-loh-*rah*-doh) (*red mole*) looks red and is made with chilies. It's spicy hot! The sauce is also called **coloradito** (koh-loh-rah-*dee*-toh).

✔ **Mole amarillo** (*moh*-leh ah-mah-*ree*-yoh) (*yellow mole*) is orangey yellow. You make it with almonds and raisins, among other ingredients. Generally, it's only mildly spicy.

✔ **Mole verde** (*moh*-leh *bvehr*-deh) (*green mole*) is made with green tomatoes, green chilies (hot peppers), and cilantro and looks green. It can be very spicy or mildly hot.

Mexicans don't eat moles every day. These delicacies are served only on special occasions. Tourists are luckier — they can find them all the time.

Cold sauces for seasoning (they're still plenty hot!)

Mexicans bring some cold sauces to the table to add more spice to your food.

✔ **Pico de gallo** (*pee*-koh deh *gah*-yoh), which translates as *rooster's beak*, is made totally with vegetables. It looks red, green, and white because it's made with tomatoes, jalapeño peppers, cilantro, and onions. Hot!

✔ **Guacamole** (goohah-kah-*moh*-leh) needs no translation. It's the dip made with avocado, **chili** (*chee*-lee) pepper, cilantro, lemon, and salt. It's sometimes spicy hot.

✔ **Salsa verde** (*sahl*-sah *bvehr*-deh) is green sauce made with green tomatoes, chilies, and cilantro. Hot!

✔ **Salsa roja** (*sahl*-sah *rroh*-Hah) is red sauce made with red tomatoes and chilies. Hot!

Ordering beverages

When ordering beverages in a Spanish speaking country, start with one of the following phrases:

Quisiera . . . (kee-see*eh*-rah . . .) (*I'd like* . . .)

Para beber, yo quiero . . . (*pah*-rah bveh-*bvehr*, yoh kee*eh*-roh . . .) (*To drink, I want* . . .)

Y para beber, favor de traer . . . (ee *pah*-rah bveh-*bvehr*, fah-*bvohr* deh trah-*ehr* . . .) (*And to drink, please bring* . . .)

Por favor dígame, ¿qué bebidas tiene? (pohr fah-*bvohr dee*-gah-meh, ¿keh bveh-*bvee*-dahs tee*eh*-neh?) (*Please tell me, what drinks do you have?*)

If you begin your drink request with one of the previous first three phrases, you can complete your order by specifying the drink of your choice:

- **una botella de agua con gas** (*ooh*-nah bvoh-*teh*-yah deh *ah*-goohah kohn gahs) (*a bottle of carbonated water*)

- **una botella de agua sin gas** (*ooh*-nah bvoh-*teh*-yah deh *ah*-goohah seen gahs) (*a bottle of uncarbonated water*)

- **una cerveza** (*ooh*-nah sehr-*bveh*-sah) (*a beer*)

- **una cerveza negra** (*ooh*-nah sehr-*bveh*-sah *neh*-grah) (*a dark beer*)

- **una cerveza rubia** (*ooh*-nah sehr-*bveh*-sah *rrooh*-bveeah) (*a lager*)

- **un jugo de manzana** (oohn *Hooh*-goh deh mahn-*sah*-nah) (*an apple juice*)

- **un jugo de naranja** (oohn *Hooh*-goh deh nah-rahn-Hah) (*an orange juice*)

- **un jugo de tomate** (oohn *Hooh*-goh deh toh-*mah*-teh) (*a tomato juice*)

- **una limonada** (*ooh*-nah lee-moh-*nah*-dah) (*a lemonade*)

- **un refresco** (oohn rreh-*frehs*-koh) (*a soft drink*)

- **un refresco de naranja** (oohn rreh-*frehs*-koh deh nah-rahn-Hah) (*an orangeade*)

- **una taza de café** (*ooh*-nah *tah*-sah deh kah-*feh*) (*a cup of coffee*)

- **un vaso de agua** (oohn *bvah*-soh deh *ah*-goohah) (*a glass of water*)

- **un vaso de leche** (oohn *bvah*-soh deh *leh*-cheh) (*a glass of milk*)

- **un vaso de vino blanco** (oohn *bvah*-soh deh *bvee*-noh *blahn*-koh) (*a glass of white wine*)

- **un vaso de vino tinto** (oohn *bvah*-soh deh *bvee*-noh *teen*-toh) (*a glass of red wine*)

Agua (*ah*-goohah) in Mexico can mean *water,* which is its exact translation, but it can also be a beverage made with water, fruit, and sugar. All fruits, and even some vegetables, make refreshing **aguas** (*ah*-goohahs). In Chile, **agüita** (ah-gooh*ee*-tah) (*little water*) can be an herb tea served after a meal.

If you're ever in Mexico (or a Mexican restaurant, for that matter) and notice someone drinking a cloudy white beverage over ice, you're probably witnessing someone partaking of **horchata** (ohr-*chah*-tah). This very unique and refreshing drink is made with rice, almonds, cinnamon, lime zest, and sugar, although there are variations on the basic recipe.

Talkin' the Talk

If you want to order a beverage to drink with your food, you may participate in a conversation similar to this one.

Waiter:	**¿Quieren algo de beber?**
	¿keee*eh*-rehn *ahl*-goh *deh* bveh-*bvehr?*
	Do you want anything to drink?
	¿Quieren un agua de frutas?
	¿keee*eh*-rehn oohn *ah*-goohah deh *frooh*-tahs?
	Do you want a fruit water?
Señora Porter:	**No, yo quiero un vaso de vino tinto de la casa.**
	noh, yoh keee*eh*-roh oohn *bvah*-soh de *bvee*-noh
	teen-toh deh lah *kah*-sah.
	No, I want a glass of house red wine.
Waiter:	**Muy bien, ¿y usted?**
	*moo*hee bveee*ehn*, ¿ee oohs-*tehd?*
	Very well, and you?
Señor Porter:	**Yo quiero una cerveza.**
	yoh keee*eh*-roh *ooh*-nah sehr-*bveh*-sah.
	I want a beer.
Waiter:	**¿Rubia o negra?**
	¿*rrooh*-bveeah oh *neh*-grah?
	Lager or dark?
Señor Porter:	**Prefiero negra.**
	preh-feee*eh*-roh *neh*-grah.
	I prefer dark.

Words to Know

beber	bveh-<u>bvehr</u>	to drink
un agua de frutas	oohn <u>ah</u>-goohah deh <u>frooh</u>-tahs	a fruit water
un vaso de vino tinto de la casa	oohn <u>bvah</u>-soh de <u>bvee</u>-noh <u>teen</u>-toh deh lah <u>kah</u>-sah	a glass of house red wine

Paying the bill

When paying the bill, you typically ask the waiter for **la cuenta** (lah koohehn-tah) (*the check*).

The following are some useful expressions when you are ready to pay your bill at a restaurant:

La cuenta, por favor. (lah koohehn-tah, pohr fah-*bvohr*.) (*The check, please.*)

¿Cuánto le debo? (¿koohahn-toh leh *deh*-bvoh?) (*How much do I owe you?*)

¿Está incluida la propina? (¿ehs-*tah* een-kloohee-dah lah proh-*pee*-nah?) (*Is the tip included?*)

Talkin' the Talk

You may have an exchange like the following as you pay your bill.

Señor Porter:	**Joven, ¿nos trae la cuenta por favor?** *Hoh*-bvehn, ¿nohs *trah*-eh lah koohehn-tah pohr fah-*bvohr*? *Waiter, will you bring us the check please?*
Waiter:	**Ya vuelvo con la cuenta.** yah bvoohehl-bvoh kohn lah koohehn-tah. *I'll be right back with the check.*
Señor Porter:	**¿Aceptan tarjetas de crédito?** ¿ah-*sehp*-tahn tahr-*Heh*-tahs deh *kreh*-dee-toh? *Do you accept credit cards?*
Waiter:	**No, lo lamento mucho, aquí no aceptamos tarjetas de crédito.** noh, loh lah-*mehn*-toh *mooh*-choh, ah-*kee* noh ah-sehp-*tah*-mohs tahr-*Heh*-tahs deh *kreh*-dee-toh. *No, I'm very sorry; we don't take credit cards here.*

Señor Porter: **Esta bien, puedo pagar en efectivo. Aquí está el dinero.**
ehs-*tah* bee*ehn*, pooheh-doh pah-*gahr* ehn eh-fehk-*tee*-bvoh. ah-*kee* ehs-*tah* ehl dee-*neh*-roh.
It's fine, I can pay cash. Here's the money.

Waiter: **Gracias. Vuelvo en seguida con su cambio.**
grah-seeahs. bvooh*ehl*-bvoh ehn seh-*gee*-dah kohn sooh *kahm*-bveeoh.
Thanks. I'll be right back with your change.

Words to Know

joven	<u>Hoh</u>-bvehn	waiter
la cuenta	lah kooh<u>ehn</u>-tah	the check
tarjetas de crédito	tahr-<u>Heh</u>-tahs deh <u>kreh</u>-dee-toh	credit cards
en efectivo	ehn eh-fehk-<u>tee</u>-bvoh	cash
el dinero	ehl dee-<u>neh</u>-roh	the money
en seguida	ehn seh-<u>gee</u>-dah	right away
el cambio	ehl <u>kahm</u>-bveeoh	the change

Going to Market

In this section, you shop for fruits, vegetables, and fish at markets that may be open or under a roof but are more informal than supermarkets. Vendors in these markets are salespeople, not just cashiers, and they may approach you to sell you goods you may or may not want. When you don't want something, you can simply say one of the following:

Ahora no, gracias. (ah-*oh*-rah noh, *grah*-seeahs.) (*Not now, thank you.*)

Ya tengo, gracias. (yah *tehn*-goh, *grah*-seeahs.) (*I already have some* [or *it*], *thanks.*)

No me interesa, gracias. (no meh een-teh-*reh*-sah, *grah*-seeahs.) (*It doesn't interest me, thank you.*)

Más tarde, gracias. (mahs *tahr*-deh, *grah*-seeahs.) (*Later, thank you.*)

No me gusta, gracias. (noh meh *goohs*-tah, *grah*-seeahs.) (*I don't like it, thanks.*)

No me moleste, ¡por favor! (noh meh moh-*lehs*-teh, ¡pohr fah-*bvohr!*) (*Don't bother me, please!*)

When you go to the market, bringing your own shopping bags or baskets to carry away the stuff you buy is a good idea. Supermarkets provide bags, of course, but at the more informal markets, the vendor simply hands you the stuff you buy and doesn't provide a container to carry it in. In these markets, you can find stalls that sell bags or baskets of all sizes. Even if you have your own carrier, you may want to buy some of these bags to take home with you — many of them are handmade and quite beautiful.

Shopping with the verb comprar

Comprar (kohm-*prahr*) means *to shop,* and **ir de compras** (eer deh *kohm*-prahs) means *to go shopping.* **Comprar** is a regular verb of the **-ar** group. The root of the verb is **compr-** (kohmpr). Here's how you conjugate **comprar** in the present tense:

Conjugation	*Pronunciation*
yo compro	yoh *kohm*-proh
tú compras	tooh *kohm*-prahs
él, ella, usted compra	ehl, *eh*-yah, oohs-*tehd kohm*-prah
nosotros, nosotras compramos	noh-*soh*-trohs, noh-*soh*-trahs kohm-*prah*-mohs
vosotros, vosotras compráis	bvoh-*soh*-trohs, bvoh-*soh*-trahs kohm-*prah*ees
ellos, ellas, ustedes compran	*eh*-yohs, *eh*-yahs, oohs-*teh*-dehs *kohm*-prahn

These phrases, based on **ir de compras** (eer deh *kohm*-prahs) (*to go shopping*), can help you at the market.

Ella está de compras. (*eh*-yah ehs-*tah* deh *kohm*-prahs.) (*She's out shopping.*)

¡Voy de compras! (¡bvoy deh *kohm*-prahs!) (*I'm going shopping!*)

¡Vamos de compras al mercado! (¡*bvah*-mohs deh *kohm*-prahs ahl mehr-*kah*-doh!) (*Let's go shopping at the market!*)

Buying fruit

Here are the names of fruits you find at the market:

- ✔ **la cereza** (lah seh-*reh*-sah) (*the cherry*)
- ✔ **la ciruela** (lah see-rooh*eh*-lah) (*the plum*)
- ✔ **el durazno** (ehl dooh-*rahs*-noh) (*the peach*)
- ✔ **la fresa** (la *freh*-sah) (*the strawberry*) (Mexico, Central America, and Spain)
- ✔ **la frutilla** (lah frooh-*tee*-yah) (*the strawberry*) (from Colombia to the South Pole)
- ✔ **la guayaba** (lah goohah-*yah*-bvah) (*the guava*)
- ✔ **el higo** (ehl *ee*-goh) (*the fig*)
- ✔ **la lima** (lah *lee*-mah) (*the lime*)
- ✔ **el limón** (ehl lee-*mohn*) (*the lemon*)
- ✔ **el mango** (ehl *mahn*-goh) (*the mango*)
- ✔ **la manzana** (lah mahn-*sah*-nah) (*the apple*)
- ✔ **el melocotón** (ehl meh-loh-koh-*tohn*) (*the peach*) (Spain)
- ✔ **el melón** (ehl meh-*lohn*) (*the melon, the cantaloupe*)
- ✔ **la mora** (lah *moh*-rah) (*the blackberry*)
- ✔ **la naranja** (lah nah-*rahn*-Hah) (*the orange*)
- ✔ **la papaya** (lah pah-*pah*-yah) (*the papaya*)
- ✔ **la pera** (lah *peh*-rah) (*the pear*)
- ✔ **el plátano** (ehl *plah*-tah-noh) (*the banana*)
- ✔ **el pomelo** (ehl poh-*meh*-loh) (*the grapefruit*) (Spain)
- ✔ **la sandía** (lah sahn-*dee*-ah) (*the watermelon*)
- ✔ **la toronja** (lah toh-*rohn*-Hah) (*the grapefruit*) (Mexico)
- ✔ **la tuna** (lah *tooh*-nah) (*the prickly pear*)
- ✔ **la uva** (lah *ooh*-bvah) (*the grape*)

Buying vegetables

Fresh vegetables are always tasty. You can easily find the following:

- ✔ **las acelgas** (lahs ah-*sehl*-gahs) (*the Swiss chard*)
- ✔ **el aguacate** (ehl ah-goohah-*kah*-teh) (*the avocado*)

- ✔ **el ají** (el ah-*Hee*) (*the hot pepper*) (South America)

- ✔ **el ajo** (ehl *ah*-Hoh) (*the garlic*)

- ✔ **el brócoli** (ehl *bʋroh*-koh-lee) (*the broccoli*)

- ✔ **la calabacita** (lah kah-lah-bvah-*see*-tah) (*the zucchini*) (Mexico)

- ✔ **las cebollas** (lahs seh-*bʋoh*-yahs) (*the onions*)

- ✔ **el chile** (ehl *chee*-leh) (*the hot pepper*) (Mexico and Guatemala)

- ✔ **el chile morrón** (ehl *chee*-leh moh-*rrohn*) (*the sweet pepper*) (Mexico)

- ✔ **la col** (lah kohl) (*the cabbage*) (Mexico)

- ✔ **la coliflor** (lah koh-lee-*flohr*) (*the cauliflower*)

- ✔ **la espinaca** (lah ehs-pee-*nah*-kah) (*the spinach*)

- ✔ **el tomate** (ehl toh-*mah*-teh) (*the tomato*)

- ✔ **la lechuga** (lah leh-*chooh*-gah) (*the lettuce*)

- ✔ **las papas** (lahs *pah*-pahs) (*the potatoes*)

- ✔ **la palta** (lah *pahl*-tah) (*the avocado*) (South America)

- ✔ **las patatas** (lahs pah-*tah*-tahs) (the potatoes) (Spain)

- ✔ **el pimentón** (ehl pee-mehn-*tohn*) (*the sweet pepper*) (Argentina, Chile, and Uruguay)

- ✔ **el repollo** (ehl rreh-*poh*-yoh) (*the cabbage*) (Argentina and Chile)

- ✔ **la zanahoria** (lah sah-nah-*oh*-reeah) (*the carrot*)

- ✔ **el zapallito** (ehl sah-pah-*yee*-toh) (*zucchini*) (Uruguay and Argentina)

Shopping for fish

These terms can help you when you're selecting seafood:

- ✔ **el camarón** (ehl kah-mah-*rohn*) (shrimp)

- ✔ **las gambas** (lahs *gahm*-bahs) (shrimp) (Spain)

- ✔ **el huachinango** (ehl oohah-chee-*nahn*-goh) (*red snapper*)

- ✔ **el langostino** (ehl lahn-gohs-*tee*-noh) (*prawn*)

- ✔ **el marisco** (ehl mah-*rees*-koh) (*seafood*)

- ✔ **el pescado** (ehl pehs-*kah*-doh) (*fish*)

- ✔ **la trucha** (lah *trooh*-chah) (*trout*)

Talkin' the Talk

 Latin Americans prepare fish and seafood in a variety of ways, all of them delicious. Here's how Amalia shops for fish. (Track 15)

Amalia:	**¿Cuánto cuesta el pescado?**
	¿koohahn-toh koohehs-tah ehl pehs-kah-doh?
	How much is the fish?
Vendor:	**Treinta pesos el kilo.**
	treheen-tah peh-sohs ehl kee-loh.
	Thirty pesos per kilo.
Amalia:	**Lo quiero fileteado, sin espinas.**
	loh keeeeh-roh fee-leh-teh-ah-doh, seen ehs-pee-nas.
	I want it filleted, boneless.
Vendor:	**¿Se lleva la cabeza para la sopa?**
	¿seh yeh-bvah lah kah-bveh-sah pah-rah lah soh-pah?
	Will you take the head for soup?
Amalia:	**Sí, aparte, por favor.**
	see, ah-pahr-teh, pohr fah-bvohr.
	Yes, separately, please.

Words to Know

fileteado	fee-leh-teh-ah-doh	filleted
sin espinas	seen ehs-pee-nas	boneless
la sopa	lah soh-pah	soup
aparte	ah-pahr-teh	separately

Shopping at the Supermercado

Of course, you can buy groceries at the **supermercado** (sooh-pehr-mehr-*kah*-doh) (*supermarket*), where you proceed very much as you do in the United States. You may also find food there that you're more accustomed to — the supermarket is a good place to go for things like cereals and canned goods.

Following are some words and a phrase that can help you at the supermarket:

- ✔ **al fondo** (ahl *fohn*-doh) (*at the back*)
- ✔ **el arroz** (ehl ah-*rrohs*) (*the rice*)
- ✔ **el atún** (ehl ah-*toohn*) (*the tuna*)
- ✔ **los cereales** (lohs seh-reh-*ah*-lehs) (*the cereals*)
- ✔ **los fideos** (ehl fee-*deh*-oh) (*the noodles*)
- ✔ **las galletas** (lahs gah-*yeh*-tahs) (*the cookies*)
- ✔ **las galletas saladas** (lahs gah-*yeh*-tahs sah-*lah*-dahs) (*the crackers*)
- ✔ **las galletas de soda** (lahs gah-*yeh*-tahs deh *soh*-dah) (*the soda crackers*)
- ✔ **Gracias, aquí está su vuelto.** (*grah*-seeahs, ah-*kee* ehs-*tah* sooh bvooh*ehl*-toh.) (*Thanks, here's your change.*)
- ✔ **la leche** (lah *leh*-cheh) (*the milk*)
- ✔ **las ollas** (lahs *oh*-yas) (*the pots*)
- ✔ **pagar** (pah-*gahr*) (*to pay*)
- ✔ **el pasillo** (ehl pah-*see*-yoh) (*the aisle*)
- ✔ **las sardinas** (lahs sahr-*dee*-nahs) (*the sardines*)
- ✔ **el tercer pasillo** (ehl tehr-*sehr* pah-*see*-yoh) (*the third aisle*)
- ✔ **el vino** (ehl *bvee*-noh) (*the wine*)
- ✔ **la vuelta** (lah bvooh*ehl*-tah) (*change* [money back]) (Spain)
- ✔ **el vuelto** (ehl bvooh*ehl*-toh) (*change*)

A Spanish-speaking friend has come to visit you. To celebrate, you take him to a fancy restaurant. Of course, the menu is in English, and your friend asks you to translate several items. Write the Spanish words in the blank following each menu item.

Beef _____

Coffee _____

Milk _____

Fried chicken _____

Green sauce _____

Beer _____

Seafood _____

After translating the menu, your friend chooses his meal. Now translate his choices into English for the waiter.

Un vaso de agua _____

Un vaso de leche _____

Una ensalada mixta _____

Mole amarillo con pollo _____

Calabacita _____

See Appendix D for the answer key.

Chapter 9

Shopping Made Easy

● ●

In This Chapter

▶ Buying personal care items at the pharmacy

▶ Shopping at department stores, specialty stores, and traditional markets

▶ Using the verbs **probarse** (*to try on*) and **llevar** (*to wear*)

▶ Expressing comparatives, superlatives, and emphasis

● ●

*W*henever and wherever you go shopping — the pharmacy, department store, specialty stores, or traditional markets — you need to know how to tell the sales clerks what you want and how you want it. This chapter takes you on a shopping spree, providing you with the words and phrases required for a successful shopping trip.

Buying Essentials at the Pharmacy and Perfumery

Most folks in the United States frequent the pharmacy for medications and personal care items. In many Latin American countries, the **farmacia** (phar-*mah*-seeah) (*pharmacy*) is exclusively for medication. For most of the other stuff you find at pharmacies in the United States — rubbing alcohol, cotton swabs, toothpaste, shaving cream, and so on — you go to the **perfumería** (pehr-fooh-mehr-*ee*-ah) (*perfumery*). To find the nearest **farmacia** or **perfumería,** the following phrases come in handy:

> **¿Dónde está la farmacia más cercana?** (¿*dohn*-deh ehs-*tah* lah fahr-*mah*-seeah mahs sehr-*kah*-nah?) (*Where is the nearest pharmacy?*)

> **¿Dónde está la perfumería más cercana?** (¿*dohn*-deh ehs-*tah* lah pehr-fooh-mehr-*ee*-ah mahs sehr-*kah*-nah?) (*Where is the nearest perfumery?*)

Another essential phrase is **Necesito . . .** (neh-seh-*see*-toh. . .) (*I need . . .*) followed by the word(s) that best describe the item you're looking for. Table 9-1 provides a list of items you're likely to want from a **farmacia** or **perfumería.**

Table 9-1	Pharmacy/Perfumery Items	
Spanish	*Pronunciation*	*English*
el acondicionador	ehl ah-kohn-dee-seeoh-nah-dohr	the hair conditioner
el alcohol	ehl ahl-koh-*ohl*	the alcohol
el antiácido	ehl ahn-tee-*ah*-see-doh	the antacid
el antihistamínico	ehl ahn-tee-ees-tah-*mee*-nee-koh	the antihistamine
el antiséptico	ehl ahn-tee-*sehp*-tee-koh	the antiseptic
la aspirina	lah ahs-pee-*ree*-nah	the aspirin
la bolsa de hielo	lah *bvohl*-sah deh ee*eh*-loh	the ice pack
el cepillo de dientes	ehl seh-*pee*-yoh deh dee-*ehn*-tehs	the toothbrush
el champú	ehl chahm-*pooh*	the shampoo
los condones	lohs kohn-*doh*-nehs	the condoms
la crema de afeitar	lah *kreh*-mah deh ah-fehee-*tahr*	the shaving cream
la crema hidratante	lah *kreh*-mah ee-drah-*tahn*-teh	the moisturizer
la curita	lah kooh-*ree*-tah	the bandage
el desodorante	ehl deh-soh-doh-*rahn*-teh	the deodorant
el enjuague bucal	ehl ehn-Hooh*ah*-geh bvooh-*kahl*	the mouthwash
el estuche portalentes	ehl ehs-*tooh*-cheh pohr-tah-*lehn*-tehs	the contact lens case
las gotas oftalmológicas lubricantes	lahs *goh*-tahs ohf-tahl-moh-*loh*-Hee-kahs looh-bvree-*kahn*-tehs	the lubricant eye drops
la hoja de afeitar	lah *oh*-Hah deh ah-fehee-*tahr*	the razor blade
el jabón	ehl Hah-*bvohn*	the soap
el jarabe para la tos	ehl Hah-*rah*-bveh *pah*-rah lah tohs	the cough syrup
el laxante	ehl lahk-*sahn*-teh	the laxative
la loción para después del afeitado	lah loh-see*ohn pah*-rah dehs-pooh*ehs* dehl ah-fehee-*tah*-doh	the aftershave
la maquinilla desechable	lah mah-kee-*nee*-yah dehs-eh-*chah*-bvleh	the disposable razor

Spanish	Pronunciation	English
la medicina antidiarrea	lah meh-deh-*see*-nah ahn-tee-deeah-*rreh*-ah	*the diarrhea medication*
la medicina para el resfriado	lah meh-dee-*see*-nah *pah*-rah ehl rrehs-free*ah*-doh	*the cold medicine*
los pañales	lohs pah-*nyah*-lehs	*the diapers*
los pañuelos de papel	lohs pah-nyooh*eh*-lohs deh pah-*pehl*	*the tissues*
el papel higiénico	ehl pah-*pehl* ee-Hee*eh*-nee-koh	*the toilet paper*
la pasta de dientes	lah *pahs*-tah deh dee*ehn*-tehs	*the toothpaste*
las pastillas para dormir	lahs pahs-*tee*-yahs *pah*-rah dohr-*meer*	*the sleeping pills*
las pastillas para la tos	lahs pahs-*tee*-yahs *pah*-rah lah tohs	*the cough drops*
el peine	ehl *peh*ee-neh	*the comb*
la solución multi-propósito para los lentes de contacto	lah soh-looh-see*ohn* moohl-tee-proh-*poh*-see-toh *pah*-rah lohs *lehn*-tehs deh kohn-*tahk*-toh	*the multipurpose solution for contact lenses*
los tampones	lohs tahm-*poh*-nehs	*the tampons*
el termómetro	ehl tehr-*moh*-meh-troh	*the thermometer*
las toallas femeninas	lahs toh-*ah*-yahs feh-meh-*nee*-nahs	*the feminine pads*

Shopping at the Department Store

When you daydream about traveling to foreign lands, you probably imagine the locals doing most of their shopping in open-air markets or small boutiques. The fact of the matter, however, is that in larger cities all around the world, people shop in department stores much as they do in the United States. When visiting a foreign country, consider scheduling a shopping trip to a major department store. This excursion is a great way to see how and where the locals get their clothes and other necessities. In department stores, you also find the prices clearly posted and labeled. And you can surely find items that have local flavor.

The basic vocabulary in Table 9-2 can help you as you shop in a store where Spanish is the primary language.

Table 9-2	Basic Shopping Terms	
Spanish	*Pronunciation*	*English*
apretado	ah-preh-*tah*-doh	*tight*
ayudar	ah-yooh-*dahr*	*to help*
barato	bvah-*rah*-toh	*inexpensive, cheap*
caro	*kah*-roh	*expensive*
grande	*grahn*-deh	*large*
liso	*lee*-soh	*plain, flat*
más	mahs	*more*
medir	meh-*deer*	*to measure*
menos	*meh*-nohs	*less*
pequeño	peh-*keh*-nyoh	*small*
el probador	ehl proh-bvah-*dohr*	*the fitting room*
probar	proh-*bvahr*	*to try*
suelto	sooh*ehl*-toh	*loose*
la talla	lah *tah*-yah	*the size*

In the following sections, you find out about a store's hours and help, specific items of clothing, the verbs *to look for* and *to try on,* different colors, and fibers and fabrics.

Looking for something with the verb buscar

Buscar (bvoohs-*kahr*) is a much-used regular verb with a number of meanings: *to look for, to try to find,* or *to search for.* Here's how you conjugate this verb in the present tense.

Conjugation	*Pronunciation*
yo busco	yoh *bvoohs*-koh
tú buscas	tooh *bvoohs*-kahs
él, ella, usted busca	ehl, *eh*-yah, oohs-*tehd bvoohs*-kah
nosotros, nosotras buscamos	noh-*soh*-trohs, noh-*soh*-trahs bvoohs-*kah*-mohs
vosotros, vosotras buscáis	bvoh-*soh*-trohs, bvoh-*soh*-trahs bvoohs-*kahees*
ellos, ellas, ustedes buscan	*eh*-yohs, *eh*-yahs, oohs-*tehd*-ehs *bvoohs*-kahn

Practice using **buscar** with these phrases:

> **Buscan un mercado.** (*bvoohs*-kahn oohn mehr-*kah*-doh.) (*They're looking for a market.*)

> **Ella busca un vestido nuevo para la fiesta.** (*eh*-yah *bvoohs*-kah oohn bvehs-*tee*-doh nooh*eh*-bvoh *pah*-rah lah feee*ehs*-tah.) (*She's looking for a new dress for the party.*)

> **Buscas una joyería.** (*bvoohs*-kahs *ooh*-nah Hoh-yeh-*ree*-ah.) (*You're looking for a jewelry store.*)

> **Busco un traje de baño nuevo para el viaje a Puerto Rico.** (*bvoohs*-koh oohn *trah*-Heh deh *bvah*-nyoh nooh*eh*-bvoh *pah*-rah ehl bveee*ah*-Heh ah pooh*ehr*-toh *rree*-koh.) (*I'm looking for a new swimsuit for the trip to Puerto Rico.*)

Asking for store hours and receiving help

Suppose you're planning your day and you want to know the store's hours. Here's how to ask for that information:

> **¿A qué hora abren?** (¿ah keh *oh*-rah *ah*-bvrehn?) (*At what time do you open?*)

> **¿A qué hora cierran?** (¿ah keh *oh*-rah seee*eh*-rrahn?) (*At what time do you close?*)

In the United States and Canada, you're probably used to browsing and shopping by yourself. In some places in Latin America, the salesperson wants to help you as soon as you enter the department. If you find the person insistent, our advice is to let yourself be helped. The salespeople aren't trying to impose anything on you; quite to the contrary, they can be very involved and helpful. Let yourself feel like royalty, being pampered as you shop. On the other hand, if you only want to browse, be firm about refusing help.

Talkin' the Talk

Here's how to tell a salesperson that you want just to browse around the store.

Salesperson: **¿Busca algo en especial?**
                       ¿bvoohs-kah *ahl*-goh ehn ehs-peh-see*ahl?*
                       Looking for something special?

Silvia: **Quiero mirar, no más.**
                       kee*eh*-roh mee-*rahr*, noh mahs.
                       I just want to look.

Salesperson:	**Me llama cuando me necesita.**
	meh *yah*-mah cooh*ahn*-doh meh neh-seh-*see*-tah.
	Call me when you need me.
Silvia:	**Sí, le voy a llamar, gracias.**
	see, leh bvohy ah yah-*mahr*, *grah*-seeahs.
	Yes, I'll call you, thank you.

Shopping for clothes

Nearly every language has a wardrobe full of words for various items of clothing **(ropa)** (*rroh*-pah). Spanish is no different. Before you go shopping, try the common clothing words in Table 9-3 on for size.

Table 9-3	Articles of Clothing	
Spanish	*Pronunciation*	*English*
el abrigo	ehl ah-*bvree*-goh	*the overcoat*
la bata de baño	lah *bvah*-tah deh *bvah*-nyoh	*the bathrobe*
la bata de casa	lah *bvah*-tah deh *kah*-sah	*the housecoat*
la bata de playa	lah *bvah*-tah deh *plah*-yah	*the beach robe*
la blusa	lah *bvlooh*-sah	*the blouse*
las botas	lahs *bvoh*-tahs	*the boots*
las bragas	lahs *bvrah*-gahs	*the panties*
la bufanda	lah bvooh-*fahn*-dah	*the scarf*
los calcetines	lohs kahl-seh-*tee*-nehs	*the socks*
la camisa	lah kah-*mee*-sah	*the shirt*
la camiseta	lah kah-mee-*seh*-tah	*the T-shirt, the undershirt*
la chaqueta	lah chah-*keh*-tah	*the jacket*
el cinturón	ehl seen-tooh-*rohn*	*the belt*
la corbata	lah kohr-*bah*-tah	*the tie*
la falda	lah *fahl*-dah	*the skirt*
los guantes	lohs gooh*ahn*-tehs	*the gloves*
el impermeable	ehl eem-pehr-meh-*ah*-bvleh	*the raincoat*
los jeans	lohs jeens	*the jeans*
los pantalones	lohs pahn-tah-*loh*-nehs	*the pants*

Spanish	Pronunciation	English
los pantalones cortos	lohs pahn-tah-*loh*-nehs *kohr*-tohs	the shorts
los piyamas	lohs pee-*yah*-mahs	the pajamas
la ropa interior	lah *rroh*-pah een-teh-ree*ohr*	the underwear
el saco	ehl *sah*-koh	the jacket
las sandalias	lahs sahn-*dah*-leeahs	the sandals
el sombrero	ehl sohm-*bvreh*-roh	the hat
el suéter	ehl sooh*eh*-tehr	the sweater
el sujetador	ehl sooh-Heh-tah-*dohr*	the bra
los tenis	lohs *teh*-nees	the sneakers
el traje de baño	ehl *trah*-Heh deh *bvah*-nyoh	the bathing suit
los vaqueros	lohs bvah-*keh*-rohs	the jeans
el vestido	ehl bvehs-*tee*-doh	the dress
los zapatos	lohs sah-*pah*-tohs	the shoes
los zapatos de salón	lohs sah-*pah*-tohs deh sah-*lohn*	the pumps

Trying on anything with the verb probarse

The verb **probarse** (proh-*bvahr*-seh) (*to try on,*) is one that you may use quite a lot when shopping. It's a reflexive verb, which requires a reflexive pronoun. That simply means that the subject is doing the action to itself. (Refer to Chapter 16 for more on reflexive verbs and how to use them.)

Probarse's root (or stem) changes from **pro-** (proh) to **prue-** (proo*eh*) in some tenses, so it's an irregular verb of the stem-changing (o to ue) variety. (For more about conjugating irregular verbs, see Chapter 2 and Appendix B.) Here is the conjugation:

Conjugation	Pronunciation
yo me pruebo	yoh meh proo*eh*-bvoh
tú te pruebas	tooh teh proo*eh*-bvahs
él, ella, usted se prueba	ehl, *eh*-yah, oohs-*tehd* seh proo*eh*-bvah
nosotros, nosotras nos probamos	noh-*soh*-trohs, noh-*soh*-trahs nohs proh-*bvah*-mohs
vosotros, vosotras os probáis	bvoh-*soh*-trohs, bvoh-*soh*-trahs ohs proh-*bvah*ees
ellos, ellas, ustedes se prueban	*eh*-yohs, *eh*-yahs, oohs-*teh*-dehs seh proo*eh*-bvahn

After you know how to use **probarse,** you can ask to try on anything before you buy it, which is always a good idea wherever you shop. Simply say, **¿Puedo probarme éste?** (¿poohe*h*-doh proh-*bvahr*-meh *ehs*-teh?) (*May I try this on?*). In some areas, people are smaller and sizes vary; the medium there may be what you consider a small. Your best bet is to try on any item before you leave the store.

Creating a colorful you

Shopping for clothes and other goods in Spanish requires some familiarity with describing colors **(colores)** (koh-*loh*-rehs) so that you can select the best match for your needs and personality. Table 9-4 gives you a handle on the Spanish color palette.

Table 9-4	Colors	
Spanish	*Pronunciation*	*English*
amarillo	ah-mah-*ree*-yoh	*yellow*
anaranjado	ah-nah-rahn-*Hah*-doh	*orange*
azul	ah-*soohl*	*blue*
blanco	*bvlahn*-koh	*white*
café	kah-*feh*	*brown*
celeste	seh-*lehs*-teh	*sky blue*
gris	grees	*grey*
marrón	mah-*rrohn*	*brown (Argentina)*
morado	moh-*rah*-doh	*purple*
negro	*neh*-groh	*black*
rojo	*rroh*-Hoh	*red*
rosado	rroh-*sah*-doh	*pink*
verde	*bvehr*-deh	*green*
violeta	bveeoh-*leh*-tah	*violet, purple*

To say you want a dark version of a color, use the adjective **oscuro** (ohs-*kooh*-roh) (*dark*). For a light color, use **claro** (*klah*-roh) (*light*).

A color ending in *-o* or *-a* acts as any other adjective in Spanish and must change endings to agree with the gender of the noun it's modifying. So a red blouse is **una blusa roja** (*ooh*-nah *bvlooh*-sah *rroh*-Hah), but a red sweater is **un suéter rojo** (oohn soohe*h*-tehr *rroh*-Hoh). Colors that end in *-e* or a consonant stay the same for both feminine and masculine nouns.

Talkin' the Talk

 Silvia accidentally split her skirt bending down to pick up some boxes at work. She needs a new one quick — one with pockets to hold the art supplies she needs as a graphic designer. She asks a salesperson for help. (Track 16)

Silvia:
¿Me ayuda, por favor?
¿meh ah-yooh-dah, pohr fah-bvohr?
Will you help me, please?

Busco una falda con bolsillos.
bvoohs-koh ooh-nah fahl-dah kohn bvohl-see-yohs.
I'm looking for a skirt with pockets.

Salesperson:
¿Qué talla tiene?
¿keh tah-yah teeeh-neh?
What's your size?

Silvia:
Talla doce americana.
tah-yah doh-seh ah-meh-ree-kah-nah.
Size 12 American.

Salesperson:
¿Me permite medirla para estar segura?
¿meh pehr-mee-teh meh-deer-lah pah-rah ehs-tahr seh-gooh-rah?
May I measure you to be sure?

Ah, su talla es treinta y ocho.
ah, sooh tah-yah ehs treheen-tah ee oh-choh.
Ah, your size is 38.

¿Qué color busca?
¿keh koh-lohr bvoohs-kah?
What color are you looking for?

Silvia:
Rojo.
rroh-Hoh.
Red.

Salesperson:
¿La quiere con flores?
¿lah keeeh-reh kohn floh-rehs?
Do you want it with flowers?

Silvia:
No, lisa, por favor.
noh, lee-sah pohr fah-bvohr.
No, plain, please.

Words to Know

¿Me ayuda por favor?	¿meh ah-<u>yooh</u>-dah pohr fah-<u>bvohr</u>?	Will you help me please?
el bolsillo	ehl bvohl-<u>see</u>-yoh	the pocket
la talla	lah <u>tah</u>-yah	the size
¿Me permite medirla?	¿meh pehr-<u>mee</u>-teh meh-<u>deer</u>-lah?	May I measure you?
con	kohn	with
flores	<u>floh</u>-rehs	flowers
liso	<u>lee</u>-soh	plain; flat

Talkin' the Talk

Here's how you may ask to try on pants.

Claudio: **¿Puedo probarme estos pantalones?**
¿poohe*h*-doh proh-*bvahr*-meh *ehs*-tohs
pahn-tah-*loh-nehs*?
May I try on these trousers?

Salesperson: **Cómo no, por aquí.**
koh-moh noh, pohr ah-*kee.*
Of course, this way.

Claudio: **Me quedan grandes.**
meh *keh*-dahn *grahn*-dehs.
They're too big. (Literally: They fit me large.)

Salesperson: **Le encuentro otros.**
leh ehn-koohe*hn*-troh *oh*-trohs.
I'll find you another pair.

Claudio: **Estos aprietan aquí.**
ehs-tohs ah-preee*h*-tahn ah-*kee.*
These are tight here.

Salesperson: **A ver éstos.**
ah bvehr *ehs*-tohs.
Let's see these.

Claudio: **¿Los tiene en verde?**
¿lohs tee*eh*-neh ehn *bvehr*-deh?
Do you have them in green?

Salesperson: **Estos, ¿a ver?**
ehs-tohs, ¿ah bvehr?
These ones, let's see?

Claudio: **Quedan muy bien.**
keh-dahn *moohee* bvee*ehn*.
They fit very well.

Words to Know

quedar	keh-<u>dahr</u>	to fit
grande	<u>grahn</u>-deh	large
a ver	ah bvehr	let's see
por aquí	pohr ah-<u>kee</u>	this way

Checking fibers and fabrics

These terms help you ask about the fibers (or fabrics **[los tejidos]** [lohs teh-*Hee*-dohs]) the garments are made of:

- **el algodón** (ehl ahl-goh-*dohn*) (*the cotton*)
- **la fibra** (lah *fee*-bvrah) (*the fiber*)
- **la lana** (lah *lah*-nah) (*the wool*)
- **por ciento** (pohr see*ehn*-toh) (*percent; percentage*)
- **pura** (*pooh*-rah) (*pure*)

And here are typical questions you may ask about fabrics:

> **¿Estos pantalones son de pura lana?** (¿*ehs*-tohs pahn-tah-*loh*-nehs sohn de *pooh*-rah *lah*-nah?) (*Are these pants made of pure wool?*)

> **No, son de lana con nylon.** (noh, sohn deh *lah*-nah kohn *nee*-lohn.) (*No, they're made of wool and nylon.*)

> **¿La camisa es de puro algodón?** (¿lah kah-*mee*-sah ehs deh *pooh*-roh ahl-goh-*dohn?*) (*Is the shirt made of pure cotton?*)

> **No, es de algodón con poliéster.** (noh, ehs deh ahl-goh-*dohn* kohn poh-lee*ehs*-tehr.) (*No, it's made of cotton and polyester.*)

> **¿Cuánto algodón tiene esta tela?** (¿kooh*ahn*-toh ahl-goh-*dohn* tee*eh*-neh *ehs*-tah *teh*-lah?) (*How much cotton does this fabric have?*)

> **Tiene cuarenta por ciento.** (tee*eh*-neh koohah-*rehn*-tah pohr see*ehn*-toh.) (*It has 40 percent.*)

> **Busco ropa de fibras naturales.** (*bvoohs*-koh *rroh*-pah deh *fee*-bvrahs nah-tooh-*rah*-lehs.) (*I'm looking for natural fiber clothes.*)

> **También tenemos.** (tahm-bvee*ehn* teh-*neh*-mohs.) (*We have them also.*)

Wearing and Taking with the Verb Llevar

In Spanish *to wear* and *to take with you* are the same verb — **llevar** (yeh-*bvahr*). Good news! This one is a regular verb of the group ending in **-ar;** its root is **llev-** (yehbv).

Conjugation	Pronunciation
yo llevo	yoh *yeh*-bvoh
tú llevas	tooh *yeh*-bvahs
él, ella, usted lleva	ehl, *eh*-yah, oohs-*tehd yeh*-bvah
nosotros, nosotras llevamos	noh-*soh*-trohs, noh-*soh*-trahs yeh-*bvah*-mohs
vosotros, vosotras lleváis	bvoh-*soh*-trohs, bvoh-*soh*-trahs yeh-*bvah*ees
ellos, ellas, ustedes llevan	*eh*-yohs, *eh*-yahs, oohs-*teh*-dehs *yeh*-bvahn

Count on these examples to help you keep track of this dressing and taking verb:

> **Me llevo esta pulsera.** (meh *yeh*-bvoh *ehs*-tah poohl-*seh*-rah.) (*I'll take this bracelet.*)

El vestido que llevas es bellísimo. (ehl bvehs-*tee*-doh keh *yeh*-bvahs ehs bveh-*yee*-see-moh.) (*The dress you have on is very beautiful.*)

Ellos llevan un regalo para ti. (*eh*-yohs *yeh*-bvahn oohn rreh-*gah*-loh *pah*-rah tee.) (*They're taking a present for you.*)

Ella siempre lleva un uniforme en su trabajo. (*eh*-yah see*ehm*-preh *yeh*-bvah oohn ooh-nee-*fohr*-meh ehn sooh trah-*bvah*-Hoh.) (*She always wears a uniform at her job.*)

La llevo. (lah *yeh*-bvoh.) (*I'll take it.*)

Another way to say *to wear* is **vestir** (bvehs-*teer*) (*to dress*), which comes from **vestido** (bves-*tee*-doh) (*dress*). The verb **vestir** is an irregular, stem-changing verb of the *e* to *i* variety, which means that the *e* in the stem changes to *i* in all of the conjugated forms except the **nosotros/nosotras** and the **vosotros/ vosotras** forms.

Making Comparisons: Good, Better, Best

When you compare one thing to another, you talk in comparatives and superlatives. In Spanish, most of the time you use the word **más** (mahs) (*more*) for comparisons and **el más** (ehl mahs), which literally means *the most,* for superlatives. An example is the word **grande** (*grahn*-deh), which means *large* in English. **Más grande** (mahs *grahn*-deh) means *larger,* and **el más grande** (ehl mahs *grahn*-deh) means *the largest.*

In English, you usually change the word's ending; in Spanish, you just add **más** or **el más.** English has a similar system of forming comparatives and superlatives for longer words such as *expensive,* where the comparative adds *more* before expensive, and the superlative adds *most.*

Table 9-5 gives you some examples of Spanish comparatives and superlatives.

Table 9-5	Spanish Adjective Comparatives and Superlatives	
Adjective	**Comparative**	**Superlative**
grande (*grahn*-deh) (*big, large*)	**más grande** (mahs *grahn*-deh) (*bigger, larger*)	**el más grande** (ehl mahs *grahn*-deh) (*the biggest; the largest*)
pequeño (peh-*keh*-nyoh) (*small*)	**más pequeño** (mahs peh-*keh*-nyoh) (*smaller*)	**el más pequeño** (ehl mahs peh-*keh*-nyoh) (*the smallest*)

(continued)

Table 9-5 *(continued)*

Adjective	Comparative	Superlative
chico (*chee*-koh) (*small, short, young*)	más chico (mahs *chee*-koh) (*smaller, shorter, younger*)	el más chico (ehl mahs *chee*-koh) (*the smallest, the shortest, the youngest*)
apretado (ah-preh-*tah*-doh) (*tight*)	más apretado (mahs ah-preh-*tah*-doh) (*tighter*)	el más apretado (ehl mahs ah-preh-*tah*-doh) (*the tightest*)
suelto (sooh*ehl*-toh) (*loose*)	más suelto (mahs sooh*ehl*-toh) (*looser*)	el más suelto (ehl mahs sooh*ehl*-toh) (*the loosest*)
caro (*kah*-roh) (*expensive*)	más caro (mahs *kah*-roh) (*more expensive*)	el más caro (ehl mahs *kah*-roh) (*the most expensive*)
barato (bvah-*rah*-toh) (*cheap*)	más barato (mahs bvah-*rah*-toh) (*cheaper*)	el más barato (ehl mahs bvah-*rah*-toh) (*the cheapest*)

Just as in English, a few exceptions exist in which the comparative form doesn't require the word **más,** such as the following examples. Notice that the English translations are also exceptions to the English rules for forming comparatives and superlatives.

✔ **bueno** (bvooh*eh*-noh) (*good*); **mejor** (meh-*Hohr*) (*better*); **el mejor** (ehl meh-*Hohr*) (*the best*)

✔ **malo** (*mah*-loh) (*bad*); **peor** (peh-*ohr*) (*worse*); **el peor** (ehl peh-*ohr*) (*the worst*)

When Superlatives Fail: Exaggerations

Spanish speakers love to exaggerate. What may seem to non-Spanish speakers to be an excessive way to talk simply adds a bit more emphasis in the Spanish-speaking mind.

To say that something is exaggeratedly this or that, you add **-ísimo** (ee-see-moh) or **-ísima** (ee-see-mah) to an adjective or an adverb. For example, to say that something **bueno** (bvooh*eh*-noh) (*good*), is exaggeratedly so, you say it's **buenísimo** (bvooheh-*nee*-see-moh) (*exceptionally good*).

Here are some additional examples:

La película es buenísima. (lah peh-*lee*-kooh-lah ehs bvooheh-*nee*-see-mah.) (*The film is exceptionally good.*)

La ciudad es grandísima. (lah seeooh-*dahd* ehs grahn-*dee*-see-mah.) (*The city is huge.*)

El hotel es malísimo. (ehl oh-*tehl* ehs mah-*lee*-see-moh.) (*The hotel is really bad.*)

Los colores son vivísimos. (lohs koh-*loh*-rehs sohn bvee-*bvee*-see-mohs.) (*The colors are exceedingly bright.*)

Los precios son carísimos. (lohs *preh*-seeohs sohn kah-*ree*-see-mohs) (*The prices are exorbitantly expensive.*)

Shopping in Specialty Stores

If you travel, you may want to shop in the specialized stores or galleries generally located on the more elegant boulevards, streets, and avenues in all Latin American countries. Seeking the finest artistic, cultural, or fashion items may include buying original art or silver in **Lima, Peru** (*lee*-mah, peh-*rooh*) and Mexico City, or shopping for paintings, sculpture, fine shoes, leather objects, and exquisite collectibles in **Buenos Aires, Argentina** (bvooheh-nohs *ahee*-rehs, ahr-Hehn-*tee*-nah).

Table 9-6 lists the types of specialty items you may be shopping for.

Table 9-6	Specialty Items	
Spanish	*Pronunciation*	*English*
el alfiler	ehl ahl-fee-*lehr*	the pin
la alfombra	lah ahl-*fohm*-bvrah	the rug
los aretes	lohs ah-*reh*-tehs	the earrings
el broche	ehl *broh*-cheh	the brooch
el colgante	ehl kohl-*gahn*-teh	the pendant
el collar	ehl koh-*yahr*	the necklace
los diamantes	lohs dee-ah-*mahn*-tehs	the diamonds
la escultura	lah ehs-koohl-*tooh*-rah	the sculpture

(continued)

Table 9-6 *(continued)*

Spanish	Pronunciation	English
los gemelos	lohs heh-*meh*-lohs	the cuff links
el grabado	ehl grah-*bvah*-doh	the etching
los huaraches	lohs ooh*ah*-rah-chehs	the leather sandals
el huipil	ehl ooh*ee*-peel	the (traditional) sleeveless blouse or dress
las joyas de oro	lahs *Hoh*-yahs deh *oh*-roh	the gold jewelry
las joyas de plata	lahs *Hoh*-yahs deh *plah*-tah	the silver jewelry
las mascaras	lahs *mahs*-kah-rahs	the masks
las perlas	lahs *pehr*-lahs	the pearls
la pintura	lah peen-*tooh*-rah	the painting
la pulsera	lah poohl-*seh*-rah	the bracelet
el reloj	ehl rreh-*loh*	the watch

You can use these phrases when shopping at a specialized store or gallery:

Busco grabados de Rufino Tamayo. (*bvoohs*-koh grah-*bvah*-dohs deh rrooh-*fee*-noh tah-*mah*-yoh.) (*I'm looking for etchings by Rufino Tamayo.*)

¿Tiene broches de plata? (¿tee*eh*-neh *bvroh*-chehs deh *plah*-tah?) (*Do you have silver brooches?*)

¿Cuánto cuesta el collar que tiene en la ventana? (¿kooh*ahn*-toh kooh*ehs*-tah ehl koh-*yahr* keh tee*eh*-neh ehn lah bvehn-*tah*-nah?) (*How much does the necklace you have in the window cost?*)

¿Y la pintura? (¿ee lah peen-*tooh*-rah?) (*And the painting?*)

¿Vende perlas del sur de Chile? (¿*bvehn*-deh *pehr*-lahs dehl soohr deh *chee*-leh?) (*Do you sell pearls from southern Chile?*)

¿De quién es la escultura en la vitrina? (¿deh kee*ehn* ehs lah ehs-koohl-*tooh*-rah ehn lah bvee-*tree*-nah?) (*By whom is the sculpture in the display case?*)

Favor de embalarlo y mandarlo a este domicilio. (fah-*bvohr* deh ehm-bvah-*lahr*-loh ee mahn-*dahr*-loh a *ehs*-teh doh-mee-*see*-leeoh.) (*Please pack it and send it to this address.*)

Shopping in Traditional Markets

You can find typical clothes and objects in the traditional markets, many of which are open every day and all year round, where bargaining and haggling are the norm. In these markets, you probably won't find any labels stating the prices because the prices aren't really fixed. (That's what the bargaining and haggling are all about.)

In the following sections, we explain how to bargain in Spanish, and we describe items that you may find in a traditional market, including items of copper, glass, clay, and wood; embroidery; and baskets.

Bargaining at a typical market

If you shop in traditional markets, getting there early is a good idea. Many merchants feel that they must make a first sale to kick off their day. If you find yourself in such a situation, you may notice that the merchant doesn't want you to leave without buying something and is therefore more willing to reduce the price to make a sale, and you can end up with a real bargain.

The following phrases help you when you need to haggle in the market place:

¿Cuánto cuesta? (¿koohahn-toh koohehs-tah?) (*How much does it cost?*)

¿Cuánto vale? (¿koohahn-toh bvah-leh?) (*How much is it worth?*)

¿A cuánto? (¿ah koohahn-toh?) (*How much?*)

Es barato. (ehs bvah-rah-toh.) (*It's cheap/inexpensive.*)

Es caro. (ehs kah-roh.) (*It's expensive.*)

Use the following set of phrases to provide emphasis. You won't use them all the time, especially the second and third ones, but they're fun to use and help you express a certain level of emotion:

¡Una ganga! (¡ooh-nah gahn-gah!) (*A bargain!*)

¡Un robo! (¡oohn rroh-bvoh!) (*A rip-off!*)

¡Un insulto! (¡oohn een-soohl-toh!) (*An insult!*)

CULTURAL WISDOM

Advice for the bargainer

In a traditional market or on the streets, when you're offered something you're interested in and price is mentioned, offer half. Of course, this bid is really outrageous, and the merchant reacts to that price with outrage. And thus a social game begins.

After offering half, you get an answer from the merchant stating a sum slightly less than what he first asked for. At this point, you know the game is on, so you offer a bit more than your first amount. And the game goes on until you believe that the merchant will go no farther and that the price is what you can afford.

Bargaining like this is a very satisfying activity for the seller and can also be so for the buyer. You establish a certain relationship while you bargain that shows your determination and that of the seller in addition to your ability to follow a certain rhythm in the operation.

Talkin' the Talk

Bargaining is sometimes a little difficult in a department store, but in traditional market places in Latin America, it's part of the deal. Listen to how Sylvia haggles over a nice rug she's spotted at an outdoor market. (Track 17)

Sylvia: **¿Cuánto cuesta esta alfombra?**
¿ kooh*ahn*-toh kooh*ehs*-tah *ehs*-tah ahl-*fohm*-bvrah?
How much does this rug cost?

Merchant: **Quinientos pesos.**
kee-neee*ehn*-tohs *peh*-sohs.
500 pesos.

Sylvia: **¿Tiene otras más baratas?**
¿tee*eh*-neh *oh*-trahs mahs bvah-*rah*-tahs?
Do you have cheaper ones?

Merchant: **Tengo ésta más pequeña.**
tehn-goh *ehs*-tah mahs peh-*keh*-nyah.
I have this smaller one.

Sylvia: **No me gusta el dibujo.**
noh meh *goohs*-tah ehl dee-*bvooh*-Hoh.
I don't like the pattern.

Merchant:	**Esta en blanco y negro, a trescientos.**
	ehs-tah ehn *bvlahn*-koh ee *neh*-groh ah
	trehs-seee*hn*-tohs.
	This black and white one, for 300.

Sylvia:	**Me gusta. ¿A doscientos?**
	meh *goohs*-tah. ¿ah dohs-seee*hn*-tohs?
	I like it. For 200?

Merchant:	**No puedo. Doscientos cincuenta. Último precio.**
	noh pooh*eh*-doh. dohs-seee*hn*-tohs seen-kooh*ehn*-
	tah. *oohl*-tee-moh *preh*-seeoh.
	I can't. 250. Last price.

Sylvia:	**Bueno, la llevo.**
	bvooh*eh*-noh, lah *yeh*-bvoh.
	Good, I'll take it.

Words to Know

alfombra	ahl-*fohm*-bvrah	rug
más baratos	mahs bvah-<u>rah</u>-tohs	cheaper
más pequeño	mahs peh-<u>keh</u>-nyoh	smaller
el dibujo	ehl dee-<u>bvooh</u>-Hoh	the pattern
último precio	<u>oohl</u>-tee-moh <u>preh</u>-seeoh	last price

Shopping for copper, glass, clay, and wood goods

Latin American artisans are well known for their fine work in copper, glass, wood, textiles, and clay, and items made of these substances are highly sought after by collectors and lovers of their hand-crafted beauty. If you're one of these people, here's some vocabulary worth knowing:

✔ **la arcilla** (lah ahr-*see*-yah) (*the clay*)

✔ **bordado** (bvohr-*dah*-doh) (*embroidered*)

✔ **la cerámica** (lah seh-*rah*-mee-kah) (*the ceramic*)

✔ **el cobre** (ehl *koh*-bvreh) (*the copper*)

✔ **hecho a mano** (*eh*-choh ah *mah*-noh) (*handmade*)

✔ **la madera** (lah mah-*deh*-rah) (*the wood*)

✔ **soplar** (soh-*plahr*) (*to blow*)

✔ **el vidrio** (ehl *bvee*-dreeoh) (*the glass*)

These phrases can help you when you shop for these specialty items:

¿Dónde venden objetos de cobre? (¿*dohn*-deh *bvehn*-dehn ohbv-*Heh*-tohs deh *koh*-bvreh?) (*Where do they sell copper objects?*)

Busco objetos de vidrio. (*bvoohs*-koh ohbv-*Heh*-tohs deh *bvee*-dreeoh.) (*I'm looking for glass objects.*)

Allí hay cerámica hecha a mano. (ah-*yee* ahy seh-*rah*-mee-kah *eh*-chah ah *mah*-noh.) (*There are some handmade ceramics.*)

Estas ollas de barro sirven para cocinar. (*ehs*-tahs *oh*-yahs deh *bvah*-rroh *seer*-bvehn *pah*-rah koh-see-*nahr.*) (*These clay pots are suitable for cooking.*)

Shopping for embroidered clothes

Who has time to embroider anymore? Well, in Latin America, you can find some wonders of embroidery skill. Here are some phrases that can help you make a good selection:

¡Qué bello este bordado! (¡keh *bveh*-yoh *ehs*-teh bvohr-*dah*-doh!) (*What beautiful embroidery!*)

¿Tiene blusitas para niña? (¿tee*eh*-neh bvlooh-*see*-tahs *pah*-rah *nee*-nyah?) (*Do you have little blouses for a girl?*)

¿Tiene vestidos bordados para mujeres? (¿tee*eh*-neh bvehs-*tee*-dohs bvohr-*dah*-dohs *pah*-rah mooh-*Hehr*-ehs?) (*Do you have ladies' embroidered dresses?*)

Shopping for baskets

You can pack everything you buy in one of those large, colorful baskets **(canastas)** (kah-*nahs*-tahs) and then use them at home for storage and as decorative accents. Because baskets come in so many materials, shapes, and sizes and are generally quite long lasting, they make a beautiful addition to any home. The following sentences help you purchase baskets:

> **Estas son canastas de mimbre.** (*ehs*-tahs sohn kah-*nahs*-tahs deh *meem*-bvreh.) (*These are wicker baskets.*)

> **¿Tiene canastas para la ropa?** (¿tee*eh*-neh kah-*nahs*-tahs *pah*-rah lah *rroh*-pah?) (*Do you have laundry baskets?*)

> **Estas canastas son de totora.** (*ehs*-tahs kah-*nahs*-tahs sohn de toh-*toh*-rah.) (*These baskets are made from a reed [found in the Andean Region].*)

> **Estas canastas son de totomoztle.** (*ehs*-tahs kah-*nahs*-tahs sohn deh toh-toh-*mohs*-tleh.) (*These baskets are made from corn leaves. [Mexico]*)

Fun & Games

Write the name of each piece of clothing next to the letter for each item in the following figure (include the correct article for each noun). See Appendix D for the answer key.

a. _____

b. _____

c. _____

d. _____

e. _____

f. _____

g. _____

h. _____

i. _____

j. _____

Chapter 10

Going Out on the Town

In This Chapter

▶ Conjugating the verb **salir** (*to go out*)

▶ Finding out what time the fun begins and ends

▶ Inviting friends and family with the verb **invitar**

▶ Enjoying movies, theater, art, and music

▶ Dancing and singing with the verbs **bailar** and **cantar**

*Y*ou have no chance of getting bored in Latin American circles. Be it music, movies, theater, or dance — you name it — you have much to see and experience.

Latinos love culture, and they rejoice in turning their cultural activities into social events — gathering with old friends and new arrivals for movies, concerts, the opera, or whatever. Latin American events combine color and costume, music and dance, artistry and passion. The people tend to be quite uninhibited and live life with great gusto. In fact, they invented the word **gusto** (*goohs*-toh) (*the pleasure* [Literally: *the taste*]).

In this chapter you find out how to enjoy yourself Latin-American style.

Going Out with the Verb Salir

Salir (sah-*leer*) (*to go out, to leave*) is an irregular verb that has many different uses. Here's how you conjugate **salir** in the present tense:

Conjugation	*Pronunciation*
yo salgo	yoh *sahl*-goh
tú sales	tooh *sah*-lehs
él, ella, usted sale	ehl, *eh*-yah, oohs-*tehd sah*-leh
nosotros, nosotras salimos	noh-*soh*-trohs, noh-*soh*-trahs sah-*lee*-mohs
vosotros, vosotras salís	bvoh-*soh*-trohs, bvoh-*soh*-trahs sah-*lees*
ellos, ellas, ustedes salen	*eh*-yohs, *eh*-yahs, oohs-*teh*-dehs *sah*-lehn

Here are just a few of the conjugated uses of this outgoing verb:

¿De dónde sale el tranvía a Callao? (¿deh *dohn*-deh *sah*-leh ehl trahn-*bvee*-ah ah kah-*yah*-oh?) (*Where does the Callao streetcar leave from?*)

Salimos a andar en trolebús. (sah-*lee*-mohs ah ahn-*dahr* ehn troh-leh-*bvoohs*.) (*We're going out to ride around in the trolleybus.*)

Ellos salen de la estación del tren. (*eh*-yohs *sah*-lehn deh lah ehs-tah-*seeohn* dehl trehn.) (*They're leaving the train station.*)

Making plans to go out is difficult when you don't know when to show up. These phrases help you set the time and place when you're ready to go out on the town (see Chapter 4 for an introduction to phrases related to time):

✔ **¿A qué hora?** (¿ah keh *oh*-rah?) (*At what time?*)

✔ **¿Cuándo comienza?** (¿koo*ahn*-doh koh-mee*ehn*-sah?) (*When does it start?*)

✔ **¿Hasta qué hora?** (¿*ahs*-tah keh *oh*-rah?) (*Until what time?*)

Inviting People with the Verb Invitar

As you make Spanish-speaking friends and acquaintances, you may want to invite them to gatherings, or find yourself invited to their events. In these situations, you need to be familiar with the verb *to invite*, which in Spanish is **invitar** (een-bvee-*tahr*). Good news! **Invitar** is a regular verb of the **-ar** variety, as you can see from the table that follows. The root of this verb is **invit-** (een-*bveet*).

Conjugation	Pronunciation
yo invito	yoh een-*bvee*-toh
tú invitas	tooh een-*bvee*-tahs
él, ella, usted invita	ehl, *eh*-yah, oohs-*tehd* een-*bvee*-tah
nosotros, nosotras invitamos	noh-*soh*-trohs, noh-*soh*-trahs een-bvee-*tah*-mohs
vosotros, vosotras invitáis	bvoh-*soh*-trohs, bvoh-*soh*-trahs een-bvee-*tah*ees
ellos, ellas, ustedes invitan	*eh*-yohs, *eh*-yahs, oohs-*teh*-dehs een-*bvee*-tahn

Use the following phrases to help you give and receive invitations:

> **Invito a mi amigo Juan al teatro.** (een-*bvee*-toh ah mee ah-*mee*-goh Hooh*ahn* ahl teh-*ah*-troh.) (*I invite my friend Juan to the theater.*)

> **Ellas invitan a sus novios al baile.** (*eh*-yahs een-*bvee*-tahn ah soohs *noh*-bveeohs ahl *bvah*ee-leh.) (*They invite their boyfriends to the dance.*)

> **Voy a invitar a mis padres al concierto.** (bvohy ah een-bvee-*tahr* ah mees *pah*-drehs ahl kohn-see*ehr*-toh.) (*I'm going to invite my parents to the concert.*)

Notice the use of **al** (ahl) (*to the*) in phrases like **al teatro** and **al baile. Teatro** and **baile** are masculine words that would normally take the article **el**. But **a el,** formed when you add the preposition **a** (ah) (*to*) to the mix, sounds unpleasant to the Spanish ear. So Spanish joins the two words into **al**, which sounds smoother.

Talkin' the Talk

Rolando decides to invite his new co-worker Julieta to a party for two of their colleagues. (Track 18)

Rolando: **Te invito a una fiesta.**
teh een-*bvee*-toh ah *ooh*-nah fee*ehs*-tah.
I invite you to a party.

Julieta: **¿Cuándo?**
¿kooh*ahn*-doh?
When?

Rolando:	**El sábado a las ocho de la noche.**
	ehl *sah*-bvah-doh ah lahs *oh*-choh deh lah *noh*-cheh.
	Saturday, at 8:00 p.m.

Julieta:	**Sí, puedo ir. ¿A qué viene la fiesta?**
	see pooh*eh*-doh eer. ¿ah keh bvee*eh*-neh lah
	fee*ehs*-tah?
	Yes, I can go. What's the party for?

Rolando:	**Mario y Lucy se van de viaje.**
	mah-reeoh ee *looh*-see seh bvahn deh bvee*ah*-Heh.
	Mario and Lucy are going on a trip.

Julieta:	**Toda ocasión es buena para bailar. Voy con mucho gusto.**
	toh-dah oh-kah-see*ohn* ehs bvooh*eh*-nah *pah*-rah
	bvahee-*lahr*. bvohy kohn *mooh*-choh *goohs*-toh.
	Any occasion is good for dancing. I'll go with pleasure.

Words to Know

la fiesta	lah fee*ehs*-tah	the party
el viaje	ehl bvee*ah*-Heh	the trip
la ocasión	lah oh-kah-see*ohn*	the occasion
el gusto	ehl *goohs*-toh	the pleasure (Literally: the taste)

GRAMMATICALLY SPEAKING

¿A qué viene?: Speaking in idioms

In Spanish the word for *idiom* is **modismo** (moh-*dees*-moh). An idiom is a phrase that can't be translated literally, such as the English phrase *raining cats and dogs*. That is to say, translating it word-for-word doesn't give you the meaning it holds. So, when you translate idioms, you have to give an equivalent phrase. **¿A qué viene?** (ah keh bvee*eh*-neh), which literally translates as *What does it come for?*, means *what for, why so, what's the occasion*, or simply *why*, when it's used in relation to a thing or an event.

When used with a pronoun or a person, **¿A qué viene?** has the same meaning as its English translation: *What does he/she come for?*

Dancing with the Verb Bailar

Bailar (bvahee-*lahr*) (*to dance*) is a beautifully regular verb, great to swing along to. The root of this verb is **bail-** (bvaheel) The conjugation of **bailar** in the present tense follows:

Conjugation	*Pronunciation*
yo bailo	yoh *bvah*ee-loh
tú bailas	tooh *bvah*ee-lahs
él, ella, usted baila	ehl, *eh*-yah, oohs-*tehd* bvahee-lah
nosotros, nosotras bailamos	noh-*soh*-trohs, noh-*soh*-trahs bvahee-*lah*-mohs
vosotros, vosotras bailáis	bvoh-*soh*-trohs, bvoh-*soh*-trahs bvahee-*lah*ees
ellos, ellas, ustedes bailan	*eh*-yohs, *eh*-yahs, oohs-*teh*-dehs, *bvah*ee-lahn

When you're talking about a dance (as a noun), you use the word **baile** (*bvah*ee-leh). These phrases can help you when you want to dance:

> **La salsa es un baile nuevo.** (lah *sahl*-sah ehs oohn *bvah*ee-leh nooh*eh*-bvoh.) (*The salsa is a new dance.*)

> **Invito a mi novia a bailar.** (een-*bvee*-toh ah mee *noh*-bveeah ah bvahee-*lahr*.) (*I invite my girlfriend to dance.*)

> **Bailamos toda la noche.** (bvahee-*lah*-mohs *toh*-dah lah *noh*-cheh.) (*We dance all night.*)

> **Bailan muy bien.** (*bvah*ee-lahn *mooh*ee bveee*ehn*.) (*They dance very well.*)

Enjoying Shows and Events

The types of events and shows available in Spanish-speaking America vary depending on where they happen. In villages or small towns, the events generally are related to celebrations of important dates, both private and public. Occasionally, a traveling show or circus may pass through a town. Larger cities offer movies, theaters, opera, concerts, literary presentations and readings, and exhibition openings. Some neighborhoods have celebrations like the kind you see in the smaller towns.

Following are some phrases that can help when you're asked or you're asking to attend an event:

Voy a buscarte a las ocho. (bvohy a bvoohs-*kahr*-teh ah lahs *oh*-choh.) (*I'll pick you up at 8:00.* [Literally: *I'll go look for you at 8:00.*])

¡Qué pena, hoy no puedo! (¡keh *peh*-nah, ohy noh pooh*eh*-doh!) (*What a pity, today I can't!*)

In the following sections, we describe several different types of events you may attend in Spanish-speaking countries: movies, plays, art exhibits, and concerts.

When you want to attend any show or event, you're most likely going to need a ticket; in Spanish, this word is **el boleto** (ehl bvoh-*leh*-toh). But be sure to buy tickets early, or they may be **agotados** (ah-goh-*tah*-dohs) (*sold out* [Literally: *exhausted*])!

At the cinema

Movies on television are fine, but they're even better in a well-equipped theater. The following are some vocabulary words related to going out to the movies:

- ✔ **el cine** (ehl *see*-neh) (*the cinema*)
- ✔ **la cartelera** (lah kahr-teh-*leh*-rah) (*the movie listings*)
- ✔ **una comedia** (*ooh*-nah koh-*meh*-deeah) (*a comedy*)
- ✔ **un drama** (oohn *drah*-mah) (*a drama*)
- ✔ **la matiné** (lah mah-tee-*neh*) (*the matinee*)
- ✔ **la película** (lah peh-*lee*-kooh-lah) (*the movie*)
- ✔ **una película de acción** (*ooh*-nah peh-*lee*-kooh-lah deh ahk-see*ohn*) (*an action picture*)
- ✔ **una película romántica** (*oohn*-nah peh-*lee*-kooh-lah rroh-*mahn*-tee-kah) (*a romance*)
- ✔ **una película de terror** (*ooh*-nah peh-*lee*-kooh-lah deh teh-*rrohr*) (*a horror movie*)

Talkin' the Talk

Cristina is a new girl in town, and Nemesio wants to spend some time with her and make a good impression. As a movie buff, Nemesio has an idea. (Track 19)

Nemesio:	**Si quieres, vamos al cine.**
	see kee*eh*-rehs *bvah*-mohs ahl *see*-neh.
	If you want, let's go to the movies.

Cristina: **¿Hay muchos cines en esta ciudad?**
¿ahy *mooh*-chohs *see*-nehs ehn *ehs*-tah seeooh-*dahd*?
Are there many cinemas in this city?

Nemesio: **Sí, hay muchos cines.**
see ahy *mooh*-chohs *see*-nehs.
Yes, there are many cinemas.

Cristina: **¿Qué dan hoy?**
¿keh dahn ohy?
What's playing today?

Nemesio: **Veamos la cartelera. ¡Ah, mira, la versión original de**
Nosferatu!
bveh-*ah*-mohs lah kahr-teh-*leh*-rah. ¡ah, *mee*-rah, lah
vehr-seeo*hn* oh-ree-Hee-*nahl* deh nohs-feh-*rah*-tooh!
Let's see the listings. Hey, look! The original version
of Nosferatu!

Cristina: **Esa película me gusta.**
ehs-ah peh-*lee*-kooh-lah meh *goohs*-tah
I like that film.

Words to Know

si quieres	see kee<u>eh</u>-rehs	if you want
el cine	ehl <u>see</u>-neh	the movies
¿Qué dan hoy?	¿keh dahn ohy?	What's playing today?
la cartelera	lah kahr-teh-<u>leh</u>-rah	the listings
la película	lah peh-<u>lee</u>-kooh-lah	the film

At the theater

Researchers have found that people learn more easily when new information is associated with emotions. And because an opportunity to explore feelings is what lures people to the movies and the theater, those places are perfect for absorbing a new language. Here are some words that can help you talk intelligently about the theater:

✔ **el actor** (ehl ahk-*tohr*) (*the actor*)

✔ **la actriz** (lah ahk-*trees*) (*the actress*)

✔ **las críticas** (lahs *kree*-tee-kahs) (*the reviews*)

✔ **la dramaturga** (lah drah-mah-*toohr*-gah) (*the playwright [feminine]*)

✔ **el dramaturgo** (ehl drah-mah-*toohr*-goh) (*the playwright [masculine]*)

✔ **la fila** (lah *fee*-lah) (*the row*)

✔ **la localidad** (lah loh-kah-lee-*dahd*) (*the seat*)

✔ **la obra** (lah *oh*-bvrah) (*the play* [Literally: *the work*])

✔ **el teatro** (ehl teh-*ah*-troh) (*the theater*)

Talkin' the Talk

Going to the theater may involve a conversation similar to this one:

Diego: **¿Quieres ir al teatro?**
¿keeeh-rehs eer ahl teh-*ah*-troh?
Do you want to go to the theater?

Gabriela: **Sí, ¡dan una obra de un dramaturgo de Chile!**
see, ¡dahn *ooh*-nah *oh*-bvrah deh oohn drah-mah-*toohr*-goh deh *chee*-leh!
Yes, they're doing a piece by a Chilean playwright!

Diego: **Tiene muy buena crítica.**
teeehn-eh *mooh*ee bvooheh-nah *kree*-tee-kah.
It has very good reviews.

Gabriela: **Los actores son excelentes.**
lohs ahk-*toh*-rehs sohn ehk-seh-*lehn*-tehs.
The actors are excellent.

Diego: **El teatro es bastante chico.**
ehl teh-*ah*-troh ehs bvahs-*tahn*-teh *chee*-koh.
The theater is quite small.

Gabriela: **Tenemos que comprar los boletos pronto.**
teh-*neh*-mohs keh kohm-*prahr* lohs bvoh-*leh*-tohs *prohn*-toh.
We have to buy the tickets soon.

Diego: **¿En qué fila te gusta sentarte?**
¿ehn keh *fee*-lah teh *goohs*-tah sehn-*tahr*-teh?
What row do you like to sit in?

Gabriela:	**Para teatro prefiero estar bien adelante.**
	pah-rah teh-*ah*-troh preh-feee*eh*-roh ehs-*tahr* bveee*ehn* ah-deh-*lahn*-teh.
	For theater I prefer to be up front.
Diego:	**Bueno. Voy a ver que puedo encontrar.**
	bvoo*heh*-noh. bvohy ah bvehr keh pooh*eh*-doh ehn-kohn-*trahr.*
	Fine. I'll see what I can find.

Words to Know

bastante	bvahs-<u>tahn</u>-teh	enough; quite
pronto	<u>prohn</u>-toh	soon
adelante	ah-deh-<u>lahn</u>-teh	in front; ahead
ver	bvehr	to see
encontrar	ehn-kohn-<u>trahr</u>	to find

At art galleries and museums

Numerous exhibitions of works by Latin-American artists appear all the time throughout the continent. Some exhibits take place in museums and public art galleries, others in private ones. Among the artists exhibited are some great names, people whose works sell for enormous amounts at art auctions. One such artist is Ecuadoran Oswaldo Guayasamín (1919–1999), who created etchings.

The following are some vocabulary words related to art:

✔ **el arte** (ehl *ahr*-teh) (*the art*)

✔ **el/la artista** (ehl/lah ahr-*tees*-tah) (*the artist*)

✔ **la escultura** (lah ehs-koohl-*tooh*-rah) (*the sculpture*)

✔ **la exhibición** (lah ek-see-bvee-see*ohn*) (*the exhibition*)

✔ **la galería** (lah gah-leh-*ree*-ah) (*the gallery*)

✔ **la pintura** (lah peen-*tooh*-rah) (*the painting*)

✔ **la subasta** (lah sooh-*bvahs*-tah) (*the auction*)

At concerts

People in every country 'round the world love their music. The Spanish-speaking world is famous for its fabulous rhythms and talented musicians. Where better to enjoy this cultural treat than at a concert? Most Spanish-American cities have important concert halls and smaller venues where young and old alike can enjoy all sorts of music influenced by local traditions. Whether the music is pop or classical, a symphony orchestra or a rock band, you'll find a following in the rhythm-loving Latino population. You can't keep from being swept up in the beat!

The following are some words you're apt to hear when you're talking about music:

- ✔ **la banda** (lah *bvahn*-dah) (*the band* [jazz or brass])
- ✔ **el/la cantante** (ehl/lah kahn-*tahn*-teh) (*the singer*)
- ✔ **el concierto** (ehl kohn-see*ehr*-toh) (*the concert*)
- ✔ **el concierto pop** (ehl kohn-see*ehr*-toh pohp) (*the pop concert*)
- ✔ **el concierto de rock** (ehl kohn-see*ehr*-toh deh rrohk) (*the rock concert*)
- ✔ **el grupo** (ehl *grooh*-poh) (*the band* [pop or rock])
- ✔ **el jazz** (ehl jHahz) (*the jazz*)
- ✔ **la música** (lah *mooh*-see-kah) (*the music, the musician* [feminine])
- ✔ **la música clásica** (lah *mooh*-see-kah *klah*-see-kah) (*the classical music*)
- ✔ **la música pop** (lah *mooh*-see-kah pohp) (*the pop music*)
- ✔ **la música rock** (lah *mooh*-see-kah rrohk) (*the rock music*)
- ✔ **el músico** (ehl *mooh*-see-koh) (*the musician* [masculine])
- ✔ **la ópera** (lah *oh*-peh-rah) (*the opera*)

The pronunciation of the word *jazz* is not the normal Spanish *j* sound (which we note as H) because this particular pronunciation has carried over some influence of the English pronunciation of *j*. So it's kind of an in-between sound — the English *j* blended with the Spanish *j*.

Talkin' the Talk

Reinaldo and Hortensia set a date to see a concert.

Reinaldo: **Te invito a un concierto con el grupo de rock Pico de Gallo.**
teh een-*bvee*-toh ah oohn kohn-see*ehr*-toh kohn ehl *grooh*-poh deh rrohk *pee*-koh deh *gah*-yoh.

	I invite you to a concert with the rock group Loudmouth.

Hortensia: **¿Cuándo?**
¿kooh*ahn*-doh?
When?

Reinaldo: **Hoy en el Teatro Esfinge. Tengo dos boletos.**
ohy ehn ehl teh-*ah*-troh ehs-*feen*-Heh. *tehn*-goh dohs
bvoh-*leh*-tohs.
Today at the Sphinx Theater. I have two tickets.

Hortensia: **Me gusta la idea.**
meh *goohs*-tah lah ee-*deh*-ah.
I like the idea.

Reinaldo: **Dicen que es un bello teatro.**
dee-sehn keh ehs oohn *bveh*-yoh teh-*ah*-troh.
They say it's a beautiful theater.

Hortensia: **Sí, y tiene muy buena acústica.**
see, ee tee*eh*-neh *mooh*ee bvooh*eh*-nah
ah-*koohs*-tee-kah.
Yes, and it has very good acoustics.

Reinaldo: **El grupo tiene muchas canciones muy populares.**
ehl *grooh*-poh tee*ehn*-eh *mooh*-chahs kahn-see*oh*-
nehs *mooh*ee poh-pooh-*lah*-rehs.
The group has a lot of very popular songs.

Words to Know

bello	*bveh*-yoh	beautiful
la acústica	lah ah-*koohs*-tee-kah	the acoustics
las canciones	lahs kahn-see*oh*-nehs	the songs

Singing with the Verb Cantar

Cantar (kahn-*tahr*) (*to sing*) is a regular verb, praise be, and its root is
cant- (kahnt). Its conjugation in the present tense follows:

Conjugation	Pronunciation
yo canto	yoh *kahn*-toh
tú cantas	tooh *kahn*-tahs
él, ella, usted canta	ehl, *eh*-yah, oohs-*tehd kahn*-tah
nosotros, nosotras cantamos	noh-*soh*-trohs, noh-*soh*-trahs kahn-*tah*-mohs
vosotros, vosotras cantáis	bvoh-*soh*-trohs, bvoh-*soh*-trahs kahn-*tah*ees
ellos, ellas, ustedes cantan	*eh*-yohs, *eh*-yahs, oohs-*teh*-dehs *kahn*-tahn

Talkin' the Talk

What a great occasion! Your favorite singer comes to sing live and in person.

Claudia: **¿Sabes si viene a cantar Shakira?**
¿*sah*-bvehs see bveee*h*-neh ah kahn-*tahr* shah-*kee*-rah?
Do you know whether Shakira is coming to sing?

Pedro: **Quizás. La anunciaron.**
kee-*sahs.* lah ah-noohn-seea*h*-rohn.
Maybe. They advertised her.

Claudia: **Espero que sí. Ella canta y baila muy bien. Es tan animada.**
ehs-*peh*-roh keh see. *eh*-yah *kahn*-tah ee *bvah*ee-lah *moo*hee bee*eh*n. ehs tahn ah-nee-*mah*-dah
I hope so. She sings and dances really well. She's so lively.

Pedro: **Es la verdad. Cuando ella canta, todos quieren bailar.**
ehs lah bvehr-*dahd.* koo*h*ahn-doh *eh*-yah *kahn*-tah, *toh*-dohs kee*eh*r-ehn bvahee-*lahr.*
It's the truth. When she sings, everyone wants to dance.

Claudia: **Yo no canto bien en absoluto, pero mis padres cantan muy bien.**
yoh noh *kahn*-toh bee*ehn* ehn ahbv-soh-*looh*-toh, *peh*-roh mees *pah*-drehs *kahn*-tahn *mooh*ee bvee*ehn.*
I don't sing well at all, but my parents sing really well.

Pedro: **Pues, no importa. Vamos al concierto de Shakira, y podemos bailar pero no cantar. ¿Bien?**
pooh*ehs,* noh eem-*pohr*-tah. *bvah*-mohs ahl kohn-see*ehr*-toh deh shah-*kee*-rah, ee poh-*deh*-mohs bvahee-*lahr peh*-roh noh kahn-*tahr.* ¿bvee*ehn?*
Well, it's not important. We'll go to Shakira's concert and we can dance but not sing. Okay?

Words to Know

quizás	<u>kee</u>-sahs	maybe
anunciar	ah-noohn-see<u>ahr</u>	to advertise; to announce
en absoluto	ehn ahbv-soh-<u>looh</u>-toh	at all
tan	tahn	so (very)
animado/a	ah-nee-<u>mah</u>-doh/dah	animated, lively

Fun & Games

The following crossword puzzle contains several Spanish words that are introduced in this chapter. Write the translation for each numbered clue into the appropriate spaces in the puzzle grid. See Appendix D for the answer key.

Across

1 cinema

3 row

4 matinee, early show

5 tickets

7 to announce

10 opera

14 listings

15 trip

16 sold out

17 theater

Down

1 review

2 singer

6 playwright (masculine)

8 concert

9 actress

11 movie

12 auction

13 party

Chapter 11

Taking Care of Business and Telecommunications

· ·

In This Chapter

▶ Understanding office-related vocabulary

▶ Issuing commands with imperatives

▶ Talking on the phone

▶ Forming the preterite (simple past) tense

▶ Performing everyday tasks around the office

· ·

*I*f you work in an office where Spanish is spoken regularly, you have an opportunity to expand your vocabulary and skills. An office is an entirely new environment with rooms, equipment, supplies, and activities you don't often meet on the street.

In this chapter, you find out common words and phrases used in an office setting. In addition, you discover two new verb forms: the imperative for giving commands and instructions and the preterit for talking about actions that occurred in the past.

Getting Around at the Office

As you're conversing with colleagues and co-workers, you need to be able to refer to the various buildings, equipment, and other stuff that comprises your business and fills the space. In the following sections, we present the Spanish words for the most common places and items you find in a business office.

Mastering your office furniture, equipment, and supplies

Every office is packed with a collection of the usual furniture, equipment, and supplies — everything from desks and chairs to photocopiers, fax machines, paper, and staples. To get started, take a tour of your office, naming your office furniture **(los muebles)** (lohs moo*heh*-bvlehs) in Spanish with the help of Table 11-1.

Table 11-1	Common Office Furniture	
Spanish	*Pronunciation*	*English*
el bote de basura	ehl *bvoh*-teh deh bvah-*sooh*-rah	*the wastebasket*
el escritorio	ehl ehs-kree-*toh*-reeoh	*the desk*
la estantería	lah ehs-tahn-teh-*ree*-ah	*the bookshelves*
el fichero	ehl fee-*cheh*-roh	*the filing cabinet*
la lámpara de escritorio	lah *lahm*-pah-rah deh ehs-kree-*toh*-reeoh	*the desk lamp*
la silla	lah *see*-yah	*the chair*

Office equipment **(el equipo)** (ehl eh-*kee*-poh) can vary a great deal but typically consists of one or more items (usually more) listed in Table 11-2.

Table 11-2	Common Office Equipment	
Spanish	*Pronunciation*	*English*
la computadora	lah kohm-pooh-tah-*doh*-rah	*the computer*
la computadora portátil	lah kohm-pooh-tah-*doh*-rah pohr-*tah*-teel	*the laptop computer*
el enfriador de agua	ehl ehn-freeah-*dohr* deh ah-goohah	*the water cooler*
la fotocopiadora	lah foh-toh-koh-peeah-*doh*-rah	*the photocopier*
la grapadora	lah grah-pah-*doh*-rah	*the stapler*
la impresora	lah eem-preh-*soh*-rah	*the printer*
la máquina de fax	lah *mah*-kee-nah deh fahks	*the fax machine*
la pizarra blanca	lah pee-*sah*-rrah bvlahn-kah	*the whiteboard*
el proyector	ehl proh-yehk-*tohr*	*the projector*
el sacagrapas	ehl sah-kah-*grah*-pahs	*the staple remover*

Spanish	Pronunciation	English
el sacapuntas	ehl sah-kah-*poohn*-tahs	the pencil sharpener
el teléfono	ehl teh-*leh*-foh-noh	the telephone
el teléfono celular	ehl teh-*leh*-foh-noh seh-looh-*lahr*	the cellphone
las tijeras	lahs tee-*Heh*-rahs	the scissors

Before sending your assistant on an errand to the supply cabinet, brush up on the Spanish names for various office supplies **(los suministros)** (lohs sooh-mee-*nees*-trohs), listed in Table 11-3.

Table 11-3	Common Office Supplies	
Spanish	Pronunciation	English
la agenda de entrevistas	lah ah-*Hehn*-dah deh ehn-treh-*bvees*-tahs	the appointment book
los bolígrafos	lohs bvoh-*lee*-grah-fohs	the pens
el calendario	ehl kah-lehn-*dah*-reeoh	the calendar
las carpetas	lahs kahr-*peh*-tahs	the file folders
un cartucho de tinta	oohn kahr-*tooh*-choh deh *teen*-tah	an ink cartridge
la cinta adhesiva	lah *seen*-tah ahd-eh-*see*-bvah	the adhesive tape
las gomas de borrar	lahs *goh*-mahs de bvoh-*rrahr*	the erasers
las grapas	lahs *grah*-pahs	the staples
los lápices	lohs *lah*-pee-sehs	the pencils
las libretas	lahs lee-*bvreh*-tahs	the notepads
las ligas	lahs *lee*-gahs	the rubber bands
los marcadores	lohs mahr-kah-*doh*-rehs	the markers
las notas autoad-hesivas despren-dibles	lahs *noh*-tahs ahooh-toh-ahd-eh-*see*-bvahs dehs-prehn-*dee*-bvlehs	the sticky notes
el papel	ehl pah-*pehl*	the paper
el papel de foto-copiadora	ehl pah-*pehl* deh foh-toh-koh-peeah-*doh*-rah	the copy paper
el pegamento	ehl peh-gah-*mehn*-toh	the glue
los sellos	lohs *seh*-yohs	the stamps
los sobres	lohs *soh*-bvrehs	the envelopes
los sujetapapeles	lohs sooh-Heh-tah-pah-*peh*-lehs	the paper clips

Looking elsewhere in the building

Although you're likely to spend most of your time in your office or other work area, you also need to be able to find your way to other rooms and areas in the building. Table 11-4 can help you brush up on the Spanish words for various rooms and areas within an office building.

Table 11-4	Office Rooms and Other Key Areas	
Spanish	*Pronunciation*	*English*
el almacén	ehl ahl-mah-*sehn*	*the warehouse*
el ascensor	ehl ah-sehn-*sohr*	*the elevator*
el baño	ehl *bvah*-nyoh	*the restroom*
el cuarto de almace-namiento	ehl kooh*ahr*-toh deh ahl-mah-seh-nah-mee*ehn*-toh	*the storage room*
el cubículo	ehl kooh-*bvee*-kooh-loh	*the cubicle*
el departamento	ehl deh-pahr-tah-*mehn*-toh	*the department*
la división	lah dee-bvee-see*ohn*	*the division*
el edificio	ehl eh-dee-*fee*-seeoh	*the building*
la escalera	lah ehs-kah-*leh*-rah	*the stairway*
la escalera mecánica	lah ehs-kah-*leh*-rah meh-*kah*-nee-kah	*the escalator*
la fábrica	lah *fah*-bvree-kah	*the plant, the factory*
la oficina	lah oh-fee-*see*-nah	*the office*
el pasillo	ehl pah-*see*-yoh	*the hallway*
la sala de copias	lah *sah*-lah deh *koh*-peeahs	*the copy room*
la sala de reuniones	lah *sah*-lah deh rrehooh-nee*oh*-nehs	*the conference room*
la sala de correos	lah *sah*-lah deh koh-*rreh*-ohs	*the mailroom*
la sala de descanso	lah *sah*-lah deh dehs-*kahn*-soh	*the break room*
la salida	lah sah-*lee*-dah	*the exit*
el vestíbulo	ehl bvehs-*tee*-bvooh-loh	*the lobby*
la zona de carga y descarga	lah *soh*-nah deh *kahr*-gah ee dehs-*kahr*-gah	*the loading dock*

Talkin' the Talk

 Inés has been transferred to her company's Mexico City office. Her new manager shows Inés to her office and helps her in gathering the supplies she needs. (Track 20)

Manager: **Inés, ésta es su oficina.**
ee-*nehs, ehs*-tah ehs sooh oh-fee-*see*-nah.
Inés, this is your office.

Inés: **Es más pequeña que mi última oficina, pero tiene una vista mejor.**
ehs mahs peh-*keh*-nyah keh mee *oohl*-tee-mah oh-fee-*see*-nah, *peh*-roh teee*eh*-neh *ooh*-nah *bvees*-tah meh-*Hohr.*
It's smaller than my last office, but it has a better view.

Manager: **La sala de descanso queda a mitad del pasillo a la izquierda.**
lah *sah*-lah deh dehs-*kahn*-soh *keh*-dah ah mee-*tahd* dehl pah-*see*-yoh ah lah ees-keee*ehr*-dah.
The break room is halfway down the hall and to the left.

Los baños están al otro lado del pasillo, enfrente de la sala de descanso.
lohs *bvah*-nyohs ehs-*tahn* ahl *oh*-troh *lah*-doh dehl pah-*see*-yoh, ehn-*frehn*-teh deh lah *sah*-lah deh dehs-*kahn*-soh.
The bathrooms are right across the hall across from the break room.

¿Hay algo que usted necesita ahora?
¿ahy *ahl*-goh keh oohs-*tehd* neh-seh-*see*-tah ah-*oh*-rah?
Is there anything that you need right now?

Inés: **Definitivamente necesito una computadora.**
deh-fee-nee-tee-bvah-*mehn*-teh neh-seh-*see*-toh *ooh*-nah kohm-pooh-tah-*doh*-rah.
I definitely need a computer.

Manager:	**Están preparando su computadora. Debe de tenerla para mañana en la mañana.** ehs-*tahn* preh-pah-*rahn*-doh sooh kohm-pooh-tah-*doh*-rah. *deh*-bveh deh teh-*nehr*-lah *pah*-rah mah-*nyah*-nah ehn lah mah-*nyah*-nah. *They are preparing your computer. You should have it by tomorrow morning.*
Inés:	**También necesito unos suministros: papel, carpetas, bolígrafos . . . .** tahm-bvee*ehn* neh-seh-*see*-toh *ooh*-nohs sooh-mee-*nees*-trohs: pah-*pehl*, kahr-*peh*-tahs, bvoh-*lee*-grah-fohs . . . . *I also need some supplies: paper, folders, pens . . . .*
Manager:	**Todos los suministros para la oficina están en el cuarto enfrente de mi oficina.** *toh*-dohs lohs sooh-mee-*nees*-trohs *pah*-rah lah oh-fee-*see*-nah ehs-*tahn* ehn ehl kooh*ahr*-toh ehn-*frehn*-teh deh mee oh-fee-*see*-nah. *All the office supplies are in the room across from my office.*
	Puede escribir un inventario de los suministros que toma. pooh*eh*-deh ehs-kree-*bveer* oohn een-bvehn-*tah*-reeoh deh lohs sooh-mee-*nees*-trohs keh *toh*-mah. *You can write an inventory of the supplies you take.*
Inés:	**Sí, entiendo.** see, ehn-tee*ehn*-doh. *Yes, I understand.*
Manager:	**Podemos reunirnos después del almuerzo para hablar. ¡Bienvenida!** poh-*deh*-mohs rrehooh-*neer*-nohs dehs-pooh*ehs* dehl ahl-mooh*ehr*-soh *pah*-rah ah-*bvlahr*. ¡bveee*ehn*-bveh-*nee*-dah! *We can meet after lunch to talk. Welcome aboard!*

Words to Know

la oficina	lah oh-fee-<u>see</u>-nah	the office
la vista	lah <u>bvees</u>-tah	the view
queda a mitad del pasillo	<u>keh</u>-dah ah mee-<u>tahd</u> dehl pah-<u>see</u>-yoh	halfway down the hall
definitivamente	deh-fee-nee-tee-bvah-<u>mehn</u>-teh	definitely
el cuarto	ehl koo<u>hahr</u>-toh	the room
el inventario	ehl een-bvehn-<u>tah</u>-reeoh	the inventory
el almuerzo	ehl ahl-moo<u>hehr</u>-soh	the lunch
bienvenida	bveeehn-bveh-<u>nee</u>-dah	welcome aboard

Phoning Made Simple

Although more and more business is being transacted via e-mail, the Web, and texting, a great deal of business is still done over the telephone. In the following sections, we provide you with phrases to help you place a call.

Checking out phone-y verbs: To call, to leave, and to listen and hear

When you're talking on the phone or talking about talking on the phone, you're likely to encounter three common verbs related to telephone conversations: **llamar** (yah-*mahr*) (*to call*), **dejar** (deh-*Hahr*) (*to leave*), and **escuchar** (ehs-kooh-*char*) (*to listen to; to hear*). All three are regular verbs belonging to the **-ar** group. If you take off the **-ar,** you get the root of each verb. And because they're all from the same group, they all have the same endings, which means if we give you the conjugation for **llamar** (and we do), you can also conjugate **dejar** and **escuchar.**

Conjugation	Pronunciation
yo llamo	yoh *yah*-moh
tú llamas	tooh *yah*-mahs
él, ella, usted llama	ehl, *eh*-yah, oohs-*tehd yah*-mah
nosotros, nosotras llamamos	noh-*soh*-trohs, noh-*soh*-trahs yah-*mah*-mohs
vosotros, vosotras llamáis	bvoh-*soh*-trohs, bvoh-*soh*-trahs yah-*mah*-ees
ellos, ellas, ustedes llaman	*eh*-yohs, *eh*-yahs, oohs-*teh*-dehs *yah*-mahn

Don't forget to try conjugating the other two verbs (**dejar** and **escuchar**) on your own. Check the verb tables in Appendix B if you're stumped.

Here are some examples that use these verbs:

> **Su madre llama todos los días.** (sooh *mah*-dreh *yah*-mah *toh*-dohs lohs *dee*-ahs.) (*Her mother calls everyday.*)

> **Yo dejo un mensaje cuando ellos no están en casa.** (yoh *deh*-Hoh oohn mehn-*sah*-Heh kooh*ahn*-doh *eh*-yohs noh ehs-*tahn* ehn *kah*-sah.) (*I leave a message when they aren't home.*)

> **Yo escucho muy cuidadosamente cuando ella habla porque tiene un acento italiano.** (yoh ehs-*kooh*-choh *mooh*ee koohee-dah-doh-sah-*mehn*-teh kooh*ahn*-doh *eh*-yah *ah*-bvlah *pohr*-keh tee*eh*-neh oohn ah-*sehn*-toh ee-tah-lee*ah*-noh.) (*I listen very carefully when she speaks because she has an Italian accent.*)

Leaving a message

When your party is unavailable or the answering machine picks up, be prepared to leave a message (**un mensaje**) (oohn mehn-*sah*-Heh). Here are some simple phrases that can help in this situation:

> ✔ **Quiero dejar un mensaje.** (kee*eh*-roh deh-*Hahr* oohn mehn-*sah*-Heh.) (*I want to leave a message.*)

> ✔ **Favor de llamarme.** (fah-*bvohr* deh yah-*mahr*-meh.) (*Please call me.*)

> ✔ **Tengo un mensaje importante para . . . .** (*tehn*-goh oohn mehn-*sah*-Heh eem-pohr-*tahn*-teh *pah*-rah . . . .) (*I have an important message for . . . .*)

> ✔ **Voy a estar en la oficina hasta las cuatro.** (bvohy ah ehs-*tahr* ehn lah oh-fee-*see*-nah *ahs*-tah lahs kooh*ahr*-toh.) (*I'm going to be in the office until 4:00.*)

✔ **Voy a llamar otra vez mañana.** (bvohy ah yah-*mahr* oh-trah bvehs mah-*nyah*-nah.) (*I'm going to call again tomorrow.*)

✔ **Quiero hablar con María.** (kee*eh*-roh ah-*bvlahr* kohn mah-*ree*-ah.) (*I want to speak with María.*)

✔ **Mi número es** . . . . (mee *nooh*-meh-roh ehs . . . .) (*My number is* . . . .)

Here's a handy rule to know when you leave (or listen to) a message: The word **tarde** (*tahr*-deh), without the article **la** (*lah*) (*the*), means *late*. But when the article **la** is in front of it, as in **la tarde,** you're talking about *the afternoon.*

Forming the Preterite Tense

Of course, in your business dealings, you're not always talking about what's happening right now. You may need to discuss past and possible future events. In this section, we show you how to form the past tense (also known as the *preterite tense*) of **llamar, dejar,** and **escuchar,** three regular **-ar** verbs that come in handy in office situations (especially when you're on the phone — see the earlier "Phoning Made Simple" section for details). We also explain how to form the preterite tense of regular **-er** and **-ir** verbs. (Check out Chapter 13 for details about forming the simple future tense.)

The regular **-ar, -er,** and **-ir** preterit endings in the following sections apply to all of the regular preterite verbs you'll ever need.

For irregular preterite verb conjugations, consult the verb tables in Appendix B.

The past tense of regular -ar verbs

Use the root of **llamar** (yah-*mahr*), which is **llam-** (*yahm*), to conjugate for the past tense.

Conjugation	Pronunciation
yo llamé	yoh yah-*meh*
tú llamaste	tooh yah-*mahs*-teh
él, ella, usted llamó	ehl, *eh*-yah, oohs-*tehd* yah-*moh*
nosotros, nosotras llamamos	noh-*soh*-trohs, noh-*soh*-trahs yah-*mah*-mohs
vosotros, vosotras llamasteis	bvoh-*soh*-trohs, bvoh-*soh*-trahs yah-mahs-*teh*ees
ellos, ellas, ustedes llamaron	*eh*-yohs, *eh*-yahs, oohs-*teh*-dehs yah-*mah*-rohn

If you missed a call, you may hear the following:

Lo llamé ayer. (loh yah-*meh* ah-*yehr.*) (*I called you* [formal] *yesterday.*)

Cuando ellos llamaron nadie contestó. (kooh*ahn*-doh *eh*-yohs yah-*mah*-rohn *nah*-deeeh kohn-tehs-*toh.*) (*When they called nobody answered.*)

Ayer no me llamaste. (ah-*yehr* noh meh yah-*mahs*-teh) (*Yesterday you* [informal] *didn't call me.*)

Si él hoy me llamó, no me enteré. (see ehl ohy meh yah-*moh*, noh meh ehn-teh-*reh.*) (*If he called me today, I didn't know about it.*)

Te llamamos por teléfono. (teh yah-*mah*-mohs pohr teh-*leh*-foh-noh.) (*We called you on the phone.*)

The words **lo** (loh) (*you* [formal]), **me** (meh) (*me*), and **te** (teh) (*you* [informal]) in these examples are direct objects, which in Spanish are placed in front of the conjugated verbs. As in English, the direct object directly receives the action of the verb — in this case revealing who is being called.

To conjugate **dejar** (deh-*Hahr*) (*to leave* [a message]) and **escuchar** (ehs-kooh-*chahr*) (*to listen to, to hear*) into the preterite tense, you use the same endings as you do for the verb **llamar.** You simply drop the **-ar** ending and add the appropriate conjugated ending based on the subject of your sentence.

The past tense of regular -er and -ir verbs

To form the preterit tense of regular **-er** and **-ir** verbs, you simply need to learn one set of endings because all regular preterite **-er** and **-ir** verbs use the same endings. We've chosen the regular verb **aprender** (ah-prehn-*dehr*) (*to learn*) to use as our example. For the verb **aprender,** follow this chart:

Conjugation	Pronunciation
yo aprendí	yoh ah-prehn-*dee*
tú aprendiste	tooh ah-prehn-*dees*-teh
él, ella, usted aprendió	ehl, *eh*-yah, oohs-*tehd* ah-prehn-dee*oh*
nosotros, nosotras aprendimos	noh-*soh*-trohs, noh-*soh*-trahs ah-prehn-*dee*-mohs
vosotros, vosotras aprendisteis	bvoh-*soh*-trohs, bvoh-*soh*-trahs ah-prehn-dees-*teh*ees
ellos, ellas, ustedes aprendieron	*eh*-yohs, *eh*-yahs, oohs-*teh*-dehs ah-prehn-dee*eh*-rohn

Here are a couple of examples of the verb aprender in the preterite form:

> **Aprendí usar la máquina de fax.** (ah-prehn-*dee* ooh-*sahr* lah *mah*-kee-nah deh fahks.) (*I learned how to use the fax machine.*)

> **Ella aprendió escribir a máquina.** (*eh*-yah ah-prehn-dee*oh* ehs-kree-*bveer* ah *mah*-kee-nah.) (*She learned how to type.*)

Getting into the Action at the Office

You may engage in highly specialized office activities depending on where you work, but some activities are common in any office setting. The following sections introduce you to frequently used words and phrases for the most common office activities.

Sending a letter or package

Mailing a letter or package seems simple enough until you arrive at the post office **(el correos)** (ehl koh-*rreh*-ohs) and find that people speak Spanish exclusively. By knowing a few key words and phrases, you can smoothly navigate your first shipping experience in Spanish.

- ✔ **el buzón** (ehl bvooh-*sohn*) (*the mailbox*)
- ✔ **la carta** (lah *kahr*-tah) (*the letter*)
- ✔ **el código postal** (ehl *koh*-dee-goh pohs-*tahl*) (*the postal code*)
- ✔ **el destinatario** (ehl dehs-tee-nah-*tah*-reeoh) (*the addressee*)
- ✔ **la dirección** (lah dee-rehk-see*ohn*) (*the address*)
- ✔ **el franqueo** (ehl frahn-*keh*-oh) (*the postage*)
- ✔ **mandar** (mahn-*dahr*) (*to send*)
- ✔ **el paquete** (ehl pah-*keh*-teh) (*the package*)
- ✔ **el sello** (ehl *seh*-yoh) (*the postage stamp*)
- ✔ **el sobre** (ehl *soh*-bvreh) (*the envelope*)
- ✔ **la tarifa de franqueo** (lah tah-*ree*-fah deh frahn-*keh*-oh) (*the postage rate*)
- ✔ **la tarjeta postal** (lah tahr-*Heh*-tah pohs-*tahl*) (*the postcard*)

The following phrases may also come in handy:

> **¿Dónde está el correos más cercano?** (¿*dohn*-deh ehs-*tah* ehl koh-*rreh*-ohs mahs sehr-*kah*-noh?) (*Where's the nearest post office?*)

¿Cuánto cuesta mandar este paquete? (¿kooh*ahn*-toh kooh*ehs*-tah mahn-*dahr ehs*-teh pah-*keh*-teh?) (*How much does it cost to send this package?*)

Quiero mandar este paquete. (kee*eh*-roh mahn-*dahr ehs*-teh pah-*keh*-teh.) (*I want to send this package.*)

¿Cuándo llega? (¿koo*ahn*-doh *yeh*-gah?) (*When does it arrive?*)

Necesito mandar esta carta urgente. (neh-seh-*see*-toh mahn-*dahr ehs*-tah *kahr*-tah oohr-*Hehn*-teh.) (*I need to send this letter express.*)

Making copies

Whether your office has a photocopy machine or you have to run out to the copy shop, the following phrases are essential in getting what you want:

¿Cuántas copias necesita? (¿koohahn-tahs *koh*-peeahs neh-seh-*see*-tah?) (*How many copies do you need?*)

Favor de hacerme dos copias de este documento. (fah-*bvohr* deh ah-*sehr*-meh dohs *koh*-peeahs deh *ehs*-teh doh-kooh-*mehn*-toh.) (*Please make me two copies of this document.*)

Prefiero las copias en color por favor. (preh-fee*eh*-roh lahs *koh*-peeahs ehn koh-*lohr* pohr fah-*bvohr*.) (*I prefer color copies please.*)

Favor de ampliar este documento por diez por ciento. (fah-*bvohr* deh ahm-plee*ahr ehs*-teh doh-kooh-*mehn*-toh pohr dee*ehs* pohr see*ehn*-toh.) (*Please enlarge this document by 10 percent.*)

Favor de reducir este documento por veinte por ciento. (fah-*bvohr* deh rreh-dooh-*seer ehs*-teh doh-kooh-*mehn*-toh pohr bveh*een*-teh pohr see*ehn*-toh.) (*Please reduce this document by 20 percent.*)

Puedo enviarle una copia. (pooh*eh*-doh ehn-bvee-*ahr*-leh *ooh*-nah *koh*-peeah.) (*I can send you a copy.*)

Using a computer

Walk into any office, and you're bound to find at least a couple of computers pitching in to help. Your first challenge is to be able to name the parts of the computer **(la computadora)** (lah kohm-pooh-tah-*doh*-rah). Figure 11-1 brings you up to speed in a hurry. Here are some important items to recognize:

- ✔ **el ordenador** (ehl ohr-deh-nah-*dor*) (*the tower case*)
- ✔ **el monitor de video** (ehl moh-nee-*tohr* deh bvee-*deh*-oh) (*the monitor*)
- ✔ **el teclado** (ehl teh-*klah*-doh) (*the keyboard*)
- ✔ **el ratón** (ehl rrah-*tohn*) (*the mouse*)

✔ **la cámara web** (lah *kah*-mah-rah wehb) (*the webcam*)

✔ **la unidad de CD/DVD-ROM** (lah oohh-nee-*dahd* deh see dee/deh bveh deh rahm) (*the CD/DVD-ROM drive*)

✔ **la impresora** (lah eem-preh-*soh*-rah) (*the printer*)

✔ **la altavoz** (lah ahl-tah-*bvohs*) (*the speaker*)

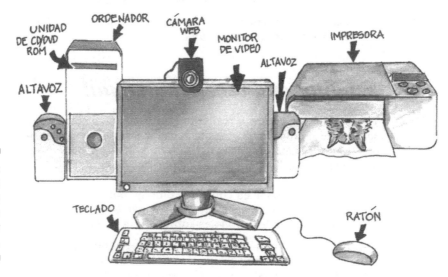

Figure 11-1:
Spanish words to describe computer components.

The following phrases describe common office activities performed on a computer and the Internet:

✔ **abrir un archivo** (ah-*bvreer* oohn ahr-*chee*-bvoh) (*to open a file*)

✔ **bajar un programa** (bvah-*Hahr* oohn proh-*grah*-mah) (*to download a program*)

✔ **conectarse a Internet** (koh-nehk-*tahr*-seh a een-tehr-*neht*) (*to connect to the Internet*)

✔ **crear una presentación de proyección de diapositivas** (kreh-*ahr* ooh-nah preh-sehn-tah-see*ohn* deh proh-yehk-see*ohn* deh deeah-poh-see-*tee*-bvahs) (*to create a slideshow presentation*)

✔ **enviar un mensaje por correo electrónico** (ehn-bvee*ahr* oohn mehn-*sah*-Heh pohr koh-*rreh*-oh eh-lehk-*troh*-nee-koh) (*to send an e-mail message*)

For more about sending e-mail, check out the following section.

✔ **escribir una carta a máquina** (ehs-kree-*bveer* ooh-nah *kahr*-tah ah *mah*-kee-nah) (*to type a letter*)

- ✔ **imprimir un documento** (eem-pree-*meer* oohn doh-kooh-*mehn*-toh) (*to print a document*)

- ✔ **leer el correo electrónico** (leh-*ehr* ehl koh-*rreh*-oh eh-lehk-*troh*-nee-koh) (*to read e-mail*)

- ✔ **navegar la Web** (nah-bveh-*gahr* lah wehbv) (*to search the Web*)

- ✔ **usar una hoja de cálculo electrónica** (ooh-*sahr* ooh-nah *oh*-Hah deh *kahl*-kooh-loh eh-lehk-*troh*-nee-kah) (*to use a spreadsheet*)

- ✔ **usar un procesador de textos** (ooh-*sahr* oohn proh-seh-sah-*dohr* deh *tehks*-tohs) (*to use a word processor*)

Sending and receiving e-mail

Two of the most common activities performed on a computer in an office setting are sending and receiving e-mail messages **(mensajes de correo electrónico)** (mehn-*sah*-Hehs deh koh-*rreh*-oh eh-lehk-*troh*-nee-koh). When managing e-mail, keep the following phrases close at hand:

Favor de ponerse en contacto conmigo por correo electrónico. (fah-*bvohr* deh poh-*nehr*-seh ehn kohn-*tahk*-toh kohn-*mee*-goh pohr koh-*rreh*-oh eh-lehk-*troh*-nee-koh.) (*Please contact me by e-mail.*)

¿Recibió Ud. el mensaje por correo electrónico que yo envié? (¿rreh-see-bvee*oh* oohs-*tehd* ehl mehn-*sah*-Heh pohr koh-*rreh*-oh eh-lehk-*troh*-nee-koh keh yoh ehn-bvee*eh*?) (*Did you receive the e-mail message I sent?*)

Necesito leer mi correo electrónico. (neh-seh-*see*-toh leh-*ehr* mee koh-*rreh*-oh eh-lehk-*troh*-nee-koh.) (*I need to read my e-mail.*)

Favor de enviarme el archivo como adjunto. (fah-*bvohr* deh ehn-bvee-*ahr*-meh ehl ahr-*chee*-bvoh *koh*-moh ahd-*Hoohn*-toh.) (*Please send me the file as an attachment.*)

Lo siento. No recibí su correo electrónico. (loh see*ehn*-toh. noh rreh-see-*bvee* sooh koh-*rreh*-oh eh-lehk-*troh*-nee-koh.) (*I'm sorry. I didn't receive your e-mail message.*)

Favor de remitir el correo electrónico a mí. (fah-*bvohr* deh rreh-mee-*teer* ehl koh-*rreh*-oh eh-lehk-*troh*-nee-koh ah mee) (*Please forward the e-mail message to me.*)

Scheduling a meeting

The office meeting **(la reunión)** (lah rrehooh-nee*ohn*) is a ritual carried out on a daily basis in countries around the world. Here are some key words and phrases you need when scheduling and talking about meetings:

✔ **celebrar una reunión** (seh-leh-*bvrahr ooh*-nah rrehooh-nee*ohn*) (*to hold a meeting*)

✔ **comenzar/terminar la reunión** (koh-mehn-*sahr*/tehr-mee-*nahr* lah rrehooh-nee*ohn*) (*to open/close the meeting*)

✔ **convocar una reunión** (kohn-bvoh-*kahr ooh*-nah rrehooh-nee*ohn*) (*to call a meeting*)

✔ **el horario** (ehl oh-*rah*-reeoh) (*the schedule*)

✔ **planear** (plah-neh-*ahr*) (*to plan*)

✔ **el programa** (ehl proh-*grah*-mah) (*the schedule*)

✔ **programar** (proh-*grah*-mahr) (*to schedule*)

✔ **la sala de reuniones** (lah *sah*-lah deh rrehooh-nee*oh*-nehs) (*the conference room*)

You may hear phrases such as the following when discussing meetings:

> **Los reunidos votaron en favor de la medida.** (lohs rrehooh-*nee*-dohs bvoh-*tah*-rohn ehn fah-*bvohr* deh lah meh-*dee*-dah.) (*The assembly voted in favor of the measure.*)

> **Tengo una reunión con el jefe esta mañana.** (*tehn*-goh *ooh*-nah rrehooh-nee*ohn* kohn ehl *Heh*-feh *ehs*-tah mah-*nyah*-nah.) (*I have a meeting with the boss this morning.*)

Talkin' the Talk

No business is safe from meetings. Here, Sr. Alvarez, the CEO of the company, and his assistant Julia try to quickly set up a meeting to discuss new developments. (Track 21)

Sr. Alvarez:	**Quiero organizar una reunión para el miércoles con todo el personal de gerencia.**
	keee*h*-roh ohr-gah-nee-*sahr ooh*-nah rrehooh-nee*ohn* *pah*-rah ehl meee*hr*-koh-lehs kohn *toh*-doh ehl pehr-soh-*nahl* deh Heh-*rehn*-seeah.
	I want to arrange a meeting for Wednesday with all the managerial staff.

Julia:	**Usted tiene disponible dos horas por la tarde.**
	oohs-*tehd* teee*h*-neh dees-poh-*nee*-bvleh dohs *oh*-rahs pohr lah *tahr*-deh.
	You have two hours available in the afternoon.

Sr. Alvarez: **Bien. Póngala en la sala de reuniones.**
bvee*ehn. pohn*-gah-lah ehn lah *sah*-lah deh
rrehooh-nee*oh*-nehs.
Good. Put it in the conference room.

Julia: **El miércoles, de cuatro a seis de la tarde en la sala de reuniones.**
ehl mee*ehr*-koh-lehs, deh kooh*ah*-troh ah *seh*ees deh
lah *tahr*-deh ehn lah *sah*-lah deh
rrehooh-nee*oh*-nehs.
Wednesday, from 4:00 to 6:00 p.m. in the conference room.

Sr. Alvarez: **Avise por correo electrónico a mi socio, por favor, y recuérdeme el día antes.**
ah-*bvee*-seh pohr koh-*rreh*-oh eh-lehk-*troh*-nee-koh
ah mee *soh*-seeoh, pohr fah-*bvohr*, ee rreh-kooh*ehr*-
deh-meh ehl *dee*-ah *ahn*-tehs.
Please let my partner know, via e-mail, and remind me the day before.

Julia: **Sin falta.**
seen *fahl*-tah.
Without fail.

Words to Know

organizar	ohr-gahn-ee-_sahr_	to organize, arrange
el personal de gerencia	ehl pehr-soh-_nahl_ deh Heh-_rehn_-seeah	the managerial staff
disponible	dees-poh-_nee_-bvleh	available
el socio	ehl _soh_-seeoh	the partner
sin falta	seen _fahl_-tah	without fail

Delegating Tasks with the Imperative

If you're in a management position, you're responsible for delegating tasks to make sure everything gets done. To do this, you use the *imperative* — a verb form for issuing commands. In the following sections, you discover how to issue formal commands so that whatever needs to get done gets done.

Issuing commands in the imperative can become fairly complicated, especially when dealing with informal commands. To keep this section simple, we focus our coverage exclusively on formal commands, which is what you really should be using in an office setting.

Forming the imperative with regular verbs

When issuing commands, you're usually telling someone to do something — *you do this*, *you do that*. English has only one form of *you*, and in commands, *you* is often implied rather than stated, as in the phrase *Make three copies.* Spanish, however, uses different types of *you*. The subjects of formal commands are **Ud.** (if you're addressing only one person) and **Uds.** (if you're addressing more than one person).

To form either an affirmative or negative formal command:

1. **Drop the final *o* from the** yo **form of the present tense.**

2. **For -ar infinitives, add *e* for** Ud. **and *en* for** Uds; **for -er or -ir infinitives, add *a* for** Ud. **and *an* for** Uds.

3. **To form the negative, simply put** no **before the verb created in Step 2.**

Table 11-5 helps you see these changes in action:

Table 11-5		Creating Formal Commands		
Infinitive Ending	*Verb*	*Present Tense yo Form*	*Singular Formal Command (Ud.)*	*Plural Formal Command (Uds.)*
-ar	**firmar** (*to sign*)	firmo	**(No) Firme.** ([*Don't*] *Sign.*)	**(No) Firmen.** ([*Don't*] *Sign.*)
-er	**leer** (*to read*)	leo	**(No) Lea.** ([*Don't*] *Read.*)	**(No) Lean.** ([*Don't*] *Read.*)
-ir	**escribir** (*to write*)	escribo	**(No) Escriba.** ([*Don't*] *Write*)	**(No) Escriban.** ([*Don't*] *Write.*)

The following list shows some regular verbs in action in formal commands.

In English, you never actually say the word *you* when you give a command or make a request. In Spanish, the use of a subject pronoun (**Ud., Uds.**) in a command is optional and not used all that frequently. You can identify the subject by taking a quick look at the verb form. (If you do use a pronoun, put it directly after the conjugated verb.)

> **Trabajen cuidadosamente.** (trah-bvah-*Hehn* koohee-dah-doh-sah-*mehn*-teh.) (*Work carefully.*)

> **No trabajen tan despacio.** (noh trah-bvah-*Hehn* tahn dehs-*pah*-seeoh.) (*Don't work so slowly.*)

> **Lea en voz alta.** (*leh*-ah ehn bvohs *ahl*-tah.) (*Read aloud.*)

> **No lea ese informe.** (noh *leh*-ah *ehs*-eh een-*fohr*-meh.) (*Don't read that report.*)

Dealing with the imperative of irregular verbs

If the first person singular (**yo**) form of the verb is irregular (such as with **traer** [*to bring*] and **venir** [*to come*]), that irregularity carries over into the formation of the command form, as in the following examples:

> **Traiga el dinero.** (*trah*ee-gah ehl dee-*neh*-roh.) (*Bring the money.*)

> **Vengan conmigo.** (*bvehn*-gahn kohn-*mee*-goh.) (*Come with me.*)

This also applies to stem-changing verbs such as **contar** (*to tell*) and **volver** (*to return*):

> **Cuénteme lo que pasó.** (kooh*ehn*-teh-me loh keh pah-*soh*.) (*Tell me what happened.*)

> **No vuelvan hasta la una.** (noh bvooh*ehl*-bvahn *ahs*-tah lah *ooh*-nah.) (*Don't return until 1:00.*)

Some spelling changes also occur in Spanish verbs in the imperative.

- For **-ar** verbs, the following changes occur: $c \rightarrow qu$, $g \rightarrow gu$, and $z \rightarrow c$ when preceding an *e*.

- For **-er** and **-ir** verbs, you change $g \rightarrow j$, $gu \rightarrow g$, and $c \rightarrow z$ when preceding an *a*.

These examples show a couple of the spelling changes in action in the imperative:

> **Saque la carpeta que necesito.** (*sah*-keh lah kahr-*peh*-tah keh neh-seh-*see*-toh.) (*Take out the file folder that I need.*)

> **Empiece la tarea antes de salir de la clase.** (ehm-pee*eh*-seh lah tah-*reh*-ah *ahn*-tehs deh sah-*leer* deh lah *klah*-seh.) (*Start the homework before leaving the classroom.*)

> **Pague el recibo.** (*pah*-geh *ehl* rreh-*see*-bvoh.) (*Pay the bill.*)

Table 11-6 presents irregular verbs that you have to memorize in order to use them in commands.

Table 11-6	Irregular Verbs in the Imperative Form	
Spanish Verbs	*Commands*	*Meaning*
dar	(No) Dé (Den).	*(Don't) Give.*
estar	(No) Esté(n).	*(Don't) Be.*
ir	(No) Vaya(n).	*(Don't) Go.*
saber	(No) Sepa(n).	*(Don't) Know.*
ser	(No) Sea(n).	*(Don't) Be.*

Here's how you include these irregular verbs in commands:

> **Estén listos a las dos.** (ehs-*tehn lees*-tohs ah lahs dohs.) (*Be ready at 2:00.*)

> **Vaya a la tienda ahora.** (*bvah*-yah ah lah tee*ehn*-dah ah-*oh*-rah.) (*Go to the store now.*)

Fun & Games

In the following figure, label the various objects found in a typical office with their Spanish names. See Appendix D for the answer key.

Chapter 12

Recreation and the Great Outdoors

· ·

In This Chapter

▶ Talking about what you like to do

▶ Keeping yourself entertained indoors with chess, reading, and writing

▶ Walking around in the great outdoors

▶ Looking at what's out there: Animal vocabulary

▶ Playing ball games and swimming

· ·

*R*ecreation is a big part of the Latin American lifestyle, and it can take many forms that fall into two basic categories — indoor and outdoor recreation. This chapter introduces you to some of the most popular recreational activities in various Spanish-speaking countries, starting with indoor activities and then expanding to the great outdoors. We provide you with words and phrases to discuss these activities and several dialogues to tune your ears to the language.

Playing Chess in Spain

El ajedrez (ehl ah-Heh-*drehs*) (*chess*) can be a fascinating game to watch or play. It has been popular in Spain since the Arab invasion of 711 A.D. In fact, some of the terms used in chess come from a combination of Arabic and Spanish words. Checkmate, for example, is derived from the Arabic word **sheik** (*sheek*) (*king*) and from the Spanish word **matar** (mah-*tahr*) (*to kill*). That's why you say checkmate **(el jaquemate)** (ehl Hah-keh-*mah*-teh) when the king is captured at the end of the game.

Talkin' the Talk

In this conversation, Gabriel and Cornelia discuss a chess tournament in Spain:

Gabriel: **Me gusta el ajedrez. Ayer estuve en una competencia.**
meh *goohs*-tah ehl ah-Heh-*drehs*. ah-*yehr* ehs-*tooh*-bveh ehn *ooh*-nah kohm-peh-*tehn*-seeah.
I like chess. Yesterday I was in a chess match.

Cornelia: **¿Quién ganó?**
¿keee*ehn* gah-*noh?*
Who won?

Gabriel: **Yo gané. Di jaquemate en sólo diez movidas.**
yoh gah-*neh*. dee Hah-keh-*mah*-teh ehn *soh*-loh dee*ehs* moh-*bvee*-dahs.
I won. I checkmated [my opponent] in only ten moves.

Cornelia: **¡Felicitaciones!**
¡feh-lee-see-tah-see*oh*-nehs!
Congratulations!

Gabriel: **Gracias. Estoy muy orgulloso de ganar a mi oponente. Él es un jugador muy formidable.**
grah-seeahs. ehs-*tohy mooh*ee ohr-gooh-*yoh*-soh deh gah-*nahr* ah mee oh-poh-*nehn*-teh. ehl ehs oohn Hooh-gah-*dohr mooh*ee fohr-mee-*dah*-bvleh.
Thanks. I'm very proud to beat my opponent. He's a very formidable player.

Words to Know

ajedrez	ah-Heh-_drehs_	chess
competencia	kohm-peh-_tehn_-seeah	contest, match
dar jaquemate	dahr Hah-keh-_mah_-teh	to checkmate
sólo	_soh_-loh	only
movidas	moh-_bvee_-dahs	moves
orgulloso	ohr-gooh-_yoh_-soh	proud
el jugador	ehl Hooh-gah-_dohr_	the player
formidable	fohr-mee-_dah_-bvleh	formidable

Reading with the Verb Leer

Reading is a pleasure, a joy, and often a wonder. Here's the verb that helps you talk about reading in Spanish: **leer** (leh-_ehr_) (*to read.*) **Leer** is a regular **-er** verb, and when you drop the **-er** ending to conjugate it, you're left with a very short stem, **le** (leh).

Conjugation	*Pronunciation*
yo leo	yoh *leh*-oh
tú lees	tooh *leh*-ehs
él, ella, usted lee	ehl, *eh*-yah, oohs-*tehd leh*-eh
nosotros, nosotras leemos	noh-*soh*-trohs, noh-*soh*-trahs leh-*eh*-mohs
vosotros, vosotras leéis	bvoh-*soh*-trohs, bvoh-*soh*-trahs leh-*eh*ees
ellos, ellas, ustedes leen	*eh*-yohs, *eh*-yahs, oohs-*teh*-dehs *leh*-ehn

Obviously, you're a great reader. Why not practice your speaking by using this reading verb?

Me gusta leer revistas. (meh *goohs*-tah leh-*ehr* rreh-*bvees*-tahs.) (*I like to read magazines.*)

Felipe lee todo el día. (feh-*lee*-peh *leh*-eh *toh*-doh ehl *dee*-ah.) (*Felipe reads all day long.*)

Talkin' the Talk

 Marisa and Aurelia are discussing reading material. (Track 22)

Marisa:	**¿Qué vas a leer?** ¿keh bvahs ah leh-*ehr*? *What are you going to read?*
Aurelia:	**Yo traje una novela.** yoh *trah*-Heh *ooh*-nah noh-*bveh*-lah. *I brought a novel.*
Marisa:	**Estoy entusiasta de una biografía.** ehs-*toy* ehn-tooh-see*ahs*-tah deh *ooh*-nah bveeoh-grah-*fee*-ah. *I'm enthusiastic about a biography.*
Aurelia:	**Hablando de biografía, ¿supiste que va a salir un libro sobre Vallejo?** ah-*bvlahn*-doh deh bveeoh-grah-*fee*-ah, ¿sooh-*pees*-teh keh bvah ah sah-*leer* oohn *lee*-bvroh *soh*-bvreh bvah-*yeh*-Hoh? *Speaking of biography, did you know that they're coming out with a book about Vallejo?*
Marisa:	**¿Quién, el poeta peruano?** ¿kee*ehn*, ehl poh-*eh*-tah peh-rooh*ah*-noh? *Who, the Peruvian poet?*
Aurelia:	**Sí, dicen que va a ser excepcional.** see, *dee*-sehn keh bvah ah sehr ehk-sehp-seeoh-*nahl*. *Yes, they say it's going to be exceptional.*

Words to Know

leer	leh-_ehr_	to read
entusiasta	ehn-tooh-see_ahs_-tah	enthusiastic
la novela	lah noh-_bveh_-lah	the novel
la biografía	lah bveeoh-grah-_fee_-ah	the biography
el libro	ehl _lee_-bvroh	the book
el poeta	ehl poh-_eh_-tah	the poet

Writing with the Verb Escribir

The writing verb **escribir** (ehs-kree-_bveer_) (_to write_) is a regular one. Its root is **escrib-** (ehs-_kreebv_). Here's how you conjugate its present tense:

Conjugation	_Pronunciation_
yo escribo	yoh ehs-_kree_-bvoh
tú escribes	tooh ehs-_kree_-bvehs
él, ella, usted escribe	ehl, _eh_-yah, oohs-_tehd_ ehs-_kree_-bveh
nosotros, nosotras escribimos	noh-_soh_-trohs, noh-_soh_-trahs ehs-kree-_bvee_-mohs
vosotros, vosotras escribís	bvoh-_soh_-trohs, bvoh-_soh_-trahs ehs-kree-_bvees_
ellos, ellas, ustedes escriben	_eh_-yohs, _eh_-yahs, oohs-_teh_-dehs ehs-_kree_-bvehn

Use these phrases to practice talking about writing:

> **Tú siempre escribes en tu diario.** (tooh see_ehm_-preh ehs-_kree_-bvehs ehn tooh dee_ah_-reeoh.) (_You always write in your journal._)

> **Mi madre escribe poemas.** (mee _mah_-dreh ehs-_kree_-bveh poh-_eh_-mahs.) (_My mother writes poems._)

Yo escribo una carta a mis padres cada semana. (yoh ehs-*kree*-bvoh *ooh*-nah *kahr*-tah ah mees *pah*-drehs *kah*-dah seh-*mah*-nah.) (*I write a letter to my parents every week.*)

When you see **le** (leh) in front of a conjugated form of **escribir** (or any verb), you know it's a Spanish *indirect object pronoun,* which indicates to or for whom the action is being performed. The full list of these pronouns is **me, te, le, nos, os,** and **les.**

Talkin' the Talk

While on vacation, Catalina has come indoors from the outdoors to write to her father, as she explains to Eduardo.

Catalina: **Escribo una carta a mi padre.**
ehs-*kree*-bvoh *ooh*-nah *kahr*-tah ah mee *pah*-dreh.
I'm writing a letter to my father.

Eduardo: **¿Le escribes regularmente?**
¿leh ehs-*kree*-bvehs rreh-gooh-*lahr*-*mehn*-teh?
Do you write him regularly?

Catalina: **Sí, por lo menos una vez a la semana.**
see, pohr loh *meh*-nohs *ooh*-nah bvehs ah lah seh-*mah*-nah.
Yes, at least once a week.

Eduardo: **¿Le escribiste alguna carta ayer?**
¿leh ehs-kree-*bvees*-teh ahl-*gooh*-nah *kahr*-tah ah-*yehr?*
Did you write him a letter yesterday?

Catalina: **No, por eso quiero escribirle una carta hoy.**
noh, pohr *eh*-soh keee*eh*-roh ehs-kree-*bveer*-leh *ooh*-nah *kahr*-tah ohy.
No, that's why I want to write him one today.

Taking It Outside (For Good or Bad)

Outdoor recreation is a big part of the Latin American lifestyle. Being outdoors can promote a quiet, contemplative feeling as you appreciate the beauty of nature, or it can pose a challenge as you expose yourself to the elements. Spanish has two ways to express the idea of going outdoors:

✔ **al aire libre** (ahl *ahee*-reh *lee*-bvreh) (*in the open air*): You use this phrase when you're talking about going out to the street, garden, or taking a walk. It implies a feeling of openness and liberty.

✔ **a la intemperie** (ah lah een-tehm-*peh*-reeeh) (*out of doors, exposed to the elements* [Literally: *in the unheated space*]): This phrase implies that you're going to be without a roof nearby and therefore will be suffering or enjoying whatever weather you may find. It gives a feeling of exposure and less safety.

The following examples can help you determine which phrase to use:

Voy a nadar en una piscina al aire libre. (bvohy ah nah-*dahr* ehn *ooh*-nah pee-*see*-nah ahl *ahee*-reh *lee*-bvreh.) (*I'm going to swim in an outdoor pool.*)

No dejes las plantas a la intemperie. (noh *deh*-Hehs lahs *plahn*-tahs ah lah een-tehm-*peh*-reeeh.) (*Don't leave the plants out in the open.*)

Strolling Along with the Verb Pasear

The verb **pasear** (pa-seh-*ahr*) (*to walk; to stroll*) has many applications, and it's a regular verb. The root of this verb is **pase-** (*pah*-seh). Here's how you conjugate its present tense:

Conjugation	Pronunciation
yo paseo	yoh pah-*seh*-oh
tú paseas	tooh pah-*seh*-ahs
él, ella, usted pasea	ehl, *eh*-yah, oohs-*tehd* pah-*seh*-ah
nosotros, nosotras paseamos	noh-*soh*-trohs, noh-*soh*-trahs pah-seh-*ah*-mohs
vosotros, vosotras paseáis	bvoh-*soh*-trohs, bvoh-*soh*-trahs pah-seh-*ah*ees
ellos, ellas, ustedes pasean	*eh*-yohs, *eh*-yahs, oohs-*teh*-dehs pah-*seh*-ahn

Take these phrases for a stroll:

¿Quieres pasear conmigo? (¿kee*eh*-rehs pah-seh-*ahr* kohn-*mee*-goh?) (*Do you want to walk with me?*)

Mi abuela pasea todas las tardes. (mee ah-bvooh*eh*-lah pah-*seh*-ah toh-dahs lahs *tahr*-dehs.) (*My grandmother walks every afternoon.*)

Checking Out the Animals

During any outdoor activity, you're bound to see at least one kind of animal. Table 12-1 introduces you to a variety of critters in Spanish.

Table 12-1	Animals Common to Central and South America and Mexico	
Spanish	**Pronunciation**	**English**
la alpaca	lah ahl-*pah*-kah	the alpaca
la ardilla	lah ahr-*dee*-yah	the squirrel
la burra	lah *bvooh*-rrah	the jenny (female donkey)
el burro	ehl *bvooh*-rroh	the male donkey
el caballo	ehl kah-*bvah*-yoh	the horse
la cabra	lah *kah*-bvrah	the goat
el ganso	ehl *gahn*-soh	the goose
el gato	ehl *gah*-toh	the cat
la gaviota	lah gah-bvee*oh*-tah	the sea gull
el gorrión	ehl goh-rree*ohn*	the sparrow
el huanaco	ehl oohah-*nah*-koh	the guanaco
la iguana	lah ee-gooh*ah*-nah	the iguana
los insectos	lohs een-*sehk*-tohs	the insects
la llama	lah *yah*-mah	the llama
el mapache	ehl mah-*pah*-cheh	the raccoon
la mariposa	lah mah-ree-*poh*-sah	the butterfly
el mono	ehl *moh*-noh	the monkey
el pájaro	ehl *pah*-Hah-roh	the bird
la paloma	lah pah-*loh*-mah	the pigeon
el pato	ehl *pah*-toh	the duck
el perro	ehl *peh*-rroh	the dog
el puma	ehl *pooh*-mah	the mountain lion
la serpiente	lah sehr-pee*ehn*-teh	the snake
la tortuga	lah tohr-*tooh*-gah	the turtle
el tucán	ehl tooh-*kahn*	the toucan
la vaca	lah *bvah*-kah	the cow

You're probably familiar with many of the animals common to both North and South America; here, we talk about animals more common to Mexico and South and Central America:

- ✔ The first breed that comes to mind is the **llama,** and its cousins the **huanaco** and **alpaca.** You find these gentle creatures, from the same family as camels, mostly in the region around the Andes — from Colombia to Chile. **Llamas** and **alpacas** are highly domesticated, but **huanacos** are more likely to run around in the wild.

- ✔ **Pumas** are South American mountain lions. They're very serious-minded, meat-eating predators. They're beautiful to behold in the zoo, but keep out of their way in the mountains.

- ✔ You can find snakes — poisonous and otherwise — monkeys, insects, and birds of all kinds in the rain forests of Bolivia, Argentina, Paraguay, Ecuador, and Mexico.

- ✔ The Galapagos Islands of Ecuador are famous for their very unique fauna, first described by Charles Darwin, who actually conceived his theory of evolution while observing the turtles and birds that live there.

- ✔ Iguanas walk around freely in the south of Mexico — until someone puts them in the soup pot — and squirrels are everywhere.

These phrases get you started talking about animals while you observe them:

Los tucanes están en la selva. (lohs tooh-*kah*-nehs ehs-*tahn* ehn lah *sehl*-bvah.) (*The toucans are in the jungle.*)

En la playa vemos gaviotas. (ehn lah *plah*-yah, *bveh*-mohs gah-bvee*oh*-tahs.) (*On the beach, we see seagulls.*)

Van a una carrera de caballos. (bvahn ah *ooh*-nah kah-*rreh*-rah deh kah-*bvah*-yohs.) (*They're going to a horse race.*)

Hay mapaches en casi todo el continente americano. (ahy mah-*pah*-chehs ehn *kah*-see *toh*-doh ehl kohn-tee-*nehn*-teh ah-meh-ree-*kah*-noh.) (*Almost all of the American continent has raccoons.*)

We could take whole books to talk about animals, but here are a few more examples:

El cerro está cubierto de mariposas. (ehl *seh*-rroh ehs-*tah* kooh-bvee*ehr*-toh deh mah-ree-*poh*-sahs.) (*The hill is covered with butterflies.*)

De paseo, vi una manada de vacas. (deh pah-*seh*-oh, bvee *ooh*-nah mah-*nah*-dah deh *bvah*-kahs.) (*While walking, I saw a herd of cows.*)

En el lago vimos patos silvestres. (ehn ehl *lah*-goh *bvee*-mohs *pah*-tohs seel-*bvehs*-trehs.) (*We saw wild ducks in the lake.*)

Talkin' the Talk

The wonderful sport of horseback riding calls for some harmony between horse and rider and allows the rider to enjoy the landscape, as Mariana explains to Dora Luz.

Mariana:	**Me encanta andar a caballo.** meh ehn-*kahn*-tah ahn-*dahr* ah kah-*bvah*-yoh. *I love riding a horse. (Literally: Riding a horse enchants [or delights] me.)*
Dora Luz:	**¿Te preparas para algún torneo?** ¿teh preh-*pah*-rahs *pah*-rah ahl-*goohn* tohr-*neh*-oh? *Are you preparing for a competition?*
Mariana:	**No, simplemente gozo el hecho de montar.** noh, seem-pleh-*mehn*-teh *goh*-soh ehl *eh*-choh deh mohn-*tahr*. *No, I simply enjoy riding.*
Dora Luz:	**¿Tienes tu propio caballo?** ¿teeeh-nehs tooh *proh*-peeoh kah-*bvah*-yoh? *Do you have your own horse?*
Mariana:	**Sí, tengo una yegua. Se llama Lirio.** see, *tehn*-goh *ooh*-nah *yeh*-goohah. seh *yah*-mah *lee*-reeoh. *Yes, I have a mare. Her name is Lirio [Lily].*
Dora Luz:	**Debe ser blanca.** *deh*-bveh sehr *bvlahn*-kah. *She must be white.*
Mariana:	**Es blanca y tiene una mancha café en la frente.** ehs *blahn*-kah ee teeeh-neh *ooh*-nah *mahn*-chah kah-*feh* ehn lah *frehn*-teh. *She's white and has a brown spot on her forehead.*

Words to Know

andar	ahn-_dahr_	to ride
el caballo	ehl kah-_bvah_-yoh	the horse
preparar	preh-pah-_rahr_	to prepare
torneo	tohr-_neh_-oh	competition; tournament
simplemente	seem-pleh-_mehn_-teh	simply
gozar	goh-_sahr_	to enjoy
el hecho de montar	ehl _eh_-choh deh mohn-_tahr_	riding
propio	_proh_-peeoh	(one's) own
la yegua	lah _yeh_-goohah	the mare
la mancha	lah _mahn_-chah	the spot
la frente	lah _frehn_-teh	the forehead

Playing with the Verb Jugar

Jugar (Hooh-_gahr_) (_to play_) is a slightly irregular verb — it's a stem-changing verb with a _u_ to _ue_ stem change. But it's a very playful and useful verb — definitely worth the effort. Here's the conjugation:

Conjugation	_Pronunciation_
yo juego	yoh Hooh_eh_-goh
tú juegas	tooh Hooh_eh_-gahs
él, ella, usted juega	ehl, _eh_-yah, oohs-_tehd_ Hooh_eh_-gah
nosotros, nosotras jugamos	noh-_soh_-trohs, noh-_soh_-trahs Hooh-_gah_-mohs
vosotros, vosotras jugáis	bvoh-_soh_-trohs, bvoh-_soh_-trahs Hooh-_gah_ees
ellos, ellas, ustedes juegan	_eh_-yohs, _eh_-yahs, oohs-_teh_-dehs Hooh_eh_-gahn

It's always good to practice on your game a little. Following are some phrases that can help when you play:

Él juega mejor que hace un mes. (ehl Hooh*eh*-gah meh-*Hohr* keh *ah*-seh oohn mehs.) (*He plays better than a month ago.*)

¿Jugamos béisbol hoy? (¿Hooh-*gah*-mohs *bveh*ees-bvohl ohy?) (*Are we playing baseball today?*)

Playing Ball Games

Most sport activities involve a ball, and the type of ball that is necessary depends on the sport you're playing. If you're talking about ball games in Spanish-speaking countries, you're probably referring to soccer **(el fútbol)** (ehl *fooht*-bvohl) or baseball **(el béisbol)** (ehl *beh*ees-bohl). In the following sections, we help you talk about these activites in Spanish, just in case you ever encounter the opportunity to involve yourself in an exciting ball game (either as a spectator or as a player).

The most popular ball game: Fútbol

Yes, **el fútbol,** called *soccer* in North American English and *football* elsewhere, is the most popular game in Latin America. This game is the talk of taverns, bars, and living rooms, and its stars are national heroes. We dare say there's more talk about **el fútbol** in Latin America than about anything else.

Here are a few **fútbol**-related terms that may come in handy:

- ✔ **el arquero** (ehl ahr-*keh*-roh) (*the goalkeeper*)
- ✔ **la cancha** (lah *kahn*-chah) (*the playing field*)
- ✔ **el equipo** (ehl eh-*kee*-poh) (*the team*)
- ✔ **ganar** (gah-*nahr*) (*to win*)
- ✔ **el gol** (ehl gohl) (*the goal*)

Perusing pre-Columbian ball games

Ball games were so important in pre-Columbian cultures that people built special playing courts. You can see these ball fields at many archeological sites in Mexico and Central America.

One such place is **Monte Albán** (*mohn*-teh ahl-*bvahn*), a city built on top of a mountain above present-day **Oaxaca** (oh-ah-*Hah*-kah), the capital of the state of the same name, in the south of Mexico. Seeing this ball court — and there are many others — you no longer wonder why ball games are so popular in Mexico. Even

the smallest village in the most difficult terrain has a ball court, more often than not in front of the municipal building.

Also, a ball game called **chueca** (chooh*eh*-kah) existed in Chile before the arrival of Europeans. And **chueca** looked like field hockey. The **araucanos** (ah-rahooh-*kah*-nohs), members of an Indian nation in the south of Chile, hit the ball with a crooked stick. So the word for *crooked* in places like Chile and Mexico is **chueco** (chooh*eh*-koh).

Talkin' the Talk

Carla and Pedro talk shop about their favorite sport, soccer. (Track 23)

Pedro: **Me divierte ver el fútbol.**
meh dee-bvee*ehr*-teh bvehr ehl *fooht*-bvohl.
I enjoy watching soccer.

Carla: **¿Adónde vas a verlo?**
¿ah-*dohn*-deh bvahs a *bvehr*-loh?
Where do you go to watch it?

Pedro: **Voy al estadio de los Guerreros.**
bvohy ahl ehs-*tah*-deeoh deh lohs geh-*rreh*-rohs.
I go to the Guerreros' stadium.

Carla: **¿Eres hincha de los Guerreros?**
¿eh-rehs *een*-chah deh lohs geh-*rreh*-rohs?
Are you a Guerreros fan?

Pedro: **Sí, hace muchos años.**
see, *ah*-seh *mooh*-chohs *ah*-nyohs.
Yes, for many years.

Carla: **¿Qué jugadores te gustan?**
¿keh Hooh-gah-*doh*-rehs teh *goohs*-tahn?
Which players do you like?

Pedro: **Prefiero a los de la defensa.**
preh-fee*ehr*-oh ah lohs deh lah deh-*fehn*-sah.
I prefer those who play defense.

Carla: **¿Y no te gustan los centro-delanteros?**
¿ee noh teh *goohs*-tahn lohs *sehn*-troh
deh-lahn-*teh*-rohs?
You don't like the center forwards?

Pedro: **Sí, pero creo que la defensa tiene un rol muy especial.**
see, *peh*-roh *kreh*-oh keh lah deh-*fehn*-sah tee*eh*-neh
oohn rrohl *moohee* ehs-peh-see*ahl.*
Yes, but I feel the defense has a very special role.

Words to Know

divertir	dee-bvehr-<u>teer</u>	to amuse, to have fun
el estadio	ehl ehs-<u>tah</u>-deeoh	the stadium
el/la hincha	ehl/lah <u>een</u>-chah	the fan
el jugador	ehl Hooh-gah-<u>dohr</u>	the player
la defensa	lah deh-<u>fehn</u>-sah	the defense
los delanteros	lohs deh-lahn-<u>teh</u>-rohs	the forwards
el rol	ehl rrohl	the role

Baseball's #2

El béisbol is definitely the second most important ball game (after **el fútbol —** see the preceding section) in Mexico, Central America, and the Caribbean. Here are some vocabulary words you may need to avoid striking out at the baseball field:

✔ **la base** (lah *bvah*-seh) (*the base*)

✔ **la base meta** (lah *bvah*-seh *meh*-tah) (*home plate*)

✔ **el bate** (ehl *bvah*-teh) (*the bat*)

✔ **el bateador** (ehl bvah-teh-ah-*dohr*) (*the batter*)

✔ **el beísbol** (ehl beh*ees*-bohl) (*the baseball*)

✔ **el jonrón** (ehl Hohn-*rohn*) (*the home run*)

✔ **el lanzador** (ehl lahn-sah-*dohr*) (*the pitcher*)

✔ **el receptor** (ehl rreh-sehp-*tohr*) (*the catcher*)

Swimming with the Verb Nadar

Water, water, everywhere — inviting you to jump right in. Before you do, you may want to know how to conjugate **nadar** (nah-*dahr*) (*to swim*). It's easy. It's a regular verb, and its root is **nad-** (nahd).

Conjugation	Pronunciation
yo nado	yoh *nah*-doh
tú nadas	tooh *nah*-dahs
él, ella, usted nada	ehl, *eh*-yah, oohs-*tehd nah*-dah
nosotros, nosotras nadamos	noh-*soh*-trohs, noh-*soh*-trahs nah-*dah*-mohs
vosotros, vosotras nadáis	bvoh-*soh*-trohs, bvoh-*soh*-trahs nah-*dah*ees
ellos, ellas, ustedes nadan	*eh*-yohs, *eh*-yahs, oohs-*teh*-dehs *nah*-dahn

Okay. Maybe you don't want to get wet right now. How about practicing your swimming here, for just a couple of laps?

Yo no sé nadar. (yoh noh seh nah-*dahr*.) (*I don't know how to swim.*)

Carlos nada como un pez. (*kahr*-lohs *nah*-dah *koh*-moh oohn pehs.) (*Carlos swims like a fish.*)

Talkin' the Talk

María Luisa likes to swim, and she wants to compete against Alvaro. But first she needs to find out how good a swimmer he is.

María Luisa:　**¿Cuándo nadas?**
　　　　　　　　¿koohahn-doh nah-dahs?
　　　　　　　　When do you go swimming?

Alvaro:	**Los martes y los viernes.**
	lohs *mahr*-tehs ee lohs bveee*hr*-nehs.
	Tuesdays and Fridays.
María Luisa:	**¿Qué estilo nadas?**
	¿keh ehs-*tee*-loh *nah*-dahs?
	What style do you swim?
Alvaro:	**Nado principalmente de pecho.**
	nah-doh preen-see-pahl-*mehn*-teh deh *peh*-choh.
	I swim mainly breaststroke.
María Luisa:	**¿Sabes nadar crol?**
	¿*sah*-bvehs nah-*dahr* krohl?
	Do you know how to swim the crawl?
Alvaro:	**Sí, y también de espalda.**
	see, ee tahm-bveee*hn* deh ehs-*pahl*-dah.
	Yes, and also the backstroke.
María Luisa:	**¿Cuánto nadas?**
	¿kooh*ahn*-toh *nah*-dahs?
	How much do you swim?
Alvaro:	**Nado un kilómetro cada vez.**
	nah-doh oohn kee-*loh*-meh-troh *kah*-dah bvehs.
	I swim one kilometer each time.
María Luisa:	**¡Que bien!**
	¡keh bveee*hn*!
	Very good!

Words to Know

nadar	nah-<u>dahr</u>	to swim
el estilo	ehl ehs-<u>tee</u>-loh	the style
nadar de pecho	nah-<u>dahr</u> deh <u>peh</u>-choh	to swim the breaststroke
nadar crol	nah-<u>dahr</u> krohl	to swim the crawl stroke
nadar de espalda	nah-<u>dahr</u> deh ehs-<u>pahl</u>-dah	to swim the backstroke

A fun swimming pun

This pun is based on the double play of the words **nada** (*nah*-dah) and **traje** (*trah*-Heh). **Nada** means both the third person of the verb **nadar** (nah-*dahr*) (*to swim*) and *nothing*. And **traje** can be the past tense of the verb **traer** (trah-*ehr*) (*to bring*) and also means *suit*.

¿No nada nada? (noh *nah*-dah *nah*-dah)
(*You aren't swimming at all?*)

No traje traje. (noh *trah*-Heh *trah*-Heh.)
(*I didn't bring a swimsuit.*)

Fun & Games

Here's your chance to let your animal magnetism show through. Write down the name for each animal in Spanish. See Appendix D for the answer key.

a. _____

b. _____

c. _____

d. _____

e. _____

f. _____

g. _____

h. _____

i. _____

j. _____

Part III
Spanish on the Go

The 5th Wave   By Rich Tennant

"I've always found my Spanish improves with a little practice, some study, and about 3 or 4 margaritas."

In this part . . .

This part gives you the tools you need to take your Spanish on the road as you travel to a Spanish-speaking country. You discover how to plan a trip, communicate with the people who handle your travel arrangements and accommodations, and deal with money in foreign lands. You also find out how to navigate an airport, travel over land in trains and taxis, secure a place to stay, and communicate in emergency situations.

Sprinkled throughout are cultural tidbits that introduce you to people, places, and things that are important in Spanish-speaking cultures.

Chapter 13
Planning a Trip

. . . .

In This Chapter

▶ Making plans to travel

▶ Handling passports and visas

▶ Using the verb *to go* and the simple future tense

▶ Getting set to pack

▶ Bringing your computer with you

. . . .

T his chapter will move you! No, you won't end up tear-soaked. Rather, you find out about moving to new worlds and new experiences and moving out of your daily routine. It's about moving into vacation, onto beaches and mountains, and into different countries and climates. It's adventure time, and this chapter provides the guidance you need to plan your adventure and navigate brave new worlds in Spanish.

Making Travel Plans

One thing you already know: Whatever your choices or your desires, you can find them in Latin America, in the Spanish-speaking countries, among the Spanish-speaking peoples. Right?

✔ **Looking for beaches?** You can find dozens of wonderful beaches everywhere, except in landlocked Bolivia and Paraguay.

✔ **Looking for waterfalls?** Head for **El Salto del Angel** (ehl *sahl*-toh dehl *ahn*-Hehl) (*The Angel's Leap*), the highest in the world, in Venezuela. Or the most spectacular one, **Las Cataratas del Iguazú** (lahs kah-tah-*rah*-tahs dehl ee-goohah-*sooh*) (*The Iguazú Falls*) in Argentina, on the border with Brazil and Paraguay.

✔ **Looking for lakes?** Consider Lake Titicaca between Peru and Bolivia or tour the lakes connecting the southern regions of Chile and Argentina.

✔ **On an ecological excursion?** Try the forests of Honduras, Venezuela, Colombia, Bolivia, Peru, Guatemala, or Costa Rica.

⌐ ✔ **Discovering ancient civilizations?** You can find literally hundreds of
places in Mexico, Guatemala, Colombia, Peru, Paraguay, and Spain.

If shopping is your heart's desire, put on some comfortable shoes and check
out these tips (see Chapter 9 for more about preparing for shopping trips):

⌐ ✔ **Looking for fine porcelain?** Head for Spain.

✔ **Shopping for leather goods?** Argentina and Mexico are prime locations.

✔ **Looking for silverware?** Try Mexico or Peru.

Here are some phrases that are helpful in making travel plans (see Chapter 15
for more details on purchasing tickets):

⌐ ✔ **el boleto de ida** (ehl bvoh-*leh*-toh deh *ee*-dah) (*one-way ticket* [Literally:
ticket to go])

✔ **el boleto de ida y vuelta** (ehl bvoh-*leh*-toh deh *ee*-dah ee bvooh*ehl*-tah)
(*round-trip ticket* [Literally: *ticket to go and return*])

✔ **el boleto de vuelta** (ehl bvoh-*leh*-toh deh bvooh*ehl*-tah) (*return ticket*)

✔ **la fecha de llegada** (lah *feh*-chah deh yeh-*gah*-dah) (*the arrival date*)

✔ **la fecha de partida** (lah *feh*-chah deh pahr-*tee*-dah) (*the departure date*)

✔ **la hora de despegue** (lah *oh*-rah deh dehs-*peh*-geh) (*the departure time*)

✔ **el vuelo con escalas** (ehl bvooh*eh*-loh kohn ehs-*kah*-lahs) (*flight with
stopovers*)

✔ **el vuelo directo** (ehl bvooh*eh*-loh dee-*rehk*-toh) (*direct flight*)

Talkin' the Talk

Sergio wants to fly from Mexico City to Cancún. He goes to a travel
agency to book his flight. (Track 24)

Sergio:	**Buenos días.**
	bvooh*eh*-nohs *dee*-ahs.
	Good morning.

Travel agent:	**Buenos días, señor. ¿En qué le puedo servir?**
	bvooh*eh*-nohs *dee*-ahs, *seh*-nyohr. ¿ehn keh leh pooh*eh*-doh sehr-*bveer?*
	Good morning, sir. How may I help you?

Sergio:	**Necesito un boleto para Cancún.**
	neh-seh-*see*-toh oohn bvoh-*leh*-toh *pah*-rah kahn-*koohn.*
	I need a ticket for Cancún.
Travel agent:	**¿En qué día le acomoda?**
	¿ehn keh *dee*-ah leh ah-koh-*moh*-dah?
	What day works for you?
Sergio:	**El viernes en la mañana.**
	ehl bvee*ehr*-nehs ehn lah mah-*nyah*-nah.
	Friday morning.
Travel agent:	**Hay un vuelo a las ocho.**
	ahy oohn bvooh*eh*-loh ah lahs *oh*-choh.
	There's a flight at 8:00.
Sergio:	**¿Un poco más tarde?**
	¿oohn *poh*-koh mahs *tahr*-deh?
	A little later?
Travel agent:	**Sí, hay otro a las nueve.**
	see, ahy *oh*-troh ah lahs nooh*eh*-bveh.
	Yes, there's another one at 9:00.
Sergio:	**Tomo ése.**
	toh-moh *eh*-seh
	I'll take that one.
Travel agent:	**¿Hasta qué día?**
	¿*ahs*-tah keh *dee*-ah?
	Until what day?
Sergio:	**Hasta el domingo por la tarde.**
	ahs-tah ehl doh-*meen*-goh pohr lah *tahr*-deh.
	Until Sunday afternoon.
Travel agent:	**Hay un vuelo a las siete de la noche.**
	ahy oohn bvooh*eh*-loh ah lahs see*eh*-teh deh lah *noh*-cheh.
	There's a flight at 7:00 p.m.
Sergio:	**Es buena hora. Hágame la reservación.**
	ehs bvooh*eh*-nah *oh*-rah. *ah*-gah-meh lah rreh-sehr-bvah-see*ohn.*
	It's a good time. Make me a reservation.

Travel agent: **Aquí está su boleto, señor. El vuelo sale de México a las nueve de la mañana.**
ah-*kee* ehs-*tah* sooh bvoh-*leh*-toh, *seh*-nyor. el bvooh*eh*-loh *sah*-leh deh *meh*-Hee-koh ah lahs nooh*eh*-bveh deh lah mah-*nyah*-nah.
Here is your ticket, sir. The flight leaves Mexico City at 9:00 a.m.

Tiene que estar en el aeropuerto una hora antes.
tee*eh*-neh keh ehs-*tahr* ehn ehl ah-eh-roh-pooh*ehr*-toh *ooh*-nah *oh*-rah *ahn*-tehs.
You have to be at the airport an hour ahead of time.

Words to Know

¿En qué le puedo servir?	¿ehn keh leh pooh<u>eh</u>-doh sehr-<u>bveer</u>?	How may I help you?
el boleto	ehl bvoh-<u>leh</u>-toh	the ticket
¿En qué día le acomoda?	¿ehn keh <u>dee</u>-ah leh ah-koh-<u>moh</u>-dah?	What day works for you?
el vuelo	ehl bvooh<u>eh</u>-loh	the flight
tomo ese	<u>toh</u>-moh <u>eh</u>-seh	I'll take that one

Mastering Visas and Passports

To enter another country, you need to go through some formalities. The requirements to enter each country can vary. Our advice is to check with a travel agent or the destination country's consulate to determine the documents and medical requirements (like shots) that you need in order to enter. Often, travel agents can make the necessary arrangements.

Always carry your passport **(el pasaporte)** (ehl pah-sah-*pohr*-teh), regardless of whether your host country requires it; you may want to go beyond your original destination. Plus, a passport is an important document to have when dealing with banking or emergencies.

When you're required to have a *visa* (**una visa**) (*ooh*-nah *bvee*-sah), a permit to visit a country, you must have a passport — the passport is where your visa is stamped. Some countries don't require visas.

Talkin' the Talk

 Patricia, a Canadian, has some questions about traveling to Mexico. (Track 25)

Patricia:	**¿Es este el Consulado de México?**
	¿ehs *ehs*-teh ehl kohn-sooh-*lah*-doh deh *meh*-Hee-koh?
	Is this the Mexican Consulate?

Consulate attendant:	**Sí, ¿en qué le puedo servir?**
	see, ¿ehn keh leh pooh*eh*-doh sehr-*bveer?*
	Yes, how can I help you?

Patricia:	**¿Necesito una visa para ir a México?**
	¿neh-seh-*see*-toh *ooh*-nah *bvee*-sah *pah*-rah eer ah *meh*-Hee-koh?
	Do I need a visa to go to Mexico?

Consulate attendant:	**Depende. ¿Es ciudadana de los Estados Unidos o de Canadá?**
	deh-*pehn*-deh. ¿ehs seeooh-dah-*dah*-nah deh lohs ehs-*tah*-dohs ooh-*nee*-dohs oh deh kah-nah-*dah?*
	That depends. Are you a citizen of the United States or Canada?

Patricia:	**Soy canadiense.**
	sohy kah-nah-dee*ehn*-seh
	I'm Canadian.

Consulate attendant:	**¿Por cuánto tiempo va?**
	¿pohr kooh*ahn*-toh tee*ehm*-poh bvah?
	How long will you be there?

Patricia:	**De noviembre a marzo.**
	deh noh-bvee*ehm*-breh ah *mahr*-soh.
	From November to March.

Consulate attendant:	**Son cinco meses. ¿Va como turista?**
	sohn *seen*-koh *meh*-sehs. ¿bvah *koh*-moh tooh-*rees*-tah?
	That's five months. Are you going as a tourist?

Patricia:	**Sí.**
	see.
	Yes.

Consulate attendant:	**Entonces no va a necesitar visa.**
	ehn-*tohn*-sehs noh bvah ah neh-seh-see-*tahr* bvee-sah.
	Then you won't need a visa.

Patricia:	**Gracias por la información.**
	grah-seeahs pohr lah een-fohr-mah-see*ohn*.
	Thank you for the information.

Consulate attendant:	**De nada.**
	deh *nah*-dah.
	You're welcome.

Words to Know

el consulado	ehl kohn-sooh-<u>lah</u>-doh	the consulate
la visa	lah <u>bvee</u>-sah	the visa
depende	deh-<u>pehn</u>-deh	that depends
el/la ciudadano/a	ehl/lah seeooh-dah-<u>dah</u>-noh/nah	the citizen
canadiense	kah-nah-dee<u>ehn</u>-seh	Canadian
el/la turista	ehl/lah tooh-<u>rees</u>-tah	the tourist

Traveling into the Simple Future with the Verb Construction Ir a Viajar

The verb **ir** (eer), like the English verb *to go,* can be used to make a kind of future tense called the *simple future.* It's like saying *I'm going to travel.* In Spanish, that phrase is **voy a viajar** (bvohy ah bveeah-*Hahr*). What follows is an example of the use of the verb **ir** with the infinitive of **viajar** (bveeah-*Hahr*) to tell about the simple future of the traveling verb. (Flip to Chapter 5 for an introduction to the verb **ir.**)

Conjugation	*Pronunciation*
yo voy a viajar	yoh bvoy ah bveeah-*Hahr*
tú vas a viajar	tooh bvahs ah bveeah-*Hahr*
él, ella, usted va a viajar	ehl, *eh-*yah, oohs-*tehd,* bvah a bveeah-*Hahr*
nosotros, nosotras vamos a viajar	noh-*soh*-trohs, noh-*soh*-trahs *bvah*-mohs ah bveeah-*Hahr*
vosotros, vosotras vais a viajar	bvoh-*soh*-trohs, bvoh-*soh*-trahs *bvah*ees ah bveeah-*Hahr*
ellos, ellas, ustedes van a viajar	*eh*-yohs, *eh*-yahs, oohs-*teh*-dehs bvahn a bveeah-*Hahr*

Practice using the simple future of **ir a viajar.** It's quite fun, so check it out:

> **Voy a viajar en avión.** (bvoy a bveeah-*Hahr* ehn ah-bvee*ohn.*) (*I'm going to travel by plane.*)

> **Vamos a viajar en tren.** (*bvah*-mohs ah bveeah-*Hahr* ehn trehn.) (*We'll be traveling by rail.*)

> **Ellos van a viajar en autobús.** (*eh*-yohs bvahn ah bveeah-*Hahr* ehn ahooh-toh-*bvoohs.*) (*They're going to travel by bus.*)

You can also use **ir** + **a** with other verbs (in the infinitive form) to say that you're going to do something. Check out these examples:

> **Voy a servir la cena a las seis.** (bvohy ah sehr-*bveer* lah *seh*-nah ah lahs se*hees.*) (*I'm going to serve dinner at 6:00.*)

> **Tú vas a ir en avión.** (tooh bvahs a eer ehn ah-bvee*ohn.*) (*You're going to go by plane.*)

Todos vamos a divertirnos. (*toh*-dohs *bvah*-mohs ah dee-bvehr-*teer*-nohs.) (*We're all going to have fun.*)

Él va a llegar cansado. (ehl bvah ah yeh-*gahr* kahn-*sah*-doh.) (*He's going to arrive tired.*)

Ella va a volver temprano. (*eh*-yah bvah ah bvohl-*bvehr* tehm-*prah*-noh.) (*She's going to return early.*)

Ellos van a llevar las maletas. (*eh*-yohs bvahn ah yeh-*bvahr* lahs mah-*leh*-tahs.) (*They're going to carry the luggage.*)

Packing: Less Is More

Of course, packing is a vital part of any trip. But before you can decide what to pack, you need to know what you're packing it in. Here are a few words to help you choose just the right carrier for your travel needs; for more on the actual clothing items you carry in them, head to Chapter 9.

- **la bolsa de viaje** (lah *bvohl*-sah deh bveea*h*-Heh) (*the overnight bag*)
- **el equipaje** (ehl eh-kee-*pah*-Heh) (*the luggage*)
- **la maleta** (lah mah-*leh*-tah) (*the suitcase*)
- **la mochila** (lah moh-*chee*-lah) (*the backpack*)
- **la talega de lona** (lah tah-*leh*-gah deh *loh*-nah) (*the duffel bag*)

While you're at it, check out these packing verbs:

- **empacar** (ehm-pah-*kahr*) (*to pack*)
- **hacer el equipaje** (ah-*sehr* ehl eh-kee-*pah*-Heh) (*to prepare the luggage*)

When visiting colonial monuments such as churches, you should plan to wear skirts, dresses, or long trousers. Shorts are great on the beach, but in cities you look more in style with longer wear. Latinos are a bit more formal than people in the United States and pay a good deal of attention to beautiful clothing. You may feel better walking on the city streets if you also have something nice to wear.

Taking Along Your Computer

For those hours between activities, you may decide to do something on your laptop computer **(computadora portátil)** (kohm-pooh-tah-*doh*-rah pohr-*tah*-teel). (For some people, work never stops, even when they're on vacation.) Here are some phrases that can help when talking about your laptop:

> **Voy a llevar conmigo la computadora portátil.** (bvohy ah yeh-*bvahr* kohn-*mee*-goh lah kohm-pooh-tah-*doh*-rah pohr-*tah*-teel.) (*I'm going to take the laptop computer with me.*)

> **No te olvides las baterías.** (noh teh ohl-*bvee*-dehs lahs bvah-teh-*ree*-ahs.) (*Don't forget the batteries.*)

> **Vas a llevar el adaptador de corriente.** (bvahs a yeh-*bvahr* ehl ah-dahp-tah-*dohr* deh koh-rreee*ehn*-teh.) (*You're going to take the voltage adapter.*)

> **Necesitamos el adaptador para cargar la batería.** (neh-seh-see-*tah*-mohs ehl ah-dahp-tah-*dohr pah*-rah kahr-*gahr* la bvah-teh-*ree*-ah.) (*We need the adapter to charge the battery.*)

Fun & Games

The following crossword puzzle contains several Spanish words introduced in this chapter. Write the translation for each numbered clue into the appropriate spaces in the puzzle grid. (See Appendix D for the answer key.)

Across

- **1** shoes
- **4** to travel
- **5** batteries
- **6** months
- **7** flight
- **9** suitcase
- **11** citizen
- **13** basement
- **14** to arrive
- **15** that depends
- **16** bus

Down

- **2** tourist
- **3** passport
- **8** luggage
- **9** backpack
- **10** tired
- **12** closet

Chapter 14

Dealing with Money in a Foreign Land

●●●

In This Chapter

▶ Checking out common terms related to money

▶ Getting money at the ATM

▶ Performing other currency transactions

▶ Exchanging dollars for pesos and other foreign currencies

●●●

$\mathbf{\mathit{y}}$ ou worked hard, you paid your dues, you earned that money. But you didn't go through all that effort just for the money. You worked for the money because it gives you the means to get not only what you need but also what you want. And now what you want is to travel to Mexico, Spain, or some other Spanish-speaking land to spend some of that money having a good time.

Well, you've come to the right place. In this chapter, you discover all the money-handling knowledge you need in all those Spanish-speaking places you plan to visit.

You probably made your money in dollars (U.S. or Canadian). If you're traveling in Latin America, you may feel that changing your money from your currency to the local currency will be confusing. As this chapter shows, financial transactions are quite a lot easier than you may suppose. That's good news!

Picking Up Common Money Terms

Just as you carry money in a purse or wallet so that you have some cash to eat out, buy souvenirs, and make other small purchases, you need to carry around some common terms and phrases about money so that you can effectively perform monetary transactions. Here are a few cash-carrying terms:

- **el banco** (ehl *bvahn*-koh) (*the bank*)
- **el billete** (ehl bvee-*yeh*-teh) (*the bill*)
- **el centavo** (ehl sehn-*tah*-bvoh) (*the cent*)
- **la compra** (lah *kohm*-prah) (*the purchase*)
- **el dinero** (ehl dee-*neh*-roh) (*the money*)
- **dinero en efectivo** (dee-*neh*-roh ehn eh-fehk-*tee*-bvoh) (*money in cash*)
- **en billetes** (ehn bvee-*yeh*-tehs) (*in bills*)
- **en monedas** (ehn moh-*neh*-dahs) (*in coins*)
- **la liquidación** (lah lee-kee-dah-see*ohn*) (*the sale [special sales event]*)
- **la moneda** (lah moh-*neh*-dah) (*the coin*)
- **una moneda de oro** (*ooh*-nah moh-*neh*-dah deh *oh*-roh) (*a gold coin*)
- **una moneda de plata** (*ooh*-nah moh-*neh*-dah deh *plah*-tah) (*a silver coin*)
- **el salario** (ehl sah-*lah*-reeoh) (*salary*)
- **la venta** (lah *bvehn*-tah) (*the sale [act of selling]*)

When you need to pay somebody for something, use the Spanish verb **pagar** (pah-*gahr*) (*to pay*). **Pagar** is a regular **-ar** verb, and its stem is **pag** (*pahg*). Here are the present tense conjugations of this useful transaction verb:

Conjugation	*Pronunciation*
yo pago	yoh *pah*-goh
tú pagas	tooh *pah*-gahs
él, ella, usted paga	ehl, *eh*-yah, oohs-*tehd pah*-gah
nosotros, nosotras pagamos	noh-*soh*-trohs, noh-*soh*-trahs pah-*gah*-mohs
vosotros, vosotras pagáis	bvoh-*soh*-trohs, bvoh-*soh*-trahs pah-*gah*ees
ellos, ellas, ustedes pagan	*eh*-yohs, *eh*-yahs, oohs-*teh*-dehs *pah*-gahn

The following little cash-carrying phrases also may come in handy:

¿Tienes algún dinero? (¿tee*eh*-nehs ahl-*goohn* dee-*neh*-roh?) (*Do you have any money?*)

¿Tienes dinero en efectivo? (¿tee*eh*-nehs dee-*neh*-roh ehn eh-fehk-*tee*-bvoh?) (*Do you have cash?*)

¿Tiene una moneda de cincuenta centavos? (¿tee*eh*-neh *ooh*-nah moh-*neh*-dah deh seen-kooh*ehn*-tah sehn-*tah*-bvohs?) (*Do you have a 50-cent coin?*)

No tenemos monedas. (noh teh-*neh*-mohs moh-*neh*-dahs.) (*We have no coins.*)

Necesitan dos monedas de diez centavos. (neh-seh-*see*-tahn dohs moh-*neh*-dahs deh dee*ehs* sehn-*tah*-bvohs.) (*They need two 10-cent coins.*)

Pagamos con dos billetes de veinte pesos. (pah-*gah*-mohs kohn dohs bvee-*yeh*-tehs deh bveh*een*-teh *peh*-sohs.) (*We paid with two 20-peso bills.*)

Aquí tiene un billete de cien colones. (ah-*kee* tee*eh*-neh oohn bvee-*yeh*-teh deh see*ehn* koh-*loh*-nehs.) (*Here you have a 100-colon bill.*)

Using an ATM

When they're in working order, ATMs (automated teller machines) can be a great way to handle your money. And more than 90 percent of the time, they do work very well.

ATMs are now available in cities and at resorts almost all over the world. They're the simplest and most discreet way to access your funds, and they may even provide a better exchange rate than a bank or currency exchange booth.

You can use your debit card and your credit card at an ATM. Simply go to the machine, punch in your personal identification number (PIN), get cash in the local currency, and on you go.

Here are some handy terms associated with ATMs:

- **la cantidad** (lah kahn-tee-*dahd*) (*the quantity, the amount*)
- **la cuenta** (lah kooh*ehn*-tah) (*the account*)
- **el débito** (ehl *deh*-bvee-toh) (*the debit*)
- **entregar** (ehn-treh-*gahr*) (*to deliver*)
- **introducir** (een-troh-dooh-*seer*) (*to insert*)
- **el número confidencial** (ehl *nooh*-meh-roh kohn-fee-dehn-see*ahl*) (*the PIN*)
- **el retiro** (ehl rreh-*tee*-roh) (*the withdrawal*)
- **el saldo** (ehl *sahl*-doh) (*the balance*)
- **la tarjeta** (lah tahr-*Heh*-tah) (*the card*)
- **teclear** (teh-kleh*ahr*) (*to type*)

We've seen ATMs that flash their signals in both Spanish and English. Just in case yours doesn't have the English display, here are the sentences you see in the order in which they appear:

Introduzca su tarjeta por favor. (een-troh-*doohs*-kah sooh tahr-*Heh*-tah pohr fah-*bvohr*.) (*Insert your card please.*)

Por favor teclee su número confidencial. (pohr fah-*bvohr* teh-*kleh*-eh sooh *nooh*-meh-roh kohn-fee-dehn-see*ahl*.) (*Please type your PIN.*)

At this point, you have to press the button that reads **Continuar** (*Continue*). After you press the button, you see the *main menu* **(menú principal),** like the one shown in Figure 14-1. Your options — **Definir las preferencias de QuickChoice** (*Set the Options of Quick Choice*) — will look something like the following, and you'll be instructed to *Select an option* **(Seleccione una opción):**

- **Estados de cuentas** (ehs-*tah*-dohs deh kooh*ehn*-tahs) (*Account Statements*)

- **Retiro en efectivo** (rreh-*tee*-roh ehn eh-fehk-*tee*-bvoh) (*Cash Withdrawal*)

- **Depósito** (deh-*poh*-see-toh) (*Deposit*)

- **Servicios adicionales** (sehr-*bvee*-seeohs ah-dee-seeoh-*nah*-lehs) (*Additional Services*)

- **Saldos de cuentas** (*sahl*-dohs deh kooh*ehn*-tahs) (*Account Balances*)

- **Dinero en efectivo rápido** (dee-*neh*-roh ehn eh-fehk-*tee*-bvoh *rrah*-pee-doh) (*Fast Cash*)

If you choose Cash Withdrawal, these other choices come up:

- **Tarjeta de crédito** (tahr-*Heh*-tah deh *kreh*-dee-toh) (*Credit card*)

- **Cuenta de cheques** (kooh*ehn*-tah deh *cheh*-kehs) (*Checking account*)

- **Débito/inversiones** (*deh*-bvee-toh/een-bvehr-see*oh*-nehs) (*Debit/investments*)

If you choose **Dinero en efectivo rápido** (*Fast Cash*), you're likely to be presented with options like the following:

- **100, 200, 300, 400, 500, 1000, 1500**

- **¿Otra cantidad?** (¿*oh*-trah kahn-tee-*dahd?*) (*Another amount?*)

Choose the desired amount, and your money comes out. Then you may see messages such as the following:

- **Entregado** (ehn-treh-*gah*-doh) (*Delivered*)

- **Saldo** (*sahl*-doh) (*Balance*)

- **Por favor tome su dinero** (pohr fah-*bvohr* *toh*-meh sooh dee-*neh*-roh) (*Please take your money*)

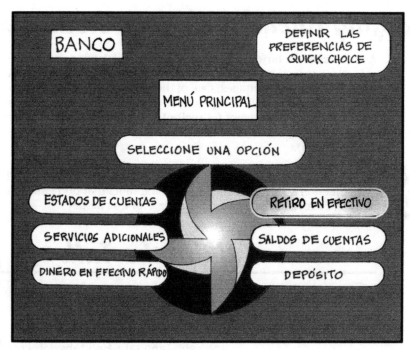

Figure 14-1:
A typical
ATM main
menu.

If you're slow about selecting an option, you may see messages such as

- ✔ **¿Requiere más tiempo?** (rreh-keee*eh*-reh mahs tee*ehm*-poh) (*Do you need more time?*)
- ✔ **Sí/No** (see/noh) (*Yes/No*)

Keep all the receipts that you get at the ATMs while traveling. If you get no receipt, or if you believe there has been an error in a transaction at an ATM, be sure to note the date, time, and place. Then, when you arrive home, check your information with your bank statement and follow your bank's policy for reporting such incidents.

On some occasions, the ATM may not work or may be out of cash. Or it can happen that the computer systems of the banks involved can't communicate (talk about not understanding a language!). When those situations occur, you can access your money only by using your credit card, as explained in the following section. These are also times when your traveler's checks come in handy. (See the section "Trading In Your Traveler's Checks" later in this chapter.)

Charging Ahead with Your Credit Card

A credit card **(la tarjeta de crédito)** (lah tahr-*Heh*-tah deh *kreh*-dee-toh) is a safe, clean way of handling money. Paying with your credit card when you travel has many advantages. One of them is that you don't have to carry cash; another is that your expenses are registered in your account. Plus, you always have a valid receipt **(el recibo)** (ehl rreh-*see*-bvoh). Problems arise only when you go to a place that doesn't take credit cards (or at least not the one you have).

Be aware that many places that take credit cards are a bit pricier than the ones that don't. You can often eat at restaurants that don't take credit cards and have excellent food and service for a lot less money.

Talkin' the Talk

Juan wants to pay for his purchase in a store. Here's how he finds out whether the store accepts his credit card. (Track 26)

Juan:	**¿Aceptan tarjetas de crédito?** ¿ah-*sehp*-tahn tahr-*Heh*-tahs deh *kreh*-dee-toh? *Do you take credit cards?*
Storekeeper:	**Con mucho gusto.** kohn *mooh*-choh *goohs*-toh. *With pleasure.*
Juan:	**Aquí tiene mi tarjeta.** ah-*kee* tee*eh*-neh mee tahr-*Heh*-tah. *Here is my card.*
Storekeeper:	**Un momento, vuelvo con su recibo.** oohn moh-*mehn*-toh, bvooh*ehl*-bvoh kohn sooh rreh-*see*-bvoh. *One moment, I'll be back with your receipt.*
	Firme aquí, por favor. *feer*-meh ah-*kee*, pohr fah-*bvohr*. *Sign here, please.*
	Aquí tiene su tarjeta y su recibo. Gracias. ah-*kee* tee*eh*-neh sooh tahr-*Heh*-tah ee sooh rreh-*see*-bvoh. *grah*-seeahs. *Here's your card and your receipt. Thank you.*

Words to Know

la tarjeta	lah tahr-_Heh_-tah	the card
firmar	feer-_mahr_	to sign

Trading In Your Traveler's Checks

Traveler's checks (**los cheques de viaje**) (lohs _cheh_-kehs deh bveeah-_Heh_) are another safe way to carry your money when you travel — you can often get the money replaced if the checks are lost or stolen. One inconvenience of traveler's checks is that you need to find the right place to cash them. Banks exchange them, and many currency exchange kiosks do as well. The better hotels also take traveler's checks.

Less-expensive hotels, restaurants, and stores may not take traveler's checks. Try to exchange your checks before you go on your forays and take just moderate amounts of cash with you.

Talkin' the Talk

Ana Maria is at a bank to cash in some traveler's checks. (Track 27)

Ana María: **¿Cuál es el cambio por dólar de los cheques de viaje?**
¿koo_ahl_ ehs eh _kahm_-bveeoh pohr _doh_-lahr deh lohs _cheh_-kehs deh bveeah-Heh?
What's the exchange per dollar for traveler's checks?

Cashier: **A nueve sesenta.**
ah nooh_eh_-bveh seh-_sehn_-tah.
_At $9.60._

Ana María: **Quiero cambiar estos cheques de viaje.**
kee_eh_-roh kahm-bvee_ahr_ ehs-tohs _cheh_-kehs deh bveeah-Heh.
I want to cash these traveler's checks.

Cashier: **¿Tiene sus documentos, por favor?**
¿tee_eh_-neh soohs doh-kooh-_mehn_-tohs, pohr fah-_bvohr_?
Do you have your identification please?

Ana María: **Mi pasaporte.**
              mee pah-sah-*pohr*-teh.
              My passport.

Cashier: **Muy bien. Ahora puede firmar sus cheques.**
              *moo*hee bveee*ehn.* ah-*oh*-rah pooheh-deh feer-*mahr*
              soohs *cheh*-kehs.
              Very good. Now you may sign your checks.

Words to Know

cambiar	kahm-bveeahr	to change
los documentos	lohs doh-kooh-mehn-tohs	identification (Literally: the documents)

Exchanging Your Dollars

Each country has its own currency **(la moneda)** (lah moh-*neh*-dah). When you travel, you generally need to use the local currency to make your transactions — businesses in some countries may not accept the dollar, and those that do typically do so because they can trick tourists into paying more for stuff when the dollar is strong relative to their currency.

When you want to exchange your dollars for the local currency, take a look at the signs telling you how much you'll get for your dollar. For example, you'll see signs stating

Dollar USA   Buy 9.70   Sell 9.80

This sign means the company or bank buys your dollars for 9.70 of the local currency. And if you want to buy dollars, they charge you 9.80 of their currency. So they're making (the equivalent of) ten cents of their currency on every dollar they handle. Don't get so hung up on the fee that you overlook the bottom line — what's most important is the amount you're getting back for each dollar.

The person who lends or exchanges money is called **el cambista** (ehl kahm-*bvees*-tah) (*money changer*). The exchange bureaus give you formal receipts, just as banks do; these receipts are the proofs of purchase you need if you discover that something is amiss with your money. So instead of exchanging your money on the street, look for the sign that says **cambio** (*kahm*-bveeoh) (*exchange*) so you know you're dealing with a legitimate entity.

These phrases come in handy when exchanging money:

> **¿Dónde puedo cambiar dólares?** (*¿dohn*-deh pooh*eh*-doh kahm-bvee*ahr doh*-lah-rehs?) (*Where can I exchange dollars?*)

> **Una cuadra a la derecha, hay una agencia.** (*ooh*-nah kooh*ah*-drah ah lah deh-*reh*-chah, ahy *ooh*-nah ah-*Hehn*-seeah.) (*One block to the right, there's an exchange bureau.*)

> **¿Dónde encuentro una casa de cambio?** (*¿dohn*-deh ehn-kooh*ehn*-troh *ooh*-nah *kah*-sah deh *kahm*-bveeoh?) (*Where can I find a place to exchange money?*)

In the following sections, we explain how to use the verb that means *to exchange,* and we name currencies in Spanish-speaking countries.

Changing money with the verb cambiar

In Spanish, *to change* and *to exchange* are expressed with the same verb, **cambiar** (kahm-bvee*ahr*). **Cambiar** is a regular verb, and its root is **cambi-** (*kahm*-bvee). Here's how you conjugate its present tense:

Conjugation	Pronunciation
yo cambio	yoh *kahm*-bveeoh
tú cambias	tooh *kahm*-bveeahs
él, ella, usted cambia	ehl, *eh*-yah, oohs-*tehd kahm*-bveeah
nosotros, nosotras cambiamos	noh-*soh*-trohs, noh-*soh*-trahs kahm-bvee*ah*-mohs
vosotros, vosotras cambiáis	bvoh-*soh*-trohs, bvoh-*soh*-trahs kahm-bvee*ah*hees
ellos, ellas, ustedes cambian	*eh*-yohs, *eh*-yahs, oohs-*teh*-dehs *kahm*-bveeahn

Try the following phrases to practice using cambiar:

> **En esa ventanilla cambian monedas.** (ehn *eh*-sah bvehn-tah-*nee*-yah *kahm*-bveeahn moh-*neh*-dahs.) (*At that window they change coins.*)

Quiero cambiar bolívares por dólares. (kee*eh*-roh kahm-bvee*ahr* bvoh-lee-bvah-rehs pohr *doh*-lah-rehs.) (*I want to exchange bolivars for dollars.*)

La casa de cambio te puede cambiar tus dólares. (lah *kah*-sah deh *kahm*-bveeoh teh pooh*eh*-deh kahm-bvee*ahr* toohs *doh*-lah-rehs.) (*The exchange house can exchange your dollars for you.*)

En el banco cambian dólares. (ehn ehl *bvahn*-koh *kahm*-bveeahn *doh*-lah-rehs.) (*At the bank they exchange dollars.*)

La comisión con que cambian es muy alta. (lah koh-mee-see*ohn* kohn keh *kahm*-bveeahn ehs *moo*hee *ahl*-tah.) (*The commission they charge for the exchange is very high.*)

Currency wise: Naming Latin American currencies

How can you impress your friends? Just ask them things like, "What is the name of the currency in Ecuador?" Take a look at Table 14-1 and then amaze your friends with your monetary knowledge.

Table 14-1	Latin American Currencies		
Country	*Currency*	*Prononunciation*	*English*
Argentina	**el peso argentino**	ehl *peh*-soh ahr-Hehn-*tee*-noh	*the Argentine peso*
Bolivia	**el boliviano**	ehl bvoh-lee-bvee*ah*-noh	*the boliviano*
Chile	**el peso chileno**	ehl *peh*-soh chee-*leh*-noh	*the Chilean peso*
Colombia	**el peso colombiano**	ehl *peh*-soh koh-lohm-bee*ah*-noh	*the Colombian peso*
Costa Rica	**el colón**	ehl koh-*lohn*	*the colón*
Cuba	**el peso cubano**	ehl *peh*-soh kooh-*bah*-noh	*the Cuban peso*
	el peso cubano convertible	ehl *peh*-soh kooh-*bvah*-noh kohn-bvehr-*tee*-bvleh	*the convertible Cuban peso*
Dominican Republic	**el peso**	ehl *peh*-soh	*the peso*
Ecuador	**el dólar**	ehl *doh*-lahr	*the dollar* (Ecuador uses the U.S. dollar)

Country	Currency	Pronunication	English
El Salvador	el dólar	ehl *doh*-lahr	*the dollar* (El Salvador uses the U.S. dollar)
Guatemala	el quetzal	ehl keh-*tsahl*	*the quetzal*
Honduras	el lempira	ehl lehm-*pee*-rah	*the lempira*
México	el peso	ehl *peh*-soh	*the peso*
Nicaragua	el córdoba	ehl *kohr*-doh-bvah	*the córdoba*
Panamá	el balboa	ehl bvahl-*bvoh*-ah	*the balboa*
	el dólar	ehl *doh*-lahr	*the dollar* (Panamá uses the U.S. dollar)
Paraguay	el guaraní	ehl goohah-rah-*nee*	*the guaraní*
Perú	el sol	ehl sohl	*the sol*
Puerto Rico	el dólar ameri-cano	ehl *doh*-lahr ah-meh-ree-*kah*-noh	*the U.S. dollar*
Spain	el euro	ehl *eh*ooh-roh	*the euro*
Uruguay	el peso	ehl *peh*-soh	*the peso*
Venezuela	el bolívar	ehl bvoh-*lee*-bvahr	*the bolívar*

Fun & Games

A quick-change artist (aren't we punny?) has rearranged the letters in several Spanish money words. Unscramble the words and then match them with their English translations.

al promca   account

al tanev   balance

cibore   bills

damones   cash

dolsa   coins

entuac   credit card

ernoid   money

jetarat ed droticé   PIN

le canob   receipt

ne votecife   the bank

romeún fendicclaion   the purchase

sibellet   the sale

tireor   withdrawal

Chapter 15

Getting Around: Planes, Trains, Taxis, and More

In This Chapter

▶ Buying tickets and bringing things with you

▶ Getting through the airport or train station

▶ Making your way through a customs checkpoint

▶ Navigating public transportation

▶ Driving a car

▶ Being early/late/on time (and waiting if necessary)

*W*hen you're traveling to and around in foreign countries, one of the biggest challenges you face is getting from point A to point B. If the signs are in English or use some sort of international symbols, that certainly helps, but you still need to be able to purchase a ticket, tell a taxi driver where you want to go, and get on the right bus. In this chapter, we help you get from point A to point B via plane, train, bus, and rental car — hopefully on schedule.

Purchasing Tickets

Whether you're traveling by airplane, train, bus, or even by boat, you typically need to purchase a ticket to board the vehicle. This transaction usually requires you to know your numbers, dates, and times (see Chapter 4) and the foreign currency (see Chapter 14). Before you head to the ticket booth, brush up on the following phrases:

Voy a Puerto Escondido. (bvohy ah pooh*ehr*-toh ehs-kohn-*dee*-doh.) (*I am going to Puerto Escondido.*)

Quiero comprar un boleto. (kee-*eh*-roh kohm-*prahr* oohn bvoh-*leh*-toh.) (*I want to purchase a ticket.*)

¿**Cuánto cuesta un boleto a Puerto Escondido?** (¿kooh*ahn*-toh
koohe*hs*-tah oohn bvoh-*leh*-toh ah pooh*ehr*-toh ehs-kohn-*dee*-doh?)
(*How much is a ticket to Puerto Escondido?*)

¿**A qué hora sale?** (¿ah keh *oh*-rah *sah*-leh?) (*What time does it leave?*)

¿**Cuándo llega a Puerto Escondido?**) (¿kooh*ahn*-doh *yeh*-gah ah
pooh*ehr*-toh ehs-kohn-*dee*-doh?) (*When does it arrive in Puerto
Escondido?*)

Necesito facturar una maleta. (neh-seh-*see*-toh fahk-tooh-*rahr* ooh-nah
mah-*leh*-tah.) (*I need to check in one suitcase.*)

¿**Dónde necesito estar para embarcar?** (¿*dohn*-deh neh-seh-*see*-toh
ehs-*tahr* pah-rah ehm-bvahr-*kahr?*) (*Where do I need to be to board?*)

Bringing Things with the Verb Traer

A useful, albeit irregular, verb is **traer** (*trah*-ehr) (*to bring*). You're always
bringing something (especially when you travel), and someone often brings
things to you. For example, you bring a camera to photograph your vacation;
at the restaurant, a waiter brings you your food and drink. Here's how you use
traer in the present tense:

Conjugation	*Pronunciation*
yo traigo	yoh *trah*ee-goh
tú traes	tooh *trah*-ehs
él, ella, usted trae	ehl, *eh*-yah, oohs-*tehd trah*-eh
nosotros, nosotras traemos	noh-*soh*-trohs, noh-*soh*-trahs trah-*eh*-mohs
vosotros, vosotras traéis	bvoh-*soh*-trohs, bvoh-*soh*-trahs trah-*eh*ees
ellos, ellas, ustedes traen	*eh*-yohs, *eh*-yahs, oohs-*teh*-dehs *trah*-ehn

It's always good to practice a new verb. Here are some phrases to try:

Traigo una cámara. (*trah*ee-goh ooh-nah *kah*-mah-rah.) (*I'm bringing a
camera.*)

¿**Traes las fotos?** (¿*trah*-ehs lahs *foh*-tohs?) (*Are you bringing the photos?*)

Lo que traemos no es problema. (loh keh trah-*eh*-mohs noh ehs
proh-*bvleh*-mah.) (*There's no problem with what we're bringing.*)

Traen cosas de uso personal. (*trah*-ehn *koh*-sahs deh *ooh*-soh
pehr-soh-*nahl.*) (*They bring things for their personal use.*)

Making Your Way through the Airport

If you happen to reach your destination by air, the personnel at the airport **(el aeropuerto)** (ehl aeh-roh-pooh*ehr*-toh) can help you get where you're going. While your luggage is being unloaded, you first go to the area where your identity papers are checked. Here are some phrases that you may hear during this process:

> **Pase a migración.** (*pah*-seh a mee-grah-see*ohn*.) (*Go to migration.*)

> **Pase a inmigración.** (*pah*-seh a een-mee-grah-see*ohn*.) (*Go to immigration.*)

> **Pase por aquí con su pasaporte en la mano.** (*pah*-seh pohr ah-*kee* kohn sooh pah-sah-*pohr*-teh ehn lah *mah*-noh.) (*Go this way with your passport in your hand.*)

You may have some specific questions of your own, especially if you need to catch a connecting flight to your final destination:

> **¿Van a transferir las maletas al vuelo de enlace?** (¿bvahn ah trahns-feh-*reer* lahs mah-*leh*-tahs ahl bvooh*eh*-loh deh ehn-*lah*-seh?) (*Will my luggage be transferred to the connecting flight?*)

> **¿Dónde voy a embarcar para el vuelo de enlace?** (¿*dohn*-deh bvohy ah ehm-bvahr-*kahr* pah-rah ehl bvooh*eh*-loh deh ehn-*lah*-seh?) (*Where will I board for my connecting flight?*)

> **¿Está a tiempo el vuelo de enlace?** (¿ehs-*tah* ah tee*ehm*-poh ehl bvooh*eh*-loh deh ehn-*lah*-seh?) (*Is my connecting flight on time?*)

> **¿Dónde recojo mis maletas?** (¿*dohn*-deh rreh-*koh*-Hoh mees mah-*leh*-tahs?) (*Where do I pick up my luggage?*)

If you need to wait in line to speak with an immigration officer at the airport, you can get ready to answer some of these questions that the officer may ask you:

> **¿Me permite su pasaporte?** (¿meh pehr-*mee*-teh sooh pah-sah-*pohr*-teh?) (*May I have your passport?*)

> **¿De dónde viene?** (¿deh *dohn*-deh bvee*eh*-neh?) (*Where do you come from?*)

> **¿En qué vuelo llegó?** (¿ehn keh bvooh*eh*-loh yeh-*goh*?) (*What flight did you come on?*)

> **¿Adónde va?** (¿ah-*dohn*-deh bvah?) (*Where are you going?*)

> **¿Cuánto tiempo quiere quedarse en el país?** (¿kooh*ahn*-toh tee*ehm*-poh kee*eh*-reh keh-*dahr*-seh ehn ehl pah*ees*?) (*How long do you want to stay in the country?*)

¿**Cuánto dinero trae consigo?** (¿koohahn-toh dee-neh-roh trah-eh kohn-see-goh?) (*How much money do you have with you?* [Literally: *How much money do you bring with you?*])

¡**Que tenga una feliz estadía!** (¡keh tehn-gah ooh-nah feh-lees ehs-tah-dee-ah!) (*Have a happy stay!*)

¡**Que lo pase muy bien!** (¡keh loh pah-seh moohee bveeehn!) (*Have a good time!*)

Pase a la aduana, por favor. (pah-seh ah lah ah-doohah-nah, pohr fah-bvohr.) (*Go on to customs, please.*)

Getting Around on the Train

Train travel is likely to be more common wherever you happen to be visiting than it is in the United States, so when you reach your destination, look for the nearest train station. The following sections can help you successfully navigate your visit to the train station.

Finding the train station

If you're looking for the train station, here are some phrases that can help:

¿**Dónde está la estación del tren?** (¿dohn-deh ehs-tah lah ehs-tah-seeohn dehl trehn?) (*Where's the train station?*)

¿**Cómo llego a la Estación Central?** (¿koh-moh yeh-goh ah lah ehs-tah-seeohn sehn-trahl?) (*How do I get to the Central Station?*)

Lléveme por favor a la estación del tren. (yeh-bveh-meh pohr fah-bvohr ah lah ehs-tah-seeohn dehl trehn.) (*Please take me to the train station.*)

Checking your documents on the train

As you're traveling on the train between two countries, the ticket collector comes at some moment and says such things as

¿**Me permiten sus pasaportes por favor?** (¿meh pehr-mee-tehn soohs pah-sah-pohr-tehs pohr fah-bvohr?) (*May I have your passports, please?*)

Me llevo sus pasaportes un rato. (meh yeh-bvoh soohs pah-sah-pohr-tehs oohn rrah-toh.) (*I'll take your passports for a while.*)

Aquí tienen de vuelta sus pasaportes. (ah-kee teeeh-nehn deh bvoohehl-tah soohs pah-sah-pohr-tehs.) (*Here are your passports back.*)

Aquí tienen sus formularios de aduana. (ah-*kee* tee*eh*-nehn soohs fohr-mooh-*lah*-reeohs deh ah-dooh*ah*-nah.) (*Here are your customs forms.*)

Llenen por favor el cuestionario. (*yeh*-nehn pohr fah-*bvohr* ehl koohehs-teeoh-*nah*-reeoh.) (*Please fill in the questionnaire.*)

Al llegar, llévelo a la aduana. (ahl yeh-*gahr* yeh-bveh-loh ah lah ah-dooh*ah*-nah.) (*When you arrive, take it to customs.*)

Talkin' the Talk

 Sonia has decided to travel to La Paz, in Bolivia. She's at the train station and wants to buy her ticket. (Track 28)

Sonia:	**Un boleto para La Paz, por favor.** oohn bvoh-*leh*-toh *pah*-rah lah pahs, pohr fah-*bvohr*. *One ticket for La Paz, please.*
Window attendant:	**¿Primera, segunda, o tercera clase?** ¿pree-*meh*-rah, seh-*goohn*-dah, oh tehr-*seh*-rah *klah*-seh? *First, second, or third class?*
Sonia:	**Primera clase, por favor.** pree-*meh*-rah *klah*-seh, pohr fah-*bvohr*. *First class, please.*
Window attendant:	**Son quinientos pesos, por favor.** sohn kee-neee*ehn*-tohs *peh*-sohs, pohr fah-*bvohr*. *That's 500 pesos, please.*
Sonia:	**Aquí los tiene. ¿A qué hora sale el tren?** ah-*kee* lohs tee*eh*-neh. ¿ah keh *oh*-rah *sah*-leh ehl trehn? *Here [is the money]. What time does the train leave?*
Window attendant:	**Sale a las 12:15.** *sah*-leh ah lahs *doh*-seh *keen*-seh. *It leaves at 12:15.*
Sonia:	**¿De qué andén sale?** ¿deh keh ahn-*dehn sah*-leh? *What platform does it leave from?*

Window attendant:	**Del andén número dos.** dehl ahn-*dehn nooh*-meh-roh dohs. *From Platform Two.*
Sonia:	**Muchas gracias, señor.** *mooh*-chahs *grah*-seeahs, seh-*nyor.* *Thank you very much, sir.*
Window attendant:	**De nada. ¡Que tenga un buen viaje!** deh *nah*-dah. ¡keh *tehn*-gah oohn bvooh*ehn* bvee*ah*-Heh! *You're welcome. Have a good trip!*

Words to Know

el boleto	ehl bvoh-<u>leh</u>-toh	the ticket
primera clase	pree-<u>meh</u>-rah <u>klah</u>-seh	first class
salir	sah-<u>leer</u>	to exit; to get out
el tren	ehl trehn	the train
andén	ahn-<u>dehn</u>	platform
¡Que tenga un buen viaje!	¡keh <u>tehn</u>-gah oohn bvooh<u>ehn</u> bvee<u>ah</u>-Heh!	Have a good trip!

Dealing with the Customs Office

When you buy your tickets, ask about the customs regulations for your destination. Each country has its own rules. Your travel agency or the consulate of the country you're visiting can give you all the customs-related information you need without any charge. Customs officers in the countries that you're likely to visit are more often than not concerned with things like cigarettes, alcoholic beverages, weapons, electrical equipment, and antique art of national interest. Take care not to carry any items that may be prohibited by law.

In the following sections, we explain how to deal with declarations and duties and register electronic equipment.

Before you embark on your journey, look up your destination country at `travel.state.gov`. This site features late-breaking travel warnings, loads of information that can steer you clear of trouble, and contact information for U.S. consulates.

Handling declarations and duties

Declare (write on the form or verbally acknowledge) anything you have that may be subject to duties or may be suspect in any way. In most cases, for example, when things are for your personal use, you can take them into the country without paying duties. The customs officials ultimately decide whether you owe any duties.

Here are some phrases to know when dealing with duties:

> **¿Este objeto paga derechos?** (*¿ehs*-teh ohbv-*Heh*-toh *pah*-gah deh-*reh*-chohs?) (*Does one pay duties on this item? [Literally: Does this object pay duties?]*)

> **¿Cuánto se paga en derechos por este objeto?** (*¿kooh*ahn*-toh se pah*-gah ehn deh-*reh*-chohs pohr *ehs*-teh ohbv-*Heh*-toh?) (*How much in duties does one pay for this thing [object]?*)

> **Debe pagar impuestos.** (*deh*-bveh pah-*gahr* eem-pooh*ehs*-tohs.) (*You have to pay duty/taxes.*)

> **Está libre de impuestos.** (ehs-*tah lee*-bvreh de eem-pooh*ehs*-tohs.) (*It's duty free.*)

Remember, the customs officer isn't out to get you. He's simply being paid to see that people don't bring unwanted or illegal items into the country.

Never joke around with a customs officer. He also has to control his sense of humor. He's there for serious business.

Talkin' the Talk

Here, Juan Carlos meets with a customs officer. (Track 29)

Customs officer: **¿Tiene algo que declarar?**
¿teee*eh*-neh *ahl*-goh keh deh-klah-*rahr?*
Do you have anything to declare?

Juan Carlos: **No, no tengo nada que declarar.**
noh, noh *tehn*-goh *nah*-dah keh deh-klah-*rahr.*
No, I have nothing to declare.

Customs officer:	**¿Trae algún material explosivo?**
	¿trah-eh ahl-goohn mah-teh-reeahl ehks-ploh-see-bvoh?
	Do you have anything explosive? [Literally: *Do you bring any explosive materials?*]
	¿Trae alguna bebida alcohólica?
	¿trah-eh ahl-gooh-nah bveh-bvee-dah ahl-koh-oh-lee-kah?
	Do you have any alcoholic beverages?
	¿Trae algún aparato eléctrico?
	¿trah-eh ahl-goohn ah-pah-rah-toh eh-lehk-tree-koh?
	Do you have any electrical devices?
Juan Carlos:	**Sólo para mi uso personal.**
	soh-loh pah-rah mee ooh-soh pehr-soh-nahl.
	Only for my personal use.
Customs officer:	**Muy bien, pase. Que disfrute su estadía.**
	moohee bveeehn, pah-seh. keh dees-frooh-teh sooh ehs-tah-dee-ah.
	Very good, go [this way]. Enjoy your stay.

Words to Know

¿Tiene algo que declarar?	¿teeeh-neh ahl-goh keh deh-klah-rahr?	Do you have any thing to declare?
algún material explosivo	ahl-goohn mah-teh-reeahl ehks-ploh-see-bvoh	anything explosive
bebida alcohólica	bveh-bvee-dah ahl-koh-oh-lee-kah	alcoholic beverage
aparato eléctrico	ah-pah-rah-toh eh-lehk-tree-koh	electrical device
uso personal	ooh-soh pehr-soh-nahl	personal use
Que disfrute su estadía.	keh dees-frooh-teh sooh ehs-tah-dee-ah.	Enjoy your stay.

Registering electrical equipment

Some countries may require that you register the serial numbers of your camera, video camera, or computer. Come to think of it, you also benefit from having that registration paper and knowing what you brought with you into the country.

Generally, you have to take the registered objects out with you (and only you) when you leave the country you're visiting. At that time, you have to show the registration documents that you got when you arrived. This step is also good — you do want to keep your goodies, don't you?

The idea behind registration is that the country's government doesn't want you to sell (or otherwise give away) or leave your dutiable objects in the country you're visiting. For obvious reasons, it doesn't want its citizens to access goods that have no duty paid on them.

Here are some phrases you may need to know when registering your electrical equipment:

Por favor llene este formulario. (pohr fah-*bvohr yeh*-neh *ehs*-teh fohr-mooh-*lah*-reeoh.) (*Please fill in this form.*)

¿Cuáles son los aparatos eléctricos que tenemos que registrar? (¿kooh*ah*-lehs sohn lohs ah-pah-*rah*-tohs eh-*lehk*-tree-kohs keh teh-*neh*-mohs keh rreh-Hees-*trahr?*) (*Which electrical devices do we have to register?*)

Al salir del país, debe presentar este formulario. (ahl sah-*leer* dehl pah*eehs*, *deh*-bveh preh-sehn-*tahr* ehs-teh fohr-mooh-*lah*-reeoh.) (*When you exit the country, you must show this form.*)

Puede pasar hacia la salida. (pooh*eh*-deh *pah*-sahr *ah*-seeah lah sah-*lee*-dah.) (*You may proceed to the exit.*)

Talkin' the Talk

The customs officer needs to see the contents of Peter's luggage.

Customs officer: **Necesitamos revisar sus maletas.**
neh-seh-see-*tah*-mohs rreh-bvee-*sahr* soohs mah-*leh*-tahs.
We need to see your suitcases.

¿Cúantas piezas tiene?
¿koohah*n*-tahs peee*eh*-sahs teee*eh*-neh?
How many pieces do you have?

Peter: **Tengo dos maletas.**
tehn-go dohs mah-*leh*-tahs.
I have two suitcases.

Customs officer: **Póngalas aquí por favor.**
pohn-gah-lahs ah-*kee* pohr fah-*bvohr.*
Put them here please.

Peter: **Aquí están.**
ah-*kee* ehs-*tahn.*
Here they are.

Customs officer: **Por favor abra esta maleta.**
pohr fah-*bvohr ah*-bvrah *ehs*-tah mah-*leh*-tah.
Please open this suitcase.

Peter: **En seguida.**
ehn seh-*gee*-dah.
Right away.

Customs officer: **¿Esto, qué es?**
¿*ehs*-toh, keh ehs?
What's this?

Peter: **Es mi máquina de afeitar eléctrica.**
ehs mee *mah*-kee-nah deh ah-fehee-*tahr*
eh-*lehk*-tree-kah.
It's my electric razor.

Customs officer: **¿Trae alguna cámara fotográfica?**
¿*trah*-eh ahl-*gooh*-nah *kah*-mah-rah
foh-toh-*grah*-fee-kah?
Do you have a camera?

                    ¿Tiene cámara de video?
¿*teeeh*-neh *kah*-mah-rah deh bvee-*deh*-oh?
Do you have a video camera?

Peter: **Aquí lo tengo.**
ah-*kee* loh *tehn*-goh.
Here [I have it].

Customs officer: **¿Trae computadora portátil?**
¿*trah*-eh kohm-pooh-tah-*doh*-rah
pohr-*tah*-teel?
Did you bring a laptop computer?

Peter: **Aquí está.**
ah-_kee_ ehs-_tah._
Here it is.

Customs officer: **Por favor pase a registrarlos en la oficina A.**
pohr fah-_bvohr pah_-seh ah rreh-Hees-_trahr_-lohs ehn lah oh-fee-_see_-nah ah.
Please go register them [your equipment] at office A.

Words to Know

revisar	rreh-bvee-<u>sahr</u>	to go through
las maletas	lahs mah-<u>leh</u>-tahs	the suitcases
las piezas	lahs pee<u>eh</u>-sahs	the pieces
abrir	ah-<u>bvreer</u>	to open
afeitar	ah-fehee-<u>tahr</u>	to shave
la cámara fotográfica	lah <u>kah</u>-mah-rah foh-toh-<u>grah</u>-fee-kah	camera
la cámara de video	lah <u>kah</u>-mah-rah deh bvee-<u>deh</u>-oh	the video camera
la computadora portátil	lah kohm-pooh-tah-<u>doh</u>-rah pohr-<u>tah</u>-teel	the laptop computer

Hailing a Taxi or Boarding a Bus

Whether you came by plane or train, you're going to leave the airport or station and search for a taxi, a bus, or the car rental office. In the following sections, we talk about taking a taxi and a bus; see the later section "Driving in a Foreign Land" for driving details.

Arranging for a taxi

These phrases help you make the arrangements you need for a taxi:

¿Dónde encuentro un taxi? (¿*dohn*-deh ehn-kooh*ehn*-troh oohn *tahk*-see?) (*Where do I find a taxi?*)

¿Hay una parada de taxis? (¿ahy *ooh*-nah pah-*rah*-dah deh *tahk*-sees?) (*Is there a taxi stop?*)

¿Pago aquí el taxi? (¿*pah*-goh ah-*kee* ehl *tahk*-see?) (*Do I pay the taxi here?*)

No. Paga el taxi al llegar a su destino. (noh. *pah*-gah ehl *tahk*-see ahl yeh-*gahr* ah sooh dehs-*tee*-noh.) (*No. You pay the taxi when you arrive at your destination.*)

Getting the bus to take you there

Here are some phrases that are useful to know when you need to take a bus from the airport or train station:

¿Hay una parada de buses? (¿ahy *ooh*-nah pah-*rah*-dah deh *bvooh*-sehs?) (*Is there a bus stop?*)

¿Hay buses para ir al centro? (¿ahy *bvooh*-sehs *pah*-rah eer ahl *sehn*-troh?) (*Are there buses for downtown?*)

¿Se compran los boletos antes? (¿seh *kohm*-prahn lohs bvoh-*leh*-tohs ahn-tehs?) (*Do I buy the tickets beforehand?*)

Getting Around with Additional Public Transportation

When you need to get around in a large city, your primary mode of travel is either your own two feet or some sort of public transportation — buses, subways, or trolleys. Following are some phrases to help you navigate the public transportation system. The places we're talking about in this section are in Buenos Aires.

En esta ciudad hay buses y trolebuses. (ehn *ehs*-tah seeooh-*dahd* ahy *bvooh*-sehs ee troh-leh-*bvooh*-sehs.) (*In this city there are buses and trolleybuses.*)

En Buenos Aires hay trenes subterráneos. (ehn bvooh*eh*-nohs *ah*ee-rehs ahy *treh*-nehs soohbv-teh-*rrah*-neh-ohs.) (*There are subways in Buenos Aires.*)

El mapa del subte está en la estación. (ehl *mah*-pah dehl *soohbv*-teh ehs-*tah* ehn lah ehs-tah-see*ohn*.) (*The subway map is in the station.*)

Sale en la estación de Callao. (*sah*-leh ehn lah ehs-tah-see*ohn* deh kah-*yah*-oh.) (*You go out at Callao station.*)

¿Aquí para el bus de Palermo? (¿ah-*kee pah*-rah ehl bvoohs deh pah-*lehr*-moh?) (*Does the Palermo bus stop here?*)

¿Este bus va por Rivadavia? (¿*ehs*-teh bvoohs bvah pohr rree-bvah-*dah*-bveeah?) (*Does this bus go on Rivadavia?*)

Hay que hacer cola. (ahy keh ah-*sehr koh*-lah.) (*You have to line up.*)

¿Qué bus tomo para Caballito? (¿keh bvoohs *toh*-moh *pah*-rah kah-bvah-*yee*-toh?) (*What bus do I take for Caballito?*)

¿El cuarenta me deja en Rivadavia con La Rural? (¿ehl koohah-*rehn*-tah meh *deh*-Hah ehn rree-bvah-*dah*-bveeah kohn lah rrooh-*rahl*?) (*Does [bus] number 40 leave me at Rivadavia and La Rural?*)

Getting around in a city can be fun but also confusing. Fortunately, many people are willing to give directions. Just ask, and you'll get answers. Most people love to help. See Chapter 7 for more about asking for and understanding directions.

Driving in a Foreign Land

Having your own car or a rental wherever you are provides you with much more freedom of movement, but obtaining a valid driver's license, understanding cryptic road signs, and actually renting a car can be a bit challenging. In the following sections, we assist you in overcoming those obstacles.

In Mexico, Spain, and most Latin American countries, you drive on the right side of the road as you do in the United States and Canada.

Getting a valid driver's license

Some countries, including Mexico, accept your valid driver's license **(licencia de conducir)** (lee-*sehn*-seeah deh kohn-dooh-*seer*) from your home country. Other countries may require an International Driver's License. You can get one from the American and Canadian automobile drivers' associations (like AAA), regardless of whether you're a member. The association itself can tell you which countries require an International Driver's License.

Deciphering road signs

Most road signs **(señales de tráfico)** (seh-*nyah*-lehs deh *trah*-fee-koh) in Latin America are based on symbols rather than words. This system makes them very easy to understand, no matter what language you speak. In fact, most driving signs have become quite universal; they're much the same everywhere:

- A *do not enter* sign is a circle in a red field, crossed by a diagonal line.
- A stop sign is always an octagonal red field with black borders. Inside is a word such as **pare** (*pah*-reh) (*stop*) or **alto** (*ahl*-toh) (*stop*), rather than the English word "stop."
- On the highway, left turns and right turns are indicated with signs that have a diamond shape with an arrow bent in the direction of the turn. A turn sign with a diagonal across it means *no turn.*

Figure 15-1 shows some common road signs that have words rather than symbols. Check out the following list for help in understanding these signs:

- **Alto** (*ahl*-toh) (*Stop*)
- **Ceda El Paso** (*seh*-dah ehl *pah*-soh) (*Yield*)
- **Conserve Su Derecha** (kohn-*sehr*-bveh sooh deh-*reh*-chah) (*Keep Right*)
- **Cruce De Ferrocarril** (*krooh*-seh deh *feh*-rroh kah-*rreel*) (*Railroad Crossing*)
- **Curva Peligrosa** (*koohr*-bvah peh-lee-*groh*-sah) (*Dangerous Curve*)
- **Despacio** (dehs-*pah*-seeoh) (*Slow*)
- **No Hay Paso** (noh ahy *pah*-soh) (*Road Closed*)
- **No Rebase** (noh rreh-*bah*-seh) (*No Passing*)
- **No E** (noh eh) (*No Parking*)
- **100 KM Máxima** (seeehn kee-*loh*-meh-trohs *mahk*-see-mah) (*Maximum Speed 100 Kilometers Per Hour*)
- **Tope** (*toh*-peh) (*Speed Bump*)

Ask at the car rental office whether you should expect any road signs that you don't understand.

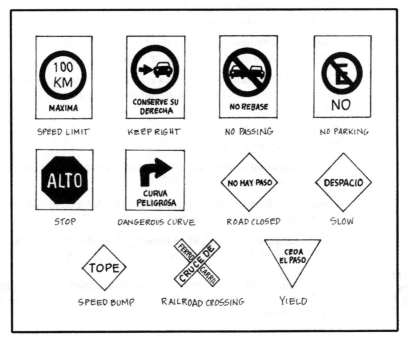

Figure 15-1:
Some
common
road signs
in Spanish.

Renting a car

Whether you're at the airport or on the street, the following two questions can come in handy when you need to rent **(arrendar)** (ah-rrehn-*dahr*) a car:

> **¿Dónde arriendan autos?** (¿*dohn*-deh ah-rreee*ehn*-dahn *a*hooh-tohs?) (*Where do they rent cars?*)

> **¿Hay oficina de renta de autos?** (¿ahy oh-fee-*see*-nah deh *rrehn*-tah deh *a*hooh-tohs?) (*Is there a car rental office?*)

Now you come to the nitty gritty of trying to rent a car. Here are some things you can say when inquiring about a rental car:

> **Quiero arrendar un auto.** (kee*eh*-roh ah-rrehn-*dahr* oohn *a*hooh-toh.) (*I want to rent a car.*)

> **¿Me puede dar la lista de precios?** (¿meh poo*eh*-deh dahr lah *lees*-tah deh *preh*-seeohs?) (*Can you give me the price list?*)

> **¿Cuánto cuesta al día?** (¿koo*ahn*-toh koo*ehs*-tah ahl *dee*-ah?) (*How much does it cost per day?*)

¿Cuánto cuesta por semana? (¿koohahn-toh koohehs-tah pohr seh-mah-nah?) (*How much does it cost per week?*)

¿Cuántos kilómetros puedo andar? (¿koohahn-tohs kee-loh-meh-trohs pooheh-doh ahn-dahr?) (*How many kilometers may I go?*)

¿Cuántos kilómetros por litro da este auto? (¿koohahn-tohs kee-loh-meh-trohs pohr lee-tro dah ehs-teh ahooh-toh?) (*How many kilometers per liter does this car get?*)

¿Cuánto cuesta el seguro? (¿koohahn-toh koohehs-tah ehl seh-gooh-roh?) (*How much is the insurance?*)

¿Tiene mapas de la región? (¿teeeh-neh mah-pahs deh lah rreh-Heeohn?) (*Do you have maps of the region?*)

¿Dónde está la rueda de repuesto? (¿dohn-deh ehs-tah lah rrooheh-dah deh rreh-poohehs-toh?) (*Where's the spare tire?*)

¿Dónde tengo que devolver el auto? (¿dohn-deh tehn-goh keh deh-bvohl-bvehr ehl ahooh-toh?) (*Where do I have to return the car?*)

TIP

If you plan to rent a car during your trip, try to find out whether arranging the rental from your home base before you go has any advantages for you. Generally, it's cheaper.

In the following sections, we describe the parts of a car in Spanish and provide handy questions to ask at the car rental office about driving conditions and roads.

Talking about the car

Whether you're renting a car or run into problems on the road, you may need to reference parts of the car. Table 15-1 provides the basic terminology.

Table 15-1	Parts of a Car	
Spanish	*Pronunciation*	*English*
Exterior		
el espejo lateral	ehl ehs-peh-Hoh lah-teh-rahl	*the sideview mirror*
el espejo retrovisor	ehl ehs-peh-Hoh rreh-troh-bvee-sohr	*the rearview mirror*
los faros delanteros	lohs fah-rohs deh-lahn-teh-rohs	*the headlights*
los limpiaparabrisas	lohs leem-peeah-pah-rah-bvree-sahs	*the windshield wipers*
el neumático	ehl nehooh-mah-tee-koh	*the tire*
el parabrisas	ehl pah-rah-bvree-sahs	*the windshield*
la puerta	lah poohehr-tah	*the door*

Spanish	Pronunciation	English
la rueda	lah rrooh*eh*-dah	*the wheel*
Interior		
el claxón	ehl klahk-*sohn*	*the horn*
el freno de mano	ehl *freh*-noh deh *mah*-noh	*the parking brake*
la guantera	lah goohahn-*teh*-rah	*the glove compartment*
el interruptor de encendido	ehl een-teh-rroohp-*tohr* deh ehn-sehn-*dee*-doh	*the ignition switch*
la palanca de cambio	lah pah-*lahn*-kah deh *kahm*-bveeoh	*the gearshift lever*
la palanca de limpiaparabrisas	lah pah-*lahn*-kah deh leem-peeah-pah-rah-*bvree*-sahs	*the windshield wiper lever*
el parasol	ehl pah-rah-*sohl*	*the sun visor*
el pedal del acelerador	ehl peh-*dahl* dehl ah-seh-leh-rah-*dohr*	*the gas pedal/ accelerator*
el pedal del embrague	ehl peh-*dahl* dehl ehm-*bvrah*-geh	*the clutch pedal*
el pedal de los frenos	ehl peh-*dahl* deh lohs *freh*-nohs	*the brake pedal*
el velocímetro	ehl bveh-loh-*see*-meh-troh	*the speedometer*
el volante	ehl bvoh-*lahn*-teh	*the steering wheel*

Getting the scoop on driving conditions

You also want to know about the driving conditions in the area you're visiting. These phrases can help you get the information you need:

¿Es difícil manejar por aquí? (¿ehs dee-*fee*-seel mah-neh-*Hahr* pohr ah-*kee?*) (*Is it hard to drive around here?*)

¿Hay que tener mucha prudencia? (¿ahy keh teh-*nehr* mooh-chah prooh-*dehn*-seeah?) (*Do you have to be very prudent/careful?*)

¿Habrá mucho tráfico en la mañana? (¿ah-*bvrah* mooh-choh *trah*-fee-koh ehn lah mah-*nyah*-nah?) (*Will there be much traffic in the morning?*)

¿Cuál es la mejor hora para salir de la ciudad? (¿kooh*ahl* ehs lah meh-*Hohr* oh-rah *pah*-rah sah-*leer* deh lah seeooh-*dahd?*) (*Which is the best time to get out of the city?*)

Asking questions about the road

The people at the car rental office may know something about the roads that you're about to explore. Here are some questions and answers you may get while you and the agent are looking at a map (see Chapter 7 for more about maps):

¿Están pavimentados los caminos? (¿ehs-*tahn* pah-bvee-mehn-*tah*-dohs lohs kah-*mee*-nohs?) (*Are the roads paved?*)

No todos. Estos son de tierra/terracería. (noh *toh*-dohs ehs-tohs sohn deh teee*h*-rrah/teh-rrah-seh-*ree*-ah.) (*Not all of them. These are dirt roads.*)

Esos caminos tienen muchos baches. (*eh*-sohs kah-*mee*-nohs teee*h*-nehn *mooh*-chohs *bvah*-chehs.) (*Those roads have a lot of potholes.*)

Estos caminos son excelentes. (*eh*-sohs kah-*mee*-nohs sohn ehk-seh-*lehn*-tehs.) (*Those roads are excellent.*)

Hay autopista. (ahy ahooh-toh-*pees*-tah.) (*There's a freeway.*)

Son caminos de cuotas/de peaje. (sohn kah-*mee*-nohs deh koohoh-tahs/ deh peh-*ah*-Heh.) (*They're toll roads.*)

Scheduling Issues: Running Late, Early, or On Time

No matter what mode of transportation you're using, it's helpful to know what kind of schedule you're on and whether you can reach your destination on time. The following list contains phrases to know when you want to schedule something and need to know whether something or someone is on time:

- **a la hora** (ah lah *oh*-rah) (*on time*)
- **adelantado** (ah-deh-lahn-*tah*-doh) (*[running] early*)
- **atrasado** (ah-trah-*sah*-doh) (*[running] late*)
- **el horario** (ehl oh-*rah*-reeoh) (*the schedule*)
- **es tarde** (ehs *tahr*-deh) (*it's [arriving] late*)
- **es temprano** (ehs tehm-*prah*-noh) (*it's [arriving] early*)

The word **tarde** (*tahr*-deh) has different meanings depending on whether you use the article. It's an adjective meaning *late* when you use it without an article, such as in the following example:

Ellos llegaron tarde. (*eh*-yohs yeh-*gah*-rohn *tahr*-deh.) (*They arrived late.*)

But when it's accompanied by the article **la, tarde** is the noun *afternoon*, such as in these examples:

Ellos llegaron a las dos de la tarde. (*eh*-yohs yeh-*gah*-rohn ah lahs dohs deh lah *tahr*-deh.) (*They arrived at 2:00 p.m. [2:00 in the afternoon].*)

Prefieren venir por la tarde. (preh-feee*h*-rehn bveh-*neer* pohr lah *tahr*-deh.) (*They prefer to come in the afternoon.*)

Sometimes the posted or printed schedule for a bus, train, or plane isn't up-to-date, and you may need to ask someone about it with the question **¿Está a tiempo el tren?** (¿ehs-*tah* ah tee*ehm*-poh ehl trehn?) (*Is the train on time?*), substituting whatever mode of transportation you're inquiring about. Here are some responses you may hear where scheduling phrases come into play:

Hay que esperar; está atrasado. (ahy keh ehs-peh-*rahr;* ehs-*tah* ah-trah-*sah*-doh.) (*You have to wait; it's late.*)

El vuelo llegó adelantado. (ehl bvooh*eh*-loh yeh-*goh* ah-deh-lahn-*tah*-doh.) (*The flight came in early.*)

El reloj está adelantado. (ehl rreh-*lohH* ehs-*tah* ah-deh-lahn-*tah*-doh.) (*The clock is fast.*)

El bus va adelantado. (ehl bvoohs bvah ah-deh-lahn-*tah*-doh.) (*The bus goes early.*)

El tren va a llegar a la hora. (ehl trehn bvah ah yeh-*gahr* ah lah *oh*-rah.) (*The train will arrive on time.*)

Esperan porque va a llegar tarde. (ehs-*peh*-rahn *pohr*-keh bvah a yeh-*gahr* tahr-deh.) (*They're waiting because it will arrive late.*)

El bus viene a la hora. (ehl bvoohs bvee*eh*-neh ah lah *oh*-rah.) (*The bus comes on time.*)

Talkin' the Talk

Susana asks for help from the airline information attendant.

Susana:	**Necesito saber, ¿cuándo sale el avión para Mendozo?**
	neh-seh-*see*-toh sah-*bvehr,* ¿koohahn-doh sah-leh ehl ah-bvee*ohn pah*-rah mehn-*doh*-soh?
	I need to know, when does the plane leave for Mendoza?
Information attendant:	**Espérame un momento. Busco la información en el horario de vuelos.**
	ehs-*peh*-rah-meh oohn moh-*mehn*-toh. bvoos-koh lah een-fohr-mah-see*ohn* ehn ehl oh-*rah*-reeoh deh bvooh*eh*-lohs.
	Wait just a moment. I'm looking for the information in the schedule of flights.

Susana:	**Gracias. También favor de chequear si es un vuelo directo.**
	grah-seeahs. tahm-bvee*ehn* fah-*bvohr* deh cheh-keh-*ahr* see ehs oohn bvooheh-loh dee-*rehk*-toh.
	Thanks. Also please check if it's a direct flight.

Information attendant:	**Según el horario, sale a las tres de la tarde y es un vuelo directo.**
	seh-*goohn* ehl oh-*rah*-reeoh, *sah*-leh ah lahs trehs deh lah *tahr*-deh ee ehs oohn bvooheh-loh dee-*rehk*-toh.
	According to the schedule, it leaves at 3:00 p.m. and it's a direct flight.

Susana:	**Necesito tener prisa, ya son las dos y media.**
	neh-seh-*see*-toh teh-*nehr* pree-sah, yah sohn lahs dohs ee *meh*-deeah.
	I need to hurry, it's already 2:30.

Information attendant:	**Ud. tiene buena suerte. La puerta está muy cerca.**
	oohs-*tehd* teee*eh*-neh bvooh*eh*-nah sooh*ehr*-teh. lah pooh*ehr*-tah ehs-*tah* moohee *sehr*-kah
	You have good luck. The gate is very close.

Words to Know

el avión	ehl ah-bvee<u>ohn</u>	the plane
chequear	cheh-keh-<u>ahr</u>	to check
buena suerte	bvooh<u>eh</u>-nah sooh<u>ehr</u>-teh	good luck
la puerta	lah pooh<u>ehr</u>-tah	the door, the gate (at an airport)
cerca	<u>sehr</u>-kah	near, close (by)
tener prisa	teh-<u>nehr</u> <u>pree</u>-sah	to hurry

Waiting with the Verb Esperar

Esperar (ehs-pehr-*ahr*) is the verb of *hoping* and *waiting* — maybe you're waiting because you're hoping, or perhaps you're hoping that you won't be waiting much longer. In any case, **esperar** is a regular verb, easy to handle, as shown in the following present-tense conjugation. The root of this verb is **esper-** (ehs-*pehr*).

Conjugation	Pronunciation
yo espero	yoh ehs-*peh*-roh
tú esperas	tooh ehs-*peh*-rahs
él, ella, usted espera	ehl, *eh*-yah, oohs-*tehd* ehs-*peh*-rah
nosotros, nosotras esperamos	noh-*soh*-trohs, noh-*soh*-trahs ehs-peh-*rah*-mohs
vosotros, vosotras esperáis	bvoh-*soh*-trohs, bvoh-*soh*-trahs ehs-peh-*rah*ees
ellos, ellas, ustedes esperan	*eh*-yohs, *eh*-yahs, oohs-*teh*-dehs ehs-*peh*-rahn

Esperar que (ehs-*peh*-rahr keh) is *hoping.* **Esperar** plain and simple is *waiting.* Here are some phrases to practice:

> **Deben esperar el avión.** (*deh*-bvehn ehs-peh-*rahr* ehl ah-bvee*ohn*.) (*They must wait for the plane.*)

> **Espero que le guste mi auto.** (ehs-*peh*-roh keh leh *goohs*-teh mee a*hooh*-toh.) (*I hope you like my car.*)

> **Espero que venga el taxi.** (ehs-*peh*-roh keh *bvehn*-gah ehl *tahk*-see.) (*I hope the taxi comes.*)

> **Espero el taxi.** (ehs-*peh*-roh ehl *tahk*-see.) (*I'm waiting for the taxi.*)

> **Espera el camión de Insurgentes.** (ehs-*peh*-rah ehl kah-mee*ohn* deh een-soohr-*Hehn*-tehs.) (*He waits for the Insurgentes bus.* [Mexico])

> **Esperamos en la cola.** (ehs-peh-*rah*-mohs ehn lah *koh*-lah.) (*We're waiting in the line.*)

> **No esperamos más el bus.** (noh ehs-peh-*rah*-mohs mahs ehl bvoohs.) (*We won't wait for the bus any longer.*)

Fun & Games

Here are illustrations of the outside and inside of a typical car. Your job: Label the parts in Spanish. See Appendix D for the answers.

a. _____   k. _____

b. _____   l. _____

c. _____   m. _____

d. _____   n. _____

e. _____   o. _____

f. _____   p. _____

g. _____   q. _____

h. _____   r. _____

i. _____   s. _____

j. _____   t. _____

Chapter 16

Finding a Place to Stay

. . . .

In This Chapter

▶ Reserving a room at a hotel or motel

▶ Checking into your room

▶ Going to sleep and waking up with the verbs **dormir** and **despertarse**

▶ Requesting towels, soap, sheets, and other stuff

. . . .

When you're travelling abroad, one of your most essential needs is a place to stay. If you have friends living in your host country, you're all set — staying anywhere else would be bordering on an insult. If you don't know someone at your destination, you need to secure accommodations at a hotel, a motel, or a hostel (depending on your budget) and then communicate with the clerk and other personnel to make sure all your needs are met.

This chapter provides the terms and phrases you need to navigate your stay in a hotel or motel.

Making Lodging Reservations

Whether you make your hotel or motel reservation over the phone or in person, you need to know a few key phrases, including the following:

> **¿Cuánto cobran por noche?** (¿kooh*ahn*-toh *koh*-bvrahn pohr *noh*-cheh?) (*How much do you charge per night?*)

> **¿Cuántas personas pueden quedarse en la habitación?** (¿kooh*ahn*-tahs pehr-*soh*-nahs pooh*eh*-dehn keh-*dahr*-seh ehn lah ah-bvee-tah-see*ohn?*) (*How many people can stay in the room?*)

> **¿Aceptan tarjetas de crédito?** (¿ah-*sehp*-tahn tahr-*Heh*-tahs deh *kreh*-dee-toh?) (*Do you accept credit cards?*)

> **¿Cuáles tarjetas de crédito aceptan?** (¿kooh*ah*-lehs tahr-*Heh*-tahs deh *kreh*-dee-toh ah-*sehp*-tahn?) (*Which credit cards do you accept?*)

> **Quiero reservar una habitación por tres noches.** (kee*eh*-roh rreh-sehr-*bvahr ooh*-nah ah-bvee-tah-see*ohn* pohr trehs *noh*-chehs.) (*I want to reserve a room for three nights.*)

Quiero . . . (kee*eh*-roh . . .) (*I want . . .*)

> **. . . una habitación cerca de la piscina.** (. . . *ooh*-nah ah-bvee-tah-see*ohn sehr*-kah deh lah pee-*see*-nah.) (. . . *a room near the pool.*)

> **. . . una habitación en la planta baja.** (. . . *ooh*-nah ah-bvee-tah-see*ohn* ehn lah *plahn*-tah *bvah*-Hah.) (. . . *a room on the ground floor.*)

> **. . . una habitación de no fumadores.** (. . . *ooh*-nah ah-bvee-tah-see*ohn* deh noh fooh-mah-*doh*-rehs.) (. . . *a non-smoking room.*)

> **. . . dos camas, por favor.** (. . . dohs *kah*-mahs pohr fah-*bvohr*.) (. . . *two beds, please.*)

> **. . . una cama doble.** (. . . *ooh*-nah *kah*-mah *doh*-bvleh.) (. . . *a double bed.*)

> **. . . una cama grande.** (. . . *ooh*-nah *kah*-mah *grahn*-deh.) (*a queen-size bed.*)

> **. . . una cama extragrande.** (. . . *ooh*-nah *kah*-mah ehks-trah-*grahn*-deh.) (. . . *a king-size bed.*)

¿Está el hotel cerca de . . . (¿ehs-*tah* ehl *oh*-tehl *sehr*-kah deh . . .) (*Is the hotel near . . .*)

> **. . . la playa?** (. . . lah *plah*-yah?) (. . . *the beach?*)

> **. . . el mercado?** (. . . ehl mehr-*kah*-doh?) (. . . *the market?*)

> **. . . la ciudad?** (. . . lah seeooh-*dahd?*) (. . . *the city?*)

> **. . . el teatro?** (. . . ehl teh-*ah*-troh?) (. . . *the theater?*)

¿Tienen las habitaciones aire acondicionado? (¿tee*eh*-nehn lahs ah-bvee-tah-see*oh*-nehs *ah*ee-reh ah-kohn-dee-seeoh-*nah*-doh?) (*Do the rooms have air conditioning?*)

Talkin' the Talk

Anita has just arrived in town, and she's at the front desk of a large hotel. She asks for a room for the night. (Track 30)

Anita:	**Necesito una habitación por favor.** neh-seh-*see*-toh *ooh*-nah ah-bvee-tah-see*ohn* pohr fah-*bvohr*. *I need a room please.*
Receptionist:	**¿Le gusta una habitación hacia la calle o hacia el patio?** ¿leh *goohs*-tah *ooh*-nah ah-bvee-tah-see*ohn ah*-seeah lah *kah*-yeh oh *ah*-seeah ehl *pah*-teeoh? *Do you like a room facing the street or the patio?*

Anita: **Prefiero hacia el patio.**
preh-fee*eh*-roh *ah*-seeah ehl *pah*-teeoh.
I prefer it toward the patio.

Receptionist: **Las del patio son muy tranquilas. Las habitaciones hacia el patio cuestan cuarenta pesos, sin desayuno.**
lahs dehl *pah*-teeoh sohn *mooh*ee trahn-*kee*-lahs. lahs ah-bvee-tah-see*oh*-nehs *ah*-seeah ehl *pah*-teeoh kooh*ehs*-tahn koohah-*rehn*-tah *peh*-sohs, seen deh-sah-*yooh*-noh.
The patio rooms are very quiet. The rooms facing the patio cost 40 pesos, without breakfast.

Anita: **¿En el primer piso?**
¿ehn ehl pree-*mehr* pee-soh?
On the first floor?

Receptionist: **No, las del segundo piso. Las del primero son a cincuenta pesos.**
noh, lahs dehl seh-*goohn*-doh pee-soh. lahs dehl pree-*meh*-roh sohn a seen-kooh*ehn*-tah *peh*-sohs.
No, the second floor ones. The first floor rooms are priced at 50 pesos.

Anita: **Prefiero una en el primer piso.**
preh-fee*eh*-roh *ooh*-nah ehn ehl pree-*mehr* pee-soh.
I prefer one on the first floor.

Receptionist: **Muy bien, señora.**
*mooh*ee bvee*ehn*, seh-nyoh-rah.
Very well, madam.

Words to Know

una habitación	<u>ooh</u>-nah ah-bvee-tah-see<u>ohn</u>	a room
hacia	<u>ah</u>-seeah	toward
preferir	preh-feh-<u>reer</u>	to prefer
tranquila	trahn-<u>kee</u>-lah	quiet
desayuno	deh-sah-<u>yooh</u>-noh	breakfast
el piso	ehl <u>pee</u>-soh	the floor

Checking Out the Hotel before Checking In

By the time you get to your hotel, you're likely to be tired from your travels. However, regardless of how tired you are, seeing the rooms before you check in is a good idea. Checking out the hotel's rooms before you check in is an even better idea if you're coming to a city or town where the tastes and levels of cleanliness may differ from your own — especially when the hotel is less than four stars. The advantage of such hotels is that they're much less expensive than the ones you book beforehand.

Knowing the following phrases before you arrive at your hotel can make getting a room much easier.

- **al interior** (ahl een-teh-ree*ohr*) (*opening to the interior*)
- **a la calle** (ah lah *kah*-yeh) (*opening to the street*)
- **con agua caliente** (kohn *ah*-goohah kah-lee*ehn*-teh) (*with hot water*)
- **con baño** (kohn *bvah*-nyoh) (*with bathroom*)
- **sólo con agua fría** (*soh*-loh kohn *ah*-goohah *free*-ah) (*with cold water only*)

Sometimes Spanish has two words for the same thing. For example, **la habitación** (lah ah-bvee-tah-see*ohn*) and **el cuarto** (ehl kooh*ahr*-toh) both mean *the room*. We've chosen to use **la habitación** in this chapter when discussing hotel room selections, but be aware that **el cuarto** is perfectly interchangeable.

Talkin' the Talk

Anita wants to be able to relax in her room. But first, she needs to make sure that it has a private bath. Otherwise, she may need to change her plans.

Receptionist: **La habitación ciento diecinueve está en el segundo patio. Es una habitación preciosa.**
lah ah-bvee-tah-see*ohn* seee*ehn*-toh deee*eh*-see-nooh*eh*-bveh ehs-*tah* ehn ehl seh-*goohn*-doh *pah*-teeoh. ehs *ooh*-nah ah-bvee-tah-see*ohn* preh-see*oh*-sah.
Room 119 is on the second patio. It's a gorgeous room.

Anita: **¿Tiene baño?**
¿teee*eh*-neh *bvah*-nyoh?
Does it have a [private] bath?

Receptionist: **Sí. Pase, por aquí está el baño.**
see. *pah*-seh, pohr ah-*kee* ehs-*tah* ehl *bvah*-nyoh.
Yes. The bathroom is this way.

Anita: **¿El baño no tiene tina?**
¿ehl *bvah*-nyoh noh teee*eh*-neh *tee*-nah?
The bathroom doesn't have a bathtub?

Receptionist: **No. Como hace calor, aquí la gente prefiere ducharse.**
noh. *koh*-moh *ah*-seh kah-*lohr*, ah-*kee* lah *Hehn*-teh preh-feee*eh*-reh dooh-*chahr*-seh.
No. Because it's hot, people here prefer to shower.

Anita: **¿Hay agua caliente?**
¿ahy *ah*-goohah kah-leee*ehn*-teh?
Is there hot water?

Receptionist: **Sí, hay agua caliente y fría todo el día.**
see, ahy *ah*-goohah kah-leee*hn*-teh ee *free*-ah *toh*-doh ehl *dee*-ah.
Yes, there's hot and cold water all day long.

Words to Know

preciosa	preh-see*oh*-sah	gorgeous, beautiful; lovely
el baño	ehl <u>bvah</u>-nyoh	the bath; the bathroom
la tina	lah <u>tee</u>-nah	the tub
ducharse	dooh-<u>chahr</u>-seh	to take a shower
caliente	kah-lee<u>ehn</u>-teh	hot
fría	<u>free</u>-ah	cold (with feminine noun)

Registering at Your Hotel

After you decide to take a room, you're often required to complete a short registration form **(el formulario de registración)** (ehl fohr-mooh-*lah*-reeoh deh rreh-Hees-trah-see*ohn*). Here are some terms to know when filling out your hotel registration form:

- **dirección permanente** (dee-rehk-see-*ohn* pehr-mah-*nehn*-teh) (*permanent address*)

- **calle, ciudad, y estado o provincia** (*kah*-yeh, seeooh-*dahd,* ee ehs-*tah*-doh oh proh-*bveen*-seeah) (*street, city, and state or province*)

- **país, código postal, teléfono** (pah*ees*, *koh*-dee-goh pohs-*tahl*, teh-*leh*-foh-noh) (*country, zip code, telephone*)

- **número de su pasaporte** (*nooh*-meh-roh deh sooh pah-sah-*pohr*-teh) (*your passport number*)

- **si viene con vehículo . . .** (see bvee*eh*-neh kohn bveh*ee*-kooh-loh . . .) (*if coming by vehicle . . .*)

- **número de placa de matrícula** (*nooh*-meh-roh deh *plah*-kah deh mah-*tree*-kooh-lah) (*plate number*)

- **fecha en que vence** (*feh*-chah ehn keh *bvehn*-seh) (*expiration date*)

Talkin' the Talk

Anita likes the hotel; there's plenty on TV, and the room is really nice. Now she needs to take care of the arrangements and check in. (Track 31)

Anita:	**Me gusta la habitación ciento diecinueve. La voy a tomar.** meh *goohs*-tah lah ah-bvee-tah-see*ohn* seeehn-toh-dee*eeh*-see-nooh*eh*-bveh. lah bvohy ah toh-*mahr*. *I like Room 119. I'm going to take it.*
Receptionist:	**¿Cuántas noches desea quedarse?** ¿kooh-*ahn*-tahs *noh*-chehs deh-*seh*-ah keh-*dahr*-seh? *How many nights do you want to stay?*
Anita:	**Me quedo por tres noches.** meh *keh*-doh pohr trehs *noh*-chehs. *I'm staying three nights.*

Receptionist:	**Haga el favor de registrarse.** *ah*-gah ehl fah-*bvohr* deh rreh-Hees-*trahr*-seh. *Please check in.*
	El desayuno no está incluido en el precio. ¿Va a hacer un depósito por la primera noche? ehl deh-sah-*yooh*-noh noh ehs-*tah* een-kloohee-doh ehn ehl *preh*-seeoh. ¿bvah ah *ah*-sehr oohn deh-*poh*-see-toh pohr lah pree-*meh*-rah *noh*-cheh? *Breakfast isn't included in the price. Are you going to make a deposit for the first night?*
Anita:	**Sí, lo voy a pagar.** see, loh bvohy ah pah-*gahr*. *Yes, I'll pay it.*
Receptionist:	**¿Cómo quiere usted pagar, con tarjeta o en efectivo?** ¿*koh*-moh keee*eh*-reh oohs-*tehd* pah-*gahr*, kohn tahr-*Heh*-tah oh enh eh-fehk-*tee*-bvoh? *How do you want to pay, with credit card or cash?*
Anita:	**Voy a pagar con mi tarjeta de crédito.** bvoy ah pah-*gahr* kohn mee tahr-*Heh*-tah deh *kreh*-dee-toh. *I'm going to pay with my credit card.*
Receptionist:	**Está bien. ¿Tiene completado el formulario de registración?** ehs-*tah* bvee*ehn*. ¿tee*eh*-neh kohm-pleh-*tah*-doh ehl fohr-mooh-*lah*-reeoh deh rreh-Hees-trah-see*ohn*? *That's fine. Have you completed the registration form?*
Anita:	**Sí, llené toda la información.** see, yeh-*neh* *toh*-dah lah een-fohr-mah-see*ohn*. *Yes, I filled in all the information.*
Receptionist:	**Gracias. Aquí está la llave para su habitación.** *grah*-seeahs. ah-*kee* ehs-*tah* lah *yah*-bveh *pah*-rah sooh ah-bvee-tah-see*ohn*. *Thank you. Here's the key for your room.*

Words to Know

quedarse	keh-<u>dahr</u>-seh	to stay
registrarse	rreh-Hees-<u>trahr</u>-seh	to check in
incluido	een-kloo<u>hee</u>-doh	included
el precio	ehl <u>preh</u>-seeoh	the price
un depósito	oohn deh-<u>poh</u>-see-toh	a deposit
con tarjeta o en efectivo	kohn tahr-<u>Heh</u>-tah oh ehn eh-fehk-<u>tee</u>-bvoh	with credit card or cash
completado	kohm-pleh-<u>tah</u>-doh	completed
llenar	yeh-<u>nahr</u>	to fill out, to fill in (information)
la llave	lah <u>yah</u>-bveh	the key

Sleeping with the Verb Dormir

After a long day, the sweet hour when you can finally rest and go to sleep comes. In Spanish, **dormir** (dohr-*meer*) (*to sleep*) is a bit irregular, much like a really tired person. **Dormir** is a stem-changing verb of the *-o* to *-ue* variety (see Chapter 6 for an introduction to stem-changing verbs).

In the following conjugation of the present tense of **dormir,** notice the differences between the singular and plural first person verb forms.

Conjugation	*Pronunciation*
yo duermo	yoh dooh*ehr*-moh
tú duermes	tooh dooh*ehr*-mehs
él, ella, usted duerme	ehl, *eh*-yah, oohs-*tehd* dooh*ehr*-meh
nosotros, nosotras dormimos	noh-*soh*-trohs, noh-*soh*-trahs dohr-*mee*-mohs
vosotros, vosotras dormís	bvoh-*soh*-trohs, bvoh-*soh*-trahs dohr-*mees*
ellos, ellas, ustedes duermen	*eh*-yohs, *eh*-yahs, oohs-*teh*-dehs dooh*ehr*-mehn

Here are some phrases to help you practice using **dormir:**

> **Yo duermo ocho horas todos los días.** (yoh dooh*ehr*-moh *oh*-choh *oh*-rahs *toh*-dohs lohs *dee*-ahs.) (*I sleep eight hours every day.*)

> **Camilo duerme en su cama.** (kah-*mee*-loh dooh*ehr*-meh ehn sooh *kah*-mah.) (*Camilo sleeps in his bed.*)

> **Dormimos en nuestra casa.** (dohr-*mee*-mohs ehn nooh*ehs*-trah *kah*-sah.) (*We sleep in our home.*)

> **Los invitados duermen en tu recámara.** (lohs een-bvee-*tah*-dohs dooh*ehr*-mehn ehn tooh rreh-*kah*-mah-rah.) (*The guests sleep in your bedroom.* [Mexico])

> **Dos gatos duermen en mi cama.** (dohs *gah*-tohs dooh*ehr*-mehn ehn mee *kah*-mah.) (*Two cats sleep in my bed.*)

Waking Up with the Verb Despertarse

You use the reflexive verb **despertarse** (dehs-pehr-*tahr*-seh) (*to awaken*) after a good night's sleep. (Chapter 3 gives you the lowdown on reflexive verbs.) You can tell that this verb is irregular when you see that the root of the verb in the first person singular form is different from that of the first person plural. This verb is a stem-changing verb of the *e* to *ie* variety (see Chapter 6 for more about stem-changing verbs).

Conjugation	*Pronunciation*
yo me despierto	yoh meh dehs-pee*ehr*-toh
tú te despiertas	tooh teh dehs-pee*ehr*-tahs
él, ella, usted se despierta	ehl, *eh*-yah, oohs-*tehd* seh dehs-pee*ehr*-tah
nosotros, nosotras nos despertamos	noh-*soh*-trohs, noh-*soh*-trahs nohs dehs-pehr-*tah*-mohs
vosotros, vosotras os despertáis	bvoh-*soh*-trohs, bvoh-soh-trahs ohs dehs-pehr-*tah*ees
ellos, ellas, ustedes se despiertan	*eh*-yohs, *eh*-yahs, oohs-*teh*-dehs seh dehs-pee*ehr*-tahn

Las mañanitas

In Mexico, someone may sing (with a band) morning songs under the window of the person that he or she wants to wake up and serenade. **Mañanita** (mah-nyah-*nee*-tah) is the Spanish word for this kind of song. In fact, every child knows a **mañanita** sung specially for birthdays, and more for the celebrations of the names of saints who coincide with people's birthdays.

You understand the previous conjugations, but you say, "I either wake up or I don't. How can I practice using this verb?" The following examples show you how to start using **despertarse:**

> **Yo me despierto temprano en la mañana.** (yoh meh dehs-pee*ehr*-toh tehm-*prah*-noh ehn lah mah-*nyah*-nah.) (*I wake up early in the morning.*)

> **Se despierta con el canto de los pájaros.** (seh dehs-pee*ehr*-tah kohn ehl *kahn*-toh deh lohs *pah*-Hah-rohs.) (*He awakens with the birds' singing.*)

> **Ellos no se despiertan de noche.** (*eh*-yohs noh seh dehs-pee*ehr*-tahn deh *noh*-cheh.) (*They don't wake up at night.*)

> **Ustedes se despiertan juntos.** (*oohs*-teh-dehs seh dehs-pee*ehr*-tahn *Hoohn*-tohs.) (*You* [formal] *wake up together.*)

Asking for Towels and Other Essentials

Whether you're staying in a hotel or motel in your mother country or in a foreign land, you may run out of essentials or need more of something like towels or clean sheets. When you need something, head to the front desk and ask:

> **Por favor puedo tener . . .** (pohr fah-*bvohr* pooh*eh*-doh teh-*nehr* . . .) (*May I please have . . .*)

followed by the item you want:

- **champú** (chahm-*pooh*) (*shampoo*)
- **dos toallas** (dohs toh-*ah*-yahs) (*two towels*)
- **papel higiénico** (pah-*pehl* ee-Hee*eh*-nee-koh) (*toilet paper*)
- **una pastilla de jabón** (*ooh*-nah pahs-*tee*-yah deh Hah-*bvohn*) (*a bar of soap*)
- **sábanas limpias** (*sah*-bvah-nahs *leem*-peeahs) (*clean sheets*)

- ✔ **suavizante** (soohah-bvee-*sahn*-teh) (*conditioner*)
- ✔ **una toallita** (*ooh*-nah toh-ah-*yee*-tah) (*a washcloth*)
- ✔ **un vaso** (oohn *bvah*-soh) (*a glass*)

Fun & Games

The following word search contains several Spanish words from this chapter. The English translations are listed here; find the Spanish equivalents and circle them. (See Appendix D for the answer key.)

```
B A L G N O C Q S A V E K Y L
Q O J O S O E D N C H A M P Ú
I I E A I L E I E I T T W Q Q
F D V C L N C E E S W T H A B
B O E G S S C I L H A H C V A
L R W Z I B L L J K S Y S G Ñ
P M J P Z Z J N U W K A U N O
D I R E C C I Ó N I L H S N V
M R E D J H M W A L D H H B O
N B P M A P V K A E Q O F O R
G A N F K K C O W Q B V X G R
B L A C O S T A R S E R B F Y
D E S P E R T A R S E M D R B
H A B I T A C I Ó N P S D Í N
F T B L W T W R V E S R M A S
```

bathroom

breakfast

to wake (oneself) up

address

to sleep

cold

room

shampoo

glass

included

to go to bed

swimming pool

price

towels

Chapter 17

Handling Emergencies

. . . .

In This Chapter

▶ Asking for help

▶ Communicating about health issues

▶ Dealing with legal problems

▶ Declining help if you don't need it

. . . .

*B*e prepared. That's the Boy Scout motto, and it's not a bad idea for any situation. You should always be prepared for emergencies, especially where you don't speak the native language. A language barrier can complicate an emergency, and part of your preparedness training for traveling to a foreign land is to learn the necessary words and phrases to ensure that doesn't happen.

This chapter looks at two main areas where you may experience an emergency:

 ✔ The first part of the chapter deals with health concerns such as breaking an arm or experiencing the stomach flu.

 ✔ The second part deals with legal emergencies — car accidents and other law infractions that may require the help of your consulate, the police, or a lawyer.

Shouting for Help

Before you start preparing for emergencies, you need to know a few important words that can quickly get you the help you need. You may find yourself in a situation in which you need to cry for help. Thumbing through your dictionary isn't quick enough, so memorize these words. You can use both versions of *Help!* interchangeably.

- ✔ **¡Auxilio!** (¡ahooh-*ksee*-leeoh!) (*Help!*)
- ✔ **¡Ayúdeme!** (¡ah-*yooh*-deh-meh!) (*Help me!*)
- ✔ **¡Incendio!** (¡een-*sehn*-deeoh!) (*Fire!*)
- ✔ **¡Inundación!** (¡ee-noohn-dah-see*ohn*!) (*Flood!*)
- ✔ **¡Maremoto!** (¡mah-reh-*moh*-toh!) (*Tidal wave!*)
- ✔ **¡Socorro!** (¡soh-*koh*-rroh!) (*Help!*)
- ✔ **¡Temblor!** (¡tehm-*bvlohr*!) (*Earth tremor!*)
- ✔ **¡Terremoto!** (¡teh-rreh-*moh*-toh!) (*Earthquake!*)

You can help speed up your request by using one of these two words:

- ✔ **¡Apúrese!** (¡ah-*pooh*-reh-seh!) (*Hurry up!*)
- ✔ **¡Rápido!** (¡*rrah*-pee-doh!) (*Quick!*)

What to say when the pot falls

You see a flower pot falling from a balcony while someone is passing by. What do you shout? All Spanish-speakers, with the exception of Mexicans, react to

   ¡Cuidado! (¡koohee-*dah*-doh) (*Watch out!* [Literally: *Care!*])

When the flower pot is falling in Mexico, however, you have to say

¡Aguas! (¡*ah*-goohahs!) (*Watch out!* [Literally: *Waters!*])

This habit most likely comes from the times when drains were nonexistent, so people in colonial cities simply tossed their dirty water out the second-floor window. They shouted **¡Aguas!** to warn passersby that dirty water was coming their way. Eventually, the habit of shouting **¡Aguas!** extended to all danger.

Handling Health Problems

When an illness or an accident jeopardizes your health, feeling overwhelmed is a common and understandable reaction, especially when you're in a foreign land where you can't explain your symptoms or problems in your native tongue. In the following sections, we guide you through some potential situations in a calm and prudent manner. Table 17-1 lists some common terms you may need to know in a medical emergency.

Table 17-1		Medical Terms
Spanish	*Pronunciation*	*English*
la ambulancia	lah ahm-bvooh-*lahn*-seeah	*the ambulance*
el analgésico	ehl ah-nahl-*Heh*-see-koh	*the painkiller*
la anestesia	lah ah-nehs-*teh*-seeah	*the anesthesia*
la camilla	lah kah-*mee*-yah	*the stretcher; the trolley; the gurney*
el corte	ehl *kohr*-teh	*the cut*
el dolor	ehl doh-*lohr*	*the pain*
el/la enfermo/a	ehl/lah ehn-*fehr*-moh/mah	*the sick person*
enyesar	ehn-yeh-*sahr*	*to set in a cast*
la fractura	lah frahk-*tooh*-rah	*the fracture/broken bone*
la herida	lah eh-*ree*-dah	*the wound*
el mareo	ehl mah-*reh*-oh	*the dizziness*
el/la médico/a	ehl/lah *meh*-dee-koh/kah	*the doctor*
los puntos	lohs *poohn*-tohs	*the stitches (surgical)*
la radiografía	lah rrah-deeoh-grah-*fee*-ah	*the x-ray picture*
los rayos X	lohs *rrah*-yohs *eh*-kees	*the x-rays*
sangrar	sahn-*grahr*	*to bleed*
el yeso	ehl *yeh*-soh	*the plaster (cast)*

If you get sick while traveling, ask for advice at your hotel's reception desk. Also, if you ask for a doctor who speaks English and are introduced to one, try to make sure that the doctor's English is better than your Spanish before you get involved with him or her. If you're having trouble being understood in English or Spanish, ask for another doctor whose language skills more nearly match your own.

Helping out with the verb ayudar

The verb **ayudar** (ah-yooh-*dahr*) (*to help*), is, as you'd expect, a very helpful word to know. It's a regular verb of the **-ar** variety, so it's very easy to conjugate. Here it is in the present tense:

Conjugation	Pronunciation
yo ayudo	yoh ah-*yooh*-doh
tú ayudas	tooh ah-*yooh*-dahs
él, ella, usted ayuda	ehl, *eh*-yah, oohs-*tehd* ah-*yooh*-dah
nosotros, nosotras ayudamos	noh-*soh*-trohs, nos-*soh*-trahs ah-yooh-*dah*-mohs
vosotros, vosotras ayudáis	bvoh-*soh*-trohs, bvoh-*soh*-trahs ah-*yooh*-dahees
ellos, ellas, ustedes ayudan	*eh*-yos, *eh*-yas, oohs-*teh*-dehs ah-*yooh*-dahn

What follows are phrases that are helpful in cases when you're talking to people you haven't met — like a doctor or some passerby. We also give you phrases for situations when those around you are closely related to you or are children.

We begin with some phrases you can use when you want to be formally helpful. The formal way of speech is more normal to use both on your part and on the part of those who are helping. It shows respect on your part to the doctor, for example, and on his part to you. Neither of you has an intimate or informal relationship with the other:

> **¿Le ayudo?** (¿leh ah-*yooh*-doh?) (*Can I help you?*)

> **Sí, necesito una ambulancia.** (see neh-seh-*see*-toh *ooh*-nah ahm-bvooh-*lahn*-seeah.) (*Yes, I need an ambulance.*)

> **Espere. Le van a ayudar.** (ehs-*peh*-reh. leh bvahn ah ah-yooh-*dahr*.) (*Wait. They'll help you.*)

> **Usted ayude al enfermo.** (oohs-*tehd* ah-*yooh*-deh ahl ehn-*fehr*-moh.) (*You go help the sick person.*)

> **¡Apúrese!** (¡ah-*pooh*-reh-seh!) (*Hurry up!*)

The following phrases are for informal situations. Remember, informality is appropriate when you talk to a child, or if the person helping you is someone you know or who is close to you.

> **¿Te ayudo?** (¿teh ah-*yooh*-doh?) (*Can I help you?*)

Sí, ayúdame. (see, ah-*yooh*-dah-meh.) (*Yes, help me.*)

Te busco un médico. (teh *bvoohs*-koh oohn *meh*-dee-koh.) (*I'll get a doctor for you.*)

¡Apúrate! (¡ah-*pooh*-rah-teh!) (*Hurry up!*)

¡Sujétame! (¡sooh-*Heh*-tah-meh!) (*Hold onto me!*)

Expressing the presence of pain with indirect object pronouns

When you're hurting, you want to be able to tell people about it so that they can help you feel better. The following sentences describe specific aches and pains with the stem-changing **-er** verb **doler** (doh-*lehr*) (*to ache, to hurt*). And, just as carrying an umbrella can prevent rain, perhaps having the phrases ready to use will prevent you from needing them!

Me duele la espalda. (meh *dooheh*-leh lah ehs-*pahl*-dah.) (*My back hurts.*)

¿Le duele la cabeza? (¿leh *dooheh*-leh lah kah-*bveh*-sah?) (*Does your head hurt?*) (Formal)

Me duele todo. (meh *dooheh*-leh *toh*-doh.) (*I hurt all over.*)

Me duelen las manos. (meh *dooheh*-lehn lahs *mah*-nohs.) (*My hands hurt.*)

¿Te duele aquí? (¿teh *dooheh*-leh ah-*kee?*) (*Does it hurt you [informal] here?*)

The ways you express pain in English and Spanish differ very little. In English, for example, you may say something like *My toe hurts,* while in Spanish, you say the equivalent of *The toe hurts to me* — with *me* acting as an indirect object pronoun. Table 17-2 lists the indirect object pronouns.

Table 17-2	Indirect Object Pronouns
Pronoun	*Translation*
me (meh)	*me*
te (teh)	*you* (informal, singular)
le (leh)	*him, her, you* (formal, singular)
nos (nohs)	*us*
os (ohs)	*you* (informal, plural)
les (lehs)	*them, you* (formal, plural)

Talking about bleeding

Following are some examples of how to get medical help for someone who's bleeding severely:

> **¡Hay una emergencia!** (¡ahy *ooh*-nah eh-mehr-*Hehn*-seeah!) (*There's an emergency!*)

> **¡Traigan un médico!** (¡*trah*ee-gahn oohn *meh*-dee-koh!) (*Bring a doctor!*)

> **¡Traigan una ambulancia!** (¡*trah*ee-gahn *ooh*-nah ahm-bvooh-*lahn*-seeah!) (*Bring an ambulance!*)

> **Lo más rápido posible.** (loh mahs *rrah*-pee-doh poh-*see*-bvleh.) (*As fast as possible.*)

> **Tiene un corte.** (*tee*eh-neh oohn *kohr*-teh.) (*You [formal] have a cut.*)

> **Necesita puntos.** (neh-seh-*see*-tah *poohn*-tohs.) (*You [formal] need stitches.*)

If you ever need to get stitches, here are some useful phrases:

> **Le vamos a poner anestesia local.** (leh *bvah*-mohs a poh-*nehr* ah-nehs-*teh*-seeah loh-*kahl*.) (*We'll use local anesthesia.*)

> **Ya se pasó el dolor.** (yah seh *pah*-soh ehl doh-*lohr*.) (*The pain is gone.*)

Telling where it hurts with words for body parts

The following list gives you several phrases that may be useful in telling someone where your injury is. Later in this section, we provide some vocabulary words that may also come in handy.

> **Me sangra la nariz.** (meh *sahn*-grah lah *nah*-rees.) (*My nose is bleeding.*)

> **No puedo ver.** (noh pooh*eh*-doh bvehr.) (*I can't see.*)

> **Me entró algo en el ojo.** (meh ehn-*troh ahl*-goh ehn ehl *oh*-Hoh.) (*Something got into my eye.*)

> **Me torcí el tobillo.** (meh tohr-*see* ehl toh-*bvee*-yoh.) (*I twisted my ankle.*)

> **Él se quebró el brazo derecho.** (ehl seh keh-*broh* ehl *bvrah*-soh deh-*reh*-choh.) (*He broke his right arm.*)

> **La herida está en el antebrazo.** (lah eh-*ree*-dah ehs-*tah* ehn ehl ahn-teh-*bvrah*-soh.) (*The wound is on the forearm.*)

> **A ella le duele la muñeca izquierda.** (ah *eh*-yah leh dooh*eh*-leh lah mooh-*nyeh*-kah ees-kee*ehr*-dah.) (*Her left wrist hurts.*)

Él se cortó el dedo índice. (ehl seh kohr-*toh* ehl *deh*-doh *een*-dee-seh.) (*He cut his index finger.*)

Ella se torció el cuello. (*eh*-yah seh tohr-see*oh* ehl kooh*eh*-yoh.) (*She twisted her neck.*)

Ahora ya no sale sangre. (ah-*oh*-rah yah noh *sah*-leh *sahn*-greh.) (*It stopped bleeding.* [Literally: *Now there is no more blood coming out.*])

Although you can usually just point to where it hurts, you may need to know the names of body parts as your doctor refers to them. Table 17-3 lists the Spanish words for various body parts.

Table 17-3	Body Parts	
Spanish	*Pronunciation*	*English*
Head and Neck Words		
las amígdalas	lahs ah-*meeg*-dah-lahs	*the tonsils*
la boca	lah *bvoh*-kah	*the mouth*
la cabeza	lah kah-*bveh*-sah	*the head*
el cuello	ehl kooh*eh*-yoh	*the neck*
la lengua	lah *lehn*-goohah	*the tongue*
la nariz	lah nah-*rees*	*the nose*
la oreja	lah oh-*reh*-Hah	*the ear*
el ojo	ehl *oh*-Hoh	*the eye*
el rostro	ehl *rrohs*-troh	*the face*
Torso Words		
el corazón	ehl koh-rah-*sohn*	*the heart*
el estómago	ehl ehs-*toh*-mah-goh	*the stomach*
el hígado	ehl *ee*-gah-doh	*the liver*
el hombro	ehl *ohm*-bvroh	*the shoulder*
el intestino	ehl een-tehs-*tee*-noh	*the bowel, the intestine, the gut*
el pecho	ehl *peh*-choh	*the chest*
el pulmón	el poohl-*mohn*	*the lung*
el riñón	ehl rree-*nyohn*	*the kidney*
Arm and Hand Words		
el antebrazo	ehl ahn-teh-*bvrah*-soh	*the forearm*
el brazo	ehl *bvrah*-soh	*the arm*
el dedo	ehl *deh*-doh	*the finger*
el dedo anular	ehl *deh*-doh ah-nooh-*lahr*	*the ring finger*

(continued)

Table 17-3 *(continued)*

Spanish	Pronunciation	English
el dedo del medio	ehl *deh*-doh dehl *meh*-deeoh	*the middle finger*
el dedo índice	ehl *deh*-doh *een*-dee-seh	*the index finger*
el dedo meñique	ehl *deh*-doh meh-*nyee*-keh	*the little finger*
la mano	lah *mah*-noh	*the hand*
la muñeca	lah mooh-*nyeh*-kah	*the wrist*
el pulgar	ehl poohl-*gahr*	*the thumb*
Leg and Foot Words		
el dedo del pie	ehl deh-doh dehl pee*eh*	*the toe*
el muslo	ehl *moohs*-loh	*the thigh*
la pantorrilla	lah pahn-toh-*rree*-yah	*the calf*
el pie	ehl pee*eh*	*the foot*
la pierna	lah pee*ehr*-nah	*the leg*
la planta del pie	lah *plahn*-tah dehl pee*eh*	*the sole of the foot*
el tobillo	ehl toh-*bvee*-yoh	*the ankle*
Left and Right		
derecho	deh-*reh*-choh	*right*
izquierdo	ees-kee*ehr*-doh	*left*

Talkin' the Talk

After a collision, Nancy is taken to a hospital and is being looked after to see whether she's broken anything.

Doctor: **¿Tiene dolor en la pierna?**
¿tee-*eh*-neh doh-*lohr* ehn lah pee-*ehr*-nah?
Does your leg hurt? [Literally: *Do you have any pain in the leg?*]

Nancy: **Sí, doctor, ¡me duele mucho!**
see, dohk-*tohr*, me dooh*eh*-leh *mooh*-choh!
Yes, doctor, it hurts a lot!

Doctor: **Vamos a sacarle rayos X.**
bvah-mohs ah sah-*kahr*-leh *rrah*-yohs eh-kees.
We'll take x-rays.

X-ray technician:	**Aquí, súbanla a la mesa.**
	ah-*kee*, *sooh*-bvahn-lah ah lah *meh*-sah.
	Here, get her on the table.
	No se mueva por favor.
	noh seh mooh*eh*-bvah pohr fah-*bvor*.
	Don't move, please.
Doctor:	**Ya está la radiografía.**
	yah ehs-*tah* lah rrah-deeoh-grah-*fee*-ah.
	The x-ray picture is ready.
	Aquí tiene una fractura.
	ah-*kee* tee*eh*-neh *ooh*-nah frahk-*tooh*-rah.
	You have a fracture here.
	Vamos a tener que enyesar su pierna.
	bvah-mohs ah teh-*nehr* keh ehn-yeh-*sahr* sooh pee*eh*hr-nah.
	We're going to have to put your leg in a cast.
	Le voy a dar un analgésico.
	leh bvohy a dahr oohn ah-nahl-*Heh*-see-koh.
	I'll give you a painkiller.

Words to Know

el dolor	*ehl doh-<u>lohr</u>*	*the pain*
la pierna	*lah pee-<u>ehr</u>-nah*	*the leg*
los rayos X	*lohs <u>rrah</u>-yohs <u>eh</u>-kees*	*the x-rays*
la radiografía	*lah rrah-deeoh-grah-<u>fee</u>-ah*	*the x-ray picture*
la fractura	*lah frahk-<u>tooh</u>-rah*	*the fracture*
enyesar	*ehn-yeh-<u>sahr</u>*	*to put in a cast*
el analgésico	*ehl ah-nahl-<u>Heh</u>-see-koh*	*the painkiller*

Describing symptoms

Table 17-4 lists common terms for medical problems that you may need to know when visiting the doctor.

Table 17-4	Helpful Words for Describing Symptoms and Getting a Prescription	
Spanish	*Pronunciation*	*English*
la cirugía	lah see-rooh-*Hee*-ah	*the surgery*
enfermo	ehn-*fehr*-moh	*sick*
el estornudo	ehl ehs-tohr-*nooh*-doh	*the sneeze*
el estreñimiento	ehl ehs-treh-nyee-mee*ehn*-toh	*the constipation*
la evacuación	lah eh-bvah-koohah-see*ohn*	*the bowel movement (Literally: the evacuation)*
la farmacia	lah fahr-*mah*-seeah	*the pharmacy*
el jarabe	ehl Hah-*rah*-bveh	*the syrup; the elixir*
la medicina	lah meh-dee-*see*-nah	*the medication; the medicine*
la náusea	lah *nah*ooh-seh-ah	*the nausea; sickness*
la orina	lah oh-*ree*-nah	*the urine*
la presión sanguínea	lah preh-see*ohn* sahn-*ghee*-neh-ah	*the blood pressure*
la receta	lah rreh-*seh*-tah	*the prescription*
la salud	lah sah-*loohd*	*the health*
la sangre	lah *sahn*-greh	*the blood*
sano	*sah*-noh	*healthy*

When you sneeze among native Spanish-speakers, you never get a chance to excuse yourself. The moment you sneeze, someone immediately says **¡Salud!** (¡sah-*loohd*!) (*Health!*) And you immediately answer **¡Gracias!** (¡grah-seeahs!) (*Thanks!*).

Talkin' the Talk

After falling and hitting her head, Julia has a headache that she can't get rid of. She finally decides that she needs to consult her doctor. After checking in with the receptionist, she's ushered into the doctor's office and begins to explain her symptoms. (Track 32)

Julia: **Me duele la cabeza.**
meh dooh*eh*-leh lah kah-*bveh*-sah.
My head hurts.

Dr. Díaz: **¿Desde cuándo?**
¿*dehs*-deh kooh*ahn*-doh?
Since when?

Julia: **Desde ayer. Me golpeé la cabeza.**
dehs-deh ah-*yehr*. meh gohl-peh-*eh* lah kah-*bveh*-sah.
Since yesterday. I banged my head.

Dr. Díaz: **¿Cómo se golpeó?**
¿*koh*-moh seh gohl-peh-*oh*?
How did you bang [it]?

Julia: **Me caí en la calle.**
meh-kah*ee* ehn lah *kah*-yeh.
I fell in the street.

Dr. Díaz: **¿Tiene mareos?**
¿tee*eh*-neh mah-*reh*-ohs?
Do you get dizzy?

Julia: **Sí, tengo mareos.**
see, *tehn*-goh mah-*reh*-ohs.
Yes, I get dizzy.

Dr. Díaz: **Vamos a tenerle en observación durante dos días.**
b*vah*-mohs ah teh-*nehr*-leh ehn ohbv-sehr-bvah-
see*ohn* dooh-*rahn*-teh dohs *dee*-ahs.
We'll keep you under observation for two days.

Words to Know

la cabeza	lah kah-<u>bveh</u>-sah	the head
golpear	gohl-peh-<u>ahr</u>	to hit; to bang
el mareo	ehl mah-<u>reh</u>-oh	the dizziness
la observación	lah obv-<u>s</u>ehr-bvah-see<u>ohn</u>	the observation

Braving the dentist

If you have a dental problem while you're in a Spanish-speaking country, getting a dentist appointment and having your problem taken care of shouldn't be much more difficult than usual, as long as you know a few key words and phrases.

Here's a summary of terms you typically hear in a dentist's office:

- **la caries** (lah *kah*-reeehs) (*the cavity*)
- **la corona** (lah koh-*roh*-nah) (*the crown*)
- **el/la dentista** (ehl/lah dehn-*tees*-tah) (*the dentist*)
- **el diente** (ehl dee*ehn*-teh) (*the tooth*)
- **el dolor de muelas** (ehl doh-*lohr* deh mooh*eh*-lahs) (*the toothache*)
- **la muela** (lah mooh*eh*-lah) (*the molar*)
- **un puente** (oohn pooh*ehn*-teh) (*a bridge*)

You may hear these phrases (or something similar) when making or attending a dentist appointment:

Necesito un dentista. (neh-seh-*see*-toh oohn dehn-*tees*-tah.) (*I need a dentist.*)

¿Me puede recomendar un dentista? (¿meh pooh*eh*-deh rreh-koh-mehn-*dahr* oohn dehn-*tees*-tah?) (*Can you recommend a dentist?*)

Doctor, tengo un dolor de muelas. (dohk-*tohr*, *tehn*-goh oohn doh-*lohr* deh mooh*eh*-lahs.) (*Doctor, I have a toothache.*)

Tiene una caries. (tee*eh*-neh *ooh*-nah *kah*-reeehs.) (*You have a cavity.*)

Quebré una muela. (keh-bv*reh ooh*-nah mooh*eh*-lah.) (*I broke a molar.*)

Voy a ponerle anestesia. (vohy ah poh-*nehr*-leh ah-nehs-*teh*-seeah.) (*I'm going to give you anesthesia.*)

Voy a taparle la caries. (vohy ah tah-*pahr*-leh lah *kah*-reeehs.) (*I'm going to fill the cavity.*)

Voy a sacarle la muela. (vohy ah sah-*kahr*-leh lah mooh*eh*-lah.) (*I'm going to take out the molar.*)

Voy a ponerle un puente. (vohy ah pohn-*ehr*-leh oohn pooh*ehn*-teh.) (*I'm going to put in a bridge.*)

Voy a ponerle una corona. (vohy ah pohn-*ehr*-leh *ooh*-nah koh-*roh*-nah.) (*I'm going to put on a crown.*)

Getting reimbursed: Insurance stuff

If you need to visit a dentist or any other health-care professional while you're traveling, be sure you get a receipt to give to your insurance carrier at home.

Call your insurance company before traveling to a foreign country to see how it recommends you proceed to make sure that your reimbursement process goes as easily as possible for everyone involved. You may also want to purchase a separate traveler's health insurance policy for the duration of your stay — such policies are usually very affordable.

The following phrases are useful in dealing with insurance questions:

¿Tiene seguro dental? (*¿*tee*eh*-neh seh-*gooh*-roh dehn-*tahl?*) (*Do you have dental insurance?*)

Sí, tengo seguro dental. (see, *tehn*-goh seh-*gooh*-roh dehn-*tahl.*) (*Yes, I have dental insurance.*)

¿Tiene seguro de salud? (*¿*tee*eh*-neh seh-*gooh*-roh deh sah-*loohd?*) (*Do you have health insurance?*)

Sí, tengo seguro de salud. (see, *tehn*-goh seh-*gooh*-roh deh sah-*loohd.*) (*Yes, I have health insurance.*)

¿Me puede dar un recibo para el seguro? (*¿*meh pooh*eh*-deh dahr oohn rreh-*see*-bvoh *pah*-rah ehl seh-*gooh*-roh?) (*Can you give me a receipt for my insurance?*)

Getting Help with Legal Problems

Most people obey the laws and usually don't engage in activities that involve the police or other aspects of the legal system. But accidents happen, and you can break a law that you know nothing about. If something like that happens to you, you need help from your consulate or a lawyer to make sure that your rights are protected.

In an emergency of any kind, but particularly in a situation involving legal officials, try to be patient and, above all, firm. Keep in mind that just as you're unfamiliar with the practices and procedures of a foreign system, the officers and administrators of that system are unaware of your legal expectations.

If you get involved in a Spanish-speaking country's legal system, try to get someone from your consulate to help you — he or she will take your interests much more to heart than a local lawyer or the local police. In fact, after you set the dates for a visit to a Spanish American area, find out where your country's closest consulate is — and when you arrive, register there in case you need emergency assistance. In some countries, you're required to register within a certain number of days.

You may also ask the following when you arrive:

> **¿Hay aquí un Consulado de los Estados Unidos?** (¿ahy ah-*kee* oohn kohn-sooh-*lah*-doh deh lohs ehs-*tah*-dohs ooh-*nee*-dohs?) (*Is there a U.S. consulate here?*)

> **¿Hay un abogado que hable inglés?** (¿ahy oohn ah-bvoh-*gah*-doh keh ah-*bvleh* een-*glehs?*) (*Is there a lawyer who speaks English?*)

If Spanish isn't your first language, and you're in a Spanish-speaking area, ask for a lawyer who speaks English and make sure the lawyer's English is better than your Spanish before you get involved with him or her. Don't accept just anyone. If you have trouble making yourself understood, get another lawyer.

The following sections note some words and phrases that are helpful in two legal situations: reporting a robbery and describing an incident to the police. The following dialogue shows you a case of legal trouble abroad. We certainly hope that you won't be involved in a situation like Silverio's, but we want to cover all your bases, and just in case, these few sentences may be useful.

Talkin' the Talk

Silverio has been pulled over by the police and is trying to understand why. (Track 33)

Police officer:	**Buenas noches, señor, ¿puedo ver su licencia para conducir por favor?** bvooh*eh*-nahs *noh*-chehs, seh-*nyohr*, ¿pooh*eh*-doh bvehr sooh lee-*sehn*-seeah *pah*-rah kohn-dooh-*seer* pohr fah-*bvohr?* *Good evening, sir, may I please see your driver's license?*
Silverio:	**Sí, señor. Aquí está.** see, seh-*nyohr.* ah-*kee* ehs-*tah.* *Yes, officer. Here it is.*
	¿Puedo saber por qué me detenía? ¿pooh*eh*-doh sah-*bvehr* pohr *keh* meh deh-teh-*nee*-ah? *May I ask why I'm being stopped?*
Police officer:	**Usted giró ilegalmente.** oohs-*tehd* hee-*roh* ee-leh-gahl-*mehn*-teh. *You made an illegal turn.*

Silverio:	**Lo siento. Pienso que estoy perdido.** loh seee*hn*-toh. peee*hn*-soh keh ehs-*tohy* pehr-*dee*-doh. *I'm sorry. I think I'm lost.*
Police officer:	**Tengo que darle una multa por la infracción de tráfico.** *tehn*-goh keh *dahr*-leh *ooh*-nah *moohl*-tah pohr lah een-frahk-see-*ohn* deh *trah*-fee-koh. *I have to give you a ticket for the traffic violation.*
Silverio:	**A lo mejor me puede decir como llegar a la plaza de toros.** ah loh meh-*Hohr* meh poohe*h*-deh deh-*seer* *koh*-moh yeh-*gahr* ah lah *plah*-sah deh *toh*-rohs. *Maybe you can tell me how to get to the bullfighting ring.*
Police officer:	**Tiene que viajar cuatro cuadras más al sur.** teee*h*-neh keh bveeah-*Hahr* kooha*h*-troh kooha*h*-drahs mahs ahl soohr. *You need to go four more blocks to the south.*
	Doblar a la izquierda y maneje un kilómetro. doh-*bvlahr* ah lah ees-keee*h*r-dah ee mah-*neh*- Heh oohn kee-*loh*-meh-troh. *Turn left and drive one kilometer.*
	La plaza de toros queda al norte. lah *plah*-sah deh *toh*-rohs *keh*-dah ahl *nohr*-teh. *The bullring is on the north side of the street.*
Silverio:	**Muchísimas gracias, señor policía, por toda su ayuda.** mooh-*chee*-see-mahs *grah*-seeahs, seh-*nyohr* poh-lee-*see*-ah, pohr *toh*-dah sooh ah-*yooh*-dah. *Thank you so much, officer, for all of your help.*
Police officer:	**Aquí está su licencia para conducir. Tenga más cuidado.** ah-*kee* ehs-*tah* sooh lee-*sehn*-seeah *pah*-rah kohn-dooh-*seer*. *tehn*-gah mahs koohee-*dah*-doh. *Here's your driver's license. Be more careful.*

Silverio: **Buenas noches.**
bvooheh-nahs *noh*-chehs.
Good evening.

Police officer: **Adiós.**
ah-dee*ohs.*
Good-bye.

Words to Know

licencia para conducir	lee-<u>sehn</u>-seeah <u>pah</u>-rah kohn-dooh-<u>seer</u>	driver's license
giró ilegalmente	hee-<u>roh</u> ee-leh-gahl-<u>mehn</u>-teh	made an illegal turn
multa	<u>moohl</u>-tah	ticket
infracción de tráfico	een-frahk-see-<u>ohn</u> deh <u>trah</u>-fee-koh	traffic violation
señor policía	seh-<u>nyohr</u> poh-lee-<u>see</u>-ah	officer

Reporting a robbery

REMEMBER

If someone robs you while you're in a Spanish-speaking area, you can attract the help you need by using these phrases:

¡Un robo! (¡oohn *rroh*-bvoh!) (*A burglary!*)

¡Un asalto! (¡oohn ah-*sahl*-toh!) (*A holdup!*)

¡Atrápenlo! (¡ah-*trah*-pehn-loh!) (*Catch him!*)

¡Policía! (¡poh-lee-*see*-ah!) (*Police!*)

We hope you never need to use them, but if you're ever robbed or attacked in a Spanish-speaking area, these phrases are important to know:

¡Llamen a la policía! (¡*yah*-mehn ah lah poh-lee-*see*-ah!) (*Call the police!*)

¡Me robó la billetera! (¡meh *rroh*-bvoh lah bvee-yeh-*teh*-rah!) (*[She/He] stole my wallet!*)

¡**Me robó el bolso!** (¡meh *rroh*-bvoh ehl *bvohl*-soh!) (*[She/He] stole my purse!*)

Haga una denuncia a la policía. (¡*ah*-gah *ooh*-nah deh-*noohn*-seeah ah la poh-lee-*see*-ah!) (*Report it to the police.* [Literally: *Make an accusation to the police.*])

Describing an incident to the police

If you do have an unpleasant encounter with a thief, here are some words that can be helpful in describing the culprit to the police:

Es un hombre bajo, corpulento. (ehs oohn *ohm*-bvreh *bvah*-Hoh, kohr-pooh-*lehn*-toh.) (*He is a short man, heavyset.*)

Tiene el pelo moreno y una barba. (tee*eh*-neh ehl *peh*-loh moh-*reh*-noh ee *ooh*-nah *bvahr*-bvah.) (*He has dark hair and a beard.*)

Lleva pantalón de mezclilla y camisa blanca. (*yeh*-bvah pahn-tah-*lohn* deh mehs-*klee*-yah ee kah-*mee*-sah *bvlahn*-kah.) (*He is wearing jeans and a white shirt.*)

Tiene unos cuarenta años. (tee*eh*-neh *ooh*-nohs koohah-*rehn*-tah *ah*-nyohs.) (*He's around 40 years old.*)

Está con una mujer delgada. (ehs-*tah* kohn *ooh*-nah mooh-*Hehr* dehl-*gah*-dah.) (*He is with a thin woman.*)

Es alta, rubia, de ojos claros. (ehs *ahl*-tah, *rrooh*-bveeah, deh *oh*-Hohs *klah*-rohs) (*She is tall, blond, with light-colored eyes.*)

The following verbs can help you describe a crime:

- ✔ **atacar** (ah-*tah*-kahr) (*to attack*)
- ✔ **robar** (*rroh*-bvahr) (*to steal; to rob*)

Talkin' the Talk

Someone has just robbed Julieta! Now she's reporting the incident to the police.

Julieta:	¡**Rápido, vengan!**
	¡*rrah*-pee-doh *bvehn*-gahn!
	Quickly, come here!
Passerby:	¿**Qué le pasó?**
	¿keh leh pah-*soh*?
	What happened to you?

Julieta:	**¡Un hombre alto con una máscara me robó el bolso!**	
	¡oohn *ohm*-bvreh *ahl*-toh kohn *ooh*-nah *mahs*-kah-rah meh rroh-*bvoh* ehl *bvohl*-soh!	
	A tall man in a mask stole my purse!	
Police officer:	**¿En qué dirección corrió?**	
	¿ehn keh dee-rehk-see*ohn* koh-rree*oh*?	
	In what direction did he run?	
Julieta:	**Cruzó la calle y corrió al norte, hacia el parque.**	
	krooh-*soh* lah *kah*-yeh ee koh-rree*oh* ahl *nohr*-teh, *ah*-seeah ehl *pahr*-keh.	
	He crossed the street and ran to the north, toward the park.	
Police officer:	**¿Puede Ud. acompañarme a la comisaría de policía para hacer un informe acerca del incidente?**	
	¿pooh*eh*-deh oohs-*tehd* ah-kohm-pah-*nyahr*-meh ah lah koh-mee-sah-*ree*-ah deh poh-lee-*see*-ah *pah*-rah ah-*sehr* oohn een-*fohr*-meh ah-*sehr*-kah dehl een-see-*dehn*-teh?	
	Can you accompany me to the police station to make a report about the incident?	
Julieta:	**Claro que sí.**	
	klah-roh keh see	
	Of course.	

Words to Know

una máscara	ooh-nah <u>mahs</u>-kah-rah	a mask
correr	koh-<u>rrehr</u>	to run
acompañar	ah-kohm-pah-<u>nyahr</u>	to accompany
la comisaría de policía	lah koh-mee-sah-<u>ree</u>-ah deh poh-lee-<u>see</u>-ah	the police station
hacer un informe	ah-<u>sehr</u> oohn een-<u>fohr</u>-meh	to make a report
claro que sí	<u>klah</u>-roh keh see	of course

Refusing Help When You Don't Really Want It

In our experience, most native Spanish-speakers are caring, gentle people who are tolerant of faulty pronunciation and very ready to help a foreigner. In fact, they may be overly helpful, leaving you with the difficult task of being firm and level-headed about your needs without hurting their feelings and being negative about their good will.

Here are some sentences to help you be just as caring and kind, but at the same time firm with your refusal for help, when you don't want any. Suppose the person trying to be helpful says things like

¡Pobrecito!, ¿le ayudo? (¡poh-breh-*see*-toh!, ¿leh ah-*yooh*-doh?) (*Oh, you poor thing* [male], *may I help you?*)

¡Vengan todos, a ayudar! (¡*bvehn*-gahn *toh*-dohs, ah ah-yooh-*dar!*) (*Come, everybody, let's help!*)

In which case, you can answer with things like

Por favor, estoy bien, no me ayude. (pohr fah-*bvohr,* ehs-*tohy* bveee*ehn,* noh meh ah-*yooh*-deh.) (*Please, I'm fine, don't help me.*)

Muchas gracias; prefiero estar solo. (*mooh*-chahs *grah*-seeahs; preh-feee*eh*-roh ehs-*tahr soh*-loh.) (*Thank you very much; I prefer to be alone.*)

Estoy muy bien, gracias; no necesito ayuda. (ehs-*tohy* mooh*ee* bveee*ehn,* *grah*-seeahs; noh neh-seh-*see*-toh ah-*yooh*-dah.) (*I'm fine, thanks; I don't need help.*)

Usted es muy gentil, gracias; no me ayude, por favor. (oohs-*tehd* ehs mooh*ee* *Hehn*-teel, *grah*-seeahs; noh meh ah-*yooh*-deh, pohr *fah*-bvohr.) (*You're very kind, thanks; don't help me, please.*)

Ustedes son muy amables, pero estoy bien. (oohs-*tehd*-ehs sohn mooh*ee* ah-*mah*-bvlehs, *peh*-roh ehs-*tohy* bveee*ehn.*) (*You* [formal] *are very kind, but I'm fine.*)

Fun & Games

Alberto doesn't know it yet, but he's going to have an accident on that surfboard of his. You see, he invited you to join him on vacation, and then he decided to take up surfing to impress a girl. The thing is, Alberto isn't nearly as good a surfer as he thinks he is, and he's going to wipe out. Good friend that you are, you're going to accompany Alberto to the doctor and explain what happened. Fill in all of Alberto's body parts (in Spanish) on the following illustration. That way, you can refer to the picture if you happen to get flustered in the excitement of the moment. (Oh, and don't worry, Alberto will be fine — just a few bumps and bruises, and some sorely wounded pride.)

Part IV
The Part of Tens

The 5th Wave   By Rich Tennant

"I know it's a popular American expression, but you just don't say 'Hasta la vista, baby' to a nun."

In this part . . .

If you're looking for easily digestible tidbits of information about Spanish, this part is for you. Here, you find ten ways to pick up Spanish quickly, ten things you should never say in Spanish, ten useful Spanish expressions to know, and ten phrases that make you sound like a native Spanish-speaker.

Chapter 18

Ten Ways to Pick Up Spanish Quickly

In This Chapter

▶ Acquiring Spanish via travel

▶ Adding Spanish to your repertoire through media

▶ Making a game of Spanish vocabulary

*Y*ou know the best way to thread a needle, drive a nail into wood, or type a letter. Just as you can acquire these skills in many ways, so can you acquire the Spanish language. The ten suggestions in this chapter are great ways for you to add this beautiful language to your life.

Go to Spanish-Speaking Places

This information probably comes as no surprise, but the absolute best way, by far, to learn Spanish is to be in an environment where everybody speaks the language and no one speaks yours. Finding this sort of environment is pretty simple if you can afford to travel. Consider immersing yourself in the language by giving yourself a Spanish-speaking vacation. With Spanish-speaking places appearing just as you come across the southern border of the United States, travel by car, bus, or plane is generally inexpensive.

Investigate Your Neighborhood

You may be able to find Spanish-speaking people in your own neighborhood or town. And among these people, you may find some who are willing to spend a few hours a week with you, doing everyday activities while you practice speaking Spanish with them. You may do volunteer work in a local library, zoo, or museum; in this way, you can reach children, who can be great teachers, along with their parents and teachers. Soon you may find yourself participating in parties, outings, and many aspects of life that utilize Spanish.

Listen to Radio and TV

Because so many people in North, Central, and South America speak Spanish, you may be lucky enough to find a radio station or a TV channel in your area that offers Spanish programming. By listening to and watching these programs, you expand your vocabulary, gain an understanding of the body language and idioms of Spanish-speaking people, and gain insight into their ideas of fun. Not to mention that the more your ears become accustomed to hearing the spoken Spanish language, the more familiar (thus less foreign) it sounds. In this case, familiarity breeds a comfort level that increases your ability to learn with greater ease.

Rent a Movie

Video centers in your area may offer films in Spanish. To get the effect of being in a Spanish-speaking country, choose a film that has no dubbing or subtitles. You may be amazed at how much you understand even the first time you see the movie, but the good thing about video is that you can play the film as many times as your whim and time allow. And it bears repeating: Repetition, repetition, repetition really helps!

Check Out Your Library

Your local library may house books, CDs, and other materials about Spanish and Spanish-speaking countries. Every bit of information you get counts in building up your mental Spanish library. Here are some items to look for:

- Atlases and maps of Spanish-speaking North, Central, and South American countries.
- Travel guides and books that describe Spanish-speaking areas.
- Novels by authors that describe Spanish places. Most of these are translations of texts by authors from countries that speak Spanish, but others are written in English.

You can also find access to the Internet through your library's computer. On the Internet, you can find an enormous amount of information and fun things related to Spanish-speaking places.

Translate Words and Phrases on Google

Computerized translation tools have come a long way, especially tools for translating Spanish to English and vice versa. If you have something to say and can't figure out how to say it, head to Google for assistance:

1. Go to www.google.com and click **Language Tools** (to the right of the search box).

2. Below **Translate text**, click **English** in the list on the left and **Spanish** in the list on the right (or vice versa, depending on which language you're translating from).

3. **Click in the text box and type what you want to translate.**

4. **Click the Translate button.**

   Google translates the word or phrase for you.

Head back to Google's Language Tools page (by using your browser's Back button or repeating Step 1 in the earlier instructions), scroll down to the section Use the Google Interface in Your Language, and click Spanish. This change displays all Google text, including buttons and links, in Spanish, so you gain additional practice with the language.

Search Google Images in Spanish

You often retain vocabulary better if you can picture in your mind what a word represents. Obviously, in this relatively brief book, we can't possibly include a picture for every new Spanish word we introduce. However, Google can. Perform a Google image search on Google's Spanish site to "see" what a word means:

1. Go to images.google.es.

2. **In the** Buscar **(bvoohs-*kahr*) (*Search*) box, type the Spanish word you want to look up and click the** Buscar **button.**

   Google displays pictures that should represent the word or come pretty close.

Create a Game

You can make up games of your own (see the sidebar "Thinking in Spanish, a little at a time" for one example). For example, you may decide to make a game of picking up a sentence a day:

1. **Put the sentence with little stickers on your refrigerator, next to your phone, on your bathroom mirror, or other places you choose.**

2. **Every time you open the refrigerator, look in the mirror, and so on, read and repeat the sentence aloud.**

Use your imagination and have fun!

Label Everything with Sticky Notes

Write the Spanish words for all the things in one room of your house on little sticky notes. Put each note on the correct item and say the Spanish word aloud every time you use (or just look at) the object. As you feel comfortable with the words, remove the sticky notes but continue saying the names aloud. If you forget the name, replace the note. When the majority of sticky notes are gone, move to another room.

You can extend this exercise beyond your home without using sticky notes — just name (either aloud or silently) every object you can in Spanish as you encounter it in your daily activities.

Say It Again, Sam

You hear a Spanish phrase in a film, you sing a line in Spanish of a song, you catch a Spanish sentence in an ad. These are treasures, and your goal is to use and polish them all the time. Several times a day, repeat those words and phrases aloud. So that you know what you're repeating, you may consult a dictionary, which can be the very one in Appendix A. Soon, the treasure is yours to keep.

Chapter 19

Ten Things Never to Say in Spanish

*P*eople often ask how to say something in Spanish, but they rarely think of asking what *not* to say, and saying the wrong thing is usually worse than saying nothing at all. In this chapter, we reveal ten things not to say in Spanish. Some of the utterances on our list include *false cognates* — Spanish words that sound like English words but mean something totally different. Others phrases are included in the list because they may offend the cultural sensibilities of the person you're talking to. Hopefully this chapter helps you avoid the embarrassment of a common Spanish or Latin American faux pas.

Soy un americano

If you're a citizen of the United States of America, describing yourself as an American by saying **Soy un americano or americana.** (*I am an American.*) comes across as being a little conceited. After all, just about everyone in the Western Hemisphere is American, and Mexicans and Canadians are North Americans, too.

When telling someone in Latin America where you're from, you're better off describing yourself as coming from the United States: **Soy de los Estados Unidos** (sohy deh lohs ehs-*tah*-dohs ooh-*nee*-dohs.) (*I'm from the United States.*). Or, you can choose to be more specific and say the state you live in; for example, **Yo vivo en California** (yoh *bvee*-bvoh ehn kah-lee-*fohr*-neeah.) (*I live in California.*).

Yo no hablo mexicano

Saying **Yo no hablo mexicano.** (*I don't speak Mexican.*) is mildly derogatory, but it also demonstrates a certain degree of ignorance regarding the speaker. Mexico is a country, not a language. The people of Mexico are considered Mexicans, but they don't speak Mexican any more than a native resident of the United States speaks United Statesean or even American. They speak Spanish. To indicate that you don't speak Spanish, say, **Yo no hablo español.** (yoh noh *ah*-bvloh ehs-pah-*nyohl.*) (*I don't speak Spanish.*)

Así no es como lo hacemos en los Estados Unidos

You've probably heard the saying, "When in Rome, do as the Romans do," which essentially means to show courtesy to your hosts by doing your best to respect their culture and traditions. When visiting a foreign land, try your best not to make value judgments concerning the culture and the way people do things there. (*Making a value judgment* consists of thinking or saying that something is right or wrong or better or worse when it's merely different.)

People from other countries have their own sense of pride and nationalism. Saying **Así no es como lo hacemos en los Estados Unidos.** (*That's not how we do it in the United States.*) implies that the United States or the way people do something in the United States is better or the right way. This statement conveys a sense of arrogance and disrespect of your hosts' culture. You may think your way is better and do it your way when nobody else is around, but try to blend in when you're in the presence of your hosts.

Tu madre lleva botas militares

In the United States, you may be able to get away with uttering a disparaging comment such as *Your mother wears army boots.* **(Tu madre lleva botas militares.)** about a friend's mother, especially if you're saying it half jokingly, but in Mexico, saying anything even mildly negative about a person's mother, especially a man's mother, is taboo.

Latin American cultures tend to be *matriarchal* — a society in which women, especially mothers, are respected and revered. Mother jokes or even mild criticism of one's mother doesn't go over big in the presence of someone who has been raised to have nothing but respect and reverence for their mother and all mother figures.

No sé

Responding **No sé.** (*I don't know.*) to a question is often perceived as a snub. When you say, *I don't know,* the other person hears, *I don't care* or *I really don't want to help you.* Instead of replying **No sé,** respond in a more positive way that conveys clearly that you want to help. For example, you may say something like **Vamos a preguntarle a Pedro. Él podría saber.** (*bvah*-mohs ah preh-goohn-*tahr*-leh ah *peh*-droh. ehl pohd-*ree*-ah sah-*bvehr*.) (*Let's ask Pedro. He may know.*)

Yo iré un poco más temprano

When invited to a party or get together, never show up early or tell your host **Yo iré un poco más temprano.** (*I'll come a little early*). Arriving at least a half hour late is considered proper etiquette. Arriving early is downright rude. Likewise, when planning a party or get together, don't be upset when your guests show up a half hour to an hour later than you specified in your invitation. They're just trying to be polite. If you really want people to start showing up at 2:00 p.m., invite them for 1:00 p.m. and be pleasantly surprised when a few of them show up "early."

¡Muy mucho!

Native Spanish speakers never, ever combine the two words **muy** (*moohee*) (*very*) and **mucho** (*mooh*-choh) (*much*) — not even if they like something very much. If you're complimenting someone on their new shoes, which you like very much you simply say **Me gustan sus zapatos nuevos muchísimo** (meh *goohs*-tahn soohs sah-*pah*-tohs nooh*eh*-bvohs mooh-*chee*-see-moh) (*I like your new shoes very much*). The **-ísimo** added to the end of **mucho** is the Spanish equivalent to the English *very* added before the *much.*

Disculpe — me siento tan embarazada

You thought you were saying *Excuse me. I feel so embarrassed.* Unfortunately, you're about to feel even more embarrassed than you thought you were. In Spanish, the word **embarazada** (ehm-bvah-rah-*sah*-dah) is the mother of all false cognates. It looks and sounds like the English word *embarrassed,* yet it translates as *pregnant.*

The usual way to say you're feeling embarrassed in Spanish is **Me siento avergonzada.** (meh see*ehn*-toh ah-bvehr-gohn-*zah*-dah.). Guys, you'd be **avergonzado** (ah-bvehr-gohn-*zah*-doh).

Necesito algo de ropa para atar el paquete

When you need some rope or string to tie up something (such as a package), you may be tempted to say something like **Necesito algo de ropa para atar el paquete,** thinking that you're asking for a piece of *rope* **(la ropa)**. Unfortunately **la ropa** is a false cognate — it means *clothing*, not *rope*. **Necesito algo de ropa para atar el paquete** means *I need some clothes to tie up the package.*

Chances are pretty good that the person you asked for a piece of clothing will catch your drift and hand you a piece of rope or string, which in Spanish is **cuerda** (kooh*ehr*-dah), but if the person chuckles a little as she does so, you'll know why.

¿Tiene hombre?, and Other Accidental Letter Changes

Most languages have many things in common, and one of these things is that changing just one little letter in a word can change the entire meaning of that word. And if you can change the meaning of one word, you can change the meaning of the statement or question. This issue is especially tricky when you're not careful about proper pronunciation. For example, to an English-speaker's ear, **hombre** (*ohm*-bvreh) (*man*) and **hambre** (*ahm*-bvreh) (*hunger*) may sound pretty much the same because *o* and *a* can have similar sounds in English. But put the wrong one in your question, and you go from asking someone if she's hungry (**¿Tiene hambre?**) to asking her if she has a man (**¿Tiene hombre?**) Now that's a different subject altogether.

Another simple slip-up can be offering to pay for someone's purchase by saying **Vos pegamos.** (bvohs peh-*gah*-mohs.) (*We'll hit you.*) rather than **Vos pagamos.** (bvohs pah-*gah*-mohs.) (*We'll pay for you.*).

And of course, there's the one about **Los Siete Pescados Mortales** (*The Seven Deadly Fish*). We think they meant **Los Siete Pecados Mortales,** (lohs see*ehh*-teh peh-*kah*-dohs mohr-*tah*-lehs) (*The Seven Deadly Sins*), in which case it's certainly much more serious. See what we mean about one little letter?

Chapter 20

Ten or So Favorite Spanish Expressions

● ●

In This Chapter

▶ Five ways to ask and answer *What's up?* or *How's it going?*

▶ Two ways to ask *How much?*, and other terms to use when shopping

▶ Toasting in Spanish

▶ Translating *Bon voyage* from French to Spanish

● ●

This chapter gives you a dozen phrases or words that Spanish speakers use all the time when meeting, greeting, and dealing with each other.

¿Qué tal?

You use the greeting **¿Qué tal?** (¿keh tahl?) (*How are things?*) when meeting someone you already know. This phrase (we introduce it in Chapter 3) is easy to pronounce and immediately gives the impression of someone speaking the language fluently.

¿Quiubo?

¿Quiubo? (¿*keeooh-boh?*) (*How are things?*) is very similar in its effect to **¿Qué tal?** but is even more colloquial. You use this phrase, which is common in Chile and a few other countries, only with someone you know well and with whom you have an informal relationship.

¿Quiubo? is a compression of the phrase **¿qué hubo?** (¿keh *ooh*-bvoh?), meaning *What happened?* To really sound like an insider, let **¿Quiubo?** just flow out of your mouth, as though you were saying queue-bvoh. (We also mention this greeting in Chapter 3.)

¿Qué pasó?

In Mexico you frequently hear **¿Qué pasó?** (¿keh pah-*soh?*) (*How are things?* [Literally: *What happened?*]) This phrase may seem funny to you at first. Someone sees another person and cries out **¿Qué pasó?** as though they've been separated just before some big event and now want to know what happened. That's what the phrase means, but its use is much broader.

Even people who barely know each other and haven't seen one another for ages can use this greeting. In any case, when you use it in Mexico, do so with someone you've seen at least once before. You'll sound like you've been there forever. (We mention this greeting in Chapter 3.)

¿Cómo van las cosas?

¿Cómo van las cosas? (¿*koh*-moh bvahn lahs *koh*-sahs?) (*How are things going?*) is a very gentle greeting that well-educated people use to express concern. People also use this phrase when they've met the other person before. (We discuss this phrase in Chapter 3.)

¿Cómo van las cosas? is more appropriate than **¿Quiubo?** or **¿Qué pasó?** when greeting someone who is older than you or someone to whom you want to show your respect.

¡Del uno!

¡Del uno! (¡dehl *ooh*-noh!) (*First rate!*) is a common phrase in Chile, but you may hear it in other places as well. Its meaning is clear, even if you haven't heard it before. Check out this little ditty:

> **"¿Cómo estamos?" dijo Ramos.** (¿*koh*-moh ehs-*tah*-mohs? dee-Hoh rrah-mohs.) (*"How are things?* [Literally: *How are we?*]*" said Ramos.*)

> **"¡Del uno!" dijo Aceituno.** (¡dehl *ooh*-noh! dee-Hoh ah-sehee-*tooh*-noh.) (*"First rate!" said Aceituno.*)

Ramos and Aceituno are just family names used to call out the rhyme. You'll sound like one of the bunch with this one.

¿Cuánto cuesta?

¿Cuánto cuesta? (¿kooh*ahn*-toh kooh*ehs*-tah?) (*How much does it cost?*) You ask this question when you're shopping and need to know the price. (See Chapter 9 for some examples.)

¿A cuánto?

¿A cuánto? (¿ah-kooh*ahn*-toh?) (*How much?*) is very similar to **¿Cuánto cuesta?**, except that this phrase may imply that you're asking the price of several things grouped together, as in **¿A cuánto la docena?** (¿ah-kooh*ahn*-toh lah doh-*seh*-nah?) (*How much for the dozen?*). You'll seem like an expert shopper when you use this one. (Flip to Chapter 9 for an example of this phrase.)

¡Un asalto!

You may think that exclaiming **¡Un asalto!** (¡oohn ah-*sahl*-toh!) (*A holdup!*) in the midst of bargaining for a lower price is hyping things up a bit. However, adding hype to your speech can be useful — at least the vendor knows that you're familiar with this phrase that shows your indignation. This phrase is also useful when you really *are* indignant. (See Chapter 17 for more on this expression.)

¡Una ganga!

Vendors often use the phrase **¡Una ganga!** (¡*ooh*-nah *gahn*-gah!) (*A bargain!*) when trying to sell you an item. You can show your familiarity with the language when you use this expression to boast about a really good buy.

¡Buen provecho!

Imagine that you're sitting at the table, soup spoon in hand, ready to begin your meal by dipping it into a cup of steaming soup. In order to sound like a native, you want to say — at this exact moment — **¡Buen provecho!** (¡bvooh*ehn* proh-*bveh*-choh!) (*Enjoy your meal!* or *Bon appetit!* [Literally: *Good profit!*]) before someone else does.

> **¡Buen provecho!** is also the right thing to say when you set a tray of food in front of your guests.

¡Salud!

¡Salud! (¡sah-*loohd!*) (*Health!*) has two usages:

- ✔ You use this word when giving a toast as a way to say *Cheers!* or *To your health!*

- ✔ You use this word after someone sneezes — it's the Spanish equivalent of *Bless you*, to which you answer, **¡Gracias!** (See Chapter 17 for more information.)

¡Buen viaje!

You hear the phrase **¡Buen viaje!** (¡bvooh*ehn* bvee*ah*-Heh!) (*Have a good trip!*) all around you in train stations, airports, and bus terminals. Use this expression when you want to wish those you care for a safe trip.

If you're reading this book as part of your preparation for travel, we say **¡Buen viaje!**

Chapter 21

Ten Phrases That Make You Sound Fluent in Spanish

In This Chapter

▶ Expressing your excitement and enthusiasm

▶ Showing your strong aversion to something

▶ Being neither here nor there

Knowing just a few words — as long as they're the right words — can convince others that you speak Spanish fluently. Certain phrases can make a big difference, too. This chapter gives you ten Spanish phrases to use at the right moments, in the right places. You'll impress your friends and have fun, too.

¡Esta es la mía!

The exclamation **¡Esta es la mía!** (¡ehs-tah ehs lah *mee-*ah!) (*This is my chance!* [Literally: *This one is mine!*]) is a natural when you see an opportunity and go for it. In this phrase, **la** (lah) (*the*) refers to **una oportunidad** (*ooh*-nah oh-pohr-tooh-nee-*dahd*) (*an opportunity*), but you can use it in the sense of *I got it!* as well.

For instance, you may be fishing, waiting for **el pez** (ehl pehs) (*the fish*). The instant the fish bites, yelling **¡Este es el mío!** (¡ehs-teh ehs ehl *mee*-oh!) (*This one is mine!*) is appropriate. (It's the same phrase as the earlier version; you're just using masculine pronouns to match the masculine noun in the sentence.) You use the same phrase when you're waiting to catch **un vuelo** (oohn bvooh*eh*-loh) (*a flight*) or **un bus** (oohn bvoohs) (*a bus*). When you see your plane or bus arrive, you say, **¡Este es el mío!**

¡Voy a ir de farra!

You frequently hear the word **farra** (*fah*-rrah) (*party, good time*) in South America. If **farras** are a jolly part of your life, you'll love this word — it even has a verb form: **farrear** (fah-rreh-*ahr*) (*to party, to have a good time*). When you're getting ready for a night on the town, you'll sound like a native if you say, **¡Voy a ir de farra!** (¡bvohy ah eer deh *fah*-rrah!) (*I'm going to party!*).

Alone, **ir de farra** means *going partying, going to have a good time,* and *going for it all the way.*

An old, woeful tango goes, **Se acabaron . . . todas las farras** (seh ah-kah-*bvah*-rohn . . . *toh*-dahs lahs *fah*-rrahs) (*The party's over* [Literally: *All the parties have ended*]). No worse news could be had.

¡La cosa va viento en popa!

The idiom **¡La cosa va viento en popa!** (¡lah *koh*-sah bvah bveee*ehn*-toh ehn *poh*-pah!) (*It's going exceedingly well!* [Literally: *It's moving with the wind from the stern.*]) comes from the language of sailing. The race is on, and the wind is coming into the sail from the stern — nothing could go faster or better. You may also say the following:

> **¡El trabajo anduvo viento en popa!** (¡ehl trah-*bvah*-Hoh ahn-*dooh*-bvoh bveee*ehn*-toh ehn *poh*-pah!) (*The job went exceedingly well!*)

> **¡El partido salió viento en popa!** (¡ehl pahr-*tee*-doh sah-lee*oh* bveee*ehn*-toh ehn *poh*-pah!) (*The game went exceedingly well!*)

> **El aprendizaje del español va viento en popa!** (¡ehl ah-prehn-dee-*sah*-Heh dehl ehs-pah-*nyohl* bvah bveee*ehn*-toh ehn *poh*-pah!) (*Learning Spanish is going exceedingly well!*)

Nos divertimos en grande

The phrase **nos divertimos en grande** (nohs dee-bvehr-*tee*-mohs ehn *grahn*-deh) means *we had a great time.* You can use **en grande** (ehn *grahn*-deh) (*a lot, much, greatly, in a big way*) for many things. For instance, you can say, **comimos en grande** (koh-*mee*-mohs ehn *grahn*-deh) (*we ate a lot*) after a feast, or **gozamos en grande** (goh-*sah*-mohs ehn *gran*-deh) (*We really, really enjoyed ourselves*) after an extraordinarily pleasant event.

The verb **divertir** (dee-bvehr-*teer*) means to amuse or divert — just like this book amuses you and diverts your attention from other, less enjoyable tasks (or so we hope). **Divertirse** (dee-bvehr-*teer*-seh) (*to amuse [oneself]*) is a reflexive form of the verb. (For more on reflexive verbs, see Chapter 3.) **Diversión** (dee-bvehr-see*ohn*) is the word for fun or entertainment.

¿Y eso con qué se come?

¿Y eso con qué se come? (¿ee *eh*-soh kohn keh seh *koh*-meh?) (*What on earth is that?* [Literally: *And what do you eat that with?*]) is a fun phrase that demonstrates considerable knowledge of the language. The phrase is quite classical, and it doesn't belong to one country or another. You say, **¿Y eso con qué se come?** when you run across something absurd or unknown. For example, say a friend has just bought a very unusual hat. He thinks it's wonderful, but you're not really too sure it's appropriate for public appearances; it's really that funny looking. But your friend just doesn't realize it, so you may say, **¿Y eso con qué se come?** to jokingly let your friend know that maybe it's not such a great hat after all.

¡Así a secas!

¡Así a secas! (¡ah-*see* ah *seh*-kahs!) (*Just like that!* [Literally: *So to dried!*]) is an idiom that conveys astonishment or disbelief. You can use this phrase in many ways — often with a snap of your fingers to help show just how quickly something happened. For instance, if you happen to know someone who always seems to be borrowing your money, you may say something like **Me pidió mil dólares, ¡así a secas!** (meh pee-dee*oh* meel *doh*-lah-rehs, ¡ah-*see* ah *seh*-kahs!) (*He asked me for $1,000, just like that!*)

Caer fatal

You use the verb phrase **caerse fatal** (kah-*ehr*-seh fah-*tahl*) (*to strongly dislike something* [Literally: *to fatally fall down*]) to say that something unpleasant has befallen you. You can use **caerse fatal** for almost anything you don't like or that hurts you in some way. For example,

- ✔ You can say, **Sus bromas me caen fatal** (soohs bvroh-mahs meh *kah*-ehn fah-*tahl*) (*I can't stand her jokes*) when someone's sense of humor really gets on your nerves.
- ✔ **La comida me cayó fatal** (lah koh-*mee*-dah meh kah-*yoh* fah-*tahl*) (*The food made me sick*) is appropriate when you're suffering some painful consequence of eating food that didn't agree with you.

You can also use **fatal** (fah-*tahl*) (*bad, rotten, unpleasant* [Literally: *fatal*]) alone to say that something wasn't good. For example, to tell someone that you saw a really rotten movie, you'd say, **La película estuvo fatal.** (lah peh-*lee*-kooh-lah ehs-*tooh*-bvoh fah-*tahl.*).

Ver negras para

The idiom **ver negras para . . .** (bvehr *neh*-grahs *pah*-rah . . .) (*to have a hard time of . . .* [Literally: *to see black for . . .*]) followed by a verb beautifully conveys that a task is hugely difficult. Following are some examples of this phrase in action:

Las vimos negras para terminarlo. (lahs *bvee*-mohs *neh*-grahs *pah*-rah tehr-mee-*nahr*-loh.) (*We had a hard time finishing it.*)

Los refugiados se las vieron negras para salir del área. (lohs rreh-fooh-Hee*ah*-dohs seh lahs bvee-*eh*-rohn *neh*-grahs *pah*-rah sah-*leer* dehl *ah*-reh-ah.) (*The refugees had a hard time leaving the area.*)

Juana se las vio negras para aprender el inglés. (Hooh*ah*-nah seh lahs bvee*oh neh*-grahs *pah*-rah ah-prehn-*dehr* ehl een-*glehs.*) (*Juana had a hard time learning English.*)

¡Ojo!

The idiom **¡Ojo!** (¡*oh*-Hoh!) (*Watch out!, Keep your eyes open!* [Literally: *Eye!*]) is a very fluent way to warn a Spanish speaker of upcoming danger or to let them know to be wary of something. For example, to warn someone of uneven cement in the sidewalk she's walking on or a sudden upcoming dip in the walkway, you can say **¡Ojo!** (or just use body language and point to your eye).

Pasó sin pena ni gloria

You generally use the phrase **pasó sin pena ni gloria** (pah-*soh* seen *peh*-nah nee *gloh*-reeah) (*it was neither here nor there*) to talk about an event that had little echo with you or the public.

The verb **pasar** in this case signals the passing of time. **Pena** (*peh*-nah) is *grief* and **gloria** (*gloh*-reeah) is *glory*. Here you're saying that the event went by without pulling you down or lifting you up — it made no difference to you. Following are some examples of how you may use this phrase:

> **El concierto pasó sin pena ni gloria.** (ehl kohn-see-*ehr*-toh pah-*soh* seen *peh*-nah nee *gloh*-reeah.) (*The concert wasn't terrible, but it wasn't great either.*)

> **La reunión pasó sin pena ni gloria.** (lah rrehooh-nee*ohn* pah-*soh* seen *peh*-nah nee *gloh*-reeah.) (*The meeting wasn't very informative.*)

> **La cena se acabó sin pena ni gloria.** (lah *seh*-nah seh ah-kah-*bvoh* seen *peh*-nah nee *gloh*-reeah.) (*The supper was just so-so.*)

Part V
Appendixes

The 5th Wave   By Rich Tennant

"Here's an idea; let's practice conjugating verbs in Spanish. Last night, you were 'viviste la vida loca'. But this morning, you are 'viviendo la vida Pepto Bismol'."

In this part . . .

This part of the book includes important information that you can use for reference. We include two mini-dictionaries (Spanish-to-English and English-to-Spanish), verb tables that show you how to conjugate regular and irregular verbs, a listing of the tracks included on the audio CD (and where in the book to find those dialogues so that you can follow along), and the all-important answer keys for the Fun & Games sections at the end of the chapters.

Spanish-English Mini-Dictionary

A

a pie (ah *pee*eh): walking (Literally: on foot)

abogado (ah-bvoh-*gah*-doh) m: lawyer

abrigo (ah-*bvree*-goh) m: overcoat

abril (ah-*bvreel*) m: April

abrir (ah-*bvreer*): to open

abuela (ah-bvooh*eh*-lah) f: grandmother

abuelo (ah-bvooh*eh*-loh) m: grandfather

acompañar (ah-kohm-pah-*nyahr*): to go with, to accompany

acostarse (ah-koh-*stahr*-seh): to go to bed

actor (ahk-*tohr*) m: actor

actriz (ahk-*trees*) f: actress

acústica (ah-*koohs*-tee-kah) f: acoustics

adelante (ah-deh-*lahn*-teh): in front, ahead

adentro (ah-*dehn*-troh): inside

adiós (ah-dee*ohs*): good-bye

aduana (ah-dooh*ah*-nah) f: customs

afuera (ah-fooh*eh*-rah): outside

agencia (ah-*Hehn*-seeah) f: agency

agosto (ah-*gohs*-toh) m: August

agua (*ah*-goohah) f: water

aguacate (ah-goohah-*kah*-teh) m: avocado

ahora (ah-*oh*-rah): now

ajedrez (ah-Heh-*drehs*) m: chess

ajo (*ah*-Hoh) m: garlic

al fondo (ahl *fohn*-doh): at the back

al frente (de) (ahl *frehn*-teh [deh]): in front (of)

al interior (ahl een-teh-ree*ohr*): opening to the interior

al lado (de) (ahl *lah*-doh [deh]): beside, next to, at the side (of)

alcohol (ahl-koh-*ohl*) m: alcohol

alfombra (ahl-*fohm*-bvrah) f: rug

algodón (ahl-goh-*dohn*) m: cotton

algún (ahl-*goohn*): some

allá (ah-*yah*): over there

allí (ah-*yee*): there

almohada (ahl-moh-*ah*-dah) f: pillow

almuerzo (ahl-mooh*ehr*-soh) m: lunch

alto (*ahl*-toh): tall; high

amarillo (ah-mah-*ree*-yoh): yellow

ambulancia (ahm-bvooh-*lahn*-seeah) f: ambulance

amígdalas (ah-*meeg*-dah-lahs) f: tonsils

anaranjado (ah-nah-rahn-*Hah*-doh): orange (color)

antebrazo (ahn-teh-*bvrah*-soh): forearm

anunciar (ah-noohn-see*ahr*): to advertise, to announce

año (*ah*-nyoh) m: year

aorta (ah-*ohr*-tah) f: aorta

aparato (ah-pah-*rah*-toh) m: machine, appliance

aprender (ah-prehn-*dehr*): to learn

apretado (ah-preh-*tah*-doh): tight

aquí (ah-*kee*): here

aretes (ah-*reh*-tehs) m, pl: earrings

armario (ahr-*mah*-reeoh) m: closet

arriba (ah-*rree*-bvah): above

arroz (ah-*rrohs*) m: rice

ascensor (ah-sehn-*sohr*) m: elevator

asiento (ah-see*ehn*-toh) m: seat

aspiradora (ahs-pee-rah-*doh*-rah) f: vacuum

atacar (ah-tah-*kahr*): attack

ático (*ah*-tee-koh) m: attic

atún (ah-*toohn*) m: tuna

auto (a*hooh*-toh) m: car (South America)

autobús (ahooh-toh-*bvoohs*) m: bus

autopista (ahooh-toh-*pees*-tah) f: freeway

avenida (ah-bveh-*nee*-dah) f: avenue

ayer (ah-*yehr*): yesterday

ayudar (ah-yooh-*dahr*): to help

azul (ah-*soohl*): blue

B

bailar (bvahee-*lahr*): to dance

bajar (bvah-*Hahr*): to descend, to go down

bajo (*bvah*-Hoh): under, below

balcón (bvahl-*kohn*) m: balcony

bañarse (bvah-*nyahr*-seh): to bathe one's self

bañera (bvah-*nyeh*-rah) f: bathtub

baño (*bvah*-nyoh) m: bathroom

barato (bvah-*rah*-toh): cheap

barrio (*bvah*-rreeoh) m: neighborhood

bastante (bvahs-*tahn*-teh): quite; enough

basurero (bvah-sooh-*reh*-roh) m: garbage can

bata de baño (*bvah*-tah deh *bvah*-nyoh) f: bathrobe

batería (bvah-teh-*ree*-ah) f: battery

batidor manual (bvah-tee-*dohr* mah-nooh-*ahl*) m: whisk

beber (bveh-*bvehr*): to drink

bello (*bveh*-yoh): beautiful

biblioteca (bvee-bvleeoh-*teh*-kah) f: library

bicicleta (bvee-see-*kleh*-tah) f: bicycle

bife (*bvee*-feh) m: steak

bigote (bvee-*goh*-teh) m: moustache

billete (bvee-*yeh*-teh) m: bill

billetera (bvee-yeh-*teh*-rah) f: wallet

biografía (bveeoh-grah-*fee*-ah) f: biography

blanco (*bvlahn*-koh): white

blusa (*bvlooh*-sah) f: blouse

boca (*bvoh*-kah) f: mouth

boleto (bvoh-*leh*-toh) m: ticket

bolígrafo (bvoh-*lee*-grah-foh) m: pen

bolsillo (bvohl-*see*-yoh) m: pocket

botas (*bvoh*-tahs) f, pl: boots

botiquín (bvoh-tee-*keen*) m: medicine cabinet

bragas (*bvrah*-gahs) f, pl: panties

brazo (*bvrah*-soh) m: arm

brillo (*bvree*-yoh) m: shine

broche (*bvroh*-cheh) m: brooch

brócoli (*bvroh*-koh-lee) m: broccoli

broma (*bvroh*-mah) f: joke

bueno (bvooh*eh*-noh): good

bufanda (bvooh-*fahn*-dah) f: scarf

bulevar (bvooh-leh-*bvahr*) m: boulevard

buscar (bvoohs-*kahr*): to search, to look for

C

caballo (kah-*bvah*-yoh) m: horse

cabeza (kah-*bveh*-sah) f: head

café (kah-*feh*) m: coffee

cajero (kah-*Heh*-roh) m: cashier (male)

calcetines (kahl-seh-*tee*-nehs) m, pl: socks

caldero (kahl-*deh*-roh) m: pot

calendario (kah-lehn-*dah*-reeoh) m: calendar

caliente (kah-lee*ehn*-teh): hot (temperature)

calle (*kah*-yeh) f: street

cama (*kah*-mah) f: bed

camarón (kah-mah-*rohn*) m: shrimp

cambiar (kahm-bvee*ahr*): to change

cambista (kahm-*bvees*-tah) m, f: money changer

camino (kah-*mee*-noh) m: road

camisa (kah-*mee*-sah) f: shirt

camiseta (kah-mee-*seh*-tah) f: T-shirt

campeón (kahm-peh-*ohn*) m, f: champion

canal (kah-*nahl*) m: channel, canal

cancelar (kahn-seh-*lahr*): to cancel

cancha (*kahn*-chah) f: playing field

cantante (kahn-*tahn*-teh) m, f: singer

cantar (kahn-*tahr*): to sing

cantidad (kahn-tee-*dahd*) f: quantity, amount

carácter (kah-*rahk*-tehr) m: character, personality

caries (*kah*-reeehs) f: cavity

caro (*kah*-roh): expensive

carpetas (kahr-*peh*-tahs) f, pl: file folders

carro (*kah*-rroh) m: car (Mexico)

carta (*kahr*-tah) f: letter

casa (*kah*-sah) f: house

cebolla (seh-*bvoh*-yah) f: onion

celeste (seh-*lehs*-teh): sky blue

cena (*seh*-nah) f: supper

cerca (*sehr*-kah): close by

cereales (seh-reh-*ah*-lehs) m, pl: cereals

cereza (seh-*reh*-sah) f: cherry

cero (*seh*-roh): zero

chaqueta (chah-*keh*-tah) f: jacket

chico (*chee*-koh): little, small

chofer (choh-*fehr*) m, f: driver

ciclismo (see-*klees*-moh) m: cycling

cine (*see*-neh) m: cinema

cinturón (seen-tooh-*rohn*) m: belt

ciruela (see-roohe*h*-lah) f: plum

cirugía (see-rooh-*Hee*ah) f: surgery

cita (*see*-tah) f: appointment

ciudad (seeooh-*dahd*) f: city

claro (*klah*-roh): light

cobija (koh-*bvee*-Hah) f: blanket

cocina (koh-*see*-nah) f: kitchen

cocinera (koh-see-*neh*-rah) f: cook (female)

coco (*koh*-koh) m: coconut

código postal (*koh*-dee-goh pohs-*tahl*) m: postal code (ZIP code)

colgar (kohl-*gahr*): to hang, to hang up

collar (koh-*yahr*) m: necklace

comer (koh-*mehr*): to eat

comida (koh-*mee*-dah) f: dinner, food

comprar (kohm-*prahr*): to buy

comprender (kohm-prehn-*dehr*): to understand

computadora (kohm-pooh-tah-*doh*-rah) f: computer

computadora portátil (kohm-pooh-tah-*doh*-rah pohr-*tah*-teel) f: laptop computer

congelador (kohn-Heh-lah-*dohr*) m: freezer

contar (kohn-*tahr*): to count

contento (kohn-*tehn*-toh) m: content, satisfied

corazón (koh-rah-*sohn*) m: heart

corbata (kohr-*bvah*-tah) f: tie

correo (koh-*rreh*-oh) m: mail, post

correo electrónico (koh-*rreh*-oh eh-lehk-*troh*-nee-koh) m: e-mail

cosa (*koh*-sah) f: thing

costar (kohs-*tahr*): to cost (in price)

cuadra (kooh*ah*-drah) f: block

cuál (koohahl): which (accented when used in a question)

cual (koohahl): which (unaccented when used in a statement or answer)

cuándo (kooh*ahn*-doh): when (accented when used in a question)

cuando (kooh*ahn*-doh): when (unaccented when used in a statement or an answer)

cuánto (kooh*ahn*-toh): how much (accented when used in a question)

cuanto (kooh*ahn*-toh): how much (unaccented when used in a statement or answer)

cuarto (kooh*ahr*-toh) m: quarter, room

cuarto (koohahr-toh): fourth

cuchara (kooh-chah-rah) f: spoon

cuchillo (kooh-chee-yoh) m: knife

cuello (kooheh-yoh) m: neck

cuenta (koohehn-tah) f: account

cuenta de cheques (koohehn-tah deh cheh-kehs) f: checking account

cuestionario (koohehs-teeoh-nah-reeoh) m: questionnaire, form

cuñada (kooh-nyah-dah) f: sister-in-law

cuñado (kooh-nyah-doh) m: brother-in-law

D

de (deh): of, from

debajo (deh-bvah-Hoh): underneath

débito (deh-bvee-toh): debit

décimo (deh-see-moh): tenth

dedo (deh-doh) m: finger

defensa (deh-fehn-sah) f: defense

dejar (deh-Hahr): to leave

dentista (dehn-tees-tah) m, f: dentist

dentro (de) (dehn-troh [deh]): inside (of)

departamento (deh-pahr-tah-mehn-toh) m: department

derecha (deh-reh-chah): right

derecho (deh-reh-choh): straight; straight ahead

desayuno (deh-sah-yooh-noh) m: breakfast

despacio (dehs-pah-seeoh): slow

despertador (dehs-pehr-tah-dohr) m: alarm clock

despertarse (dehs-pehr-tahr-seh): to wake up

día (dee-ah) m: day

diamantes (deeah-mahn-tehs) m, pl: diamonds

diario (deeah-reeoh) m: newspaper, daily

dibujo (dee-bvooh-Hoh) m: drawing, pattern

diciembre (dee-seeehm-bvreh) m: December

diente (deeehn-teh) m: tooth

difícil (dee-fee-seel): difficult

dinero (dee-neh-roh): money

dirección (dee-rehk-see-ohn) f: address

disponible (dees-poh-nee-bvleh): available

divertido (dee-bvehr-tee-doh): amusing; funny

doblar (doh-bvlahr): turn

doble (doh-bvleh): double

doctor (dohk-tohr) m: male doctor

doctora (dohk-toh-rah) f: female doctor

documento (doh-kooh-mehn-toh) m: document; paper

dolor (doh-lohr) m: pain

dolor de muelas (doh-lohr deh mooheh-lahs) m: toothache

domingo (doh-meen-goh) m: Sunday

dormitorio (dohr-mee-toh-reeoh) m: bedroom

ducha (dooh-chah) f: shower

dulce (doohl-seh) m: sweet

durante (dooh-rahn-teh): during

durazno (dooh-rahs-noh) m: peach

E

edad (eh-dahd) f: age

edificio (eh-dee-fee-seeoh) m: building

él (ehl) m: he

electricista (eh-lehk-tree-sees-tah) m, f: electrician (male or female)

ella (eh-yah) f: she

ellas (eh-yahs) f: they (feminine)

ellos (eh-yohs) m: they (masculine, or mixed group)

empezar (ehm-peh-sahr): to begin; to start

empleo (ehm-pleh-oh) m: job

encima (de) (ehn-see-mah [deh]): on top (of)

encontrar (ehn-kohn-*trahr*): to find

enero (eh-*neh*-roh) m: January

enfermera (ehn-fehr-*meh*-rah) f: nurse

enfermo (ehn-*fehr*-moh): sick

ensalada (ehn-sah-*lah*-dah) f: salad

entender (ehn-tehn-*dehr*): to understand

entrada (ehn-*trah*-dah) f: entrance, entryway

entradas (ehn-*trah*-dahs) f, pl: hors d'oeuvres

entregar (ehn-treh-*gahr*): to deliver

enviar (ehn-bvee*ahr*): send

equipo (eh-*kee*-poh) m: team

escalera (ehs-kah-*leh*-rah) f: staircase

escribir (ehs-kree-*bveer*): to write

escritorio (ehs-kree-*toh*-reeoh) m: desk

escuchar (ehs-kooh-*chahr*): to listen to, to hear

escuela (ehs-kooh*eh*-lah) f: school

escultura (ehs-koohl-*tooh*-rah) f: sculpture

escurridor (ehs-kooh-rree-*dohr*) m: colander

especial (ehs-peh-see*ahl*): special

espejo (ehs-*peh*-Hoh) m: mirror

esperar (ehs-peh-*rahr*): to wait for, to hope

espinaca (ehs-pee-*nah*-kah) f: spinach

esposa (ehs-*poh*-sah) f: wife

esposo (ehs-*poh*-soh) m: husband

esquí (ehs-*kee*) m: ski

esquina (ehs-*kee*-nah) f: corner

estación (ehs-tah-see*ohn*) f: station, season

estacionamiento (ehs-tah-seeoh-nah-mee*ehn*-toh) m: parking

estadio (ehs-*tah*-deeoh) m: stadium

estado (ehs-*tah*-doh) m: state

estar (ehs-*tahr*): to be (temporary)

este (*ehs*-teh) m: east, this

estilo (ehs-*tee*-loh) m: style

estómago (ehs-*toh*-mah-goh) m: stomach

estreñimiento (ehs-treh-nyee-mee*ehn*-toh) m: constipation

estudio (ehs-*tooh*-deeoh) m: study

estufa (eh-*stooh*-fah) f: stove

evacuación (eh-bvah-kooah-see*ohn*) f: bowel movement (Literally: evacuation)

examen (ehk-*sah*-mehn) m: test

F

fábrica (*fah*-bvree-kah) f: plant, factory

fácil (*fah*-seel): easy

falda (*fahl*-dah) f: skirt

farmacia (fahr-*mah*-seeah) f: pharmacy

febrero (feh-*bvreh*-roh) m: February

fecha (*feh*-chah) f: date

feliz (feh-*lees*): happy

feo (*feh*-oh): ugly

fideo (fee-*deh*-oh) m: noodle

fiebre (fee*eh*-bvreh) f: fever

fila (*fee*-lah) f: row, line, line-up

firmar (feer-*mahr*): to sign

formulario (fohr-mooh-*lah*-reeoh) m: form

fotocopiadora (foh-toh-koh-peeah-*doh*-rah) f: photocopier

fotógrafo (foh-*toh*-grah-foh) m: photographer

fractura (frahk-*tooh*-rah) f: fracture, broken bone

franqueo (frahn-*keh*-oh) m: postage

fregadero (freh-gah-*deh*-roh) m: sink (kitchen)

fresa (*freh*-sah) f: strawberry

fría (*free*-ah): cold

fruta (*frooh*-tah) f: fruit

fuera (fooh*eh*-rah): outside

G

gabinete (gah-bvee-*neh*-teh) m: cabinet

galleta (gah-*yeh*-tah) f: cookie; cracker

ganar (gah-*nahr*): to win

gancho (*gahn*-choh) m: clothes hanger

garantía (gah-rahn-*tee*-ah) f: warranty

garganta (gahr-*gahn*-tah) f: throat

gente (*Hehn*-teh) f: people

gerente (Heh-*rehn*-teh) m, f: manager

gol (gohl) m: goal, hit

golpear (gohl-peh-*ahr*): to hit, to bang

gracias (*grah*-seeahs): thank you

grande (*grahn*-deh): big; large

grapadora (grah-pah-*doh*-rah) f: stapler

grapas (*grah*-pahs) f, pl: staples

gris (grees): grey

grupo (*grooh*-poh) m: group

guantes (gooh*ahn*-tehs) m, pl: gloves

guerra (*geh*-rrah) f: war

guía (*gee*ah) m, f: guide

gustar (goohs-*tahr*): to be pleasing, to like

H

hablar (ah-*bvlahr*): to talk

hacia (*ah*-seeah): toward

hambre (*ahm*-bvreh) f: hunger

hecho a mano (*eh*-choh ah *mah*-noh): handmade

herida (eh-*ree*-dah) f: wound

hermana (ehr-*mah*-nah) f: sister

hermano (ehr-*mah*-noh) m: brother

hija (*ee*-Hah) f: daughter

hijo (*ee*-Hoh) m: son

hombre (*ohm*-bvreh) m: man

hombro (*ohm*-bvroh) m: shoulder

hora (*oh*-rah) f: hour

horario (oh-*rah*-reeoh) m: schedule

horno (*ohr*-noh) m: oven

horno microondas (*ohr*-noh mee-kroh *ohn*-dahs) m: microwave

hoy (ohy): today

hueso (ooh*eh*-soh) m: bone

huevo (ooh*eh*-bvoh) m: egg

I

identificación (ee-dehn-tee-fee-kah-see*ohn*) f: identification

idioma (ee-dee*oh*-mah) m: language

impermeable (eem-pehr-meh-*ah*-bvleh) m: raincoat

impresora (eem-preh-*soh*-rah) f: printer

imprimir (eem-pree-*meer*): to print

incluido (een-klooh*ee*-doh): included

ingeniero (een-Heh-neee*ehr*-roh) m: engineer

inmigración (een-mee-grah-see*ohn*) f: immigration

intestino (een-tehs-*tee*-noh) m: bowel, intestine, gut

invitar (een-bvee-*tahr*): to invite

ir (eer): to go

ir de compras (eer deh *kohm*-prahs): to go shopping

isla (*ees*-lah) f: island

izquierda (ees-keee*ehr*-dah): left

J

jardín (Hahr-*deen*) m: garden

jeans (jeens) m, pl: jeans

juego (Hooh*eh*-goh) m: game

jueves (Hooh*eh*-bvehs) m: Thursday

jugador (Hooh-gah-*dohr*) m: player

jugar (Hooh-*gahr*): to play

julio (*Hooh*-leeoh) m: July

junio (*Hooh*-neeoh) m: June

junto (*Hoohn*-toh): together

L

lámpara (*lahm*-pah-rah) f: lamp

lana (*lah*-nah) f: wool

lápiz (*lah*-pees) m: pencil

lástima (*lahs*-tee-mah) f: pity, shame

lavadora (lah-bvah-*doh*-rah) f: washing machine

lavamanos (lah-bvah-*mah*-nohs) m: sink (bathroom)

lavaplatos (lah-bvah-*plah*-tohs) m: dishwasher

leche (*leh*-cheh) f: milk

lechuga (leh-*chooh*-gah) f: lettuce

leer (leh-*ehr*): to read

libre (*lee*-bvreh): free

libreta (lee-*bvreh*-tah) f: notepad

libro (*lee*-bvroh) m: book

lima (*lee*-mah) f: lime

limón (lee-*mohn*) m: lemon

limpiar (leem-pee-*ahr*): to clean

línea (*lee*-neh-ah) f: line

liso (*lee*-soh): plain; flat

listada (lees-*tah*-dah): striped

llamar (yah-*mahr*): to call

llamarse (yah-*mahr*-seh): to call oneself

llave (*yah*-bveh) f: key

llegar (yeh-*gahr*): to arrive

llevar (yeh-*bvahr*): to carry, to wear

lluvia (*yooh*-bveeah) f: rain

luna (*looh*-nah) f: moon

lunes (*looh*-nehs) m: Monday

M

madera (mah-*deh*-rah) f: wood

madre (*mah*-dreh) f: mother

madrina (mah-*dree*-nah) f: godmother

maleta (mah-*leh*-tah) f: luggage; suitcase

malo (*mah*-loh): bad

mañana (mah-*nyah*-nah) f: morning

mañana (mah-*nyah*-nah): tomorrow

manejar (mah-neh-*Hahr*): to drive (a car)

manga (*mahn*-gah) f: sleeve

mano (*mah*-noh) f: hand

manzana (mahn-*sah*-nah) f: apple, block (length of street)

mapa (*mah*-pah) m: map

máquina de fax (*mah*-kee-nah deh fahks) f: fax machine

mar (mahr) m: sea

maravilloso (mah-rah-bvee-*yoh*-soh): wonderful

marcador (mahr-kah-*dohr*) m: marker

marcar (mahr-*kahr*): to mark, to dial, to punch in the number

mariposa (mah-ree-*poh*-sah) f: butterfly

marisco (mah-*rees*-koh) m: seafood

marrón (mah-*rrohn*): brown

martes (*mahr*-tehs) m: Tuesday

martillo (mahr-*tee*-yoh): hammer

marzo (*mahr*-soh) m: March

más (mahs): more

máscara (*mahs*-kah-rah) f: mask

matiné (mah-tee-*neh*) f: early show

mayo (*mah*-yoh) m: May

mecánico (meh-*kah*-nee-koh) m: mechanic

medianoche (meh-deeah-*noh*-cheh) f: midnight

médica (*meh*-dee-kah) f: physician (female), doctor (female)

médico (*meh*-dee-koh) m: physician (male), doctor (male)

medio (*meh*-deeoh) m: half, middle

medio baño (*meh*-deeoh *bvah*-nyoh) m: half-bathroom (a bathroom with no shower or tub)

mediodía (meh-deeoh-*dee*-ah) m: noon

medir (meh-*deer*): to measure

mejor (meh-*Hohr*): better

menos (*meh*-nohs): less

mes (mehs) m: month

mesa (*meh*-sah) f: table

miércoles (meee*ehr*-koh-lehs) m: Wednesday

minuto (mee-*nooh*-toh) m: minute

moneda (moh-*neh*-dah) f: coin

monitor de video (moh-*nee*-tohr deh *bvee*-deh-oh) m: monitor

montaña (mohn-*tah*-nyah) f: mountain

morado (moh-*rah*-doh): purple

mucho (*mooh*-choh): a lot, much

mueble (mooh*eh*-bvleh) m: furniture

muela (mooh*eh*-lah) f: molar

mujer (mooh-*Hehr*) f: woman

muñeca (mooh-*nyeh*-kah) f: wrist

museo (mooh-*seh*-oh) m: museum

muslo (*moohs*-loh) m: thigh

N

nadar (nah-*dahr*): to swim

naranja (nah-*rahn*-Hah) f: orange (fruit)

nariz (nah-*rees*) f: nose

náusea (*nah*ooh-seh-ah) f: nausea, sickness

negro (*neh*-groh): black

nevera (neh-*bveh*-rah) f: refrigerator

nieta (neee*eh*-tah) f: granddaughter

nieto (neee*eh*-toh) m: grandson

ningún (neen-*goohn*): none

niña (*nee*-nyah) f: girl

niño (*nee*-nyoh) m: boy

noche (*noh*-cheh) f: night

norte (*nohr*-teh) m: north

nosotras (noh-*soh*-trahs) f: we (feminine)

nosotros (noh-*soh*-trohs) m: we (masculine, and mixed group)

notas autoadhesivas desprendibles (*noh*-tahs ahooh-toh-ahd-eh-*see*-bvahs dehs-prehn-*dee*-bvlehs) f, pl: sticky notes

novela (noh-*bveh*-lah) f: novel

noveno (noh-*bveh*-noh): ninth

novia (*noh*-bveeah) f: girlfriend

noviembre (noh-bveee*ehm*-bvreh) m: November

novio (*noh*-bveeoh) m: boyfriend

nuera (nooh*eh*-rah) f: daughter-in-law

número (*nooh*-meh-roh) m: number

O

obra (*oh*-bvrah) f: play (Literally: the work)

observación (obv-sehr-bvah-seee*ohn*) f: observation

octavo (ohk-*tah*-bvoh): eighth

octubre (ohk-*tooh*-bvreh) m: October

ocupado (oh-kooh-*pah*-doh): occupied busy

oeste (oh-*ehs*-teh) m: west

oficina (oh-fee-*see*-nah) f: office

ojo (*oh*-Hoh) m: eye

olla (*oh*-yah) f: pot

olvidarse de (ohl-bvee-*dahr*-seh [deh]): to forget (about)

once (*ohn*-seh): eleven

ordenador (ohr-deh-nah-*dohr*) m: tower case

oreja (oh-*reh*-Hah) f: ear

orina (oh-*ree*-nah) f: urine

oro (*oh*-roh) m: gold

oscuro (ohs-*kooh*-roh): dark

otro (*oh*-troh): the other one, another

P

padre (*pah*-dreh) m: father

padrino (pah-*dree*-noh) m: godfather

pagar (pah-*gahr*): to pay

país (pah*ees*) m: country

pájaro (*pah*-Hah-roh) m: bird

palta (*pahl*-tah) f: avocado (in South America)

pantalones (pahn-tah-*loh*-nehs) m, pl: trousers, pants

pantalones cortos (pahn-tah-*loh*-nehs *kohr*-tohs) m, pl: shorts

pantorrilla (pahn-toh-*rree*-yah) f: calf (of the leg)

pañales (pah-*nyah*-lehs) m, pl: diapers

pañuelos de papel (pah-nyooh*eh*-lohs deh pah-*pehl*) m, pl: tissues

papas (*pah*-pahs) f, pl: potatoes

papas fritas (*pah*-pahs *free*-tahs) f: potato chips, French fries

papaya (pah-*pah*-yah) f: papaya

papel (pah-*pehl*) m: paper

papel de fotocopiadora (pah-*pehl* deh foh-toh-koh-peeah-*doh*-rah) m: copy paper

papel higiénico (pah-*pehl* ee-Hee*eh*-nee-koh) m: toilet paper

paquete (pah-*keh*-teh) m: package

parada (pah-*rah*-dah) f: stop

pared (pah-*rehd*) f: wall

parque (*pahr*-keh) m: park

partir (pahr-*teer*): to start

pasaporte (pah-sah-*pohr*-teh) m: passport

pasear (pah-seh-*ahr*): to walk; to stroll

paseo (pah-*seh*-oh) m: walk

pasillo (pah-*see*-yoh) m: aisle, hallway

patatas (pah-*tah*-tahs) f, pl: potatoes (in Spain)

pato (*pah*-toh) m: duck

pavimento (pah-bvee-*mehn*-toh) m: pavement

peaje (peh-*ah*-Heh) m: toll

pecho (*peh*-choh) m: chest

pegamento (peh-gah-*mehn*-toh) m: glue

peinarse (peh*ee*-*nahr*-seh): to comb one's hair

peine (*peh*ee-neh) m: comb

pelea (peh-*leh*-ah) f: fight

pelo (*peh*-loh) m: hair

pena (*peh*-nah) f: shame; pity

pensar (pehn-*sahr*): to think

peor (peh-*ohr*): worse

pequeño (peh-*keh*-nyoh): small

pera (*peh*-rah) f: pear

perla (*pehr*-lah) f: pearl

personal (pehr-soh-*nahl*) m: staff

pescado (pehs-*kah*-doh) m: fish

picante (pee-*kahn*-teh): hot; spicy (flavor)

pie (pee*eh*) m: foot

pierna (pee*ehr*-nah) f: leg

piyamas (pee-*yah*-mahs) m, pl: pajamas

piloto (pee-*loh*-toh) m: pilot

pimentón (pee-mehn-*tohn*) m: sweet pepper (in Argentina, Chile, and Uruguay)

piña (*pee*-nyah) f: pineapple

pintar (peen-*tahr*): to paint

pintura (peen-*tooh*-rah) f: painting

piscina (pees-*see*-nah) f: swimming pool

piso (*pee*-soh) m: floor

pizarra blanca (pee-*sah*-rrah b*vlahn*-kah) f: whiteboard

plancha (*plahn*-chah) f: iron

planear (plah-neh-*ahr*): to plan

planta del pie (*plahn*-tah dehl pee*eh*) f: sole of the foot

plátano (*plah*-tah-noh) m: plantain

plato (*plah*-toh) m: plate

playa (*plah*-yah) f: beach

plaza (*plah*-sah) f: square

plomo (*ploh*-moh) m: lead

poco (*poh*-koh) m: a bit, a small amount

poeta (poh-*eh*-tah) m: poet

policía (poh-lee-*see*-ah) m, f: police officer

pollo (*poh*-yoh) m: chicken

pomelo (poh-*meh*-loh) m: grapefruit (in Mexico)

por ciento (pohr see*ehn*-toh): percent, percentage

por qué (pohr *keh*): why

portal (pohr-*tahl*) m: portal, entrance, doorway

potable (poh-*tah*-bvleh): drinkable

precio (*preh*-seeoh) m: price

precioso (preh-see*oh*-soh): precious, gorgeous, beautiful, lovely

preferir (preh-feh-*reer*): to prefer

preguntar (preh-goohn-*tahr*): to ask (a question)

preocuparse (por) (preh-oh-kooh-*pahr*-seh [pohr]): to worry (about)

preparar (preh-pah-*rahr*): to prepare

presión sanguínea (preh-see*ohn* sahn-*gee*-neh-ah) f: blood pressure

prima (*pree*-mah) f: cousin (female)

primera clase (pree-*meh*-rah *klah*-seh) f: first class

primero (pree-*meh*-roh): first

primo (*pree*-moh) m: cousin (male)

probador (proh-bvah-*dohr*) m: fitting room

probar (proh-*bvahr*): to try

programa (proh-*grah*-mah) m: program, schedule

programar (proh-*grah*-mahr): to schedule

pronto (*prohn*-toh): right away, soon

propio (*proh*-peeoh): one's own

proyector (proh-yehk-*tohr*) m: projector

puente (pooh*ehn*-teh) m: bridge

puerta (pooh*ehr*-tah) f: door

pulgar (poohl-*gahr*) m: thumb

pulmón (poohl-*mohn*) m: lung

pulsera (poohl-*seh*-rah) f: bracelet

puntos (*poohn*-tohs) m, pl: stitches (surgical)

pura (*pooh*-rah): pure

Q

que (keh): that, than

qué (keh): what (accented when used in a question)

quedarse (keh-*dahr*-seh): to stay, to remain

quejarse (de) (keh-*Hahr*-seh [deh]): to complain (about)

querer (keh-*rehr*): to want, to wish

queso (*keh*-soh) m: cheese

quién (kee*ehn*): who (accented when used in a question)

quien (kee*ehn*): who (unaccented when used in a statement or answer)

quinto (*keen*-toh): fifth

quitarse (kee-*tahr*-seh): to take off, remove clothing

R

radiografía (rrah-deeoh-grah-*fee*-ah) f: x-ray picture

raqueta (rrah-*keh*-tah) f: racket

ratón (rrah-*tohn*) m: mouse

receta (rreh-*seh*-tah) f: prescription, recipe

recibidor (rreh-see-bvee-*dohr*) m: entrance hall

recibo (rreh-*see*-bvoh) m: receipt

recogedor (rreh-koh-Heh-*dohr*) m: dustpan

reembolsar (rreh-ehm-bvol-*sahr*): to refund

registrarse (rreh-Hees-*trahr*-seh): to check in

reglamentos (rrehg-lah-*mehn*-tohs) m: rules

reírse (de) (rreh*eer*-seh [deh]): to laugh (at, about)

reloj (rreh-*loh*) m: watch

repetir (rreh-peh-*teer*): to repeat

repollo (rreh-*poh*-yoh) m: cabbage (in Argentina and Chile)

reservación (rreh-sehr-bvah-see-*ohn*) f: reservation

reservar (rreh-sehr-*bvahr*): to reserve

responder (rrehs-pohn-*dehr*): to answer

restaurante (rrehs-tahooh-*rahn*-teh) m: restaurant

retiro (rreh-*tee*-roh) m: withdrawal

reunión (rrehooh-nee*ohn*) f: meeting

revisar (rreh-bvee-*sahr*): to go through, to check

riñón (rree-*nyohn*) m: kidney

río (*rree*-oh) m: river

robar (rroh-*bvahr*): to steal, to rob

rojo (*rroh*-Hoh): red

rol (rrohl) m: role

romántico (rroh-*mahn*-tee-koh): romantic

ropa (*rroh*-pah) f: clothes

ropa interior (*rroh*-pah een-teh-ree*ohr*) f: underwear

rosado (rroh-*sah*-doh): pink

rostro (*rrohs*-troh) m: face

ruinas (rrooh*ee*-nahs) f, pl: ruins

S

sábado (*sah*-bvah-doh) m: Saturday

sábana (*sah*-bvah-nah) f: sheet

sacagrapas (sah-kah-*grah*-pahs) m: staple remover

sacapuntas (sah-kah-*poohn*-tahs) m: pencil sharpener

sala (*sah*-lah) f: living room

sala de copias (*sah*-lah deh *koh*-peeahs) f: copy room

sala de correos (*sah*-lah deh koh-*rreh*-ohs) f: mailroom

sala de descanso (*sah*-lah deh dehs-*kahn*-soh) f: break room

sala de reuniones (*sah*-lah deh rrehooh-nee*oh*-nehs) f: conference room

salado (sah-*lah*-doh): salty

saldo (*sahl*-doh) m: balance (financial)

salir (sah-*leer*): to exit, to leave, to go out

salud (sah-*loohd*) f: health

sandalias (sahn-*dah*-leeahs) f, pl: sandals

sandía (sahn-*dee*-ah) f: watermelon

sangrar (sahn-*grahr*): to bleed

sangre (*sahn*-greh) f: blood

sano (*sah*-noh): healthy

sardinas (sahr-*dee*-nahs) f, pl: sardines

sartén (sahr-*tehn*) f: frying pan

secadora (seh-kah-*doh*-rah) f: dryer

seco: *seh*-koh: dry

sed (sehd) f: thirst

seguir (seh-*geer*): to follow, to continue

segundo (seh-*goohn*-doh) m: second

sello (*seh*-yoh) m: stamp

semana (seh-*mah*-nah) f: week

señor (Sr.) (seh-*nyor*) m: Mr. or sir

señora (Sra.) (seh-*nyor*-ah) f: Mrs. or madam

señorita (Srta.) (seh-nyor-*ee*-tah) f: Miss

sentarse (sehn-*tahr*-seh): to sit down

sentirse (sehn-*teer*-seh): to feel

septiembre (sehp-tee*ehm*-bvreh) m: September

séptimo (*sehp*-tee-moh): seventh

ser (sehr): to be (permanent)

serrucho (seh-*rrooh*-choh) m: saw (tool)

servilleta (sehr-bvee-*yeh*-tah) f: napkin

servir (sehr-*bveer*): to serve, to be of service

sexto (*sehks*-toh): sixth

si (see): if

sí (see): yes

siguiente (see-gee*ehn*-teh): next

silla (*see*-yah) f: chair

sillón reclinable (see-*yohn* rreh-klee-*nah*-bvleh) m: recliner

sobre (*soh*-bvreh) m: envelope

sofá (soh-*fah*) m: sofa

sol (sohl) m: sun

sombrero (sohm-*bvreh*-roh) m: hat

soplar (soh-*plahr*): to blow

sótano (*soh*-tah-noh) m: basement

subir (sooh-*bveer*): to go up; to ascend

subterráneo (soohbv-teh-*rrah*-neh-oh): underground

suelo (sooh*eh*-loh) m: floor

suelto (sooh*ehl*-toh): loose

suéter (sooh*eh*-tehr) m: sweater

sujetador (sooh-Heh-tah-*dohr*) m: bra

sujetapapeles (sooh-Heh-tah-pah-*peh*-lehs) m, pl: paper clips

sur (soohr) m: south

T

tabla (*tah*-bvlah) f: board (wood)

tabla de cortar (*tah*-bvlah deh kohr-*tahr*) f: cutting board

tabla de planchar (*tah*-bvlah deh plahn-*chahr*) f: ironing board

talla (*tah*-yah) f: size

también (tahm-bvee*ehn*): also

tampones (tahm-*poh*-nehs) m, pl: tampons

tapa (*tah*-pah) f: lid

tarde (*tahr*-deh) f: afternoon, late

tarea (tah-*reh*-ah) f: homework

tarifa de franqueo (tah-*ree*-fah deh frahn-*keh*-oh) f: postage rate

tarjeta (tahr-*Heh*-tah) f: card

tarjeta de crédito (tahr-*Heh*-tah deh *kreh*-dee-toh) f: credit card

tarjeta postal (tahr-*Heh*-tah pohs-*tahl*) f: postcard

taza (*tah*-sah) f: cup

tazón (tah-*sohn*) m: bowl

té (teh) m: tea

techo (*teh*-choh) m: ceiling

teclado (tehk-*lah*-doh) m: keyboard

tele (*teh*-leh) f: TV (colloquial)

teléfono (teh-*leh*-foh-noh) m: telephone

teléfono celular (teh-*leh*-foh-noh seh-looh-*lahr*) m: cellphone

televisor (teh-leh-bvee-*sohr*) m: television set

tenedor (teh-neh-*dohr*) m: fork

tener (teh-*nehr*): to have

tercero (tehr-*seh*-roh): third

termómetro (m): tehr-*moh*-meh-troh m: thermometer

tía (*tee*-ah) f: aunt

tierra (tee*eh*-rrah) f: land

tijeras (tee-*Heh*-rahs) f, pl: scissors

tina (*tee*-nah) f: tub

tío (*tee*-oh) m: uncle

típica (*tee*-pee-kah): typical

toalla (toh-*ah*-yah) f: towel

toallas femeninas (toh-*ah*-yahs feh-meh-*nee*-nahs) f, pl: feminine pads

toallita (toh-ah-*yee*-tah) f: washcloth

tobillo (toh-*bvee*-yoh) m: ankle

todavía (toh-dah-*bvee*-ah): yet; still

tomar (toh-*mahr*): to take, to drink

tomar el sol (toh-*mahr* ehl sohl): to sunbathe

toronja (toh-*rohn*-Hah) f: grapefruit

tos (tohs) f: cough

tostador (tohs-tah-*dohr*) m: toaster

trabajar (trah-bvah-*Hahr*): to work

traer (*trah*-ehr): to bring

tráfico (*trah*-fee-koh) m: traffic

traje de baño (*trah*-Heh deh *bvah*-nyoh) m: bathing suit

tranquilo (trahn-*kee*-loh): quiet, calm, tranquil

trapeador (trah-peh-ah-*dohr*) m: mop

tren (trehn) m: train

trolebús (troh-leh-*bvoohs*) m: trolley bus

trucha (*trooh*-chah) f: trout

tú (tooh): you (singular, informal)

tuna (*tooh*-nah) f: prickly pear

U

unidad de CD/DVD-ROM (ooh-nee-*dahd* deh see-dee/deh-bveh-deh rohm) f: CD/DVD-ROM drive

uso personal (*ooh*-soh pehr-soh-*nahl*) m: personal use

usted (Ud.) (oohs-*tehd*): you (formal, singular)

ustedes (Uds.) (oohs-*teh*-dehs): you (formal, plural)

uva (*ooh*-bvah) f: grape

V

vaqueros (bvah-*keh*-rohs) m, pl: jeans

vaso (*bvah*-soh) m: glass

vehículo (bveh-*ee*-kooh-loh) m: vehicle

velocímetro (bveh-loh-*see*-meh-troh) m: speedometer

venta (*bvehn*-tah) f: sale

ventana (bvehn-*tah*-nah) f: window

ventanilla (bvehn-tah-*nee*-yah) f: little window

ver (bvehr): to see

verde (*bvehr*-deh): green

vestíbulo (bvehs-*tee*-bvooh-loh) m: lobby

vestido (bvehs-*tee*-doh) m: dress

vestirse (bvehs-*teer*-seh): to get dressed

viaje (bvee*ah*-Heh) m: trip

viajero (bveeah-*Heh*-roh) m: traveler

vida (*bvee*-dah) f: life

viernes (bvee*ehr*-nehs) m: Friday

vino (*bvee*-noh) m: wine

violeta (bveeoh-*leh*-tah): violet; purple

violín (bveeoh-*leen*) m: violin

vivir (bvee-*bveer*): to live

vosotras (bvoh-*soh*-trahs) f, pl: you (informal) (feminine)

vosotros (bvoh-*soh*-trohs) m, pl: you (informal) (masculine, or mixed group)

vuelo (bvooh*eh*-loh) m: flight

vuelo con escalas (bvooh*eh*-loh kohn ehs-*kah*-lahs) m: flight with stopovers

vuelo directo (bvooh*eh*-loh dee-*rehk*-toh) m: direct flight

vuelta (bvooh*ehl*-tah) f: change (money back) (in Spain)

vuelto (bvooh*ehl*-toh) m: change (money back)

Y

yerno (*yehr*-noh) m: son-in-law

yeso (*yeh*-soh) m: plaster (in casts or walls)

yo (yoh): I

Z

zanahoria (sah-nah-*oh*-reeah) f: carrot

zapallito (sah-pah-*yee*-toh) m: zucchini (in Uruguay and Argentina)

zapatos (sah-*pah*-tohs) m, pl: shoes

zapatos de salón (sah-*pah*-tohs deh sah-*lohn*) m, pl: pumps

zona de carga y descarga (*soh*-nah deh *kahr*-gah ee dehs-*kahr*-gah) f: loading dock

English-Spanish Mini-Dictionary

A

a bit, a small amount: **poco** (*poh*-koh) m

a lot, much: **mucho** (*mooh*-choh)

above: **arriba** (ah-*rree*-bvah)

account: **cuenta** (kooh*ehn*-tah) f

acoustics: **acústica** (ah-*koohs*-tee-kah) f

actor: **actor** (ahk-*tohr*) m

actress: **actriz** (ahk-*trees*) f

address: **dirección** (dee-rehk-see-*ohn*) f

to advertise, to announce: **anunciar** (ah-noohn-see*ahr*)

afternoon: **tarde** (*tahr*-deh) f

age: **edad** (eh-*dahd*) f

agency: **agencia** (ah-*Hehn*-seeah) f

aisle, hallway: **pasillo** (pah-*see*-yoh) m

alarm clock: **despertador** (dehs-pehr-tah-*dohr*) m

alcohol: **alcohol** (ahl-koh-*ohl*) m

also: **también** (tahm-bvee*ehn*)

ambulance: **ambulancia** (ahm-bvooh-*lahn*-seeah) f

amusing, funny: **divertido** (dee-bvehr-*tee*-doh)

ankle: **tobillo** (toh-*bvee*-yoh) m

to answer: **responder** (rrehs-pohn-*dehr*)

aorta: **aorta** (ah-*ohr*-tah) f

apple: **manzana** (mahn-*sah*-nah) f

appointment: **cita** (*see*-tah) f

April: **abril** (ah-*bvreel*) m

arm: **brazo** (*bvrah*-soh) m

to arrive: **llegar** (yeh-*gahr*)

to ask (a question): **preguntar** (preh-goohn-*tahr*)

at the back: **al fondo** (ahl *fohn*-doh)

to attack: **atacar** (ah-tah-*kahr*)

attic: **ático** (*ah*-tee-koh) m

August: **agosto** (ah-*gohs*-toh) m

aunt: **tía** (*tee*-ah) f

available: **disponible** (dees-poh-*nee*-bvleh)

avenue: **avenida** (ah-bveh-*nee*-dah) f

avocado: **aguacate** (ah-goohah-*kah*-teh) m

avocado (in South America): **palta** (*pahl*-tah) f

B

bad: **malo** (*mah*-loh)

balance (financial): **saldo** (*sahl*-doh) m

balcony: **balcón** (bvahl-*kohn*) m

basement: **sótano** (*soh*-tah-noh) m

to bathe one's self: **bañarse** (bvah-*nyahr*-seh)

bathing suit: **traje de baño** (*trah*-Heh deh *bvah*-nyoh) m

bathrobe: **bata de baño** (*bvah*-tah deh *bvah*-nyoh) f

bathroom: **baño** (*bvah*-nyoh) m

bathtub: **bañera** (bvah-*nyeh*-rah) f

battery: **batería** (bvah-teh-*ree*-ah) f

to be (permanent): **ser** (sehr)

to be (temporary): **estar** (ehs-*tahr*)

to be pleasing, to like: **gustar** (goohs-*tahr*)

beach: **playa** (*plah*-yah) f

beautiful: **bello** (*bveh*-yoh)

bed: **cama** (*kah*-mah) f

bedroom: **dormitorio** (dohr-mee-*toh*-reeoh) m

to begin, to start: **empezar** (ehm-peh-*sahr*)

belt: **cinturón** (seen-tooh-*rohn*) m

beside, next to, at the side (of): **al lado (de)** (ahl *lah*-doh [deh])

best: **el la mejor** (ehl lah meh-*Hohr*)

better: **mejor** (meh-*Hohr*)

bicycle: **bicicleta** (bvee-see-*kleh*-tah) f

big, large: **grande** (*grahn*-deh)

bill: **billete** (bvee-*yeh*-teh) m

biography: **biografía** (bveeoh-grah-*fee*-ah) f

bird: **pájaro** (*pah*-Hah-roh) m

black: **negro** (*neh*-groh)

blanket: **cobija** (koh-*bvee*-Hah) f

to bleed: **sangrar** (sahn-*grahr*)

block: **cuadra** (kooh*ah*-drah) f

blood: **sangre** (*sahn*-greh) f

blood pressure: **presión sanguínea** (preh-see*ohn* sahn-*gee*-neh-ah) f

blouse: **blusa** (*bvlooh*-sah) f

blow: **soplar** (soh-*plahr*)

blue: **azul** (ah-*soohl*)

board (wood): **tabla** (*tah*-bvlah) f

bone: **hueso** (ooh*eh*-soh) m

book: **libro** (*lee*-bvroh) m

boots: **botas** (*bvoh*-tahs) f, pl

boulevard: **bulevar** (bvooh-leh-*bvahr*) m

bowel, intestine, gut: **intestino** (een-tehs-*tee*-noh) m

bowel movement (Literally: evacuation): **evacuación** (eh-bvah-kooh*ah*-seeoh*n*) f

bowl: **tazón** (tah-*sohn*) m

boy: **niño** (*nee*-nyoh) m

boyfriend: **novio** (*noh*-bveeoh) m

bra: **sujetador** (sooh-Heh-tah-*dohr*) m

bracelet: **pulsera** (poohl-*seh*-rah) f

break room: **sala de descanso** (*sah*-lah deh dehs-*kahn*-soh) f

breakfast: **desayuno** (deh-sah-*yooh*-noh) m

bridge: **puente** (pooh*ehn*-teh) m

to bring: **traer** (*trah*-ehr)

broccoli: **brócoli** (*bvroh*-koh-lee) m

brooch: **broche** (*bvroh*-cheh) m

brother: **hermano** (ehr-*mah*-noh) m

brother-in-law: **cuñado** (kooh-*nyah*-doh) m

brown: **marrón** (mah-*rrohn*)

building: **edificio** (eh-dee-*fee*-seeoh) m

bus: **autobús** (ahooh-toh-*bvoohs*) m

butterfly: **mariposa** (mah-ree-*poh*-sah) f

to buy: **comprar** (kohm-*prahr*)

by taxi: **en taxi** (ehn *tahk*-see)

C

cabbage (in Argentina and Chile): **repollo** (rreh-*poh*-yoh) m

cabinet: **gabinete** (gah-bvee-*neh*-teh) m

calendar: **calendario** (kah-lehn-*dah*-reeoh) m

calf: **pantorrilla** (pahn-toh-*rree*-yah) f

to call: **llamar** (yah-*mahr*)

to call oneself: **llamarse** (yah-*mahr*-seh)

to cancel: **cancelar** (kah-seh-*lahr*)

car (Mexico): **carro** (*kah*-rroh) m

car (S. America): **auto** (*ahooh*-toh) m

card: **tarjeta** (tahr-*Heh*-tah) f

carrot: **zanahoria** (sah-nah-*oh*-reeah) f

to carry, to wear: **llevar** (yeh-*bvahr*)

cashier (male): **cajero** (kah-*Heh*-roh) m

cavity: **caries** (*kah*-reeehs) f

CD/DVD-ROM drive: **unidad de CD/DVD-ROM** (ooh-nee-*dahd* deh see-dee/deh-bveh-deh rohm) f

ceiling: **techo** (*teh*-choh) m

cellphone: **teléfono celular** (teh-*leh*-foh-noh seh-looh-*lahr*) m

cereals: **cereales** (seh-reh-*ah*-lehs) m, pl

chair: **silla** (*see*-yah) f

champion: **campeón** (kahm-peh-*ohn*) m

change (money back): **vuelto** (bvooh*ehl*-toh) m

change (money back, in Spain): **vuelta** (bvooh*ehl*-tah) f

to change: **cambiar** (kahm-bvee*ahr*)

channel: **canal** (kah-*nahl*) m

character, personality: **carácter** (kah-*rahk*-tehr) m

cheap: **barato** (bvah-*rah*-toh)

to check in: **registrarse** (rreh-Hees-*trahr*-seh)

checking account: **cuenta de cheques** (kooh*ehn*-tah deh *cheh*-kehs) f

cheese: **queso** (*keh*-soh) m

cherry: **cereza** (seh-*reh*-sah) f

chess: **ajedrez** (ah-Heh-*drehs*) m

chest: **pecho** (*peh*-choh) m

chicken: **pollo** (*poh*-yoh) m

cinema: **cine** (*see*-neh) m

city: **ciudad** (seeooh-*dahd*) f

to clean: **limpiar** (leem-pee*ahr*)

close by: **cerca** (*sehr*-kah)

closet: **armario** (ahr-*mah*-reeoh) m

clothes: **ropa** (*rroh*-pah) f

clothes hanger: **gancho** (*gahn*-choh) m

coconut: **coco** (*koh*-koh) m

coffee: **café** (kah-*feh*) m

coin: **moneda** (moh-*neh*-dah) f

colander: **escurridor** (ehs-kooh-*rree*-dohr) m

cold: **fría** (*free*-ah)

comb: **peine** (*peh*ee-neh) m

to comb one's hair: **peinarse** (pehee-*nahr*-seh)

to complain (about): **quejarse (de)** (keh-*Hahr*-seh [deh])

computer: **computadora** (kohm-pooh-tah-*doh*-rah) f

conference room: **sala de reuniones** (*sah*-lah deh rrehooh-nee*oh*-nehs) f

constipation: **estreñimiento** (ehs-treh-nyee-mee*ehn*-toh) m

content, satisfied: **contento** (kohn-*tehn*-toh)

cook (female): **cocinera** (koh-see-*neh*-rah) f

cookies, crackers: **galletas** (gah-*yeh*-tahs) f

copy paper: **papel de fotocopiadora** (pah-*pehl* deh foh-toh-koh-peeah-*doh*-rah) m

copy room: **sala de copias** (*sah*-lah deh *koh*-peeahs) f

corner: **esquina** (ehs-*kee*-nah) f

to cost: **costar** (kohs-*tahr*)

cotton: **algodón** (ahl-goh-*dohn*) m

cough: **tos** (tohs) f

to count: **contar** (kohn-*tahr*)

country: **país** (pah*ees*) m

cousin (female): **prima** (*pree*-mah) f

cousin (male): **primo** (*pree*-moh) m

credit card: **tarjeta de crédito** (tahr-*Heh*-tah deh *kreh*-dee-toh) f

cup: **taza** (*tah*-sah) f

customs: **aduana** (ah-dooh*ah*-nah) f

cutting board: **tabla de cortar** (*tah*-bvlah deh kohr-*tahr*) f

cycling: **ciclismo** (see-*klees*-moh) m

D

to dance: **bailar** (bvahee-*lahr*)

dark: **oscuro** (ohs-*kooh*-roh)

date: **fecha** (*feh*-chah) f

daughter: **hija** (*ee*-Hah) f

daughter-in-law: **nuera** (nooh*eh*-rah) f

day: **día** (*dee*ah) m

debit: **débito** (*deh*-bvee-toh) m

December: **diciembre** (dee-see*ehm*-bvreh) m

defense: **defensa** (deh-*fehn*-sah) f

to deliver: **entregar** (ehn-treh-*gahr*)

dentist: **dentista** (dehn-*tees*-tah) m, f

department: **departamento** (deh-pahr-tah-*mehn*-toh) m

to descend, to go down: **bajar** (bvah-*Hahr*)

desk: **escritorio** (ehs-kree-*toh*-reeoh) m

diamonds: **diamantes** (dee-ah-*mahn*-tehs) m, pl

diapers: **pañales** (pah-*nyah*-lehs) m, pl

difficult: **difícil** (dee-*fee*-seel)

dinner: **comida** (koh-*mee*-dah) f

direct flight: **vuelo directo** (bvooh*eh*-loh dee-*rehk*-toh) m

dishwasher: **lavaplatos** (lah-bvah-*plah*-tohs) m

doctor: **doctor** (dohk-*tohr*), **médico** (*meh*-dee-koh) m

document, paper: **documento** (doh-kooh-*mehn*-toh) m

door: **puerta** (pooh*ehr*-tah) f

double: **doble** (*doh*-bvleh)

drawing, pattern: **dibujo** (dee-*bvooh*-Hoh) m

dress: **vestido** (bvehs-*tee*-doh) m

to drink: **beber** (bveh-*bvehr*)

drinkable: **potable** (poh-*tah*-bvleh)

to drive (a car): **manejar** (mah-neh-*Hahr*)

driver: **chofer** (choh-*fehr*) m

dry: **seco** (*seh*-koh)

dryer: **secadora** (seh-kah-*doh*-rah) f

duck: **pato** (*pah*-toh) m

during: **durante** (dooh-*rahn*-teh)

dustpan: **recogedor** (rreh-koh-Heh-*dohr*) m

E

ear: **oreja** (oh-*reh*-Hah) f

early show: **matiné** (mah-tee-*neh*) f

earrings: **aretes** (ah-*reh*-tehs) m, pl

east: **este** (*ehs*-teh) m

easy: **fácil** (*fah*-seel)

to eat: **comer** (kohm-*ehr*)

egg: **huevo** (ooh*eh*-bvoh) m

eighth: **octavo** (ohk-*tah*-bvoh)

electrician: **electricista** (eh-lehk-tree-*sees*-tah) m, f

elevator: **ascensor** (ah-sehn-*sohr*) m

eleven: **once** (*ohn*-seh)

e-mail: **correo electrónico** (koh-*rreh*-oh eh-lehk-*troh*-nee-koh) m

engineer: **ingeniero** (een-Heh-neee*eh*-roh) m

entrance, entryway: **entrada** (ehn-*trah*-dah) f

entrance hall: **recibidor** (rreh-see-bvee-*dohr*) m

envelope: **sobre** (*soh*-bvreh) m

to exit, to leave, to go out: **salir** (sah-*leer*)

expensive: **caro** (*kah*-roh)

eye: **ojo** (*oh*-Hoh) m

F

face: **rostro** (*rrohs*-troh) m

father: **padre** (*pah*-dreh) m

fax machine: **máquina de fax** (*mah*-kee-nah deh fahks) f

February: **febrero** (feh-*bvreh*-roh) m

to feel: **sentirse** (sehn-*teer*-seh)

female doctor: **doctora** (dohk-*toh*-rah) f

feminine pads: **toallas femeninas** (toh-*ah*-yahs feh-meh-*nee*-nahs) f, pl

fever: **fiebre** (fee*eh*-bvreh) f

fifth: **quinto** (*keen*-toh)

fight: **pelea** (peh-*leh*-ah) f

file folders: **carpetas** (kahr-*peh*-tahs) f, pl

to find: **encontrar** (ehn-kohn-*trahr*)

finger: **dedo** (*deh*-doh) m

first: **primero** (pree-*meh*-roh)

first class: **primera clase** (pree-*meh*-rah *klah*-seh) f fish: **pescado** (pehs-*kah*-doh) m

fitting room: **probador** (ehl proh-bvah-*dohr*) m

flight: **vuelo** (bvooh*eh*-loh) m

flight with stopovers: **vuelo con escalas** (bvooh*eh*-loh kohn ehs-*kah*-lahs) m

floor: **piso** (*pee*-soh) m (level in a building)

floor: **suelo** (sooh*eh*-loh) m (bottom of a room)

to follow, to continue: **seguir** (seh-*geer*)

foot: **pie** (pee*eh*) m

forearm: **antebrazo** (ahn-teh-*bvrah*-soh) m

to forget (about): **olvidarse (de)** (ohl-bvee-*dahr*-seh [deh])

fork: **tenedor** (teh-neh-*dohr*) m

form: **formulario** (fohr-mooh-*lah*-reeoh) m

fourth: **cuarto** (kooh*ahr*-toh)

fracture, broken bone: **fractura** (frahk-*tooh*-rah) f

free: **libre** (*lee*-bvreh)

freeway: **autopista** (ahooh-toh-*pees*-tah) f

freezer: **congelador** (kohn-Heh-lah-*dohr*) m

Friday: **viernes** (bvee*ehr*-nehs) m

fruit: **fruta** (*frooh*-tah) f

frying pan: **sartén** (sahr-*tehn*) f

furniture: **mueble** (mooh*eh*-bvleh) m

G

game: **juego** (Hooh*eh*-goh) m

garbage can: **basurero** (bvah-sooh-*reh*-roh) m

garden: **jardín** (Hahr-*deen*) m

garlic: **ajo** (*ah*-Hoh) m

to get dressed: **vestirse** (bvehs-*teer*-seh)

girl: **niña** (*nee*-nyah) f

girlfriend: **novia** (*noh*-bveeah) f

glass: **vaso** (*bvah*-soh) m

gloves: **guantes** (gooh*ahn*-tehs) m, pl

glue: **pegamento** (peh-gah-*mehn*-toh) m

to go: **ir** (eer)

to go shopping: **ir de compras** (eer deh *kohm*-prahs)

to go through, to check: **revisar** (rreh-bvee-*sahr*)

to go to bed: **acostarse** (ah-koh-*stahr*-seh)

to go up, to ascend: **subir** (sooh-*bveer*)

to go with, to accompany: **acompañar** (ah-kohm-pah-*nyahr*)

godfather: **padrino** (pah-*dree*-noh) m

godmother: **madrina** (mah-*dree*-nah) f

gold: **oro** (*oh*-roh) m

good: **bueno** (bvooh*eh*-noh)

good-bye: **adiós** (ah-dee*ohs*)

gorgeous, beautiful, lovely: **precioso** (preh-see*oh*-soh)

granddaughter: **nieta** (nee*eh*-tah) f

grandfather: **abuelo** (ah-bvooh*eh*-loh) m

grandmother: **abuela** (ah-bvooh*eh*-lah) f

grandson: **nieto** (nee*eh*-toh) m

grape: **uva** (*ooh*-bvah) f

grapefruit: **toronja** (toh-*rohn*-Hah) f

grapefruit (in Mexico): **pomelo** (poh-*meh*-loh) m

green: **verde** (*bvehr*-deh)

grey: **gris** (grees)

group: **grupo** (*grooh*-poh) m

guava: **guayaba** (gooah-*yah*-bvah) f

guide: **guía** (*gee*-ah) m, f

H

hair: **pelo** (*peh*-loh) m

half: **medio** (*meh*-deeoh) m

half-bathroom (a bathroom with no shower or tub): **medio baño** (*meh*-deeoh *bvah*-nyoh) m

hammer: **martillo** (mahr-*tee*-yoh) m

hand: **mano** (*mah*-noh) f

hand made: **hecho a mano** (*eh*-choh ah *mah*-noh)

to hang, to hang up: **colgar** (kohl-*gahr*)

happy: **feliz** (feh-*lees*)

hat: **sombrero** (sohm-*bʋreh*-roh) m

to have: **tener** (teh-*nehr*)

he: **él** (ehl) m

head: **cabeza** (kah-*bʋeh*-sah) f

health: **salud** (sah-*loohd*) f

healthy: **sano** (*sah*-noh)

heart: **corazón** (koh-rah-*sohn*) m

to help: **ayudar** (ah-yooh-*dahr*)

here: **aquí** (ah-*kee*)

hit, goal: **gol** (gohl) m

to hit, to bang: **golpear** (gohl-peh-*ahr*)

homework: **tarea** (tah-*reh*-ah) f

hors d'oeuvres: **entradas** (ehn-*trah*-dahs) f, pl

horse: **caballo** (kah-*bʋah*-yoh) m

hot, spicy (flavor): **picante** (pee-*kahn*-teh)

hot (temperature): **caliente** (kah-lee*ehn*-teh)

hour: **hora** (*oh*-rah) f

house: **casa** (*kah*-sah) f

how much: **cuánto** (kooh*ahn*-toh) (accented when used in a question)

hunger: **hambre** (*ahm*-bʋreh) f

husband: **esposo** (ehs-*poh*-soh) m

I

I: **yo** (yoh)

identification: **identificación** (ee-dehn-tee-fee-kah-see*ohn*) f

if: **si** (see)

immigration: **inmigración** (een-mee-grah-see*ohn*) f

in front (of): **al frente (de)** (ahl *frehn*-teh [deh])

in front, ahead: **adelante** (ah-deh-*lahn*-teh)

included: **incluido** (een-klooh-*ee*-doh)

inside: **adentro** (ah-*dehn*-troh)

inside (of): **dentro (de)** (*dehn*-troh [deh])

to invite: **invitar** (een-bʋee-*tahr*)

iron: **plancha** (*plahn*-chah) f

ironing board: **tabla de planchar** (*tah*-bʋlah deh plahn-*chahr*) f

island: **isla** (*ees*-lah) f

J

jacket: **chaqueta** (chah-*keh*-tah) f

January: **enero** (eh-*neh*-roh) m

jeans: **jeans** (jeens), **vaqueros** (bʋah-*keh*-rohs) m, pl

job: **empleo** (ehm-*pleh*-oh) m

joke: **broma** (*broh*-mah) f

July: **julio** (*Hooh*-leeoh) m

June: **junio** (*Hooh*-neeoh) m

K

key: **llave** (*yah*-bʋeh) f

keyboard: **teclado** (tehk-*lah*-doh) m

kidney: **riñón** (rree-*nyohn*) m

kitchen: **cocina** (koh-*see*-nah) f

knife: **cuchillo** (kooh-*chee*-yoh) m

L

lamp: **lámpara** (*lahm*-pah-rah) f

land: **tierra** (tee*eh*-rrah) f

language (Literally: tongue): **lengua** (*lehn*-goohah) f

language: **idioma** (ee-dee*oh*-mah) m

laptop computer: **computadora portátil** (kohm-pooh-tah-*doh*-rah pohr-*tah*-teel) f

late: **tarde** (*tahr*-deh)

to laugh (at, about): **reírse (de)** (rreh*eer*-seh [deh])

lawyer: **abogado** (ah-bvoh-*gah*-doh) m

lead: **plomo** (*ploh*-moh) m

to learn: **aprender** (ah-prehn-*dehr*)

to leave: **dejar** (deh-*Hahr*)

left: **izquierda** (ees-kee*ehr*-dah)

leg: **pierna** (pee*ehr*-nah) f

lemon: **limón** (lee-*mohn*) m

less: **menos** (*meh*-nohs)

letter: **carta** (*kahr*-tah) f

lettuce: **lechuga** (leh-*chooh*-gah) f

library: **biblioteca** (bvee-bvleeoh-*teh*-kah) f

lid: **tapa** (*tah*-pah) f

life: **vida** (*bvee*-dah) f

light: **claro** (*klah*-roh)

to like: **gustar** (goohs-*tahr*)

lime: **lima** (*lee*-mah) f

line: **línea** (*lee*-neh-ah) f

to listen, to hear: **escuchar** (ehs-kooh-*chahr*)

little, small: **chico** (*chee*-koh)

little window: **ventanilla** (bvehn-tah-*nee*-yah) f

live: **vivir** (bvee-*bvee*r)

living room: **sala** (*sah*-lah) f

loading dock: **zona de carga y descarga** (*soh*-nah deh *kahr*-gah ee dehs-*kahr*-gah) f

lobby: **vestíbulo** (bvehs-*tee*-bvooh-loh) m

loose: **suelto** (sooh*ehl*-toh)

luggage, suitcase: **maleta** (mah-*leh*-tah) f

lunch: **almuerzo** (ahl-mooh*ehr*-soh) m

lung: **pulmón** (poohl-*mohn*) m

M

machine, appliance: **aparato** (ah-pah-*rah*-toh) m

mail, post: **correo** (koh-*rreh*-oh) m

mailroom: **sala de correos** (*sah*-lah deh koh-*rreh*-ohs) f

man: **hombre** (*ohm*-bvreh) m

manager: **gerente** (Heh-*rehn*-teh) m

map: **mapa** (*mah*-pah) m

March: **marzo** (*mahr*-soh) m

to mark, to dial, to punch in the number: **marcar** (mahr-*kahr*)

marker: **marcador** (mahr-kah-*dohr*) m

mask: **máscara** (*mahs*-kah-rah) f

May: **mayo** (*mah*-yoh) m

to measure: **medir** (meh-*deer*)

mechanic: **mecánico** (meh-*kah*-nee-koh) m

medicine cabinet: **botiquín** (bvoh-tee-*keen*) m

meeting: **reunión** (rrehooh-nee*ohn*) f

microwave: **horno microondas** (*ohr*-noh mee-kroh-*ohn*-dahs) m

midnight: **medianoche** (meh-deeah-*noh*-cheh) f

milk: **leche** (*leh*-cheh) f

minute: **minuto** (mee-*nooh*-toh) m

mirror: **espejo** (ehs-*peh*-Hoh) m

Miss: **señorita** (Srta.) (seh-nyor-*ee*-tah) f

molar: **muela** (mooh*eh*-lah) f

Monday: **lunes** (*looh*-nehs) m

money: **dinero** (dee-*neh*-roh) m

money changer: **cambista** (kahm-*bvees*-tah) m, f

monitor: **monitor de video** (moh-*nee*-tohr deh *bvee*-deh-oh) m

month: **mes** (mehs) m

moon: **luna** (*looh*-nah) f

mop: **trapeador** (trah-peh-ah-*dohr*) m

more: **más** (mahs)

morning: **mañana** (mah-*nyah*-nah) f

mother: **madre** (*mah*-dreh) f

mountain: **montaña** (mohn-*tah*-nyah) f

mouse: **ratón** (rrah-*tohn*) m

moustache: **bigote** (bvee-*goh*-teh) m

mouth: **boca** (*bvoh*-kah) f

Mr., sir: **señor (Sr.)** (seh-*nyor*) m

Mrs., madam: **señora (Sra.)** (seh-*nyor*-ah) f

much: **mucho** (*mooh*-choh)

museum: **museo** (mooh-*seh*-oh) m

N

napkin: **servilleta** (sehr-bvee-*yeh*-tah) f

nausea, sickness: **náusea** (*nah*ooh-seh-ah) f

neck: **cuello** (kooh*eh*-yoh) m

necklace: **collar** (koh-*yahr*) m

neighborhood: **barrio** (*bvah*-rreeoh) m

newspaper, daily: **diario** (dee*ah*-reeoh) m

next: **siguiente** (see-gee*ehn*-teh)

night: **noche** (*noh*-cheh) f

ninth: **noveno** (noh-*bveh*-noh)

none: **ningún** (neen-*goohn*)

noodle: **fideo** (fee-*de*-oh) m

noon: **mediodía** (*meh*-deeoh-*dee*-ah) m

north: **norte** (*nohr*-teh) m

nose: **nariz** (nah-*rees*) f

notepad: **libreta** (lee-*bvreh*-tah) f

novel: **novela** (noh-*bveh*-lah) f

November: **noviembre** (noh-bvee*ehm*-breh) m

now: **ahora** (ah-*oh*-rah)

number: **número** (*nooh*-meh-roh) m

nurse: **enfermera** (ehn-fehr-*meh*-rah) f

O

observation: **observación** (obv-sehr-bvah-see*ohn*) f

occupied, busy: **ocupado** (oh-kooh-*pah*-doh)

October: **octubre** (ohk-*tooh*-bvreh) m

of, from: **de** (deh)

office: **oficina** (oh-fee-*see*-nah) f

on top (of): **encima (de)** (ehn-*see*-mah [deh])

one's own: **propio** (*proh*-peeoh)

onions: **cebollas** (seh-*bvoh*-yahs) f, pl

to open: **abrir** (ah-*bvreer*)

opening to the interior: **al interior** (ahl een-teh-ree*ohr*)

orange (color): **anaranjado** (ah-nah-rahn-*Hah*-doh)

orange (fruit): **naranja** (nah-*rahn*-Hah) f

other one, another: **otro** (*oh*-troh)

outside: **afuera** (ah-fooh*eh*-rah), **fuera** (fooh*eh*-rah)

oven: **horno** (*ohr*-noh) m

over there: **allá** (ah-*yah*)

overcoat: **abrigo** (ah-*bvree*-goh) m

P

package: **paquete** (pah-*keh*-teh) m

paid for: **pagado** (pah-*gah*-doh)

pain: **dolor** (doh-*lohr*) m

to paint: **pintar** (peen-*tahr*)

painting: **pintura** (peen-*tooh*-rah) f

pajamas: **piyamas** (pee-*yah*-mahs) f, pl

panties: **bragas** (*bvrah*-gahs) f, pl

papaya: **papaya** (pah-*pah*-yah) f

paper: **papel** (pah-*pehl*) m

paper clips: **sujetapapeles** (sooh-Heh-tah-pah-*peh*-lehs) m, pl

park: **parque** (*pahr*-keh) m

parking: **estacionamiento** (ehs-tah-seeoh-nah-mee*ehn*-toh) m

passport: **pasaporte** (pah-sah-*pohr*-teh) m

pavement: **pavimento** (pah-bvee-*mehn*-toh) m

to pay: **pagar** (pah-*gahr*)

peach: **durazno** (dooh-*rahs*-noh) m

pear: **pera** (*peh*-rah) f

pearl: **perla** (*pehr*-lah) f

pen: **bolígrafo** (bvoh-*lee*-grah-foh) m

pencil: **lápiz** (*lah*-pees) m

pencil sharpener: **sacapuntas** (sah-kah-*poohn*-tahs) m

people: **gente** (*Hehn*-teh) f

percent, percentage: **por ciento** (pohr see*ehn*-toh)

personal use: **uso personal** (*ooh*-soh pehr-soh-*nahl*) m

pharmacy: **farmacia** (fahr-*mah*-seeah) f

photocopier: **fotocopiadora** (foh-toh-koh-peeah-*doh*-rah) f

photographer: **fotógrafo** (foh-*toh*-grah-foh) m

physician: **médico/a** (*meh*-dee-koh/kah) m, f

pillow: **almohada** (ahl-moh-*ah*-dah) f

pilot: **piloto** (pee-*loh*-toh) m

pineapple: **piña** (*pee*-nyah) f

pink: **rosado** (rroh-*sah*-doh)

pity, shame: **lástima** (*lahs*-tee-mah) f

plain, flat: **liso** (*lee*-soh)

to plan: **planear** (plah-neh-*ahr*)

plant, factory: **fábrica** (*fah*-bvree-kah) f

plantain: **plátano** (*plah*-tah-noh) m

plaster (in casts or walls): **yeso** (yeh-soh) m

plate: **plato** (*plah*-toh) m

to play: **jugar** (Hooh-*gahr*)

play (Literally: the work): **obra** (*oh*-bvrah) f

player: **jugador** (Hooh-gah-*dohr*) m

playing field: **cancha** (*kahn*-chah) f

plum: **ciruela** (see-rooh*eh*-lah) f

pocket: **bolsillo** (bvohl-*see*-yoh) m

poet: **poeta** (poh-*eh*-tah) m, f

police officer: **policía** (poh-lee-*see*-ah) m, f

portal, entrance, doorway: **portal** (pohr-*tahl*) m

postage: **franqueo** (frahn-*keh*-oh) m

postage rate: **tarifa de franqueo** (tah-*ree*-fah deh frahn-*keh*-oh) f

postal code (ZIP code): **código postal** (*koh*-dee-goh pohs-*tahl*) m

postcard: **tarjeta postal** (tahr-*Heh*-tah pohs-*tahl*) f

pot: **caldero** (kahl-*deh*-roh) m

potato chips, French fries: **papas fritas** (*pah*-pahs *free*-tahs) f, pl

potatoes: **papas** (*pah*-pahs) f, pl

potatoes (in Spain): **patatas** (pah-*tah*-tahs) f, pl

precious, gorgeous, beautiful, lovely: **precioso** (preh-see*oh*-soh)

to prefer: **preferir** (preh-feh-*reer*)

to prepare: **preparar** (preh-pah-*rahr*)

prescription: **receta** (rreh-*seh*-tah) f

price: **precio** (*preh*-seeoh) m

prickly pear: **tuna** (*tooh*-nah) f

print: **imprimir** (eem-pree-*meer*)

printer: **impresora** (eem-preh-*soh*-rah) f

profession: **carrera** (kah-*rreh*-rah) f

program, schedule: **programa** (proh-*grah*-mah) m

projector: **proyector** (proh-yehk-*tohr*) m

pumps: **zapatos de salón** (sah-*pah*-tohs deh sah-*lohn*) m, pl

pure: **pura** (*pooh*-rah)

purple: **morado** (moh-*rah*-doh)

Q

quantity, amount: **cantidad** (kahn-tee-*dahd*) f

quarter: **cuarto** (kooh*ahr*-toh) m

questionnaire, form: **cuestionario** (koohehs-teeoh-*nah*-reeoh) m

quiet, calm, tranquil: **tranquilo** (trahn-*kee*-loh)

quite, enough: **bastante** (bvahs-*tahn*-teh)

R

race: **carrera** (kah-*rreh*-rah) f

racket: **raqueta** (rrah-*keh*-tah) f

rain: **lluvia** (*yooh*-bveeah) f

raincoat: **impermeable** (eem-pehr-meh-*ah*-bvleh) m

to read: **leer** (leh-*ehr*)

receipt: **recibo** (rreh-*see*-bvoh) m

recliner: **sillón reclinable** (see-*yohn* rreh-klee-*nah*-bvleh) m

red: **rojo** (*rroh*-Hoh)

refrigerator: **nevera** (neh-*bveh*-rah) f

to refund: **reembolsar** (rreh-ehm-bvol-*sahr*)

repeat: **repetir** (rreh-peh-*teer*)

reservation: **reservación** (rreh-sehr-bvah-see*ohn*) f

to reserve: **reservar** (rreh-sehr-*bvahr*)

restaurant: **restaurante** (rrehs-tahooh-*rahn*-teh) m

rice: **arroz** (ah-*rros*) m

right: **derecha** (deh-*reh*-chah)

right away, soon: **pronto** (*prohn*-toh)

river: **río** (*rree*-oh) m

road: **camino** (kah-*mee*-noh) m

role: **rol** (rrohl) m

romantic: **romántico** (rroh-*mahn*-tee-koh)

room: **cuarto** (kooh*ahr*-toh) m

row, line, line-up: **fila** (*fee*-lah) f

rug: **alfombra** (ahl-*fohm*-bvrah) f

ruins: **ruinas** (rrooh*ee*-nahs) f

rules: **reglamentos** (rrehg-lah-*mehn*-tohs) m

S

salad: **ensalada** (ehn-sah-*lah*-dah) f

sale: **venta** (*bvehn*-tah) f

salty: **salado** (sah-*lah*-doh)

sandals: **sandalias** (sahn-*dah*-leeahs) f, pl

sardines: **sardinas** (sahr-*dee*-nahs) f, pl

Saturday: **sábado** (*sah*-bvah-doh) m

saw (tool): **serrucho** (seh-*rrooh*-choh) m

scarf: **bufanda** (bvooh-*fahn*-dah) f

schedule: **horario** (oh-*rah*-reeoh) m

to schedule: **programar** (proh-*grah*-mahr)

school: **escuela** (ehs-kooh*eh*-lah) f

scissors: **tijeras** (tee-*Heh*-rahs) f, pl

sculpture: **escultura** (ehs-koohl-*tooh*-rah) f

sea: **mar** (mahr) m

seafood: **marisco** (mah-*rees*-koh) m

to search, to look for: **buscar** (bvoohs-*kahr*)

seat: **asiento** (ah-see*ehn*-toh) m

second: **segundo** (seh-*goohn*-doh) m

to see: **ver** (bvehr)

to send: **enviar** (ehn-bvee*ahr*)

September: **septiembre** (sehp-tee*ehm*-bvreh) m

to serve, to be of service: **servir** (sehr-*bveer*)

seventh: **séptimo** (*sehp*-tee-moh)

shame, pity: **pena** (*peh*-nah) f

she: **ella** (*eh*-yah) f

sheet: **sábana** (*sah*-bvah-nah) f

shine: **brillo** (*bvree*-yoh) m

shirt: **camisa** (kah-*mee*-sah) f

shoes: **zapatos** (sah-*pah*-tohs) m, pl

shorts: **pantalones cortos** (pahn-tah-*loh*-nehs *kohr*-tohs) m, pl

shoulder: **hombro** (*ohm*-bvroh) m

shower: **ducha** (*dooh*-chah) f

shrimp: **camarón** (kah-mah-*rohn*) m

sick: **enfermo** (ehn-*fehr*-moh)

sick person: **enfermo/a** (ehn-*fehr*-moh/mah) m, f

to sign: **firmar** (feer-*mahr*)

to sing: **cantar** (kahn-*tahr*)

singer: **cantante** (kahn-*tahn*-teh) m, f

sink (bathroom): **lavamanos** (lah-bvah-*mah*-nohs) m

sink (kitchen): **fregadero** (freh-gah-*deh*-roh) m

sister: **hermana** (ehr-*mah*-nah) f

sister-in-law: **cuñada** (kooh-*nyah*-dah) f

to sit down: **sentarse** (sehn-*tahr*-seh)

sixth: **sexto** (*sehks*-toh)

size: **talla** (*tah*-yah) f

skate: **patín** (pah-*teen*) m

ski: **esquí** (ehs-*kee*) m

skirt: **falda** (*fahl*-dah) f

sky blue: **celeste** (seh-*lehs*-teh)

to sleep: **dormir** (dohr-*meer*)

sleeve: **manga** (*mahn*-gah) f

slow: **despacio** (dehs-*pah*-seeoh)

small: **pequeño** (peh-*keh*-nyoh)

small amount: **poco** (*poh*-koh) m

socks: **calcetines** (kahl-seh-*tee*-nehs) m, pl

sofa: **sofá** (soh-*fah*) m

sole of the foot: **planta del pie** (*plahn*-tah dehl pee*eh*) f

some: **algún** (ahl-*goohn*)

son: **hijo** (*ee*-Hoh) m

son-in-law: **yerno** (*yehr*-noh) m

south: **sur** (soohr) m

special: **especial** (ehs-peh-see*ahl*)

speedometer: **velocímetro** (bveh-loh-*see*-meh-troh) m

spinach: **espinaca** (ehs-pee-*nah*-kah) f

spoon: **cuchara** (kooh-*chah*-rah) f

square: **plaza** (*plah*-sah) f

stadium: **estadio** (ehs-*tah*-deeoh) m

staff: **personal** (pehr-soh-*nahl*) m

staircase: **escalera** (ehs-kah-*leh*-rah) f

stamp: **sello** (*seh*-yoh) m

staple remover: **sacagrapas** (sah-kah-*grah*-pahs) m

stapler: **grapadora** (grah-pah-*doh*-rah) f

staples: **grapas** (*grah*-pahs) f, pl

to start: **partir** (pahr-*teer*)

state: **estado** (ehs-*tah*-doh) m

station, season: **estación** (ehs-tah-*seeohn*) f

to stay, to remain: **quedarse** (keh-*dahr*-seh)

steak: **bife** (*bvee*-feh) m

to steal, to rob: **robar** (rroh-*bvahr*)

sticky notes: **notas autoadhesivas desprendibles** (*noh*-tahs ahooh-toh-ahd-eh-*see*-bvahs dehs-prehn-*dee*-bvlehs) f, pl

stitches (surgical): **puntos** (*poohn*-tohs) m, pl

stomach: **estómago** (ehs-*toh*-mah-goh) m

stop: **parada** (pah-*rah*-dah) f

stove: **estufa** (eh-*stooh*-fah) f

straight, straight ahead: **derecho** (deh-*reh*-choh)

strawberry (from Colombia to the South Pole): **frutilla** (frooh-*tee*-yah) f

strawberry (Mexico, Central America, and Spain): **fresa** (*freh*-sah) f

street: **calle** (*kah*-yeh) f

striped: **listada** (lees-*tah*-dah)

study: **estudio** (ehs-*tooh*-deeoh) m

style: **estilo** (ehs-*tee*-loh) m

sun: **sol** (sohl) m

to sunbathe: **tomar el sol** (toh-*mahr* ehl sohl)

Sunday: **domingo** (doh-*meen*-goh) m

supper: **cena** (*seh*-nah) f

surgery: **cirugía** (see-rooh-*Hee*-ah) f

sweater: **suéter** (sooh*eh*-tehr) m

sweet: **dulce** (*doohl*-seh)

sweet pepper (in Argentina, Chile, and Uruguay): **pimentón** (pee-mehn-*tohn*) m

to swim: **nadar** (nah-*dahr*)

swimming pool: **piscina** (pees-*see*-nah) f

syrup, elixir: **jarabe** (Hah-*rah*-bveh) m

T

table: **mesa** (*meh*-sah) f

to take, to drink: **tomar** (toh-*mahr*)

to take off, remove clothing: **quitarse** (kee-*tahr*-seh)

to talk: **hablar** (ah-*bvlahr*)

tall, high: **alto** (*ahl*-toh)

tampons: **tampones** (tahm-*poh*-nehs) m, pl

tea: **té** (teh) m

team: **equipo** (eh-*kee*-poh) m

telephone: **teléfono** (teh-*leh*-foh-noh) m

television set: **televisor** (teh-leh-bvee-*sohr*) m

tenth: **décimo** (*deh*-see-moh)

test: **examen** (ehk-*sah*-mehn) m

thank you: **gracias** (*grah*-seeahs)

that, than: **que** (keh)

there: **allí** (ah-*yee*)

thermometer: **termómetro** (tehr-*moh*-meh-troh) m

they (feminine): **ellas** (*eh*-yahs) f

they (masculine, or mixed group): **ellos** (*eh*-yohs) m

thigh: **muslo** (*moohs*-loh) m

thing: **cosa** (*koh*-sah) f

to think: **pensar** (pehn-*sahr*)

third: **tercero** (tehr-*seh*-roh)

thirst: **sed** (sehd) f

this one: **este** (*ehs*-teh)

throat: **garganta** (gahr-*gahn*-tah) f

thumb: **pulgar** (poohl-*gahr*) m

Thursday: **jueves** (Hooh*eh*-bvehs) m

ticket: **boleto** (bvoh-*leh*-toh) m

tie: **corbata**: (kohr-*bvah*-tah) f

tight: **apretado** (ah-preh-*tah*-doh)

tissues: **pañuelos de papel** (pah-nyooh*eh*-lohs deh pah-*pehl*) m, pl

toaster: **tostador** (tohs-tah-*dohr*) m

today: **hoy** (ohy)

together: **junto** (*Hoohn*-toh)

toilet paper: **papel higiénico** (pah-*pehl* ee-Heee*eh*-nee-koh) m

toll: **peaje** (peh-*ah*-Heh) m

tomorrow: **mañana** (mah-*nyah*-nah)

tonsils: **amígdalas** (ah-*meeg*-dah-lahs) f, pl

tooth: **diente** (dee*eh*-teh) m

toothache: **dolor de muelas** (doh-*lohr* deh mooh*eh*-lahs) m

toward: **hacia** (*ah*-seeah)

towel: **toalla** (toh-*ah*-yah) f

tower case: **ordenador** (ohr-deh-*nah*-dor) m

traffic: **tráfico** (*trah*-fee-koh) m

train: **tren** (trehn) m

traveler: **viajero** (bveeah-*Heh*-roh) m

trip: **viaje** (bveeah-*Heh*) m

trolley bus: **trolebús** (troh-leh-*bvoohs*) m

trousers: **pantalones** (pahn-tah-*loh*-nehs) m, pl

trout: **trucha** (*trooh*-chah) f

to try: **probar** (proh-*bvahr*)

T-shirt: **camiseta** (kah-mee-*seh*-tah) f

tub: **tina** (*tee*-nah) f

Tuesday: **martes** (*mahr*-tehs) m

tuna: **atún** (ah-*toohn*) m

to turn: **doblar** (doh-*bvlahr*)

TV: **tele** (*teh*-leh) f

typical: **típica** (*tee*-pee-kah)

U

ugly: **feo** (*feh*-oh)

uncle: **tío** (*tee*-oh) m

under, below: **bajo** (*bvah*-Hoh)

underground: **subterráneo** (soohbv-teh-*rrah*-neh-oh)

underneath: **debajo** (deh-*bvah*-Hoh)

to understand: **comprender** (kohm-prehn-*dehr*)

to understand: **entender** (ehn-tehn-*dehr*)

underwear: **ropa interior** (*rroh*-pah een-teh-ree*ohr*) f

urine: **orina** (oh-*ree*-nah) f

V

vacuum: **aspiradora** (ahs-pee-rah-*doh*-rah) f

vehicle: **vehículo** (bveh-*ee*-kooh-loh) m

violet, purple: **violeta** (bveeoh-*leh*-tah)

violin: **violín** (bveeoh-*leen*) m

W

to wait: **esperar** (ehs-peh-*rahr*)

to wake up: **despertarse** (dehs-pehr-*tahr*-seh)

walk: **paseo** (pah-*seh*-oh) m

to walk, to stroll: **pasear** (pah-seh-*ahr*)

walking (Literally: on foot): **a pie** (ah pee*eh*)

wall: **pared** (pah-*rehd*) f

wallet: **billetera** (bvee-yeh-*teh*-rah) f

to want, to wish: **querer** (keh-*rehr*)

war: **guerra** (*geh*-rrah) f

warranty: **garantía** (gah-rahn-*tee*-ah) f

washcloth: **toallita** (toh-ah-*yee*-tah) f

washing machine: **lavadora** (lah-bvah-*doh*-rah) f

watch: **reloj** (rreh-*loh*) m

water: **agua** (*ah*-goohah) f

watermelon: **sandía** (sahn-*dee*-ah) f

we (feminine): **nosotras** (noh-*soh*-trahs) f

we (masculine, or mixed group): **nosotros** (noh-*soh*-trohs) m

Wednesday: **miércoles** (mee*ehr*-koh-lehs) m

week: **semana** (seh-*mah*-nah) f

west: **oeste** (oh-*ehs*-teh) m

what (accented when used in a question): **qué** (keh)

what (unaccented when used in a statement or answer): **que** (keh)

when (accented when used in a question): **cuándo** (kooh*ahn*-doh)

when (unaccented when used in a statement or an answer): **cuando** (kooh*ahn*-doh)

which (accented when used in a question): **cuál** (kooh*ahl*)

which (unaccented when used in a statement or answer): **cual** (kooh*ahl*)

whisk: **batidor manual** (bvah-tee-*dohr* mah-nooh*ahl*) m

white: **blanco** (*bvlahn*-koh)

whiteboard: **pizarra blanca** (pee-*sah*-rrah *bvlahn*-kah) f

who (accented when used in a question): **quién** (kee*ehn*)

who (unaccented when used in a statement or answer): **quien** (kee*ehn*)

why: **por qué** (pohr keh)

wife: **esposa** (ehs-*poh*-sah) f

to win: **ganar** (gah-*nahr*)

window: **ventana** (bvehn-*tah*-nah) f

windshield: **parabrisas** (pah-rah-*bvree*-sahs) m

wine: **vino** (*bvee*-noh) m

withdrawal: **retiro** (rreh-*tee*-roh) m

woman: **mujer** (mooh-*Hehr*) f

wonderful: **maravilloso** (mah-rah-bvee-*yoh*-soh)

wood: **madera** (mah-*deh*-rah) f

wool: **lana** (*lah*-nah) f

to work: **trabajar** (trah-bvah-*Hahr*)

to worry (about): **preocuparse (por)** (preh-oh-kooh-*pahr*-seh [pohr])

worse: **peor** (peh-*ohr*)

wound: **herida** (eh-*ree*-dah) f

wrist: **muñeca** (mooh-*nyeh*-kah) f

to write: **escribir** (ehs-kree-*bveer*)

X

x-ray picture: **radiografía** (rrah-deeoh-grah-*fee*-ah) f

Y

year: **año** (*ah*-nyoh) m

yellow: **amarillo** (ah-mah-*ree*-yoh)

yes: **sí** (see)

yesterday: **ayer** (*ah*-yehr)

yet, still: **todavía** (toh-dah-*bvee*-ah)

you (formal, plural): **ustedes (Uds.)** (oohs-*teh*-dehs)

you (formal, singular): **usted (Ud.)** (oohs-*tehd*)

you (informal, plural) (feminine): **vosotras** (bvoh-*soh*-trahs)

you (informal, plural) (masculine, or mixed group): **vosotros** (bvoh-*soh*-trohs)

you (informal, singular): **tú** (tooh)

Z

zero: **cero** (*seh*-roh)

zucchini (in Uruguay and Argentina): **zapallito** (sah-pah-*yee*-toh) m

Appendix B
Verb Tables

● ●

Regular Spanish Verbs

Regular Verbs Ending in -ar
For example: hablar (to speak)

Past Participle: hablado (spoken); Gerund: hablando (speaking)

	Present	Past	Future
yo (I)	hablo	hablé	hablaré
tú (you, informal)	hablas	hablaste	hablarás
Ud. (you, formal)	habla	habló	hablará
él/ella (he/she)	habla	habló	hablará
nosotros/nosotras (we)	hablamos	hablamos	hablaremos
vosotros/vosotras (you, informal)	habláis	hablasteis	hablaréis
Uds. (you, formal)	hablan	hablaron	hablarán
ellos/ellas (they)	hablan	hablaron	hablarán

Regular Verbs Ending in -er
For example: comer (to eat)

Past Participle: comido (eaten); Gerund: comiendo (eating)

	Present	Past	Future
yo (I)	como	comí	comeré
tú (you, informal)	comes	comiste	comerás
Ud. (you, formal)	come	comió	comerá
él/ella (he/she)	come	comió	comerá
nosotros/nosotras (we)	comemos	comimos	comeremos

	Present	Past	Future
vosotros/vosotras (you, informal)	coméis	comisteis	comeréis
Uds. (you, formal)	comen	comieron	comerán
ellos/ellas (they)	comen	comieron	comerán

Regular Verbs Ending in -ir
For example: vivir (to live)

Past Participle: vivido (lived); Gerund: viviendo (living)

	Present	Past	Future
yo (I)	vivo	viví	viviré
tú (you, informal)	vives	viviste	vivirás
Ud. (you, formal)	vive	vivió	vivirá
él/ella (he/she)	vive	vivió	vivirá
nosotros/nosotras (we)	vivimos	vivimos	viviremos
vosotros/vosotras (you, informal)	vivís	vivisteis	viviréis
Uds. (you, formal)	viven	vivieron	vivirán
ellos/ellas (they)	viven	vivieron	vivirán

Irregular Spanish Verbs

		Present	Past	Future
conocer	yo (I)	conozco	conocí	conoceré
to know (be acquainted with)	tú (you, informal)	conoces	conociste	conocerás
Past participle: conocido (known)	Ud. (you, formal)	conoce	conoció	conocerá
Gerund: conociendo (knowing)	él/ella (he/she)	conoce	conoció	conocerá
	nosotros/ nosotras (we)	conocemos	conocimos	conoceremos
	vosotros/vosotras (you, informal)	conocéis	conocisteis	conoceréis
	Uds. (you, formal)	conocen	conocieron	conocerán
	ellos/ellas (they)	conocen	conocieron	conocerán

		Present	Past	Future
dar	*yo (I)*	doy	di	daré
to give	*tú (you, informal)*	das	diste	darás
Past participle: dado (gave)	*Ud. (you, formal)*	da	dio	dará
Gerund: dando (giving)	*él/ella (he/she)*	da	dio	dará
	nosotros/ nosotras (we)	damos	dimos	daremos
	vosotros/vosotras (you, informal)	dais	disteis	daréis
	Uds. (you, formal)	dan	dieron	darán
	ellos/ellas (they)	dan	dieron	darán

		Present	Past	Future
estar	*yo (I)*	estoy	estuve	estaré
to be (location, state of condition)	*tú (you, informal)*	estás	estuviste	estarás
Past participle: estado (been)	*Ud. (you, formal)*	está	estuvo	estará
Gerund: estando (being)	*él/ella (he/she)*	está	estuvo	estará
	nosotros/ nosotras (we)	estamos	estuvimos	estaremos
	vosotros/vosotras (you, informal)	estáis	estuvisteis	estaréis
	Uds. (you, formal)	están	estuvieron	estarán
	ellos/ellas (they)	están	estuvieron	estarán

		Present	Past	Future
hacer	*yo (I)*	hago	hice	haré
to do, to make	*tú (you, informal)*	haces	hiciste	harás
Past participle: hecho (done, made)	*Ud. (you, formal)*	hace	hizo	hará
Gerund: haciendo (doing, making)	*él/ella (he/she)*	hace	hizo	hará
	nosotros/ nosotras (we)	hacemos	hicimos	haremos
	vosotros/vosotras (you, informal)	hacéis	hicisteis	haréis
	Uds. (you, formal)	hacen	hicieron	harán
	ellos/ellas (they)	hacen	hicieron	harán

		Present	Past	Future
ir	*yo (I)*	voy	fui	iré
to go	*tú (you, informal)*	vas	fuiste	irás
Past participle: ido (gone)	*Ud. (you, formal)*	va	fue	irá
Gerund: yendo (going)	*él/ella (he/she)*	va	fue	irá
	nosotros/ nosotras (we)	vamos	fuimos	iremos
	vosotros/vosotras (you, informal)	vais	fuisteis	iréis
	Uds. (you, formal)	van	fueron	irán
	ellos/ellas (they)	van	fueron	irán

		Present	Past	Future
lavarse	*yo (I)*	me lavo	me lavé	me lavaré
to wash one's self	*tú (you, informal)*	te lavas	te lavaste	te lavarás
Past participle: lavado (washed one's self)	*Ud. (you, formal)*	se lava	se lavó	se lavará
Gerund: lavándose (washing one's self)	*él/ella (he/she)*	se lava	se lavó	se lavará
	nosotros/ nosotras (we)	nos lavamos	nos lavamos	nos lavaremos
	vosotros/vosotras (you, informal)	os laváis	os lavasteis	os lavaréis
	Uds. (you, formal)	se lavan	se lavaron	se lavarán
	ellos/ellas (they)	se lavan	se lavaron	se lavarán

		Present	Past	Future
leer	*yo (I)*	leo	leí	leeré
to read	*tú (you, informal)*	lees	leíste	leerás
Past participle: leído (read)	*Ud. (you, formal)*	lee	leyó	leerá
Gerund: leyendo (reading)	*él/ella (he/she)*	lee	leyó	leerá
	nosotros/ nosotras (we)	leemos	leímos	leeremos
	vosotros/vosotras (you, informal)	leéis	leísteis	leeréis
	Uds. (you, formal)	leen	leyeron	leerán
	ellos/ellas (they)	leen	leyeron	leerán

		Present	Past	Future
oir	*yo (I)*	oigo	oí	oiré
to hear	*tú (you, informal)*	oyes	oíste	oirás
Past Participle: oído (heard)	*Ud. (you, formal)*	oye	oyó	oirá
Gerund: oyendo (hearing)	*él/ella (he/she)*	oye	oyó	oirá
	nosotros/ nosotras (we)	oímos	oímos	oiremos
	vosotros/vosotras (you, informal)	oís	oísteis	oiréis
	Uds. (you, formal)	oyen	oyeron	oirán
	ellos/ellas (they)	oyen	oyeron	oirán

		Present	Past	Future
poner	*yo (I)*	pongo	puse	pondré
to put	*tú (you, informal)*	pones	pusiste	pondrás
Past participle: puesto (put)	*Ud. (you, formal)*	pone	puso	pondrá
Gerund: poniendo (putting)	*él/ella (he/she)*	pone	puso	pondrá
	nosotros/ nosotras (we)	ponemos	pusimos	pondremos
	vosotros/vosotras (you, informal)	ponéis	pusisteis	pondréis
	Uds. (you, formal)	ponen	pusieron	pondrán
	ellos/ellas (they)	ponen	pusieron	pondrán

		Present	**Past**	**Future**
querer	*yo (I)*	quiero	quise	querré
to want, to wish	*tú (you, informal)*	quieres	quisiste	querrás
Past participle: querido (wanted, wished)	*Ud. (you, formal)*	quiere	quiso	querrá
Gerund: queriendo (wanting, wishing)	*él/ella (he/she)*	quiere	quiso	querrá
	nosotros/ nosotras (we)	queremos	quisimos	querremos
	vosotros/vosotras (you, informal)	queréis	quisisteis	querréis
	Uds. (you, formal)	quieren	quisieron	querrán
	ellos/ellas (they)	quieren	quisieron	querrán

		Present	**Past**	**Future**
saber	*yo (I)*	sé	supe	sabré
to know something	*tú (you, informal)*	sabes	supiste	sabrás
Past participle: sabido (known)	*Ud. (you, formal)*	sabe	supo	sabrá
Gerund: sabiendo (knowing)	*él/ella (he/she)*	sabe	supo	sabrá
	nosotros/ nosotras (we)	sabemos	supimos	sabremos
	vosotros/vosotras (you, informal)	sabéis	supisteis	sabréis
	Uds. (you, formal)	saben	supieron	sabrán
	ellos/ellas (they)	saben	supieron	sabrán

		Present	Past	Future
salir	*yo (I)*	salgo	salí	saldré
to leave, to go out	*tú (you, informal)*	sales	saliste	saldrás
Past participle: salido (left)	*Ud. (you, formal)*	sale	salió	saldrá
Gerund: saliendo (leaving)	*él/ella (he/she)*	sale	salió	saldrá
	nosotros/ nosotras (we)	salimos	salimos	saldremos
	vosotros/vosotras (you, informal)	salís	salisteis	saldréis
	Uds. (you, formal)	salen	salieron	saldrán
	ellos/ellas (they)	salen	salieron	saldrán

		Present	Past	Future
ser	*yo (I)*	soy	fui	seré
to be (permanent state of condition)	*tú (you, informal)*	eres	fuiste	serás
Past participle: sido (been)	*Ud. (you, formal)*	es	fue	será
Gerund: siendo (being)	*él/ella (he/she)*	es	fue	será
	nosotros/ nosotras (we)	somos	fuimos	seremos
	vosotros/vosotras (you, informal)	sois	fuisteis	seréis
	Uds. (you, formal)	son	fueron	serán
	ellos/ellas (they)	son	fueron	serán

		Present	Past	Future
tener	*yo (I)*	tengo	tuve	tendré
to have	*tú (you, informal)*	tienes	tuviste	tendrás
Past participle: tenido (had)	*Ud. (you, formal)*	tiene	tuvo	tendrá
Gerund: teniendo (having)	*él/ella (he/she)*	tiene	tuvo	tendrá
	nosotros/ nosotras (we)	tenemos	tuvimos	tendremos
	vosotros/vosotras (you, informal)	tenéis	tuvisteis	tendréis
	Uds. (you, formal)	tienen	tuvieron	tendrán
	ellos/ellas (they)	tienen	tuvieron	tendrán

		Present	Past	Future
traer	*yo (I)*	traigo	traje	traeré
to bring	*tú (you, informal)*	traes	trajiste	traerás
Past participle: traído (brought)	*Ud. (you, formal)*	trae	trajo	traerá
Gerund: trayendo (bringing)	*él/ella (he/she)*	trae	trajo	traerá
	nosotros/ nosotras (we)	traemos	trajimos	traeremos
	vosotros/vosotras (you, informal)	traéis	trajisteis	traeréis
	Uds. (you, formal)	traen	trajeron	traerán
	ellos/ellas (they)	traen	trajeron	traerán

		Present	Past	Future
venir	*yo (I)*	vengo	vine	vendré
to come	*tú (you, informal)*	vienes	viniste	vendrás
Past participle: venido (came)	*Ud. (you, formal)*	viene	vino	vendrá
Gerund: viniendo (coming)	*él/ella (he/she)*	viene	vino	vendrá
	nosotros/ nosotras (we)	venimos	vinimos	vendremos
	vosotros/vosotras (you, informal)	venís	vinisteis	vendréis
	Uds. (you, formal)	vienen	vinieron	vendrán
	ellos/ellas (they)	vienen	vinieron	vendrán

		Present	Past	Future
ver	*yo (I)*	veo	vi	veré
to see	*tú (you, informal)*	ves	viste	verás
Past participle: visto (seen)	*Ud. (you, formal)*	ve	vio	verá
Gerund: viendo (seeing)	*él/ella (he/she)*	ve	vio	verá
	nosotros/ nosotras (we)	vemos	vimos	veremos
	vosotros/vosotras (you, informal)	veis	visteis	veréis
	Uds. (you, formal)	ven	vieron	verán
	ellos/ellas (they)	ven	vieron	verán

Spanish Verbs with e to i Stem Changes

		Present	Past	Future
conseguir	*yo (I)*	consigo	conseguí	conseguiré
to attain, to get	*tú (you, informal)*	consigues	conseguiste	conseguirás
Past participle: conseguido (attained, got)	*Ud. (you, formal)*	consigue	consiguió	conseguirá
Gerund: consiguiendo (attaining,getting)	*él/ella (he/she)*	consigue	consiguió	conseguirá
	nosotros/ nosotras (we)	conseguimos	conseguimos	conseguiremos
	vosotros/vosotras (you, informal)	conseguís	conseguisteis	conseguiréis
	Uds. (you, formal)	consiguen	consiguieron	conseguirán
	ellos/ellas (they)	consiguen	consiguieron	conseguirán

		Present	Past	Future
pedir	*yo (I)*	pido	pedí	pediré
to ask for, to request	*tú (you, informal)*	pides	pediste	pedirás
Past participle: pedido (asked for, requested)	*Ud. (you, formal)*	pide	pidió	pedirá
Gerund: pidiendo (asking for, requesting)	*él/ella (he/she)*	pide	pidió	pedirá
	nosotros/ nosotras (we)	pedimos	pedimos	pediremos
	vosotros/vosotras (you, informal)	pedís	pedisteis	pediréis
	Uds. (you, formal)	piden	pidieron	pedirán
	ellos/ellas (they)	piden	pidieron	pedirán

		Present	**Past**	**Future**
repetir	*yo (I)*	repito	repetí	repetiré
to repeat	*tú (you, informal)*	repites	repetiste	repetirás
Past participle: repetido (repeated)	*Ud. (you, formal)*	repite	repitió	repetirá
Gerund: repitiendo (repeating)	*él/ella (he/she)*	repite	repitió	repetirá
	nosotros/ nosotras (we)	repetimos	repetimos	repetiremos
	vosotros/vosotras (you, informal)	repetís	repetisteis	repetiréis
	Uds. (you, formal)	repiten	repitieron	repetirán
	ellos/ellas (they)	repiten	repitieron	repetirán

		Present	**Past**	**Future**
servir	*yo (I)*	sirvo	serví	serviré
to serve	*tú (you, informal)*	sirves	serviste	servirás
Past participle: servido (served)	*Ud. (you, formal)*	sirve	sirvió	servirá
Gerund: sirviendo (serving)	*él/ella (he/she)*	sirve	sirvió	servirá
	nosotros/ nosotras (we)	servimos	servimos	serviremos
	vosotros/vosotras (you, informal)	servís	servisteis	serviréis
	Uds. (you, formal)	sirven	sirvieron	servirán
	ellos/ellas (they)	sirven	sirvieron	servirán

		Present	Past	Future
vestir	*yo (I)*	visto	vestí	vestiré
to dress	*tú (you, informal)*	vistes	vestiste	vestirás
Past participle: vestido (dressed)	*Ud. (you, formal)*	viste	vistió	vestirá
Gerund: vistiendo (dressing)	*él/ella (he/she)*	viste	vistió	vestirá
	nosotros/ nosotras (we)	vestimos	vestimos	vestiremos
	vosotros/vosotras (you, informal)	vestís	vestisteis	vestiréis
	Uds. (you, formal)	visten	vistieron	vestirán
	ellos/ellas (they)	visten	vistieron	vestirán

Spanish Verbs with e to ie Stem Changes

		Present	Past	Future
cerrar	*yo (I)*	cierro	cerré	cerraré
to close	*tú (you, informal)*	cierras	cerraste	cerrarás
Past participle: cerrado (closed)	*Ud. (you, formal)*	cierra	cerró	cerrará
Gerund: cerrando (closing)	*él/ella (he/she)*	cierra	cerró	cerrará
	nosotros/ nosotras (we)	cerramos	cerramos	cerraremos
	vosotros/vosotras (you, informal)	cerráis	cerrasteis	cerraréis
	Uds. (you, formal)	cierran	cerraron	cerrarán
	ellos/ellas (they)	cierran	cerraron	cerrarán

		Present	Past	Future
empezar	*yo (I)*	empiezo	empecé	empezaré
to begin	*tú (you, informal)*	empiezas	empezaste	empezarás
Past participle: empezado (begun)	*Ud. (you, formal)*	empieza	empezó	empezará
Gerund: empezando (beginning)	*él/ella (he/she)*	empieza	empezó	empezará
	nosotros/ nosotras (we)	empezamos	empézamos	empezaremos
	vosotros/vosotras (you, informal)	empezáis	empezasteis	empezaréis
	Uds. (you, formal)	empiezan	empezaron	empezarán
	ellos/ellas (they)	empiezan	empezaron	empezarán

		Present	Past	Future
entender	*yo (I)*	entiendo	entendí	entenderé
to understand	*tú (you, informal)*	entiendes	entendiste	entenderás
Past participle: entendido (understood)	*Ud. (you, formal)*	entiende	entendió	entenderá
Gerund: entendiendo (understanding)	*él/ella (he/she)*	entiende	entendió	entenderá
	nosotros/ nosotras (we)	entendemos	entendimos	entenderemos
	vosotros/vosotras (you, informal)	entendéis	entendisteis	entenderéis
	Uds. (you, formal)	entienden	entendieron	entenderán
	ellos/ellas (they)	entienden	entendieron	entenderán

		Present	Past	Future
pensar	*yo (I)*	pienso	pensé	pensaré
to think	*tú (you, informal)*	piensas	pensaste	pensarás
Past participle: pensado (thought)	*Ud. (you, formal)*	piensa	pensó	pensará
Gerund: pensando (thinking)	*él/ella (he/she)*	piensa	pensó	pensará
	nosotros/ nosotras (we)	pensamos	pensamos	pensaremos
	vosotros/vosotras (you, informal)	pensáis	pensasteis	pensaréis
	Uds. (you, formal)	piensan	pensaron	pensarán
	ellos/ellas (they)	piensan	pensaron	pensarán

		Present	Past	Future
perder	*yo (I)*	pierdo	perdí	perderé
to lose	*tú (you, informal)*	pierdes	perdiste	perderás
Past participle: perdido (lost)	*Ud. (you, formal)*	pierde	perdió	perderá
Gerund: perdiendo (losing)	*él/ella (he/she)*	pierde	perdió	perderá
	nosotros/ nosotras (we)	perdemos	perdimos	perderemos
	vosotros/vosotras (you, informal)	perdéis	perdisteis	perderéis
	Uds. (you, formal)	pierden	perdieron	perderán
	ellos/ellas (they)	pierden	perdieron	perderán

Spanish Verbs with o to ue Stem Changes

		Present	Past	Future
almorzar	*yo (I)*	almuerzo	almorcé	almorzaré
to have lunch	*tú (you, informal)*	almuerzas	almorzaste	almorzarás
Past participle: almorzado (had lunch)	*Ud. (you, formal)*	almuerza	almorzó	almorzará
Gerund: almorzando (having lunch)	*él/ella (he/she)*	almuerza	almorzó	almorzará
	nosotros/ nosotras (we)	almorzamos	almorzamos	almorzaremos
	vosotros/vosotras (you, informal)	almorzáis	almorzasteis	almorzaréis
	Uds. (you, formal)	almuerzan	almorzaron	almorzarán
	ellos/ellas (they)	almuerzan	almorzaron	almorzarán

		Present	Past	Future
dormir	*yo (I)*	duermo	dormí	dormiré
to sleep	*tú (you, informal)*	duermes	dormiste	dormirás
Past participle: dormido (slept)	*Ud. (you, formal)*	duerme	durmió	dormirá
Gerund: durmiendo (sleeping)	*él/ella (he/she)*	duerme	durmió	dormirá
	nosotros/ nosotras (we)	dormimos	dormimos	dormiremos
	vosotros/vosotras (you, informal)	dormís	dormisteis	dormiréis
	Uds. (you, formal)	duermen	durmieron	dormirán
	ellos/ellas (they)	duermen	durmieron	dormirán

		Present	Past	Future
encontrar	*yo (I)*	encuentro	encontré	encontraré
to find	*tú (you, informal)*	encuentras	encontraste	encontrarás
Past participle: encontrado (found)	*Ud. (you, formal)*	encuentra	encontró	encontrará
Gerund: encontrando (finding)	*él/ella (he/she)*	encuentra	encontró	encontrará
	nosotros/ nosotras (we)	encontramos	encontramos	encontraremos
	vosotros/vosotras (you, informal)	encontráis	encontrasteis	encontraréis
	Uds. (you, formal)	encuentran	encontraron	encontrarán
	ellos/ellas (they)	encuentran	encontraron	encontrarán

		Present	Past	Future
poder	*yo (I)*	puedo	pude	podré
to be able to	*tú (you, informal)*	puedes	pudiste	podrás
Past participle: podido (was able to)	*Ud. (you, formal)*	puede	pudo	podrá
Gerund: pudiendo (being able to)	*él/ella (he/she)*	puede	pudo	podrá
	nosotros/ nosotras (we)	podemos	pudimos	podremos
	vosotros/vosotras (you, informal)	podéis	pudisteis	podréis
	Uds. (you, formal)	pueden	pudieron	podrán
	ellos/ellas (they)	pueden	pudieron	podrán

		Present	Past	Future
volver	*yo (I)*	vuelvo	volví	volveré
to return	*tú (you, informal)*	vuelves	volviste	volverás
Past participle: vuelto (returned)	*Ud. (you, formal)*	vuelve	volvió	volverá
Gerund: volviendo (returning)	*él/ella (he/she)*	vuelve	volvió	volverá
	nosotros/ nosotras (we)	volvemos	volvimos	volveremos
	vosotros/vosotras (you, informal)	volvéis	volvisteis	volveréis
	Uds. (you, formal)	vuelven	volvieron	volverán
	ellos/ellas (they)	vuelven	volvieron	volverán

A Spanish Verb with a u to ue Stem Change

		Present	Past	Future
jugar	*yo (I)*	juego	jugué	jugaré
to play a game or sport	*tú (you, informal)*	juegas	jugaste	jugarás
Past participle: jugado (played)	*Ud. (you, formal)*	juega	jugó	jugará
Gerund: jugando (playing)	*él/ella (he/she)*	juega	jugó	jugará
	nosotros/ nosotras (we)	jugamos	jugamos	jugaremos
	vosotros/vosotras (you, informal)	jugáis	jugasteis	jugaréis
	Uds. (you, formal)	juegan	jugaron	jugarán
	ellos/ellas (they)	juegan	jugaron	jugarán

Appendix C

On the CD

. . . .

Track Listing

*T*he following is a list of the tracks that appear on this book's audio CD. Note that this is an audio-only CD — it'll play in any standard CD player or in your computer's CD-ROM drive.

Track 1: Introduction and Pronunciation Guide

Track 2: Discussing dinner preparations with the verb **preparar** (Chapter 2)

Track 3: Discussing age with the verb **tener** (Chapter 2)

Track 4: Getting formal with strangers (Chapter 3)

Track 5: Practicing the verb **estar** (Chapter 3)

Track 6: Talking about vacation plans with dates and times (Chapter 4)

Track 7: Bargaining over the prices and weights of oranges and bananas (Chapter 4)

Track 8: Moving into a new home (Chapter 5)

Track 9: Talking about daily plans before leaving for school (Chapter 5)

Track 10: Asking about weather (Chapter 6)

Track 11: Describing jobs (Chapter 6)

Track 12: Locating the restaurant and the pool at a hotel (Chapter 7)

Track 13: Getting step-by-step directions to a museum (Chapter 7)

Track 14: Ordering food at a restaurant (Chapter 8)

Track 15: Shopping for fish at a market (Chapter 8)

Track 16: Shopping for a skirt (Chapter 9)

Track 17: Bargaining for a rug (Chapter 9)

Track 18: Being invited to a party (Chapter 10)

Track 19: Making plans to see a movie (Chapter 10)

Track 20: Starting a new office job and gathering supplies (Chapter 11)

Track 21: Setting up a business meeting (Chapter 11)

Track 22: Discussing reading material (Chapter 12)

Track 23: Talking about soccer (Chapter 12)

Track 24: Booking a flight (Chapter 13)

Track 25: Asking about visas (Chapter 13)

Track 26: Using credit cards (Chapter 14)

Track 27: Cashing in traveler's checks (Chapter 14)

Track 28: Buying a train ticket (Chapter 15)

Track 29: Meeting a customs officer (Chapter 15)

Track 30: Asking for a hotel room (Chapter 16)

Track 31: Checking in to a hotel (Chapter 16)

Track 32: Describing symptoms to a doctor (Chapter 17)

Track 33: Talking to a police officer after being pulled over (Chapter 17)

Customer Care

If you have trouble with the CD, please call Wiley Product Technical Support at 877-762-2974. Outside the United States, call 317-572-3993. You can also contact Wiley Product Technical Support at support.wiley.com. Wiley Publishing will provide technical support only for installation and other general quality control items.

To place additional orders or to request information about other Wiley products, please call 877-762-2974.

Appendix D

Answer Keys

. . . .

*T*he following are all the answers to the Fun & Games activities.

Chapter 1: Spanish in a Nutshell

```
L  T  U  A  J  T  J  B  K  S  O  L  A  H  O  R  A
N  C  O  M  E  D  O  R  P  I  K  A  J  C  A  E  M
P  X  K  C  Y  V  I  A  R  H  A  B  L  A  M  O  S
H  O  L  A  R  A  P  O  R  A  Z  Z  D  R  X  Y  O
J  N  H  Y  Í  A  T  O  E  B  G  G  Z  S  A  Y  F
M  A  R  D  M  I  N  V  T  L  R  Q  K  U  R  W  I
N  Q  Q  G  M  U  I  B  Z  O  A  Y  U  T  P  G  C
Z  E  Q  R  B  P  R  E  I  V  C  I  K  H  B  Z  I
D  A  O  O  O  A  A  G  D  R  I  W  A  Z  H  A  N
M  D  P  F  O  D  R  E  S  T  A  C  I  Ó  N  W  A
N  Q  W  A  M  F  J  F  H  Z  S  M  F  Y  C  U  Z
J  N  X  J  T  A  E  U  C  W  E  L  W  W  I  O  D
A  N  T  T  R  O  N  P  N  W  R  N  A  D  U  N  O
B  L  G  E  I  W  S  P  Z  N  Y  J  D  H  D  Ñ  D
Ó  G  V  O  S  I  Y  G  L  L  S  W  I  F  A  A  F
N  E  K  Z  P  U  C  G  Q  V  Z  H  Ó  B  D  W  Q
N  P  K  T  R  E  N  X  B  J  P  N  S  O  D  I  X
```

good-bye: **adiós**   now: **ahora**   bathroom: **baño**
city: **ciudad**   dining room: **comedor**   day: **día**
bedroom: **dormitorio**   station: **estación**   thank you: **gracias**
we talk: **hablamos**   I talk: **hablo**   hello: **hola**
soap: **jabón**   map: **mapa**   refrigerator: **nevera**
office: **oficina**   train: **tren**   shoes: **zapatos**

Chapter 2: Warming Up with Spanish Grammar Basics

Across: 1 **vive,** 3 **retiran,** 7 **barre,** 8 **soplan,** 9 **viajo,** 12 **preparamos,** 13 **habla,** 14 **camina.**

Down: 1 **venden,** 2 **visitáis,** 4 **abre,** 5 **mencionas,** 6 **como,** 7 **bailas,** 8 **sospecha,** 10 **desea,** 11 **nadan.**

Chapter 3: Getting Started with Basic Expressions

✔ Good afternoon! **¡Buenas tardes!**

✔ My name is Mr. Kendall. **Me llamo Sr. Kendall.**

✔ A pleasure, ma'am. **Mucho gusto, señora.**

✔ My name is Jane Wells. **Me llamo Jane Wells.**

✔ Where are you from? **¿De dónde es Ud.?**

✔ I'm from Canada. **Soy de Canadá.**

✔ What city are you from? **¿De qué ciudad es Ud.?**

✔ I'm from New York. **Soy de Nueva York.**

✔ Is that a very large city? **¿Es ésa una ciudad muy grande?**

✔ Yes, it is a very large city. **Sí, es una ciudad muy grande.**

✔ We are on vacation. **Estamos de vacaciones.**

✔ Are you satisfied? **¿Están contentos?**

✔ We are very happy. **Estamos muy felices.**

Chapter 4: Getting Your Numbers, Times, and Measurements Straight

Across: 1 **verano,** 4 **ocho,** 7 **mes,** 8 **segundo,** 11 **agosto,** 13 **cincuenta,** 14 **mayo,** 15 **primavera,** 18 **treinta,** 20 **cien,** 21 **ochenta,** 22 **tres,** 23 **invierno,** 25 **once.**

Down: 1 **viernes,** 2 **quinto,** 3 **domingo,** 5 **hoy,** 6 **quince,** 7 **martes,** 9 **enero,** 10 **cuatro,** 12 **semana,** 16 **marzo,** 17 **jueves,** 19 **nueve,** 20 **catorce,** 24 **noveno.**

Chapter 5: Speaking Spanish at Home

1. **el dormitorio** 2. **el baño** 3. **la cocina** 4. **el comedor**
5. **el salón** 6. **el sótano** 7. **la lavandería**

a. **la cama**   b. **el gavetero**   c. **el excusado**   d. **la bañera**
e. **la nevera**   f. **la estufa**   g. **el gabinete**   h. **el fregadero**
i. **la silla**   j. **la mesa**   k. **el televisor**   l. **el sofá**
m. **la lavadora**   n. **la secadora**

Chapter 6: Getting to Know You: Making Small Talk

female cousin: **prima**   which: **cuál**   uncle: **tío**
granddaughter: **nieta**   grandmother: **abuela**   godfather: **padrino**
grandfather: **abuelo**   father: **padre**   when: **cuándo**
why: **por qué**   godmother: **madrina**   son: **hijo**
son-in-law: **yerno**   daughter-in-law: **nuera**   mother: **madre**
sister: **hermana**   brother-in-law: **cuñado**   brother: **hermano**
grandson: **nieto**   male cousin: **primo**   sister-in-law: **cuñada**
aunt: **tía**   what: **qué**   daughter: **hija**

Chapter 7: Asking for Directions

✔ Go to the square. **Vaya a la plaza.**

✔ Walk two blocks to the small park. **Camine dos cuadras al jardín.**

✔ Go straight to Alabaster Ave. **Vaya derecho a la Avenida Alabaster.**

✔ Turn left. **Doble a la izquierda.**

✔ Continue north to Camisa St. **Siga al norte a la Calle Camisa.**

✔ Turn right. **Doble a la derecha.**

✔ Continue two more blocks and turn left on Reina Blvd. **Siga dos cuadras más y doble a la izquierda en el Bulevar Reina.**

✔ My house is behind the park. **Mi casa está detrás del parque.**

Chapter 8: Dining Out and Going to the Market

beef: **carne**   coffee: **café**   milk: **leche**
fried chicken: **pollo frito**   green sauce: **salsa verde**   beer: **cerveza**
seafood: **marisco**

un vaso de agua: a glass of water
un vaso de leche: a glass of milk
una ensalada mixta: a mixed salad
mole amarillo con pollo: chicken with yellow mole (sauce)
calabacita: zucchini

Chapter 9: Shopping Made Easy

a. **el cinturón**
b. **la blusa**
c. **la falda**
d. **los pantalones**
e. **la camisa**
f. **los calcetines**
g. **los zapatos**
h. **los zapatos de salón**
i. **la corbata**
j. **la chaqueta** or **el saco**

Chapter 10: Going Out on the Town

Across: 1 **cine**, 3 **fila**, 4 **matiné**, 5 **boletos**, 7 **anunciar**, 10 **ópera**, 14 **cartelera**, 15 **viaje**, 16 **agotados**, 17 **teatro**.

Down: 1 **crítica**, 2 **cantante**, 6 **dramaturgo**, 8 **concierto**, 9 **actriz**, 11 **película**, 12 **subasta**, 13 **fiesta**.

Chapter 11: Taking Care of Business and Telecommunications

the desk: **el escritorio**
the chair: **la silla**
the desk lamp: **la lámpara de escritorio**
the computer: **la computadora**
the bookshelves: **la estantería para libros**
the calendar: **el calendario**
the pen: **el bolígrafo**
the pencil sharpener: **el sacapuntas**
the stapler: **la grapadora**
the telephone: **el teléfono**
the waste basket: **el bote de basura**

Chapter 12: Recreation and the Great Outdoors

a. **la ardilla:** the squirrel
b. **la cabra:** the goat
c. **el caballo:** the horse
d. **la vaca:** the cow
e. **el ganso:** the goose
f. **el gornón:** the sparrow
g. **la mariposa:** the butterfly
h. **el perro:** the dog
i. **el burro:** the donkey
j. **el gato:** the cat

Chapter 13: Planning a Trip

Across: 1 **zapatos**, 4 **viajar**, 5 **baterías**, 6 **meses**, 7 **vuelo**, 9 **maleta**, 11 **ciudadana**, 13 **sótano**, 14 **llegar**, 15 **depende**, 16 **autobús**.

Down: 2 **turista**, 3 **pasaporte**, 8 **equipaje**, 9 **mochila**, 10 **cansado**, 12 **armario**.

Chapter 14: Dealing with Money in a Foreign Land

la compra: the purchase
recibo: receipt
saldo: balance
dinero: money
el banco: the bank
número confidencial: PIN
retiro: withdrawal

la venta: the sale
monedas: coins
cuenta: account
tarjeta de crédito: credit card
en efectivo: cash
billetes: bills

Chapter 15: Getting Around: Planes, Trains, Taxis, and More

Exterior

a. headlights: **los faros delanteros**
b. windshield wipers: **los limpiaparabrisas**
c. windshield: **el parabrisas**
d. rearview mirror: **el espejo retrovisor**
e. sideview mirror: **el espejo lateral**
f. door: **la puerta**
g. wheel: **la rueda**
h. tire: **el neumático**

Interior

i. steering wheel: **el volante**
j. sun visor: **el parasol**
k. speedometer: **el velocímetro**
l. windshield wiper lever: **la palanca de limpiaparabrisas**
m. horn: **el claxón**
n. clutch pedal: **el pedal del embrague**
o. brake pedal: **el pedal de los frenos**
p. gas pedal: **el pedal del acelerador**
q. ignition switch: **el interruptor de encendido**
r. parking brake: **el freno de mano**
s. gear shift lever: **la palanca de cambio**
t. glove compartment: **la guantera**

Chapter 16: Finding a Place to Stay

```
B A L G N O C Q S A V E K Y L
Q O J O S O E D N C H A M P Ú
I I E A I L E I E I T T W Q Q
F D V C L N C E E S W T H A B
B O E G S S C I L H A H C V A
L R W Z I B L L J K S Y S G Ñ
P M J P Z Z J N U W K A U N O
D I R E C C I Ó N I L H S N V
M R E D J H M W A L D H H B O
N B P M A P V K A E Q O F O R
G A N F K K C O W Q B V X G R
B L A C O S T A R S E R B F Y
D E S P E R T A R S E M D R B
H A B I T A C I Ó N P S D Í N
F T B L W T W R V E S R M A S
```

to go to bed: **acostarse**	bathroom: **baño**
shampoo: **champú**	breakfast: **desayuno**
to wake up: **despertarse**	address: **dirección**
to sleep: **dormir**	cold: **fría**
room, bedroom: **habitación**	included: **incluido**
swimming pool: **piscina**	price: **precio**
glass: **vaso**	towels: **toallas**

Chapter 17: Handling Emergencies

a. the eye: **el ojo**	b. the nose: **la nariz**
c. the mouth: **la boca**	d. the shoulder: **el hombro**
e. the chest: **el pecho**	f. the hand: **la mano**
g. the finger: **el dedo**	h. the stomach: **el estómago**
i. the thigh: **el muslo**	j. the ankle: **el tobillo**
k. the toe: **el dedo del pie**	l. the foot: **el pie**
m. the leg: **la pierna**	n. the wrist: **la muñeca**
o. the thumb: **el pulgar**	p. the arm: **el brazo**
q. the neck: **el cuello**	r. the ear: **la oreja**
s. the head: **la cabeza**	t. the face: **el rostro**

Index

• N •

• O •

• Q •

• R •

• S •

Notes

Notes

Wiley Publishing, Inc.
End-User License Agreement

READ THIS. You should carefully read these terms and conditions before opening the software packet(s) included with this book "Book". This is a license agreement "Agreement" between you and Wiley Publishing, Inc. "WPI". By opening the accompanying software packet(s), you acknowledge that you have read and accept the following terms and conditions. If you do not agree and do not want to be bound by such terms and conditions, promptly return the Book and the unopened software packet(s) to the place you obtained them for a full refund.

1. **License Grant.** WPI grants to you (either an individual or entity) a nonexclusive license to use one copy of the enclosed software program(s) (collectively, the "Software") solely for your own personal or business purposes on a single computer (whether a standard computer or a workstation component of a multi-user network). The Software is in use on a computer when it is loaded into temporary memory (RAM) or installed into permanent memory (hard disk, CD-ROM, or other storage device). WPI reserves all rights not expressly granted herein.

2. **Ownership.** WPI is the owner of all right, title, and interest, including copyright, in and to the compilation of the Software recorded on the physical packet included with this Book "Software Media". Copyright to the individual programs recorded on the Software Media is owned by the author or other authorized copyright owner of each program. Ownership of the Software and all proprietary rights relating thereto remain with WPI and its licensers.

3. **Restrictions on Use and Transfer.**

   (a) You may only (i) make one copy of the Software for backup or archival purposes, or (ii) transfer the Software to a single hard disk, provided that you keep the original for backup or archival purposes. You may not (i) rent or lease the Software, (ii) copy or reproduce the Software through a LAN or other network system or through any computer subscriber system or bulletin-board system, or (iii) modify, adapt, or create derivative works based on the Software.

   (b) You may not reverse engineer, decompile, or disassemble the Software. You may transfer the Software and user documentation on a permanent basis, provided that the transferee agrees to accept the terms and conditions of this Agreement and you retain no copies. If the Software is an update or has been updated, any transfer must include the most recent update and all prior versions.

4. **Restrictions on Use of Individual Programs.** You must follow the individual requirements and restrictions detailed for each individual program in the "About the CD" appendix of this Book or on the Software Media. These limitations are also contained in the individual license agreements recorded on the Software Media. These limitations may include a requirement that after using the program for a specified period of time, the user must pay a registration fee or discontinue use. By opening the Software packet(s), you agree to abide by the licenses and restrictions for these individual programs that are detailed in the "About the CD" appendix and/or on the Software Media. None of the material on this Software Media or listed in this Book may ever be redistributed, in original or modified form, for commercial purposes.

5. **Limited Warranty.**

    (a) WPI warrants that the Software and Software Media are free from defects in materials and workmanship under normal use for a period of sixty (60) days from the date of purchase of this Book. If WPI receives notification within the warranty period of defects in materials or workmanship, WPI will replace the defective Software Media.

    (b) WPI AND THE AUTHOR(S) OF THE BOOK DISCLAIM ALL OTHER WARRANTIES, EXPRESS OR IMPLIED, INCLUDING WITHOUT LIMITATION IMPLIED WARRANTIES OF MERCHANTABILITY AND FITNESS FOR A PARTICULAR PURPOSE, WITH RESPECT TO THE SOFTWARE, THE PROGRAMS, THE SOURCE CODE CONTAINED THEREIN, AND/ OR THE TECHNIQUES DESCRIBED IN THIS BOOK. WPI DOES NOT WARRANT THAT THE FUNCTIONS CONTAINED IN THE SOFTWARE WILL MEET YOUR REQUIREMENTS OR THAT THE OPERATION OF THE SOFTWARE WILL BE ERROR FREE.

    (c) This limited warranty gives you specific legal rights, and you may have other rights that vary from jurisdiction to jurisdiction.

6. **Remedies.**

    (a) WPI's entire liability and your exclusive remedy for defects in materials and workmanship shall be limited to replacement of the Software Media, which may be returned to WPI with a copy of your receipt at the following address: Software Media Fulfillment Department, Attn.: *Spanish For Dummies,* 2nd Edition, Wiley Publishing, Inc., 10475 Crosspoint Blvd., Indianapolis, IN 46256, or call 1-800-762-2974. Please allow four to six weeks for delivery. This Limited Warranty is void if failure of the Software Media has resulted from accident, abuse, or misapplication. Any replacement Software Media will be warranted for the remainder of the original warranty period or thirty (30) days, whichever is longer.

    (b) In no event shall WPI or the author be liable for any damages whatsoever (including without limitation damages for loss of business profits, business interruption, loss of business information, or any other pecuniary loss) arising from the use of or inability to use the Book or the Software, even if WPI has been advised of the possibility of such damages.

    (c) Because some jurisdictions do not allow the exclusion or limitation of liability for consequential or incidental damages, the above limitation or exclusion may not apply to you.

7. **U.S. Government Restricted Rights.** Use, duplication, or disclosure of the Software for or on behalf of the United States of America, its agencies and/or instrumentalities "U.S. Government" is subject to restrictions as stated in paragraph (c)(1)(ii) of the Rights in Technical Data and Computer Software clause of DFARS 252.227-7013, or subparagraphs (c) (1) and (2) of the Commercial Computer Software - Restricted Rights clause at FAR 52.227-19, and in similar clauses in the NASA FAR supplement, as applicable.

8. **General.** This Agreement constitutes the entire understanding of the parties and revokes and supersedes all prior agreements, oral or written, between them and may not be modified or amended except in a writing signed by both parties hereto that specifically refers to this Agreement. This Agreement shall take precedence over any other documents that may be in conflict herewith. If any one or more provisions contained in this Agreement are held by any court or tribunal to be invalid, illegal, or otherwise unenforceable, each and every other provision shall remain in full force and effect.